"Richard Kopley and the many distinguished contributors effectively rebut the widespread notion that textual scholarship and documentary editing are anachronistic critical endeavors. These bellwether essays provoke and challenge this and the next generation of Americanists to a higher standard of scholarly achievement—to 'make it new' and not merely glib or fashionable."

—Gary Scharnhorst
Professor of English, University of New Mexico

"Under the able editorship of Professor Kopley, *Prospects* is a truly valuable guide to the scholarship on sixteen important writers in American literature, assessing the current status of critical investigation and pointing the way to the future of serious inquiry. No beginning scholar or graduate student in American literature should be without this book."

—James Nagel
Eidson Distinguished Professor, University of Georgia

"A splendid roster of notable scholars sizes up the imperatives for future critical work in the ever-evolving world of American literary studies. By honing in on exemplary cases such as Emerson and Douglass, Stowe and Cather, Faulkner and Wright, these essays clarify the challenges and indicate the directions that sophisticated scholarship will most likely take in the years ahead."

—Martha Banta
Professor of English, University of California, Los Angeles

"An impressive collection of analytical, bibliographical essays on major American authors. It not only summarizes current scholarly trends but also points in future directions. This volume will prove extremely useful to scholars of American literature."

—David S. Reynolds
Distinguished Professor of American Literature and American Studies,
Baruch College and the Graduate School of the City University of New York

Prospects for the
Study of American Literature

A Guide for Scholars and Students

EDITED BY

Richard Kopley

New York University Press
NEW YORK AND LONDON

NEW YORK UNIVERSITY PRESS
New York and London

Library of Congress Cataloging-in-Publication Data
Prospects for the study of American literature: a guide for scholars and
students / edited by Richard Kopley.
    p. cm.
    Includes bibliographical references and index.
    ISBN 0–8147–4666–7 (clothbound).—ISBN 0–8147–4698–5 (paperback)
    1. American literature—History and criticism—Theory, etc.
    2. American literature—Study and teaching—Theory, etc.
    3. American literature—Outlines, syllibi, etc. I. Kopley,
Richard.
PS25.P76 1997   97–15555
810.9—dc21   CIP

We wish to thank Pennsylvania State University Press for granting us
permission to quote from Kent P. Ljungquist, "Prospects for the Study of
Edgar Allan Poe," *Resources for American Literary Study* 21, no. 2 (fall 1995):
173–88; Wilson J. Moses, "Prospects for the Study of Frederick Douglass,"
Resources for American Literary Study 23, no. 1 (spring 1997): 1–15; Ed
Folsom, "Prospects for the Study of Walt Whitman," *Resources for American
Literary Study* 20, no. 1 (spring 1994): 1–15; Linda Wagner-Martin,
"Prospects for the Study of Edith Wharton," *Resources for American Literary
Study* 22, no. 1 (spring 1996): 1–15; Susan J Rosowski, "Prospects for the
Study of Willa Cather," *Resources for American Literary Study* 22, no. 2 (fall
1996): 147–64; Michael S. Reynolds, "Prospects for the Study of Ernest
Hemingway," *Resources for American Literary Study* 21, no. 1 (spring 1995):
1–15.

New York University Press books are printed on acid-free paper,
and their binding materials are chosen for strength and durability.

Manufactured in the United States of America
10 9 8 7 6 5 4 3 2 1

To Victor A. Doyno, generous friend and mentor

Contents

Acknowledgments

I am delighted to express my great appreciation for the excellent support I've enjoyed with *Prospects* over the years.

In 1992, Carla Mulford, one of the editors of *Resources for American Literary Study*, graciously invited me to become associate editor of the journal, and her invitation enabled me to initiate the "Prospects" series in *RALS*. Jackson R. Bryer, also an editor of *RALS*, and Robert Secor, who became an editor of that journal, provided welcome encouragement and advice regarding both the "Prospects"series in *RALS* and this volume. Nina Baym, Alan Gribben, Michael Meyer, and Linda Wagner-Martin provided expert counsel regarding possible contributors. Raymond E. Lombra, Associate Dean for Research and Graduate Studies in the College of the Liberal Arts at Penn State, and the RGSO Committee offered funding support at an early stage of the project's development. Mary M. Dupuis, former Director of Academic Affairs at the Penn State, DuBois Campus, furnished additional support, as did Robert Secor, former Head of Penn State's English Department (and present Vice Provost of the University), and Don Bialostosky, current Head of the Department.

Donna Brantlinger Black, editorial assistant for *RALS*, offered expert editorial skills with regard to the "Prospects" series in *RALS*, six installments of which are included in this volume. She also helped with regard to the final revisions of the book. Sanford Thatcher, Director of the Penn State Press, and Jan Wilson, Permissions Editor at the Press, helped vitally regarding permissions. My secretary Belinda Peters ably assisted with formatting the manuscript and managing last-minute communications. Donna Harpster also offered needed secretarial aid, and Richard Cunningham provided critical research assistance. Cynthia Myers effectively managed department support, and Thomas Minsker invaluably assisted by creating camera-ready copy.

I would like to offer a special thanks to the expert editors at New York University Press. I am very grateful to former editor Katherine Gill, who first expressed an interest in publishing *Prospects*. I am also grateful to Managing Editor Despina Papazoglou Gimbel, who oversaw the final stages of pre-production on this book, and to Design and Production Manager Elyse Strongin, who assisted in these final stages. And I am much indebted to Editor in Chief and present Director of the NYU Press, Niko Pfund, who has critically guided my work on *Prospects* throughout the past three years. Without his enthusiasm for the project and his sound advice regarding the process, there would be no *Prospects*.

Finally, I wish to thank two people who always believed in the prospective value of *Prospects:* my wife, Amy Golahny, and my mother, Irene Kopley.

Contributors

MICHAEL AWKWARD, Professor of English at The University of Pennsylvania, is the author of *Inspiriting Influences: Tradition, Revision, and Afro-American Women's Novels* (Columbia UP, 1989) and *Negotiating Difference: Race, Gender, and the Politics of Positionality* (U of Chicago P, 1995) and editor of *New Essays on "Their Eyes Were Watching God"* (Cambridge UP, 1990).

JOHN BRYANT, Professor of English at Hofstra University, is author of *Melville and Repose* (Oxford UP, 1993) and has written numerous articles on Melville in such journals as *American Literature, Nineteenth-Century Literature, New England Quarterly, Arizona Quarterly,* and *Resources for American Literary Study.* He is editor of *Melville Society Extracts* and *A Companion to Melville Studies* (Greenwood P, 1986). At present he is working on a study of the *Typee* manuscript and a book titled *The Fluid Text.*

DANIEL MARK FOGEL, Professor of English, Dean of the Graduate School, and Vice Provost at Louisiana State University, founded the *Henry James Review* and served as its editor from 1979 to 1995. His books include *"Daisy Miller": A Dark Comedy of Manners* (Twayne, 1990), *Covert Relations: James Joyce, Virginia Woolf, and Henry James* (UP of Virginia, 1990), and *A Companion to Henry James Studies* (Greenwood P, 1993). In addition, he edited *Henry James Novels: 1886–1890* for The Library of America, and his essays have been published in *Diacritics, Studies in Bibliography, Modern Fiction Studies,* and other learned journals.

ED FOLSOM is Professor of English at the University of Iowa, where he edits the *Walt Whitman Quarterly Review.* He is the author of *Walt Whitman's Native Representations* (Cambridge UP, 1994), editor of *Walt Whitman: The Centennial Essays* (U of Iowa P, 1994), and, with the late

Gay Wilson Allen, coeditor of *Walt Whitman and the World* (U of Iowa P, 1995).

JOAN D. HEDRICK, Director of Women's Studies, Trinity College, is the author of the Pulitzer Prize–winning biography, *Harriet Beecher Stowe: A Life* (Oxford UP, 1994), and of *Solitary Comrade: Jack London and His Work* (U of North Carolina P, 1982).

MICHELLE JOHNSON is Assistant Professor of English at The University of Wisconsin, Milwaukee.

KENETH KINNAMON, Ethel Pumphrey Stephens Professor of English at The University of Arkansas, is the author of *The Emergence of Richard Wright: A Study in Literature and Society* (U of Illinois P, 1972), the editor of *New Essays on "Native Son"* (Cambridge UP, 1990), a coeditor of *Conversations with Richard Wright* (UP of Mississippi, 1993), and the compiler of *A Richard Wright Bibliography: Fifty Years of Criticism and Commentary, 1933–1982* (Greenwood P, 1988).

MICHAEL J. KISKIS is Associate Professor of American Literature at Elmira College, Elmira, New York, where he teaches courses in nineteenth-century American literature and serves on the advisory board of the Center for Mark Twain Studies at Quarry Farm. He is editor of *Mark Twain's Own Autobiography: The Chapters from the "North American Review"* (Wisconsin UP, 1990) and has published on Mark Twain as well as on issues related to non-traditional students, autobiographical writing, and academic program development. He is currently president of the Mark Twain Circle of America and editor of *Studies in American Humor.*

RICHARD KOPLEY, Associate Professor of English at The Pennsylvania State University, DuBois Campus, is editor of *Poe's "Pym": Critical Explorations* (Duke UP, 1992), coeditor of *Resources for American Literary Study*, and author of *Edgar Allan Poe and "The Philadelphia Saturday News"* (Poe Society, 1991) and a variety of essays on Poe, Hawthorne, and Melville in such journals as *ATQ, Studies in American Fiction*, and *Studies in the American Renaissance.*

KENT P. LJUNGQUIST, Professor of English at Worcester Polytechnic Institute, is author of *The Grand and the Fair: Poe's Landscape Aesthetics and Pictorial Techniques* (Scripta Humanistica, 1984), coeditor of Cooper's

The Deerslayer (SUNY Press, 1987), and editor of the *Facts on File Bibliography of American Fiction to 1865* (Facts on File, 1994). He has published articles in *American Literature, ESQ, Resources for American Literary Study, Studies in the American Renaissance,* and contributed to a number of reference volumes.

THOMAS L. MCHANEY is Kenneth M. England Professor of Southern Literature at Georgia State University in Atlanta. He has published critical, textual, biographical, and bibliographical work on William Faulkner and essays on several other Southern writers. He was one of the general editors of *William Faulkner Manuscripts* (25 vols.; Garland, 1987–89), with sole responsibility for ten titles. He is the principal editor, and author of historical and textual introductions, for a forthcoming facsimile and transcription of a recently discovered holograph manuscript draft of Faulkner's second novel, *Mosquitoes* (Bibliographical Society of the University of Virginia, 1997).

WILSON J. MOSES, Professor of History at The Pennsylvania State University, is the author of *The Golden Age of Black Nationalism* (Oxford UP, 1978), *Black Messiahs and Uncle Toms* (Penn State UP, 1982), *Alexander Crummell* (Oxford UP, 1989), *The Wings of Ethiopia* (Iowa State UP, 1990), and editor of *Destiny and Race: Sermons and Addresses by Alexander Crummell* (U of Massachusetts P, 1992) and *Classical Black Nationalism* (New York UP, 1996).

JOEL MYERSON, Carolina Distinguished Professor of American Literature at the University of South Carolina, has published descriptive primary and annotated secondary bibliographies of Emerson, edited *Emerson Centenary Essays* (Southern Illinois UP, 1982) and *Emerson and Thoreau: The Contemporary Reviews* (Cambridge UP, 1992), coedited *Critical Essays on Ralph Waldo Emerson* (G. K. Hall, 1983) and *Emerson's Antislavery Writings* (Yale UP, 1995), and has in press an edition of Emerson's *Selected Letters*. He is presently coediting *The Later Lectures of Ralph Waldo Emerson.*

MICHAEL S. REYNOLDS, Professor of English Emeritus, North Carolina State University, is a Hemingway biographer. His most recent publication is *Hemingway: The 1930s* (Norton, 1997). He is working on *Hemingway —The Final Years* (Norton, 1999).

SUSAN J. ROSOWSKI, Adele Hall Professor, University of Nebraska–Lincoln, is General Editor of the *Willa Cather Scholarly Edition*, Editor-in-Chief of *Cather Studies*, author of *The Voyage Perilous: Willa Cather's Romanticism* (U of Nebraska P, 1986) and of many essays on Cather and other American authors. She has served as president of the Western Literature Association and has directed four international seminars on Willa Cather. She is currently completing a book on gender, creativity, and the American West.

SANFORD SCHWARTZ teaches literature at The Pennsylvania State University. The author of *The Matrix of Modernism: Pound, Eliot, and Early Twentieth-Century Thought* (Princeton UP, 1985) and various essays on modern intellectual, cultural, and literary history, he is currently president of the T. S. Eliot Society (1994–97) and engaged in a book on American culture after World War II.

DAVID E. E. SLOANE, Professor of English at the University of New Haven, is author of *Mark Twain's Humor: Critical Essays* (Garland, 1993), *"Adventures of Huckleberry Finn": American Comic Vision* (Twayne-Macmillan, 1988), *American Humor Magazines and Comic Periodicals* (Greenwood, 1987), *The Literary Humor of the Urban Northeast: 1830–1890* (Louisiana State UP, 1983), and *Mark Twain as a Literary Comedian* (Louisiana State UP, 1979). He is past president of the Mark Twain Circle and the American Humor Studies Association.

LINDA WAGNER-MARTIN is Hanes Professor of English and Comparative Literature at University of North Carolina, Chapel Hill. An editor of the *Heath Anthology of American Literature*, she is coeditor of *The Oxford Companion to Women's Writing in the United States* (Oxford UP, 1995) and its accompanying anthology, and editor of *New Essays on "Go Down, Moses"* (Cambridge UP, 1996). Among other recent books are *"Favored Strangers": Gertrude Stein and Her Family* (Rutgers UP, 1995), *The Midcentury American Novel, 1935–1965* (Twayne, 1997), and *Wharton's "The Age of Innocence": A Novel of Ironic Nostalgia* (Twayne, 1996).

ELIZABETH HALL WITHERELL, Librarian at the University of California at Santa Barbara, is the Editor-in-Chief for the Princeton University Press edition, *The Writings of Henry David Thoreau*.

Prospects for the Study of American Literature

Introduction

Richard Kopley

In 1990, I started to think about the potential usefulness of some regular consideration of the future of American literary study—a prospective complement to the indispensable retrospective series, *American Literary Scholarship* (Durham, NC: Duke UP, 1963–). No doubt Alfred Bendixen's success in creating the American Literature Association helped me to consider a project concerning the field as a whole. I imagined that experts in various author fields could offer to all Americanists, from graduate students to senior scholars, valuable guidance regarding needed future work in these fields. They could suggest revealing syntheses of prior interpretations and approaches (both traditional and theoretical), promising new interpretations and approaches, vital research in manuscript archives and periodicals collections, the investigation of new sources and influences, the editing and annotation of important texts, the examination of neglected areas in the author's life, the compiling of primary and secondary bibliographies and concordances and collections, and much other work that these experts would consider worthwhile. They could provide what would amount to annotated bibliographies of work yet to be done. The discipline's sense of possibility could be greatly expanded— we could light out for the territory a little sooner, perhaps. Discussing the idea with fellow Americanists, I found encouragement; accepting an editorial position with *Resources for American Literary Study* in the spring of 1992, I found an opportunity. With the support of editors Jackson R. Bryer and Robert Secor, I initiated the series "Prospects for American Literary Study," and we offered as our first installment, in the Spring 1994 issue of *RALS*, Ed Folsom's excellent assessment of the future of Whitman studies, "Prospects for the Study of Walt Whitman." The work was well received, and well profiled in the *Chronicle of Higher Education*

1

("Hot Type," 29 June 1994: A10). Subsequent issues of *RALS* offered additional "Prospects" essays, and these became a popular feature of the journal. To develop a book of "Prospects" essays, I combined the journal installments with essays specifically commissioned for the book: the result is the present volume.

Reading the sixteen essays gathered here may well prompt a mixture of pride and exhaustion—pride in the work that the profession has already accomplished, highlighted throughout these essays, and exhaustion regarding the work that we have yet to do. Fortunately, the community of Americanists has the time and the will and the skill. And exhaustion should yield to excitement as readers come across the project that is right for them or as they are stimulated to imagine that project. Certainly these essays invite us to a wide variety of scholarly adventures.

Joel Myerson's essay on Ralph Waldo Emerson suggests, among many other projects, the exploration of Emerson's account books and of the letters he received that remain unpublished (manuscripts held by Harvard's Houghton Library), the creation of a concordance for Emerson's writings, and the examination of Emerson's critical relationships with women. Elizabeth Hall Witherell's essay on Henry David Thoreau proposes, among a similar plethora of scholarly efforts, the reconstruction of Thoreau's lectures, the investigation of Thoreau's unpublished Kalendar, and the design of a computer database of Thoreau manuscripts. Kent P. Ljungquist recommends in his piece on Edgar Allan Poe numerous scholarly endeavors, including the development of a reader's guide to Poe's short fiction, the analysis of Poe's exposure to Freemasonry in 1830s Baltimore, and the recovery of important Poe material in neglected nineteenth-century newspapers of the Midwest. John Bryant offers in his essay on Herman Melville a wealth of opportunities, including the study of the Augusta Papers at the New York Public Library; the assessment of Melville's compositional practice in the manuscripts of such works as *Typee*, the late poetry, and *Billy Budd*; and the interrelating of Melville's compositional practice with his rhetorical strategies (and the regarding of both with equal eye).

Among the many opportunities in Frederick Douglass studies noted by Wilson J. Moses are the contextualizing of Douglass's experience as a mulatto, the elaboration of Douglass's involvement with the East Baltimore Mental Improvement Society, the analysis of Douglass's speeches in the tradition of nineteenth-century political oratory, and the delineation of Douglass's changing use of the Bible through his life. Joan D.

Hedrick describes numerous opportunities in the study of Harriet Beecher Stowe, from the determining of Stowe's debt to the eighteenth-century stylists to a treatment of Stowe's visual imagination in her writings and her amateur art; from a study of Stowe as businesswoman, with consideration of her business-related correspondence and the Ticknor and Fields business records, to an edition of Stowe's correspondence with her husband Calvin. Ed Folsom identifies a broad array of scholarly projects needed in Whitman studies, including the creation of a hypertext version of *Leaves of Grass* and other Whitman books; the examination of recently discovered Whitman notebooks (now digitized), letters, and manuscripts; the investigation of the Horace Traubel Collection at the Library of Congress (and perhaps the writing of a thorough biography of Whitman-devotee Traubel himself); and the writing of a Whitman biography based on the view that Whitman was gay. David E. E. Sloane and Michael J. Kiskis identify many projects for the Twainian, such as appraisal of Twain's use of his private writing in his published work, inquiry into Twain's varied collaborative efforts, scrutiny of the literary sources identified in Alan Gribben's *Mark Twain's Library: A Reconstruction* and the anticipated supplement, and reexamination of Twain and issues of class and race.

The great project in Henry James studies, Daniel Mark Fogel notes, is the planned complete edition of the correspondence. Future biographical scholarship will inevitably be shaped by the much-needed volumes. Fogel mentions, too, such research needs as the study of Leon Edel's notebooks at McGill University, which apparently feature transcriptions of one hundred otherwise unknown James letters; the CD publication of an ambitious variorum edition of James and a facilitating concordance; and the precise dating of James's literary work. Linda Wagner-Martin recommends in her essay on Edith Wharton, among other projects, the assembling of a volume of valuable previously published critical essays (*Edith Wharton: Six Decades of Criticism* [or *Seven*]), the editing of a volume including Wharton's *The Writing of Fiction* and her related pieces (*Edith Wharton on Writing*), the cataloguing of the most substantial collections of Wharton manuscripts and correspondence, and the continued inspection of the manuscript revisions in Wharton's works and the publishing histories of these works. Susan J. Rosowski sets forth an abundance of scholarly efforts, including the updating and expansion of previous editions of Cather's journalistic writings, research on Cather's companion Edith Lewis, interpretation of Cather's fiction in its periodical context, discussion of Cather and race with reference to her review of the Vos exhibition, and study of Cather's audience. Sanford Schwartz anticipates that Eliot scholars will not cease from exploration; he cites, among a variety of worthy projects, the study of Eliot's early years in New England and St. Louis, the illumination of Eliot's relationship to a range of theatrical traditions, the reconsideration of his Christianity, the analysis of his influence on modern poets and critics, and the reinterpretation of his work in light of revisionary understandings of modernism.

There is no dearth of work to do in the study of Ernest Hemingway; Michael S. Reynolds outlines plentiful projects, from the creation of on-line bibliographies to the dating of manuscripts to the eventual editing of standard and variorum editions of the texts to the probing of Hemingway's thirties in Key West and Havana and the still-mysterious World War II years to the editing of the correspondence between Hemingway and Ezra Pound and Archibald MacLeish, and that between Hemingway and Scribner's publishing house. Michael Awkward and Michelle Johnson, in their essay on Zora Neale Hurston, advocate much scholarly investigation, including the elaboration of the relationship of her anthropological work to her literary work, the analysis of her changing views of Hoodoo and of slavery, the comparative examination of Hurston's work and that of her friend Langston Hughes, and the exploration of her connection to later African American writers. Thomas L. McHaney, in his piece on William Faulkner, recommends that scholars undertake, among other efforts, the identification and analysis of Faulkner's reading; the study of the African American communities in Oxford, Mississippi; a search for new Faulkner manuscripts in the hands of lesser-known acquaintances and their heirs; and Bakhtinian interpretations of Faulkner's works. And Keneth Kinnamon, writing on the future study of Richard Wright, offers, among varied scholarly projects, the creation of a thorough chronology of Wright's life; the writing of a new biography with a focus on both the man and the author; the publication of Wright's correspondence and his numerous unpublished works in the Beinecke Library, including fiction, nonfiction, and poetry; and the elaboration of a book-length reception study.

The scholarly adventures suggested here are bountiful and beguiling; in all areas of study, rich opportunities and challenges await. My expectations for the essays have been well surpassed; I congratulate the contributors and wish readers a satisfying provocation.

Because of inevitable space limitations, numerous important American writers are not represented in this volume; I look forward to including prospective essays on many of these writers in future issues of *RALS* and, I hope, in future volumes of *Prospects*. We could eventually return to the writers considered in this volume, in which case we could then gauge the impact of the original "Prospects" essays and think ahead anew. Meanwhile, I would be glad to learn readers' views on the usefulness of this volume and their suggestions for improvement.

When Americanists—particularly nineteenth-century Americanists—think of the achievement of excellence, they may well call to mind Henry David Thoreau's remarkable figure in *Walden*, "the artist of Kouroo"—he who fashions a perfect staff out of the best material, with great art and an indifference to time, and who thereby triumphs. Perhaps what is said of this exemplary artist may be said, too, of the exemplary scholar. Perhaps each of us may aspire to be a scholar of Kouroo—one who could offer a work of the sturdiest wood—wood carved, smoothed, and polished with an art born not only of great knowledge of the considered writings, their author and his or her world, and the ablest criticism and scholarship, but also of a tremendously sympathetic imagination and that hard-to-attain indifference to time. The work would certainly be extraordinary: as Thoreau wrote of the artist of Kouroo, "The material was pure, and his art was pure; how could the result be other than wonderful?" My hope for *Prospects* is that the good words of its contributors will help readers to make exceptional staffs—scholarly works that endure—achievements that could not be "other than wonderful."

Ralph Waldo Emerson

Joel Myerson

When I was in graduate school in the late 1960s, it was still possible to "work up" Emerson for study rather easily. There were ten volumes of journals and twelve volumes of published writings in the old Houghton Mifflin Centenary Edition, six volumes of the new *Journals and Miscellaneous Notebooks of Ralph Waldo Emerson* (*JMN*) carried Emerson's life through 1838, another seven volumes contained superb editions of Emerson's letters (including his correspondence with Thomas Carlyle), and less than a shelf of recent secondary works existed to wade through, including a very fine biography (Ralph L. Rusk's). There was a lot that needed to be done in Emerson studies, and scholars were busily providing the basic materials with which to do it. In 1984, Robert E. Burkholder and I provided an assessment of the resources for studying Emerson that had been published through 1981. In the present essay, then, I plan to bring Emersonians up to date and make some suggestions about future directions for Emerson studies.

Future scholars will not have to worry about doing bibliographical work on Emerson. My primary bibliography presents a biblio-biography of Emerson that helps place him within the nineteenth-century literary marketplace. Anyone thinking that Emerson spent his life with his head in the clouds need only look at his record as a professional author to dispel this rather quaint idea. (I am preparing a supplement to this work and would be glad to share information with interested scholars.) In 1985 Burkholder and I published an annotated bibliography of writings about Emerson that covered the period from 1816 to 1979, then brought that up to date in 1994 with an annotated bibliography for the years 1980 through 1991. Manfred Putz's bibliography includes foreign-language sources that we did not include. Until our next supplement, readers can consult the comprehensive listings of Emerson criticism published in *Emerson Society Papers* and the excellent bibliographical essays in *American Literary Scholarship*. (The semiannual *Emerson Society Papers* contains not only bibliographical listings, but also scholarly notes and general information on Emerson and Emersonian activities.)

The most exciting work in Emerson studies in the last thirty years has been editorial. Rarely has the scholarship on an author been affected as much by editorial work as has that on Emerson. After all, most of the editorial work for other American Renaissance authors essentially involved establishing authoritative texts of materials that had been available in less acceptable forms. Since 1960, Emerson editors have added some two dozen generally thick volumes of primary writings to Emerson's canon, most of which are private writings. This astonishing amount of material has allowed us a view into Emerson's mind that was not possible before 1960, has allowed us to see how his ideas took shape and how they were reworked from the first point of inspiration through their appearances in print. Our journeying is made easier by the detailed annotations and many cross-references to where material was used in the published works. Despite the whining of a few people early on about the "barbed wire" of the editorial symbols in the *JMN*, nearly all scholars seem to be delighted with the inclusive textual policy of all these editions and have been able to use the information about levels of revision in their interpretations of Emerson's writings. Each edition has been marked by the highest standards of textual scholarship; after all, there were the examples of Rusk's editing and the editing of the *JMN*, and a number of editors from the *JMN* went on to do volumes in the other editions. Joel Porte has made a good one-volume selection from the *JMN*, but serious scholars should never substitute it for the original.

In order to fit their edition of Emerson's journals into "only" sixteen volumes, the editors of the *JMN* had to leave out some otherwise excellent works from their edition. The best of these omitted journals have been published in three volumes as *The Topical Notebooks of Ralph Waldo Emerson*, edited by Ronald A. Bosco, Glen M. Johnson, and Susan Sutton Smith, under chief editor Ralph H. Orth. Included in this edition are eighteen journals or notebooks, including ones dealing with the preparation of lectures, compiling biographical notes and reminiscences of Emerson's acquaintances, and treating such topics as "Fate," "Beauty and Art," "Natural History of Intellect," "England and America," "Theory of Poetry," "Rhetoric," "Philosophy," and "Literature." Bosco ("Blessed") has also edited a topical notebook for journal publication. Another edition goes a long way toward proving Emerson's assertion to his future wife Lidian Jackson in 1835 that "I am born a poet. . . . That is my nature & vocation" (*Letters*, 1:435). *The Poetry Notebooks of Ralph Waldo Emerson*, edited by Orth, Albert J. von Frank, Linda Allardt, and David W. Hill, presents the contents of nine poetry notebooks and the texts of poems in additional manuscripts in one massive (990-page) volume. Of especial value is a long section called "Analysis of the Poems" that gives the composition and publication histories of each work. Another four volumes appeared in *The Letters of Ralph Waldo Emerson*, edited by Eleanor M. Tilton.

Rusk's edition had omitted letters that had appeared in print, and these are now included in Tilton's edition, along with many other letters not available to Rusk. Of special note are the letters to Arthur Hugh Clough, William Henry Furness, John Sterling, Henry David Thoreau, Samuel Gray Ward, and Caroline Sturgis Tappan (whose letters to Emerson are liberally quoted in notes). Like Rusk's edition, Tilton's is sumptuously annotated.

Two other editions present different views of Emerson from what we have seen before. Until 1989, the only evidence we had of the literary work during Emerson's early career as a minister was a one-volume selected edition of twenty-five of the more than 170 of his sermons. That situation changed with the publication of the first of the four volumes in *The Complete Sermons of Ralph Waldo Emerson*, edited by Ronald A. Bosco, Andrew Delbanco, Wesley T. Mott, and Teresa Toulouse, with Albert J. von Frank as general editor. Now we have available for study all of Emerson's sermons, and this edition gives us a wonderful glimpse into the beginnings of a long career. Any future study of Emerson's literary artistry must begin with these volumes. An interesting collection is *Emerson's Antislavery Writings*, edited by Len Gougeon and me, which collects in one place all of Emerson's writings against slavery, including unpublished and uncollected works.

Even more manuscript material exists for future editors. The Ralph Waldo Emerson Memorial Association collection at the Houghton Library of Harvard University contains many unpublished nuggets (particularly in the large collection of letters written to Emerson) and some real gems, such as Emerson's account books and later lectures. Ronald A. Bosco and I are editing the later lectures, but I fear that, in the present bleak climate of scholarly publishing, the account books may not see publication. This is a shame because these detailed factual accounts of Emerson's material life provide information about his publishing career, financial support of friends and relatives, and life in Concord that are not available elsewhere.

The Collected Works of Ralph Waldo Emerson, with Joseph Slater as general editor and Douglas Emory Wilson as textual editor, has published five volumes (*Nature, Addresses, and Lectures; Essays: First Series; Essays: Second Series; Representative Men; English Traits*) and will continue with *The Conduct of Life, Letters and Social Aims, Society and Solitude, Poems*, and a collection of miscellaneous writings. The two-volume collection of Emerson in the Library of America series is the most comprehensive shorter collection available.

With all this primary material now available, it is shocking that the only published concordance to Emerson's writings is George Shelton Hubbell's of the poetry, done in 1932. We desperately need to employ computer technology to get a handle on all the texts of Emerson's public and private writings. Given Emerson's penchant for using and reusing material, this concordance is a prime desideratum.

Emerson's long and full life has been examined in three large biographies. Gay Wilson Allen describes the development of Emerson's philosophy and particularly the oriental influences on it. John McAleer examines Emerson's social and cultural contexts in a biography that emphasizes and is organized around his most important friendships. Robert D. Richardson, Jr., is the first to attempt an intellectual biography (similar to what he did for Thoreau), and his discussion of how Emerson became one of the major figures of American literature is fascinating and suggestive. Richardson is particularly good in tracing the influence of Emerson's reading upon his ideas. Albert J. von Frank's chronology of Emerson's life is an invaluable guide to the many people and events that populated it, and is also the best single source for following Emerson's career as a lecturer. The early years of Emerson's life (up to the publication of *Nature*) are the subject of Richard A. Hutch's Eriksonian biography and of Evelyn Barish's psychological biography, which devotes considerable space to the influence of his parents, aunt Mary Moody Emerson, first wife Ellen Tucker Emerson, and his tuberculosis and eye problems. Barish has also done an illustrated study of Emerson in Italy. Delores Bird Carpenter has edited a life of Lidian Emerson (written by her daughter Ellen) and a selected edition of her letters. Edith W. Gregg presents much detail about family life in her edition of *The Letters of Ellen*

Tucker Emerson. Nancy Craig Simmons shows how James Elliot Cabot, along with Emerson's daughters, helped to assemble his later works as his memory and creative powers failed.

But even with all this work, a good bit remains to be done. All the biographies of Emerson rightly focus on his role as a founder of American literature and his friendships with important people. We need, also, to gain insight into Emerson as a family man and the role the family played in his writings, one that goes beyond the obvious influence of young Waldo's death on "Threnody." Biographies of Emerson begin to lose steam after they reach about 1855, and we need more works dealing with discrete periods of Emerson's later life—works such as A. B. Paulson's analysis of Emerson's aphasia. While Christina Zwarg has done a provocative study of Emerson's relations with Margaret Fuller, and Jerome Loving a comprehensive discussion of Emerson's bringing Whitman to a boil, we still need studies of the other important friendships in Emerson's life, such as those with Anna Barker Ward and Caroline Sturgis. (For major or minor figures, Merton M. Sealts, Jr.'s study of Emerson and Melville and Robert Sattelmeyer's of Emerson and Thoreau might serve as models.) Indeed, it is remarkable that there is not a single sustained study of Emerson and women, especially when we consider how important women were to his emotional and intellectual development, and how much writing he has left on the subject. Nor is there a study of Emerson's role in popular culture, as he assumed the mantle of "The Sage of Concord" and was turned to by succeeding generations for inspiration and guidance.

A number of studies have been done on Emerson's reading, but they are all partial ones, focusing on either one type of literature (such as Asian literature, classical writers, or the novel) or borrowings from one library (such as Harvard or the Boston Athenaeum). We need a comprehensive account, similar to the account done by Merton M. Sealts, Jr., on Melville and the one provided by Robert Sattelmeyer on Thoreau. Incredibly, there is only one major study of Emerson's use of the Bible, Zink's seventy-page article published in 1935. Emerson, an ex-minister, might be thought of as using the Bible as a stylistic or metaphorical source for his writings, but we have no extended study of this topic.

Much remains to be done with Emerson's career as a lecturer and his other career as a professional author, both of which put food on the table and, as such, were important to him. Emerson was one of the most popular lecturers of his time, and he delivered hundreds of lectures to all sorts of audiences. Many Americans knew Emerson first or solely from his podium appearances. Emerson's British lecture tours have been described in some detail, but not his American ones. This is surprising because many of his lecture tours tried out materials that later appeared in his books. At present, all we have are a couple of calendars of his American lecture engagements and scattered prose accounts of individual lectures and lecture series. Brief works like Mark R. Winchell's merely whet our appetite for more. And the earlier studies of both his British and American lecture tours are very much out of date, particularly as regards the many editions of letters and journals of people who knew Emerson that have been published in the last forty years.

Emerson's dealings with various lyceums show him to be a good businessman, as do his relations with his publishers. Emerson's business activity is a field ripe for investigation, as the subject of book history is taking off. Emerson was one of the few nineteenth-century authors to pass up taking royalties in order to own the plates of his books, paying publishers a percentage for distributing them. His signing with Ticknor and Fields (later to become Houghton Mifflin) made him a part of the firm's continued campaign to establish a constellation of "classic" American authors, all of whom happened to be published by the firm, and the establishment of this constellation was one of the earliest examples of canon formation in American literature. There are disappointingly few studies of Emerson as a professional author, even though the published and manuscript materials for such an investigation are readily available. Studies of Emerson as lecturer and as professional author will provide an important counterweight to the long-standing assumption that Emerson always had his head in empyrean heights.

Emerson's numerous works and long life have cast a long shadow, and many of the critical studies of his writings place him in one or another American literary tradition. Joseph G. Kronick explores how Emerson's concept of history influenced later writers. Emerson's role in the history of philosophy has long intrigued Stanley Cavell, and his works on this subject are always interesting. Similarly, Teresa Toulouse studies the relationship between Emerson's sermons and Coleridge's writings, and Richard Poirier (*Poetry*) sees Emerson as the beginning of a line of American pragmatism. Lawrence Buell places Emerson within the context of New England literary culture, and especially its oratorical tradition. Philip F. Gura also studies Emerson's use of language. How the age reponded to Emerson's optimism is the subject of Irving Howe's book. Emerson's part in the British influence on American literature is examined by Robert Weisbuch, and Armida Gilbert deals specifically with his debt to the English Romantic poets. Leon Chai discusses Emerson's formative role in the beginnings of American Romanticism. Emerson's place in the long tradition of New England dissenters, particularly that which stemmed from Anne Hutchinson, is discussed by Amy Schrager Lang. Larry J. Reynolds compares Emerson's reactions to the European revolutions of midcentury to those of his contemporaries. David Leverenz places Emerson in the tradition of manhood in the American Renaissance. Emerson's role as a participant in the literary marketplace is the subject of studies by Stephen Railton and R. Jackson Wilson. Arthur Versluis argues for Emerson's debt to Asian literatures.

Books dealing entirely with Emerson abound. For an author whom many have accused of being dry, there is no scarcity of studies of Emerson and sexuality (that is, of a linguistic or philosophical nature; no dirty linen here), especially those by Eric Cheyfitz and Erik Ingvar Thurin. Wesley T. Mott and Susan L. Roberson study in detail Emerson's ministerial career and his sermons; the importance of this background to the development of his personal and literary career is dealt with by David M. Robinson (*Apostle*). Mary Kupiec Cayton looks at Emerson's career as an example of the response to the new capitalist order of America. To Merton M. Sealts, Jr., understanding Emerson's views on the scholar is essential to understanding his writings. Leonard Neufeldt's analysis of Emerson's development as a writer is solid and convincing, as is Barbara Packer's discussion of Emerson's use of fables of the fall (*Fall*). The growth of Emerson's style and its connection to the Romantic sublime is Julie Ellison's subject, while Russell B. Goodman places Emerson in the history of American Romantic philosophy. David Van Leer argues for a serious consideration of the philosophical qualities of Emerson's essays. Emerson's developing position on one of the great issues of the day, abolition, is detailed by Len Gougeon. Gertrude Reif Hughes studies Emerson's later works as challenging and sees optimism as a consistent force through his career, whereas Robinson, studying the period through *The Conduct of Life*, sees pragmatism as the major philosophical force. Other books deal with very specific topics: Donald L. Gelpi on the idea of the religious quest; Alan D. Hodder on the influence of Revelation; Robert J. Loewenberg on the "Jewish idea"; John Michael on skepticism; George J. Stack on Nietzsche; Gustaaf Van Cromphout on Goethe; and John B. Williams on Emerson's influence on Melville.

Not that all has been sweetness and light for Emerson. The then-president of Yale, A. Bartlett Giamatti, attacks Emerson for the essay "Power," which he feels licensed American politicians to forget the lessons of the past. Howard Horwitz shows how the Standard Oil Trust appropriated Emersonian ideas for its own ends. David Marr argues that Emerson's belief in the private man discourages political involvement. Fortunately, Emerson is not without defenders, including John Updike, who offers a general assessment of Emerson's importance to American culture, and Richard Poirier, who furnishes a spirited defense of Emerson's call to discard the past (*Renewal*). Emerson has also been made to fit the readings of certain schools of criticism, including the deconstructive (David L. Smith), psychoanalytic (Mark Edmundson), and Marxist (Carolyn Porter; but see Grusin's argument against a Marxist interpretation ["'Put God'"]). However, pedagogical studies of Emerson are few. I find it hard to believe that Emerson is so easy to teach that virtually no literature about the subject is available to help instruct others. Burkholder's essay ("Re-seeing") is a model of this kind; we need more works like it.

Those wishing to find handy collections of essays on Emerson are in luck: see the volumes edited by Bloom, Buell, Burkholder and Myerson, Cady and Budd, Donadio et al., Myerson, and Porte. (Myerson has also compiled a large selection of the contemporary reviews of Emerson's works.) Those bewildered by the large number of selections and seeking comfort in one broad yet short overview can find it in Barbara Packer's work ("Emerson").

Other, briefer works are suggestive of what might be good approaches in future Emerson studies. The examinations of the influence of higher biblical criticism on Emerson's development by Barbara Packer ("Origin") and Richard Grusin (*Hermeneutics*) show that we have a lot more to understand about the influence of religious studies on Emerson's philosophical development. Emerson's literary development, on a micro level, can be seen from studies of how he wrote or revised or compiled individual works (see Ronald A. Bosco ["'Poetry'"], Glen M. Johnson ["Craft," "'Immortality'"], and Nancy Craig Simmons ["Arranging"]); with all the new information available from the various editions of Emerson's private and public writings, it is almost sinful not to follow up with studies of his compositorial habits. Another fruitful line of inquiry is how Emerson worked within specific literary genres, a line pursued by William H. Gass (on the essay) and Lawrence Rosenwald (on the diary).

The application of commodity theory by Ian F. A. Bell indicates potential in its application to Emerson's writings.

How Emerson's thought developed, and the stages it went through, will always interest scholars. We seem to have gone past the period when everyone was responding to Stephen Whicher's theory and into a time when new ideas are proposed, such as Robert Milder's concept of conversions. More ideas are needed. But the concentration on ideas should not let us forget that Emerson was a delightful literary stylist, as Michael J. Colacurcio makes clear, and we need to understand better his literary artistry and devices. And by all means let us not forget that many of Emerson's writings were in direct response to the events of his times; studies like those of Robert E. Burkholder ("Kneeland," "Radical Emerson"), Len Gougeon, and Linck C. Johnson continue to remind us of this fact. Similarly, Emerson reflected his times as a cultural construct, as Buell ("Context") shows us.

Most of all, we need contextual studies of Emerson, ones that place him within his times and interpret his relationship to those times (as, for example, works by Cayton and Reynolds do). Recent critical approaches such as book history and new historicism combine the best of the historians of the past and the critical theorizers of today. At present, though, most studies of Emerson that attempt to contextualize him tend to place him at the head of a tradition or as a major point along its development. That Emerson is one of the enduring major authors of American literature has been accepted since the late nineteenth century, so these studies often invoke Emerson's presence as a reflexive justification of their own worth (as in "Emerson's adoption of the interpretation I have proposed is evidence of its value"). But these attempts to place Emerson within a literary tradition, while useful, often tell us little about Emerson. Emerson was a product of his times: literary scholars often fail to appreciate and explain this, and, as a result, their work often lacks the solidity and interconnectedness that mark the work of the best historians (such as Robert A. Gross, who writes on this period). A knowledge of the intellectual trends of the time (both social and theological) are essential to understanding what traditions helped to form Emerson, what he revolted against, and why his rebellion became, within one generation, embraced by the establishment. As we approach the bicentennial celebration of Emerson's birth in 2003, we need to know more about why Emerson has become such a fixture in our literary history, and we now have available most of the primary documents necessary to find the answers. We may discover that the next circle, as we move into the twenty-first century, is indeed the nineteenth century, and that this may, in a sense, lead us back to the future.

WORKS CITED

Allen, Gay Wilson. *Waldo Emerson: A Biography.* New York: Viking, 1981.

Barish, Evelyn. *Emerson in Italy.* New York: Henry Holt, 1989.

———. *Emerson: The Roots of Prophecy.* Princeton, NJ: Princeton UP, 1989.

Bell, Ian F. A. "The Hard Currency of Words: Emerson's Fiscal Metaphor in Nature." *ELH* 52 (1985): 733–53.

Bloom, Harold, ed. *Ralph Waldo Emerson.* New York: Chelsea House, 1985.

Bosco, Ronald A. "'Blessed Are They Who Have No Talent': Emerson's Unwritten Life of Amos Bronson Alcott." *ESQ: A Journal of the American Renaissance* 36 (1990): 1–36.

———. "'Poetry for the World of Readers' and 'Poetry for Bards Proper': Poetic Theory and Textual Integrity in Parnassus." *Studies in the American Renaissance 1989.* Ed. Joel Myerson. Charlottesville: UP of Virginia, 1989. 257–312.

Buell, Lawrence. "Emerson in His Cultural Context." Buell, *Ralph Waldo Emerson: A Collection of Critical Essays.* 48–60.

———. *New England Literary Culture: From Revolution through Renaissance.* New York: Cambridge UP, 1986.

———, ed. *Ralph Waldo Emerson: A Collection of Critical Essays.* Englewood Cliffs, NJ: Prentice Hall, 1993.

Burkholder, Robert E. "Emerson, Kneeland, and the Divinity School Address." *American Literature* 58 (1986): 1–14.

———. "The Radical Emerson: Politics in 'The American Scholar.'" *ESQ: A Journal of the American Renaissance* 34 (1988): 37–57.

———. "Transcendental Re-seeing: Teaching Revision Using the Works of Emerson and Thoreau." *Teaching English in the Two-Year College* 12 (1985): 14–21.

Burkholder, Robert E., and Joel Myerson. *Emerson: An Annotated Secondary Bibliography.* Pittsburgh: U of Pittsburgh Press, 1985.

———. "Ralph Waldo Emerson." *The Transcendentalists: A Review of Research and Criticism.* Ed. Myerson. New York: Modern Language Association, 1984. 135–66.

———. *Ralph Waldo Emerson: An Annotated Bibliography of Criticism, 1980–1991.* Westport, CT: Greenwood, 1994.

———, eds. *Critical Essays on Ralph Waldo Emerson.* Boston: G. K. Hall, 1983.

Cady, Edwin H., and Louis J. Budd, eds. *On Emerson: The Best from "American Literature."* Durham, NC: Duke UP, 1988.

Cavell, Stanley. *Conditions Handsome and Unhandsome: The Constitution of Emersonian Perfectionism.* Chicago: U of Chicago P, 1990.

———. *In Quest of the Ordinary: Lines of Skepticism and Romanticism.* Chicago: U of Chicago P, 1988.

———. *The Senses of Walden: An Expanded Edition.* San Francisco: North Point, 1981.

———. *This New Yet Unapproachable America: Lectures after Emerson after Wittgenstein.* Albuquerque, NM: Living Batch P, 1989.

Cayton, Mary Kupiec. *Emerson's Emergence: Self and Society in the Transformation of New England, 1800–1845.* Chapel Hill: U of North Carolina P, 1989.

Chai, Leon. *The Romantic Foundations of the American Renaissance.* Ithaca, NY: Cornell UP, 1987.

Cheyfitz, Eric. *The Trans-Parent: Sexual Politics in the Language of Emerson.* Baltimore: Johns Hopkins UP, 1981.

Colacurcio, Michael J. "'Pleasing God': The Lucid Style of Emerson's 'Address.'" *ESQ: A Journal of the American Renaissance* 37 (1991): 141–212.

Donadio, Stephen, et al., eds. *Emerson and His Legacy: Essays in Honor of Quentin Anderson.* Carbondale: Southern Illinois UP, 1986.

Edmundson, Mark. *Towards Reading Freud: Self-Creation in Milton, Wordsworth, Emerson, and Sigmund Freud.* Princeton, NJ: Princeton UP, 1990.

Ellison, Julie. *Emerson's Romantic Style.* Princeton, NJ: Princeton UP, 1984.

Emerson, Ellen Tucker. *The Letters of Ellen Tucker Emerson.* Ed. Edith W. Gregg. 2 vols. Kent, OH: Kent State UP, 1982.

———. *The Life of Lidian Jackson Emerson.* Ed. Delores Bird Carpenter. Boston: Twayne, 1980.

Emerson, Lidian Jackson. *The Selected Letters of Lidian Jackson Emerson.* Ed. Delores Bird Carpenter. Columbia: U of Missouri P, 1987.

Emerson, Ralph Waldo. *The Collected Works of Ralph Waldo Emerson.* Ed. Joseph Slater et al. 5 vols. to date. Cambridge, MA: Harvard UP, 1971–.

———. *The Complete Sermons of Ralph Waldo Emerson.* Ed. Albert J. von Frank et al. 4 vols. Columbia: U of Missouri P, 1989–92.

———. *Emerson in His Journals.* Ed. Joel Porte. Cambridge, MA: Harvard UP, 1982.

———. *Emerson's Antislavery Writings.* Ed. Len Gougeon and Joel Myerson. New Haven, CT: Yale UP, 1995.

———. *The Journals and Miscellaneous Notebooks of Ralph Waldo Emerson.* Ed. William H. Gilman et al. 16 vols. Cambridge, MA: Harvard UP, 1960–82.

————. *The Letters of Ralph Waldo Emerson.* Ed. Ralph L. Rusk (vols. 1–6) and Eleanor M. Tilton (vols. 7–10). 10 vols. New York: Columbia UP, 1939; 1990–95.

————. *The Poetry Notebooks of Ralph Waldo Emerson.* Ed. Ralph H. Orth et al. Columbia: U of Missouri P, 1986.

————. *Ralph Waldo Emerson,* 2 vols. (vol. 1: *Essays and Lectures,* 1983; vol. 2: *Collected Poems and Translations,* 1994). New York: Library of America, 1983–94.

————. *The Topical Notebooks of Ralph Waldo Emerson.* Ed. Ralph H. Orth et al. 3 vols. Columbia: U of Missouri P, 1990–94.

Emerson, Ralph Waldo, and Thomas Carlyle. *The Correspondence of Emerson and Carlyle.* Ed. Joseph Slater. New York: Columbia UP, 1964.

Gass, William H. "Emerson and the Essay." *Yale Review* 71 (1982): 321–62.

Gelpi, Donald L. *Endless Seeker: The Religious Quest of Ralph Waldo Emerson.* Lanham, MD: UP of America, 1991.

Giamatti, A. Bartlett. "Power, Politics, and a Sense of History: The Baccalaureate Address." *Yale Alumni Magazine* (1981): 10–13.

Gilbert, Armida. *Emerson and the English Romantic Poets.* Kent, OH: Kent State UP, forthcoming.

Goodman, Russell B. *American Philosophy and the American Tradition.* New York: Cambridge UP, 1990.

Gougeon, Len. *Virtue's Hero: Emerson, Antislavery, and Reform.* Athens: U of Georgia P, 1990.

Gross, Robert A. *Books and Libraries in Thoreau's Concord.* Worcester, MA: American Antiquarian Society, 1988.

Grusin, Richard A. "'Put God in Your Debt': Emerson's Economy of Expenditure." *PMLA* 103 (1988): 35–44.

————. *Transcendentalist Hermeneutics: Institutional Authority and the Higher Criticism of the Bible.* Durham, NC: Duke UP, 1991.

Gura, Philip F. *The Wisdom of Words: Language, Theology, and Literature in the New England Renaissance.* Middletown, CT: Wesleyan UP, 1981.

Hodder, Alan. D. *Emerson's Rhetoric of Revelation: Nature, the Reader and the Apocalypse Within.* University Park: Pennsylvania State UP, 1989.

Horwitz, Howard. "The Standard Oil Trust as Emersonian Hero." *Raritan* 6.4 (1987): 97–119.

Howe, Irving. *The American Newness: Culture and Politics in the Age of Emerson.* Cambridge, MA: Harvard UP, 1986.

Hubbell, George Shelton. *A Concordance to the Poems of Ralph Waldo Emerson.* New York: H. W. Wilson, 1932.

Hughes, Gertrude Reif. *Emerson's Demanding Optimism.* Baton Rouge: Louisiana State UP, 1984.

Hutch, Richard A. *Emerson's Optics: Biographical Process and the Dawn of Religious Leadership*. Washington, DC: UP of America, 1983.

Johnson, Glen M. "Emerson's Craft of Revision: The Composition of *Essays* (1841)." *Studies in the American Renaissance 1980*. Ed. Joel Myerson. Boston: Twayne, 1980. 51–72.

———. "Emerson's Essay 'Immortality': The Problem of Authorship." *American Literature* 56 (1984): 313–30.

Johnson, Linck C. "Reforming the Reformers: Emerson, Thoreau, and the Sunday Lectures at Amory Hall, Boston." *ESQ: A Journal of the American Renaissance* 37 (1991): 235–89.

Kronick, Joseph G. *American Poetics of History: From Emerson to the Moderns*. Baton Rouge: Louisiana State UP, 1984.

Lang, Amy Schrager. *Prophetic Woman: Anne Hutchinson and the Problem of Dissent in the Literature of New England*. Berkeley: U of California P, 1987.

Leverenz, David. *Manhood and the American Renaissance*. Ithaca, NY: Cornell UP, 1989.

Loewenberg, Robert J. *An American Idol: Emerson and the "Jewish Idea."* Lanham, MD: UP of America, 1984.

Loving, Jerome. *Emerson, Whitman, and the American Muse*. Chapel Hill: U of North Carolina P, 1982.

Marr, David. *American Worlds since Emerson*. Amherst: U of Massachusetts P, 1988.

McAleer, John. *Ralph Waldo Emerson: Days of Encounter*. Boston: Little, Brown, 1984.

Michael, John. *Emerson and Skepticism*. Baltimore: Johns Hopkins UP, 1988.

Milder, Robert. "Emerson's Two Conversions." *ESQ: A Journal of the American Renaissance* 33 (1987): 20–34.

Mott, Wesley T. *"The Strains of Eloquence": Emerson and His Sermons*. University Park: Pennsylvania State UP, 1989.

Myerson, Joel. *Ralph Waldo Emerson: A Descriptive Bibliography*. Pittsburgh: U of Pittsburgh P, 1982.

———, ed. *Emerson and Thoreau: The Contemporary Reviews*. New York: Cambridge UP, 1982.

———, ed. *Emerson Centenary Essays*. Carbondale: Southern Illinois UP, 1982.

Neufeldt, Leonard. *The House of Emerson*. Lincoln: U of Nebraska P, 1982.

Packer, Barbara. *Emerson's Fall: A New Interpretation of the Major Essays*. New York: Continuum, 1982.

———. "Origin and Authority: Emerson and the Higher Criticism." *Reconstructing American Literary History*. Ed. Sacvan Bercovitch. Cambridge, MA: Harvard UP, 1986. 67–92.

———. "Ralph Waldo Emerson." *Cambridge Literary History of the United States*. Ed. Emory Elliott. New York: Columbia UP, 1988. 381–98.

Paulson, A. B. "Emerson and Aphasia." *Language and Style* 14 (1981): 155–71.

Poirier, Richard. *Poetry and Pragmatism.* Cambridge, MA: Harvard UP, 1992.

———. *The Renewal of Literature: Emersonian Reflections.* New York: Random House, 1987.

Porte, Joel, ed. *Emerson: Prospect and Retrospect.* Cambridge, MA: Harvard UP, 1982.

Porter, Carolyn. *Seeing and Being: The Plight of the Participant Observer in Emerson, James, Adams, and Faulkner.* Middletown, CT: Wesleyan UP, 1981.

Putz, Manfred. *Ralph Waldo Emerson: A Bibliography of Twentieth-Century Criticism.* New York: Peter Lang, 1986.

Railton, Stephen. *Authorship and Audience: Literary Performance in the American Renaissance.* Princeton, NJ: Princeton UP, 1991.

Reynolds, Larry J. *European Revolutions and the American Literary Renaissance.* New Haven, CT: Yale UP, 1988.

Richardson, Robert D., Jr. *Emerson: The Mind on Fire.* Berkeley: U of California P, 1995.

Roberson, Susan L. *Emerson in His Sermons.* Columbia: U of Missouri P, 1994.

Robinson, David M. *Apostle of Culture: Emerson as Preacher and Lecturer.* Philadelphia: U of Pennsylvania P, 1982.

———. *Emerson and the Conduct of Life: Pragmatism and Ethical Purpose in the Later Work.* New York: Cambridge UP, 1993.

Rosenwald, Lawrence. *Emerson and the Art of the Diary.* New York: Oxford UP, 1988.

Rusk, Ralph L. *The Life of Ralph Waldo Emerson.* New York: Scribners, 1949.

Sattelmeyer, Robert. *Thoreau's Reading.* Princeton, NJ: Princeton UP, 1988.

———. "'When He Became My Enemy': Emerson and Thoreau, 1848–49." *New England Quarterly* 62 (1989): 187–204.

Sealts, Merton M., Jr. *Emerson on the Scholar.* Columbia: U of Missouri P, 1992.

———. "Melville and Emerson's Rainbow." *ESQ: A Journal of the American Renaissance* 26 (1980): 53–78.

———. *Melville's Reading,* rev. and enl. ed. Columbia: U of South Carolina P, 1988.

Simmons, Nancy Craig. "Arranging the Sibylline Leaves: James Elliot Cabot's Work as Emerson's Literary Executor." *Studies in the American Renaissance 1983.* Ed. Joel Myerson. Charlottesville: UP of Virginia, 1983. 335–89.

———. "Man without a Shadow: The Life and Work of James Elliot Cabot, Emerson's Biographer and Literary Executor." Diss. Princeton U, 1980.

Smith, David L. "Emerson and Deconstruction: The End(s) of Scholarship." *Soundings* 64 (1984): 379–98.

Stack, George J. *Nietzsche and Emerson: An Elective Affinity.* Athens: Ohio UP, 1992.

Thurin, Erik Ingvar. *Emerson as Priest of Pan: A Study in the Metaphysics of Sex.* Lawrence: Regents P of Kansas, 1981.

Toulouse, Teresa. *The Art of Prophesying: New England Sermons and the Shaping of Belief.* Athens: U of Georgia P, 1987.

Updike, John. "Emersonianism." *New Yorker* (4 June 1984): 112, 115–20, 123–28, 131–32.

Van Cromphout, Gustaaf. *Emerson's Modernity and the Example of Goethe.* Columbia: U of Missouri P, 1990.

Van Leer, David. *Emerson's Epistemology: The Argument of the Major Essays.* New York: Cambridge UP, 1986.

Versluis, Arthur. *American Transcendentalism and Asian Religions.* New York: Oxford UP, 1983.

von Frank, Albert J. *An Emerson Chronology.* New York: G. K. Hall, 1994.

Weisbuch, Robert. *Atlantic Double-Cross: American Literature and British Influence in the Age of Emerson.* Chicago: U of Chicago P, 1986.

Whicher, Stephen E. *Freedom and Fate: An Inner Life of Ralph Waldo Emerson.* Philadelphia: U of Pennsylvania P, 1953.

Williams, John B. *White Fire: The Influence of Emerson on Melville.* Long Beach: California State U, Long Beach, 1991.

Wilson, R. Jackson. *Figures of Speech: American Writers and the Literary Marketplace, from Benjamin Franklin to Emily Dickinson.* New York: Knopf, 1989.

Winchell, Mark R. "Ralph Waldo Emerson." *American Orators before 1900.* Ed. Bernard K. Duffy and Halford R. Ryan. Westport, CT: Greenwood, 1987. 154–61.

Zink, Harriet Rodgers. "Emerson's Use of the Bible." *University of Nebraska Studies in Language, Literature, and Criticism* 14 (1935): 5–75.

Zwarg, Christina. *Feminist Conversations: Fuller, Emerson, and the Play of Reading.* Ithaca, NY: Cornell UP, 1995.

2

Henry David Thoreau

Elizabeth Hall Witherell

Among the writers included in the traditional canon of American literature, Thoreau has always provoked the strongest popular reactions, both
positive and negative. He is an icon of American individualism, the
father of environmentalism, and in general much better known for what
he is thought to represent than for what he actually wrote. In the words
of Jane Bennett, Thoreau and the location of his experiment in living,
Walden Pond, have been "elevated to the status of floating signifiers,
whose possibility of meaning exceeds any specific referent or singular
theme" (84).

Specific referents and singular themes are still the bread and butter of
academics who study Thoreau, of course, but as more diverse areas of
interest have been accepted as legitimate, the popular view of Thoreau
has been included among the topics worthy of treatment in serious scholarship. As Cecelia Tichi puts it, "literary studies" of the American
Renaissance and its major and minor figures "become cultural studies"
(224). This broader field is available from one end of the spectrum of
response, where the contextualizing theorists—Marxists, feminists, New
Historicists—open fresh areas of investigation, to the other, where a
project to re-edit the texts of Thoreau's writings and his journal continues
to provide new primary material to be considered. The result for all
readers of Thoreau—teachers and students alike—has been a fascinating
and fruitful complication of our view of the man and his writing that
opens myriad possibilities for continued exploration.

Four review essays in *ESQ*—by Richard Schneider in 1981, Robert
Sattelmeyer in 1985, Philip Gura in 1992, and William Rossi in 1996—are
useful for charting the highlights in Thoreau scholarship from 1977
through 1995. Two recent collections of essays, one growing out of a

two-week symposium that celebrated the fiftieth anniversary of the founding of the Thoreau Society (Schofield and Baron) and another intended to "help readers read Thoreau better" (Myerson xi) are also good sources of information about current areas of interest that are worthy of further inquiry. Richard Schneider's introductory material in the volume of essays he collected on teaching Thoreau (*Approaches* 1–27) surveys old and new works with an eye to their pedagogical usefulness. But the most comprehensive single source of information about what has been done and what remains to be done in Thoreau scholarship is Walter Harding and Michael Meyer's *The New Thoreau Handbook*, published in 1980. A brief review of how scholars and critics have filled the gaps identified in *The New Thoreau Handbook* incidentally indicates where Thoreau studies have aligned with and diverged from the general course of developments in American literary studies during the last seventeen years.

The *Handbook* authors' prediction that there will never be "a 'definitive' biography of Thoreau to satisfy all times and all people" (24) is undoubtedly true, although Harding's is the most comprehensive in its detail (the 1982 revised edition includes notes not printed in the first edition). However, Harding and Meyer also suggested that each generation needs its own biography: for our generation, that is Richardson's *Henry Thoreau: A Life of the Mind*. Focusing on the intellectual development that underlies Thoreau's art, Richardson brings greater depth and richness than ever before to our picture of the complexities and contradictions of his subject.

That said, it is also the case that a number of areas of Thoreau's life would yield to closer scrutiny or to re-viewing: a prime example is his sexuality. The contemporaneous description provided by a pupil in the Thoreau brothers' school, Horace Hosmer, is sweetly innocent of psychological theorizing: he "did not have the 'love-idea' in him; i.e. he did not appear to feel the *sex*-attraction" (131). In 1976, Jonathan Katz claimed Thoreau for the community of gay American writers. More recently, Harding has dealt with this issue in "Thoreau's Sexuality" by presenting textual evidence of Thoreau's interest in the male body; Michael Warner has discussed this issue as well. But the subject is far from exhausted, and a full exploration of the evidence in the context of nineteenth-century American sexual manners and mores and of Thoreau's relationships would be extremely helpful. As a young man, he tended toward romantic infatuations with older and somehow unattainable women; many of his friendships with men were somewhat defensive and ritualized—this is the case in different ways with Emerson, with Sanborn, with Blake and the Worcester circle. Thoreau's reaction to William Ellery Channing, the unnamed partner on many of his excursions, while apparently more spontaneous, was complex: it would be worthwhile to reexamine the friendship.

To counterbalance the absence of women in Thoreau's writings, it is useful to remember that for most of his life he was surrounded by women who loved and supported him, and whom he loved in return—his mother, his sisters, his aunts, Mary Moody Emerson. An examination of these relationships would be of interest; a study of Henry and his sister Sophia that discussed her role in the family could be fascinating.

In 1958, Sherman Paul noted that "much that Thoreau wrote has not been closely read" (viii); at that time, most of what was available was several printed generations away from what Thoreau wrote. Now, thanks to support from the National Endowment for the Humanities and sponsoring institutions including the State University College of New York at Geneseo; Princeton University; the University of California, Santa Barbara; and Georgia State University, scholars are producing a new thirty-volume edition of Thoreau's books, essays, Journal, and correspondence, *The Writings of Henry D. Thoreau*. In addition to *Walden*, the project's first publication, there are ten more volumes containing newly edited texts for *A Week on the Concord and Merrimack Rivers, The Maine Woods,* and *Cape Cod;* for Thoreau's earliest essays, his reform essays, and his literary translations from Greek, Latin, and French; and for four volumes of the Journal covering the years 1837 to 1852. Each of these texts, based on manuscripts or a first edition emended to represent a definable stage of Thoreau's intention for the work, will support the closest reading. All of the volumes in the Thoreau Edition (sometimes known as the Princeton Edition because Princeton University Press has published the project's work from the start) include introductions that present historical and textual information—the history of composition, publication, and reception, for example; descriptions of physical features of the source texts; and the principles governing editorial decisions—as well as notes and tables documenting the editorial work.

The scope of the Thoreau Edition extends to all of Thoreau's writings for publication, his complete Journal (forty-seven manuscript volumes), and his correspondence (a chronological list of all of the letters in the Thoreau Edition files as well as all of those known to have existed but no longer extant was published by Kappes et al. in 1982). When Walter

Harding started his work as the first editor-in-chief of this project, in 1965, the most authoritative texts of the published writings were to be found in first or second editions, which had gone through the hands of fewer editors and compositors than twentieth-century versions. The only available text of Thoreau's Journal—now considered by many to be his most important work—was incomplete in large and small ways: this edition, published in 1906, lacked half of the text of the original Journal for 1837 through 1849, and from the Journal for 1850 through 1861 the editors omitted quotations, lists and charts of plants, and early drafts of works published later.

Although the Thoreau Edition will be a work-in-progress for some time to come, both the volumes that are published and the project's files, used as a resource by scholars, have encouraged close readings and made possible new intertextual interpretations. J. Lyndon Shanley's study of the drafts of *Walden* and Ronald Clapper's "Genetic Text" were an essential basis for such studies as Sattelmeyer's of the development of the book through its seven versions, but the availability of the new Journal volumes was also important. Considering Thoreau's attitude toward sexual desire, Warner compares the Journal draft of a passage with its use in "Love" and finds that the draft "challenges what the essay version pretends to celebrate" (53). Thoreau drafted passages in his Journal for many of his lectures, essays, and books, and comparisons such as Warner's can be illuminating. Beginning with *Journal 2*, Thoreau Edition volumes of the Journal include a table of cross-references to published versions that should make intertextual studies easier.

The New Thoreau Handbook states flatly that "no final order of composition of Thoreau's works can be established" (32), but the new texts and contexts allow the complicated interrelationships among the many versions of a given work—Journal passages, drafts, lecture notes—and between works that were under way at the same time to be studied with more confidence. Linck Johnson has studied such interrelationships for *A Week*, including an edition of the first draft, and Stephen Adams and Donald Ross, Jr., have examined the major works. In a model that could productively be followed for any of Thoreau's works first presented to the public as a lecture, Bradley P. Dean has reconstructed the lecture versions of what was published as "Life without Principle." This reconstructive work depends partly on the kind of basic digging in contemporary newspapers and other publications that Dean and Gary Scharnhorst have done for reviews of *Walden*, and that forms the basis of

Scharnhorst's *Annotated Bibliography*. A published list of Thoreau's lectures, updating Harding's checklist, would be helpful. Eventually, it may in fact be possible to chart Thoreau's creative path in and among all his works, allowing for interpretations that complicate and enrich the final, public version of each of them.

Computer technology offers exciting new possibilities for gaining access to and studying Thoreau's texts. Libraries around the country are considering the benefits of digitizing manuscript material, both to make it more widely available and to protect it from overuse (microfilm and other forms of photocopy serve this purpose now). Once digitized, material can, theoretically, be manipulated at will: the proper equipment is necessary, of course. With hypertext, successive manuscript versions of a work can be linked with transcripts and edited text to create resources customized by the user to suit his or her research or teaching needs. Concordance programs can be run to study Thoreau's use of language. Dean has made a preliminary survey of Thoreau texts in machine-readable form, and a planned Media Center at the new Thoreau Institute in Lincoln, Massachusetts, described in greater detail below, will gather these materials and, to the extent possible under current copyright restrictions, make them available.

Despite the progress made, it will be true for some time to come that primary materials essential to a full study of Thoreau are not easily available, or are available only in incomplete versions. In addition to the later Journal volumes, which are scheduled to appear in sequence in the Edition, there are the manuscripts that contain his natural history work— what he called his "Kalendar" (see Howarth 306–31). Preparing these manuscripts for publication is not part of the scope of the Thoreau Edition, and although several scholars, including Witherell and Dean, are currently working on them, they are an open field for research. They consist of almost a thousand manuscript pages that need to be brought under control in several ways before their significance can be fully appreciated. A data base would seem to be the most appropriate way to organize the material and would be a worthy project for a team of scholars familiar with Thoreau's hand.

Recent publications have only hinted at the complexity and richness of this material (H. Daniel Peck reproduces a page [164–65], as does Dean [Thoreau, *Faith* 222]). Not only will the Kalendar and the related manuscripts provide a clearer picture of how Thoreau developed as a natural scientist and how he responded to Darwin, but also they will provide the basis for informed speculation about the direction Thoreau's work would have taken had he lived. Related to the Journal and to several unfinished essays, these manuscripts will help to answer the lingering question of exactly what Thoreau was doing after *Walden*. In addition, they may be of real use to botanists and ecologists seeking to document indigenous plant species and changes in animal habitats. At his death, Thoreau left several unfinished natural history essays that are closely related to the Kalendar material. Dean has edited one of these, "The Dispersion of Seeds" (Thoreau, *Faith*), and is working on others.

Thoreau's commonplace books are also rich sources of information. Several have been published in facsimile by Kenneth Walter Cameron. Recent articles by Hongbo Tan and Suzanne Rose offer good examples of the uses that can be made of unpublished material. An accessible, machine-readable transcript of Thoreau's Indian Books at the Pierpont Morgan Library in New York would be a great benefit to the field; at least one early transcript exists, at the Morgan, and it might serve as a basis.

Those who begin to work with manuscripts soon realize that they are an endless source of insight. William Howarth's *The Literary Manuscripts of Henry David Thoreau* is the best starting point for investigating the manuscripts themselves. Since it was published in 1974, a number of individual leaves of manuscript have surfaced, and some have changed hands; in addition, more is known about Thoreau's habits of composition. A revised version of the book, presented as a computer data base, would not only document these changes but also serve as a flexible basis for recording information about new manuscripts.

Scholars who want to use the manuscripts find that these documents are spread across the country (see Witherell, "Availability," for a partial account of how they came to be where they are: more work in this area would be a contribution to a history of Thoreau's reputation as well as of collecting). Four research libraries hold most of the material; the following brief account lists only highlights. The Morgan Library has all but one of the bound manuscript volumes of the Journal; the Henry W. and Albert A. Berg Collection of the New York Public Library has a number of letters and reams of Kalendar notes; the Houghton Library at Harvard has drafts of *A Week* and *The Maine Woods*; the Huntington Library in San Marino, California, has much of the seven drafts of *Walden*. The Abernethy Library at Middlebury College, the Concord Free Public Library, and the Barrett Library at the University of Virginia have substantial collections as well. In many cases, microfilm of manuscript material is available for purchase; scholars may apply to the library in question.

Occasionally, Thoreau manuscript material comes up for sale: single leaves can be offered at several thousand dollars. Most of these leaves were at one time tipped into the first volume of a set of the twenty-volume Manuscript Edition, which was published by Houghton Mifflin in 1906. Some still are part of a set: at last count, about 165 of the six hundred or so sets produced had been located, and of those, about 130 still had their manuscripts (Dean, "Checklist"). Over the years, the manuscripts have been removed from many of these sets and sold separately. Very rarely, a group of several leaves comes onto the market—in recent years, the draft of an essay, a multi-page letter, and a few pages that Thoreau removed from one of his Journal volumes have been for sale. The asking prices have ranged from tens to hundreds of thousands of dollars, depending on the provenance of the material and whether the contents have been published.

Of the studies that focus on structure and interpretation of these contents, Harding and Meyer's observation that "the vast majority" center on *Walden* (198) still holds true, but that magic circle is widening. Johnson's study of *A Week* and Dean's of "Life without Principle" have been noted; "Walking" is becoming a more popular subject of scrutiny, as are the essays that make up *The Maine Woods*, especially "Ktaadn." The Journal has received useful and sometimes provocative attention from, among others, Howarth, Sharon Cameron, and Peck. As new volumes of the Thoreau Edition Journal become available, interpretations of it and Thoreau's use of it should evolve. Thoreau's poetry has been placed in the context of his literary career, and a group of poems that represent the culmination of his literary apprenticeship has been identified and made available (Witherell). He has not been studied as a letter writer perhaps because the number of letters is small; nevertheless, an examination of the relationship of the letters to the Journal would be interesting.

Harding and Meyer's call for closer examination of the subject of Thoreau's language and his literary theories (198) has begun to be answered by the work of Richard Dillman, Frederick Garber, and Henry Golemba. Dillman also applies reader-response techniques, as does Irene Goldman. Goldman provides one of the few feminist approaches to Thoreau; a handful of others appears in a special issue of *ISLE: Interdisciplinary Studies in Literature and Environment*. In a 1990 dissertation, Linda Frost views *The Maine Woods* from a more linguistically oriented feminist perspective; the success of her analysis suggests that new dimensions of other works might be revealed by applying the technique.

In the area of influence studies, *The New Thoreau Handbook* suggested investigating Eastern sources more thoroughly (94), and extending the examination of these sources beyond *A Week on the Concord and Merri-mack Rivers* and *Walden* (114). The work of Tan and Versluis, discussed elsewhere in this essay, is part of a response to this call. American students, rarely required to be fluent in another language, often overlook Thoreau's facility in this area: he read German, French, Spanish, and some Italian, as well as Latin and Greek, and he knew many of the classics of those languages in their original forms. His own interest in the roots of words and in linguistic theories is manifest in his conscious attention to language; Michael West and Gura (*Wisdom*) are basic readings in this area. An examination of the effect of Thoreau's reading in other languages on his linguistic study would extend our knowledge of his version of this standard Transcendentalist preoccupation. In terms of the influence of an entire culture, Thoreau's debt to Goethe remains largely unexplored, although Ingrid Fry's dissertation is a start.

Thoreau's appreciation of the visual arts had a significant effect on his writings: connections have been drawn with landscape painting as well as with theories of representation, by Barbara Novak, Barton Levi St. Armand, and Schneider. Thoreau was impressed by William Gilpin's works, a fact that could be the basis for a new study of the writer's understanding of the relation between visual and linguistic description.

Thoreau's influence on American political culture into the 1970s is documented by Meyer; an examination of his use by current movements advocating voluntary simplicity would be helpful. Buell (*Environmental Imagination*), Scott Slovic, and Gary Snyder, among others, treat and display the influence of Thoreau's nature writing: it would be interesting to study the evolution of Thoreau's ideas about the preservation of nature in the light of the maturing environmental movement and its associated backlash. Thoreau's influence on the work of other poets of the nineteenth and twentieth centuries, especially Emily Dickinson and Robert Frost, has been noted; currently more attention is focused on prose writers.

Harding and Meyer noted the need for "a selective annotated bibliography to guide the student through the great morass of duplicative and redundant material" (226). This need is met in part by the annual publication *American Literary Scholarship*, in which a succession of reviewers has given pithy summaries of publications on "Emerson, Thoreau, and Transcendentalism" (Margaret Fuller achieved title status in 1994). In addition to publishing the standard primary bibliography, Raymond Borst has published an annotated secondary bibliography covering the years 1835 to 1899. Amplifications and corrections appear in Scharnhorst's fuller bibliography covering roughly the same time period. Schneider cites Annette Woodlief for literary criticism focused on *Walden* through 1973, and he notes the lack of a "comprehensive single checklist . . . for criticism on *Walden* after 1973" (*Approaches* 14).

Harding and Meyer called attention to the absence of a well-developed context in Thoreau studies: while there are many critical interpretations of his writings, *Walden* and "Civil Disobedience" in particular, in general there has been "comparatively little attempt to place Thoreau against the background of his times" (107). They mentioned the importance of knowing Thoreau's sources (91) and singled out the need for "a comprehensive and balanced study of T[horeau]'s religious attitudes that places in perspective his use of Eastern and Western religious beliefs and practices" and that for a "book-length comprehensive treatment of T[horeau]'s politics" (155).

Some of these needs have been met and some have not. The effort to ground Thoreau's life and work in contemporaneous culture has been under way for some time and has produced solid and exciting new work. Raymond Borst's log of Thoreau's life, like the Dickinson and Melville logs, offers a wealth of raw material—biographical and historical details drawn from Thoreau's Journal and his letters and from other contemporary sources—in the form of a chronology. The best of the contextualizing studies have illuminated areas of the background that were not known to be dark and will serve as models for future work. Among these are Robert Gross's fascinating studies of Thoreau's Concord, Johnson's examination of Thoreau's place in the contemporary reform tradition, Leonard Neufeldt's analysis of the economic conditions of Thoreau's times, and Steven Fink's portrait of Thoreau the writer accommodating to the literary market. General treatments of popular culture in the nineteenth-century, such as Joan Burbick's, are useful for understanding the material and psychological conditions of Thoreau's existence. Sattelmeyer's treatment of Thoreau's reading is accompanied by an invaluable bibliography that includes the most reliable information available about where Thoreau found each title, what edition he used, and where he quoted from it. Some editions have not yet been identified.

In a piece soon to be published in a collection of essays about the Transcendentalists and religion, K. P. Van Anglen has raised the issue of Thoreau's attitude toward the New England religious tradition; much remains to be explored here. Arthur Versluis on Transcendentalism in general and Alan Hodder on *Walden* in particular deal with Eastern religious sources. Still, the definitive study of Thoreau's spirituality and his indebtedness to the scriptures of other cultures is yet to appear.

In her introduction to a useful collection of Thoreau's political writings, Nancy L. Rosenblum makes the astute comment that "Thoreau is not [seen as] a political philosopher . . . less because his style of thought is unsystematic or his references to the history of political thought are few, and more because of his insistence that political society's claim on us is conditional and intermittent, and that government's contribution to a well-spent life is only comparatively important" (vii). A thoroughgoing exploration of Thoreau's understanding of the history of political thought from the perspective of Rosenblum's premise would be enlightening. Thoreau's involvement with the abolitionist movement could be profitably reviewed, as well, and Schneider points out that "[n]o books deal specifically with Thoreau's response to slavery" (*Approaches* 13).

Thoreau's relationship to nineteenth-century science has become one of the hottest new topics in Thoreau studies. Richardson, Rossi, and Laura Dassow Walls have improved our understanding of both terms of this subject. However, as discussed above, Thoreau's detailed records of his observations as a natural scientist are still in manuscript, untranscribed and unsorted. The picture of exactly how these records contributed to his writing will not be complete until all of the evidence is available.

Another recent area of investigation is the development of Thoreau's reputation: some of this work is in the context, described by Tichi, of remaking the canon of American literature in general and the literature of New England in particular. Articles by Lawrence Buell ("Henry Thoreau Enters the American Canon") and Nina Baym frame Thoreau's acceptance as a canonical author with a movement organized by what Tichi characterizes as "academic-publishing elites rooted in Boston" (216). This is a useful point of view from which to rethink the information in studies of Thoreau's reputation by Fritz Oehlschlaeger and George Hendrick, Meyer, and Scharnhorst. Whether or not Thoreau serves an establishment purpose at a given time depends on the nature of the establishment: an analysis of how his place in the curriculum has changed over the years would be revealing. In the spirit of current efforts to understand a culture's reading habits, it would be interesting to devise a way to determine how and when Thoreau is currently being read.

As in the 1960s those protesting the war in Vietnam turned to "Civil Disobedience" for guidance, now the leaders in both ecological and ecocritical movements find inspiration in his writing: Thoreau is the ultimate "green" writer. Buell's subtle study of Thoreau as a writer of environmental prose and of his predecessors and inheritors in this tradition came out in 1995. Four years before, Don Henley and Dave Marsh edited *Heaven Is under Our Feet*, a collection of almost seventy celebratory pieces (many by well-known actors, performers, and politicians), contributed to raise funds to preserve land around Walden Pond. The ecological approach, academic and populist alike, reveals as much about the current culture as about Thoreau or what he wrote; similarly revealing are the uses of Thoreauvian soundbites in popular literature and in advertising. Research in these and related areas would be entertaining as well as useful.

It is worth noting that the Thoreau Society has entered into a partnership with Don Henley's Walden Woods Project to create the Thoreau Institute, located in Walden Woods in Lincoln, Massachusetts. The Institute, established with a challenge grant from the National Endowment for the Humanities, comprises both a building and a broad educational effort. The building will house a library that will make available a comprehensive collection of Thoreau material: the initial accessions—all donations—are the collections of Walter Harding, Raymond Adams, and Roland Robbins. The Institute will also house a media center, which will be equipped to provide educational materials about Thoreau to teachers at all levels and in all parts of the country. The Thoreau Institute is expected to open in 1997. The Thoreau Society has also revived its annual *Concord Saunterer*; the loss of *Studies in the American Renaissance* makes all the more important a serious publication in the area of Thoreau studies.

Those who are teaching Thoreau at advanced levels now have the guidance of peers in Schneider's *Approaches to Teaching Thoreau's "Walden" and Other Works*. As usual, students have for the most part escaped all knowledge of the contextualization now popular in academic discourse: as Schneider notes, a major challenge to those teaching Thoreau is "to overcome students' misconception that he was a uniquely isolated figure retreating from the turmoil of his time" (*Approaches* 25). The success of Thoreau's self-mythologizing makes this a continuing challenge to all who read him now, almost a century and a half after he wrote; carefully annotated texts are a great help in teaching. Harding's new *Annotated Walden* is a good example of the usefulness of having information about the events, assumptions, and lexicon of Thoreau's time readily available. Similarly definitive treatments of other works would be most welcome, to aid both students and teachers.

Some specific texts and contexts in Thoreau studies that would benefit from closer examination have been described here. I do not mean to slight in rpretive work; if I have given it short shrift, it is only because, in my position as editor-in-chief of the Thoreau Edition, I see so much basic textual work to be done. A good general Thoreauvian rule is that a careful reexamination of anything that has been accepted as given will yield new information. As the Thoreau Edition produces the complete Journal, and as the manuscripts that document Thoreau's relation to nineteenth-century science and represent his work as a natural historian become more readily accessible, new views of Thoreau will be possible. When the materials are all available, a new biography will be needed, one that concentrates on Thoreau's work from 1850 until his death in 1862 and that reflects the valuable historicization under way now. In the meantime, as the new texts and contexts are interpreted, evidence for a fuller understanding of Thoreau accumulates, like the details that Thoreau's careful observer in "A Winter Walk" could use to reveal the history of the dry beech leaf that he sees balanced against a pebble on the shore of Walden Pond:

> A skillful engineer, methinks, might project its course since it fell from the parent stem. Here are all the elements for such a calculation. Its present position, the direction of the wind, the level of the pond, and how much more is given. In its scarred edges and veins is its log rolled up. (*Natural History Essays* 63)

WORKS CITED

Adams, Stephen, and Donald Ross, Jr. *Revising Mythologies: The Composition of Thoreau's Major Works.* Charlottesville: UP of Virginia, 1988.

Baym, Nina. "Early Histories of American Literature: A Chapter in the Institution of New England." *Feminism and American Literary History: Essays.* New Brunswick, NJ: Rutgers UP, 1992.

Bennett, Jane. *Thoreau's Nature: Ethics, Politics, and the Wild*. Thousand Oaks, CA: Sage Publications, 1994.

Borst, Raymond R. *Henry David Thoreau: A Descriptive Bibliography*. Pittsburgh: U of Pittsburgh P, 1982.

———. *Henry David Thoreau: A Reference Guide, 1835–1899*. Boston: G. K. Hall, 1987.

———. *The Thoreau Log: A Documentary Life of Henry David Thoreau, 1817–1862*. New York: G. K. Hall, 1992.

Buell, Lawrence. *The Environmental Imagination: Thoreau, Nature Writing, and the Formation of American Culture*. Cambridge, MA: Belknap Press of Harvard UP, 1995.

———. "Henry Thoreau Enters the American Canon." *New Essays on "Walden."* Ed. Robert F. Sayre. Cambridge, England: Cambridge UP, 1992. 23–52.

Burbick, Joan. *Healing the Republic: The Language of Health and the Culture of Nationalism in Nineteenth-Century America*. Cambridge, England: Cambridge UP, 1994.

Cameron, Sharon. *Writing Nature: Henry Thoreau's Journal*. New York: Oxford UP, 1985.

Clapper, Ronald. "The Development of *Walden*: A Genetic Text." Diss. U of California, Los Angeles, 1967.

Dean, Bradley P. "A Checklist of 1906 Manuscript Edition Sets." *Thoreau Research Newsletter* 2.2 (1991): 5–7.

———. "A Preliminary Checklist of Machine-Readable Thoreau Texts." *Thoreau Research Newsletter* 2 (1991): 7–8.

———. "Reconstructions of Thoreau's Early 'Life without Principle' Lectures." *Studies in the American Renaissance 1987*. Ed. Joel Myerson. Charlottesville: UP of Virginia, 1987. 285–364.

Dean, Bradley P., and Gary Scharnhorst. "The Contemporary Reception of *Walden*." *Studies in the American Renaissance 1990*. Ed. Joel Myerson. Charlottesville: UP of Virginia, 1990. 293–328.

Dillman, Richard. *Essays on Henry David Thoreau: Rhetoric, Style and Audience*. West Cornwall, CT: Locust Hill P, 1993.

"Emerson, Thoreau, and Transcendentalism." *American Literary Scholarship: An Annual*. Ed. James Woodress, et al. Durham, NC: Duke UP, 1965–1993.

"Emerson, Thoreau, Fuller, and Transcendentalism." *American Literary Scholarship: An Annual*. Ed. David J. Nordloh and Gary Scharnhorst. Durham, NC: Duke UP, 1994–.

Fink, Steven. *Prophet in the Marketplace: Thoreau's Development as a Professional Writer*. Princeton, NJ: Princeton UP, 1992.

Frost, Linda. "Thinking Language to Be a Body of Thought: Reading Ralph Waldo Emerson, Henry David Thoreau, Louisa May Alcott and Margaret Fuller Ossoli." Diss. State U of New York at Stony Brook, 1990.

Fry, Ingrid Elisabeth. "Elective Affinities: Johann Wolfgang von Goethe's Concept of Bildung and Its Influence on the American Transcendental Writers Emerson, Fuller, and Thoreau." Diss. Washington U, 1994.

Garber, Frederick. *Thoreau's Fable of Inscribing.* Princeton, NJ: Princeton UP, 1991.

Goldman, Irene. "Feminism, Deconstruction, and the Universal: A Case Study on *Walden.*" *Conversations: Contemporary Critical Theory and the Teaching of Literature.* Ed. Charles Moran and Elizabeth Penfield. Urbana: National Council of Teachers of English, 1990. 120–31.

Golemba, Henry. *Thoreau's Wild Rhetoric.* New York: New York UP, 1990.

Gross, Robert A. *Books and Libraries in Thoreau's Concord.* Worcester, MA: American Antiquarian Society, 1988.

———. "Culture and Cultivation: Agriculture and Society in Thoreau's Concord." *Journal of American History* 69 (1982): 42–61.

———. "The Great Bean Field Hoax: Thoreau and Agricultural Reformers." *Virginia Quarterly Review* 61 (1985): 483–97.

———. "'The Most Estimable Place in All the World': A Debate on Progress in Nineteenth-Century Concord." *Studies in the American Renaissance 1978.* Ed. Joel Myerson. Boston: Twayne Publishers, 1978. 1–15.

———. "Young Men and Women of Fairest Promise: Transcendentalism in Concord." *Concord Saunterer* 2.1 (1994): 5–18.

Gura, Philip F. "Travelling Much in Concord: A Sampling of Recent Thoreau Scholarship." *ESQ: A Journal of the American Renaissance* 38 (1992): 71–86.

———. *The Wisdom of Words: Language, Theology, and Literature in the New England Renaissance.* Middletown, CT: Wesleyan UP, 1981.

Harding, Walter. "A Check List of Thoreau's Lectures." *Bulletin of the New York Public Library* 52 (1948): 78–87.

———. *The Days of Henry Thoreau.* New York: Alfred A. Knopf, 1965. Princeton, NJ: Princeton UP, 1982.

———. "Thoreau's Sexuality." *Journal of Homosexuality* 21.3 (1991): 23–45.

Harding, Walter, and Michael Meyer. *The New Thoreau Handbook.* New York: New York UP, 1980.

Henley, Don, and Dave Marsh, eds. *Heaven Is under Our Feet.* Stamford, CT: Longmeadow, 1991.

Hodder, Alan D. "'Ex oriente lux': Thoreau's Ecstasies and the Hindu Texts." *Harvard Theological Review* 86 (1993): 403–39.

Hosmer, Horace. *Remembrances of Concord and the Thoreaus: Letters of Horace Hosmer to Dr. S. A. Jones.* Ed. George Hendrick. Urbana: U of Illinois P, 1977.

Howarth, William L. *The Literary Manuscripts of Henry David Thoreau.* Columbus: Ohio State UP, 1974.

ISLE: Interdisciplinary Studies in Literature and Environment 1.1 (1993):
Kirkland, Leigh. "Sexual Chaos in Walden Pond." 131–36.
Scijag, Leonard M., and Nancy Craig Simmons. "Ecofeminist Cosmology in Thoreau's *Walden.*" 121–29.
Walls, Laura Dassow. "*Walden* as Feminist Manifesto." 137–44.
Westling, Louise. "Thoreau's Ambivalence toward Mother Nature." 145–50.

Johnson, Linck C. "Reforming the Reformers: Emerson, Thoreau, and the Sunday Lectures at Amory Hall, Boston." *ESQ: A Journal of the American Renaissance* 37 (1991): 235–89.

———. *Thoreau's Complex Weave: The Writing of "A Week on the Concord and Merrimack Rivers."* Charlottesville: UP of Virginia, 1986.

Kappes, Carolyn, Walter Harding, Randy F. Nelson, and Elizabeth Witherell. "A Calendar of the Correspondence of Henry D. Thoreau." *Studies in the American Renaissance 1982.* Ed. Joel Myerson. Boston: Twayne Publishers, 1982. 325–99.

Katz, Jonathan. *Gay American History.* New York: Crowell, 1976.

Meyer, Michael. *Several More Lives to Live: Thoreau's Political Reputation in America.* Westport, CT: Greenwood P, 1977.

Myerson, Joel, ed. *The Cambridge Companion to Henry David Thoreau.* Cambridge, England: Cambridge UP, 1995.

Neufeldt, Leonard. *The Economist: Henry Thoreau and Enterprise.* New York: Oxford UP, 1989.

Novak, Barbara. *Nature and Culture.* New York: Oxford UP, 1980.

Oehlschlaeger, Fritz, and George Hendrick, eds. *Toward the Making of Thoreau's Modern Reputation: Selected Correspondence of S. A Jones, A. W. Hosmer, H. S. Salt, H. G. O. Blake, and D. Ricketson.* Urbana: U of Illinois P, 1980.

Paul, Sherman. *The Shores of America: Thoreau's Inward Exploration.* Urbana: U of Illinois P, 1958.

Peck, H. Daniel. *Thoreau's Morning Work: Memory and Perception in "A Week on the Concord and Merrimack Rivers," the Journal, and "Walden."* New Haven, CT: Yale UP, 1990.

Richardson, Robert D., Jr. *Henry Thoreau: A Life of the Mind.* Berkeley: U of California P, 1986.

———. "Thoreau and Science." In *American Literature and Science.* Ed. Robert Scholnick. Lexington: UP of Kentucky, 1992. 110–27.

Rose, Suzanne. "Following the Trail of Footsteps from the Indian Notebooks to *Walden.*" *New England Quarterly* 67 (1994): 77–91.

Rossi, William. "Education in the Field: Recent Thoreau Criticism and Environment." *ESQ: A Journal of the American Renaissance* 42 (1996).

———. "Poetry and Progress: Thoreau, Lyell, and the Geological Principles of *A Week on the Concord and Merrimack Rivers*." *American Literature* 66 (1994): 275–301.

———. "Roots, Leaves, and Method: Henry Thoreau and Nineteenth-Century Natural Science." *Journal of American Studies Association of Texas* 19 (1988): 1–22.

Sattelmeyer, Robert. "The Remaking of *Walden*." *Writing the American Classics*. Ed. James Barbour and Tom Quirk. Chapel Hill: U of North Carolina P, 1990. 53–78.

———. "Study Nature and Know Thyself: Recent Thoreau Criticism." *ESQ: A Journal of the American Renaissance* 31 (1985): 190–208.

———. *Thoreau's Reading: A Study in Intellectual History with Bibliographical Catalogue*. Princeton, NJ: Princeton UP, 1988.

Scharnhorst, Gary. *Henry David Thoreau: An Annotated Bibliography of Comment and Criticism before 1900*. New York: Garland Publishing, 1992.

———. *Henry David Thoreau: A Case Study in Canonization*. Columbia, SC: Camden House, 1993.

Schneider, Richard J. *Approaches to Teaching Thoreau's "Walden" and Other Works*. New York: Modern Language Association, 1996.

———. "Humanizing Henry David Thoreau." *ESQ: A Journal of the American Renaissance* 27 (1981): 57–71.

———. "Thoreau and Nineteenth-Century American Landscape Painting." *ESQ: A Journal of the American Renaissance* 31 (1985): 67–88.

Schofield, Edmund A., and Robert C. Baron, eds. *Thoreau's World and Ours: A Natural Legacy*. Golden, CO: North American P, 1993.

Shanley, J. Lyndon. *The Making of "Walden."* Chicago: U of Chicago P, 1957.

Slovic, Scott. *Seeking Awareness in American Nature Writing: Henry Thoreau, Annie Dillard, Edward Abbey, Wendell Berry, Barry Lopez*. Salt Lake City: U of Utah P, 1992.

Snyder, Gary. *The Practice of the Wild*. San Francisco: North Point, 1990.

St. Armand, Barton Levi. "Luminism in the Work of Henry David Thoreau: The Dark and the Light." *Canadian Review of American Studies* 32 (1980): 143–66.

Tan, Hongbo. "Confucius at Walden Pond: Thoreau's Unpublished Confucian Translations." *Studies in the American Renaissance 1993*. Ed. Joel Myerson. Charlottesville: UP of Virginia, 1993. 275–303.

Thoreau, Henry D. *Cape Cod*. Ed. Joseph J. Moldenhauer. Princeton, NJ: Princeton UP, 1988.

————. [Commonplace Books in print; see also Howarth 281–307]:

Thoreau's Canadian Notebook and Record of Surveys: Selected Chapters from Transcendentalist Climate. Ed. Kenneth Walter Cameron. Hartford: Transcendental Books, [1967].

Thoreau's Fact Book in the Harry Elkins Widener Collection in the Harvard College Library. Ed. Kenneth Walter Cameron. 3 vols. Hartford: Transcendental Books, [1966–c.1987].

Thoreau's Literary Notebook in the Library of Congress. Ed. Kenneth Walter Cameron. Hartford: Transcendental Books, [c.1964].

————. *Early Essays and Miscellanies.* Ed. Joseph J. Moldenhauer et al. Princeton, NJ: Princeton UP, 1975.

————. *Faith in a Seed: "The Dispersion of Seeds" and Other Late Natural History Writings.* Ed. Bradley P. Dean. Washington, DC: Island P, 1993.

————. *Journal 1: 1837–1844.* Ed. Elizabeth Hall Witherell et al. Princeton, NJ: Princeton UP, 1981.

————. *Journal 2: 1842–1848.* Ed. Robert Sattelmeyer. Princeton, NJ: Princeton UP, 1984.

————. *Journal 3: 1848–1851.* Ed. Robert Sattelmeyer et al. Princeton, NJ: Princeton UP, 1990.

————. *Journal 4: 1851–1852.* Ed. Leonard N. Neufeldt and Nancy Craig Simmons. Princeton, NJ: Princeton UP, 1992.

————. *The Maine Woods.* Ed. Joseph J. Moldenhauer. Princeton, NJ: Princeton UP, 1972.

————. *The Natural History Essays.* Ed. Robert Sattelmeyer. Salt Lake City: Peregrine Smith Books, 1980.

————. *Political Writings.* Ed. Nancy L. Rosenblum. Cambridge, England: Cambridge UP, 1996.

————. *Reform Papers.* Ed. Wendell Glick. Princeton, NJ: Princeton UP, 1973.

————. *Translations.* Ed. K. P. Van Anglen. Princeton, NJ: Princeton UP, 1986.

————. *Walden.* Ed. J. Lyndon Shanley. Princeton, NJ: Princeton UP, 1971.

————. *Walden: An Annotated Edition.* Ed. Walter Harding. Boston: Houghton Mifflin, 1995.

————. *A Week on the Concord and Merrimack Rivers.* Ed. Carl F. Hovde et al. Princeton, NJ: Princeton UP, 1980.

Tichi, Cecelia. "American Literary Studies to the Civil War." *Redrawing the Boundaries: The Transformation of English and American Literary Studies.* Ed. Stephen Greenblatt and Giles Gunn. New York: Modern Language Association, 1992. 209–31.

Van Anglen, K. P. "Reading Transcendentalist Texts Religiously: Emerson, Thoreau and the Myth of Secularization." *Literature and Religion: Essays in*

Critical Theory and Practice. Ed. John L Mahoney. New York: Fordham UP, 1997.

Versluis, Arthur. *American Transcendentalism and Asian Religions.* New York: Oxford UP, 1993.

Walls, Laura Dassow. *Seeing New Worlds: Henry David Thoreau and Nineteenth-Century Natural Science.* Madison: U of Wisconsin P, 1995.

Warner, Michael. "Thoreau's Bottom." *Raritan* 11 (1992): 53–79.

West, Michael. "Scatology and Eschatology: The Heroic Dimensions of Thoreau's Wordplay." *PMLA* 89 (1974): 1043–64.

Witherell, Elizabeth Hall. "The Availability of Thoreau's Texts and Manuscripts from 1862 to the Present." *Thoreau's World and Ours: A Natural Legacy.* Ed. Edmund A. Schofield and Robert C. Baron. Golden, CO: North American P, 1993. 107–20.

———. "Thoreau as Poet." *The Cambridge Companion to Henry David Thoreau.* Ed. Joel Myerson. Cambridge, England: Cambridge UP, 1995. 57–70.

———. "Thoreau's Watershed Season as a Poet: The Hidden Fruits of the Summer and Fall of 1841." *Studies in the American Renaissance 1990.* Ed. Joel Myerson. Charlottesville: UP of Virginia, 1990. 49–106.

Woodlief, Annette. "*Walden:* A Checklist of Literary Criticism through 1973." *Resources for American Literary Study* 5 (1975): 15–57.

3

Edgar Allan Poe

Kent P. Ljungquist

Observing the contradiction between the massive amount of published work on Poe and its inferior quality, J. Albert Robbins lamented, in the inaugural issue of the *Poe Newsletter* (1968), the sorry state of Poe studies. Noting a steady stream of unilluminating books and articles, source studies, and impressionistic interpretations, Robbins pronounced Poe a "critical orphan," a term reflecting a lack of sophistication and comprehensiveness in Poe scholarship vis-à-vis that of other major American authors. Robbins then recorded a list of scholarly and critical needs. From the perspective of the twenty-nine years since Robbins's essay, one clearly sees that several of the needs he enunciated have been met. Poe scholars now have access to Stovall's and Mabbott's capably edited volumes of the poems and tales, two serviceable bibliographies, a chronological source book modeled after Jay Leyda's *The Melville Log*, several collections of reprinted criticism, and, in Kenneth Silverman's *Edgar A. Poe: Mournful and Never-ending Remembrance*, a biography that supersedes Quinn's by dint of its thorough research and narrative consistency.

On the scholarly and critical fronts, however, one problem identified by Robbins and a host of other commentators has continued to plague Poe studies. Noting that Poe criticism often fails to be cumulative, these commentators observe how students of Poe often repeat the claims of previous books or articles, or, even worse, how errors, half truths, or misperceptions are repeated (Levine; Thompson, "The Poe Case"). If Poe's writings appeal to readers' deepest apprehensions, they can also cause critical responses to be highly subjective or to follow the vagaries of critical fashion. Despite the best efforts of specialist publications like *Poe Studies* (formerly the *Poe Newsletter*) and the *Poe Studies Association*

Newsletter, whose review columns are designed to monitor and correct errors and inconsistencies, the lack of cumulative dialogue among students of Poe appears to be a greater problem today than it was in 1968. With the advent of poststructuralism and decentering strategies that minimize the centrality of the author and his or her control over texts, moreover, the obligation to build constructively on a common body of discoveries appears problematic, if not explicitly challenged. As critics have aligned themselves with a variety of theoretical schools, Poe scholarship has lost even the uncertain focus it once had. Despite the important advances noted above, Poe remains the least comprehensively researched major author of the American Renaissance.

Esther F. Hyneman's *Edgar Allan Poe: An Annotated Bibliography of Books and Articles in English, 1827–1973* and J. Lasley Dameron and Irby B. Cauthen, Jr.'s *Edgar Allan Poe: A Bibliography of Criticism, 1827–1967* were both published in 1974. Used in tandem, they offer serviceable if unspectacular bibliographical guidance to nineteenth-century reviews and modern secondary criticism. After Dameron published his volume, he continued to work on annual updatings in *Poe Studies,* compilations generally limited to current secondary criticism. These checklists have continued in *Poe Studies* in other hands, despite that journal's irregular publication.

The current status and incompleteness of Poe bibliography can be gauged by comparison with work done on other major authors of the American Renaissance. For example, in 1992 *Melville Society Extracts* presented a special issue titled "Melville in Review" that offered over ninety newly discovered items (reprinted in full) from dozens of nineteenth-century periodicals. Parallel compilations, like Burton R. Pollin's "A Posthumous Assessment: The 1849–1850 Periodical Press Response to Edgar Allan Poe" and Benjamin Franklin Fisher's bibliographical gleanings from the 1890s, are highly desirable, especially given Poe's immersion in the nineteenth-century periodical milieu. Discoveries along such lines, however, have been scanty. Poe scholars have no volume that approaches the comprehensiveness of Kevin Hayes's and Hershel Parker's *Checklist of Melville Reviews,* though Pollin's "Poe 'Viewed and Reviewed': An Annotated Checklist of Contemporaneous Notices" and I. M. Walker's *Edgar Allan Poe: The Critical Heritage* offer good starting points for sampling nineteenth-century responses. Since 1980, only a handful of supplements to Pollin's checklist has surfaced (Kopley, *Poe and "The Philadelphia Saturday News"*; Ljungquist, "Poe in Boston

Newspapers"), none with the thoroughness applied to Melville or other major authors of the American Renaissance. (Graham Clarke's *Edgar Allan Poe: Critical Assessments* is apparently a compilation of previous scholarship with new errors added.) A volume for Poe like Gary Scharnhorst's *Henry David Thoreau: An Annotated Bibliography of Comment and Criticism before 1900*, which roughly doubles the number of known items in books, magazines, and newspapers, would be a primary benefit to Poe studies since both the Hyneman bibliography and the Dameron and Cauthen bibliography cover only the most well-known newspaper items. Such a volume need not devolve into an exercise in enumeration of trivial or obscure materials. Some items, like those in Pollin's census of obituary notices, are well worthy of reprinting ("A New Englander's Obituary Notice of Poe"). Like Scharnhorst's book, such a compilation can provide indices to the growth of an author's reputation, insights into the values and expectations of an author's readers and critics, and indications of how an author's works were imitated and parodied.

Pollin has applied and modified the plan of the Harvard edition of the tales and poems for his own edition of Poe's longer narratives, the Brevities ("Marginalia," "Pinakidia," etc.), and the contributions to the *Broadway Journal*. In reviews over the years, the editorial policies of both Mabbott's edition and Pollin's edition have been questioned, and I have commented on errors and inconsistencies, results of either haphazard proofreading or an imperfect synthesis of the textual apparatus ("Growth of Poe Texts" and "Poe"). No such problems detract from G. R. Thompson's Library of America edition of the *Essays and Reviews*, though the selection is not as inclusive as one might hope, and the omission of numerous short notices is particularly regrettable. It would be helpful to have all of Poe's critical notices available, even ones later incorporated into longer reviews. It would also be useful to collect his self-promotional pieces: his Baltimore newspaper puffs for his own pieces in the *Southern Literary Messenger* (Jackson), his unsigned defense of his "Autography" (Ljungquist, "Poe's 'Autography'"), and the autobiographical sketch that he wrote for the Philadelphia *Saturday Museum* in 1843 (Pollin, "Poe's Authorship"). With additional work in Pollin's edition in the offing, such as J. V. Ridgely's *Southern Literary Messenger* volume, it is hoped that a fuller portrait of Poe as a literary critic and cultural arbiter can emerge.

Whatever one's opinion of the editorial policies of the Mabbott and Pollin editions, these editions provide a wealth of fully annotated materials for the study of the textual changes that Poe sanctioned as poems, tales, and essays were revised or expanded for new contexts in periodicals or books. It is therefore somewhat surprising that so few textual studies based on these editions have been attempted. (One might also consider whether scholars have taken full advantage of Pollin's *Word Index to Poe's Fiction* or Elizabeth Wiley's *Concordance to the Poetry of Edgar Allan Poe*.) Fisher's *Poe at Work: Seven Textual Studies*, published before Mabbott's *Tales and Sketches* made its impact, offers a number of possibilities for the study of classic tales. Similar attention could be directed at heavily revised pieces such as "Loss of Breath" (originally titled "A Decided Loss") and "Hans Pfaall." Poe's work on the latter tale represented a process of substantial if intermittent revision, including the addition of explanatory notes that were designed to enhance verisimilitude. This technique, also evident in notes Poe attached to the satirical "The Thousand-and-Second Tale of Scheherezade," may reflect practices that combine Poe's talents as a fiction maker and his skills as a magazine editor.

Even less attention has focused on textual cruxes in Poe's critical writings, though we know that a number of manuscripts for his critical articles (e.g., materials in the Koester collection at the University of Texas) bear significant variants from the printings in the Harrison edition. We know also that in the mid-1840s Poe contemplated a book on American authors, a project begun with the "Autography," adapted in "The Literati of New York City," and revisited in his unpublished notes for *The Living Writers of America*. Pollin's editing of the last set of documents offers opportunities for further study of Poe's overall plan for the project and Poe's changing perspectives on a book about American authors, a vision shaped by circumstances that the author confronted at each stage in the volume's conception. Perhaps because critical attention has focused on discrete short works in the Poe canon, broader contextual studies of such larger scale projects have been rare. In this regard, it would be helpful to learn more about overall plans and publishing exigencies for *Tales of the Grotesque and Arabesque* and *Tales*. In a recent study, Ezra Greenspan showed how the latter volume fulfilled the plan for Wiley and Putnam's Library of American Books, a subject that may repay further attention.

The poetry remains the least extensively studied part of the Poe canon. Although debts to major Romantic poets have been traced in significant detail, the ample notes on eighteenth-century writers (e.g., Pope, Young) in the Pollin edition may suggest an earlier line of potential influence. Silverman's biography may mark a return to biographical readings of the poems, perhaps reminiscent of the numerous (and sometimes highly debatable) connections drawn in Mabbott's edition; more specifically, Silverman's contention that the poems provide insights into important psychological preoccupations will undoubtedly invite the kind of scrutiny that connects these texts to Poe's attitudes about death, loss, and gender relations.

Poe's important relationships to the Aesthetic movement and the Symbolist movement and his call to read a poem for the poem's sake have perhaps obscured his debts to poetic forms in popular culture. Studies such as Pollin's "Poe as a Writer of Songs," which establish a context for his lyrics in the tradition of popular ballad and song, offer promise for more detailed inquiry. Future investigation might focus on Poe's less extensively studied poems (e.g., "The Valley of Unrest," "Dream-Land") within the context of the periodical milieu. Poe's so-called "dreamscapes" might appear less exotic or idiosyncratic when compared and contrasted with similar fare in nineteenth-century magazines and newspapers.

Critical theory has asserted more influence on the study of Poe's fiction than on the study of his poems. As veteran students of Poe have long known, Poe could be rhetorically extravagant in stating his poetic credo and aesthetic goals, but he was comparatively orthodox in practice. A mix of theoretical and traditional strategies might explore the tension (perhaps even the disjunction) between his poetic theory and his handling of the nuts and bolts of rhyme and meter. The late Helen Ensley published two significant short studies along such lines, but a full-scale treatment of this subject might determine how extensively Poe's heady poetic rationale was limited and constrained by the formal pressures of verse conventions.

With Poe's comic tales and science fiction both available in commercial paperbacks (Galloway; Beaver), one can no longer lament that any substantial segment of his fictional canon is wholly neglected. "Usher," "Ligeia," "Cask," "Masque," and "The Purloined Letter" remain the most frequently studied short works, and *The Narrative of Arthur Gordon Pym*, once regarded as an anomaly in the Poe canon, is now the subject of two recent book-length treatments (Kennedy; Kopley, *Poe's "Pym"*). The most intensively studied segment of the canon over the past decade has been the fiction of ratiocination, which has invited scrutiny of Poe's sources (Kopley, *Poe and "The Philadelphia Saturday News"*) and of his signifying practices (Irwin; Muller and Richardson). His role as a pioneer in the popular detective story is amply documented, though much more work could be done on his wide-ranging influence on individual practitioners—male and female; American and British; turn-of-the-century, modern, and contemporary—in the fields of crime and detection.

With generic categories blurred and aesthetic hierarchies challenged, if not totally dismantled, critics now take at face value what was once a point of controversy: the so-called split between Poe's humorous works and his serious works. Poe's early satires, once dismissed as inferior hackwork, now constitute an important foreground for Poe's fictional career, in which the serious and the comic, the grotesque and the arabesque, romantic transport and ironic detachment play complementary roles, even when categories are held in disequilibrium or tension. Once the object of guesswork or speculation, the tales earmarked for Poe's abortive collection, *Tales of the Folio Club*, represent a sophisticated satirical rendering of the world of American letters in the early 1830s. Despite our increased knowledge of the journalistic and social contexts of these works, one can only lament that the pioneering work on these early satires by Hammond, Richard, and others—work scattered throughout a range of scholarly journals—has not been synthesized into a more manageable compass. A compact reader's guide to Poe's short fiction, similar to volumes available on Hawthorne and Melville, would constitute an important scholarly tool for these works and for all of Poe's fiction. Such a volume might offer a synthesis of Poe's sources for individual tales, along with a synopsis of existing interpretations, allowing the student and scholar alike to gauge the validity of new claims. New sources for Poe's satires are bound to surface, as shown in John E. Reilly's recent discovery of a piece called "Raising the Wind" (the original title of Poe's piece on swindling or "Diddling") in the Philadelphia *Public Ledger* of 1838. Discoveries such as this one have implications for placing individual tales at strategic points in Poe's career, thus illuminating the circumstances governing his compositions, as well as his artistic development.

One approach to Poe's fiction—a line of interpretation extending from N. Bryllion Fagin's biographical treatment in *The Histrionic Mr. Poe* to Thompson's influential *Poe's Fiction: Romantic Irony in the Gothic Tales*— addresses Poe as a self-conscious critic of Romantic fads and Gothic conventions. With ironic distance from pain, death, and loss, Thompson contends, Poe exposed Romantic excesses through irony, satire, parody, and hoax, techniques that anticipated avant-garde literature and criticism in the latter part of our century (Thompson, "Romantic Arabesque"). This mode of interpretation offers prospects for further development, though a more earnest set of readings, in all likelihood, will derive from Silverman's biography. If Robbins dubbed Poe a "critical orphan," Silverman, in the psychological argument by which he traces the direct emotional investment of Poe in his works, stresses literally the orphan status of Poe, that is, the loss of his parents and his sense of abandonment by John Allan. Poe's tales thus enact a series of memorializing gestures in homage to his actor parents. Although Silverman's thesis will stimulate further psychological readings, particularly of those classic horror tales in which powerful female figures appear as surrogates for the women in Poe's life, the cautionary note struck by Robbins and others merits restatement. One might ask whether such psychological readings are really "new," whether they mark a refinement or merely a redeployment of Marie Bonaparte's controversial psychoanalytic argument. These potential readings—psychological, feminist, or a combination of both—can devolve into worn-out redraftings of older interpretations, such as Jeffrey Meyers's portrait of the alienated, self-destructive artist. Cynthia Jordan's reading, which claims that Poe relegates women's concerns to a second-story status, all but ignores previous scholarship and lacks a rich contextual view that would incorporate Poe's responses to specific women writers.

The real and potential perils of neglecting or downplaying the cumulative weight of the scholarly record is strikingly evident in readings of tales with racial themes, concerns to which critics will inevitably return, given the current academic climate. Building on readings of *The Narrative of Arthur Gordon Pym* and "The Gold-Bug," critics will, in all likelihood, continue to trace Poe's charged if indirect response to antebellum debates on race and slavery. Though interpretation of this subject may be designed to correct the image of Poe as a figure divorced from historical controversies, an impressionistic view long ago refuted, the claim for Poe's historicity, in several cases, has been more rhetorical than real. Future students of Poe's racial attitudes need to resist the naive faith invested by Dana D. Nelson, Joan C. Dayan ("Romance and Race," "Amorous Bondage"), and others in the claim that Poe wrote a controversial defense of slavery in the *Southern Literary Messenger* in 1836. Nathaniel Beverley Tucker's unequivocal claim to the review was noted long ago by William Doyle Hull II, and a meticulous analysis of Poe's alleged authorship of the so-called "Paulding-Drayton Review" has more recently been undertaken by J. V. Ridgely, whose work is being supplemented by Terence Whalen. The future publication of Whalen's findings on the subject in *Edgar Allan Poe and the Masses* should finally lay to rest the myth of Poe's authorship of this notorious text.

Other subjects—Poe's Gothic and fantastic techniques, his "Germanism," his application of the categories of the "grotesque" and "arabesque"—will continue to exercise students of Poe's fiction. As connections are drawn between Poe's tales and changes in antebellum America, attention will inevitably focus on certain social movements. Scholars usually trace Poe's interest in Freemasonry to "The Cask of Amontillado" (Sorenson), a tale from the mid-1840s, but his interest in this social movement may have been sparked earlier by the activities of the Delphian Club, which served as one model for the Folio Club. A number of the Delphians were Masons, several rising to Grand Master status. Another social movement that attracted Poe's interest was Transcendentalism. To the extent that a heroic version of Transcendentalism has been challenged by social historians, Poe's critiques of the movement may now seem more pertinent than ever. Whether scholars see Poe as a "psychal" Transcendentalist fascinated by strong psychological energies (Carlson) or as a biting critic of the movement's stylistic vagueness and excess (Dayan, *Fables*), they need to build on the foundations established by Ottavio Casale. Casale distinguished a New England brand of Transcendentalism, which Poe detested in its political and aesthetic manifestations, from a "profound and ennobling" philosophy that attracted his inquiring mind and aspiring imagination. In "The Temperance Movement and Its Friends Look at Poe," Pollin explored yet another reform group and the aspersions it cast on Poe for his notorious drinking habits. Picking up suggestions from Pollin and Fisher (*The Very Spirit of Cordiality*), scholars might further explore tales that provide renderings of the world of alcohol in its diverse social and literary manifestations. Whatever social or psychological sources Poe used for his varied effects, theorists will mine the heightened consciousness or the incoherencies of his deranged narrators, the discontinuities in his longer narratives, the endlessly deferred attempts at closure—but they should be reminded that much of the best work on Poe's theory of prose fiction remains unpublished (Conron).

Poe wrote only one piece of drama—the verse play *Politian*—but few readers will contest the notion that his works in all genres have a decided histrionic quality. Their intensity may have its biographical source in the acting careers of Poe's parents, most notably in the theatrical achievement of his mother (see Geddeth Smith). Poe was an astute critic of dramatic writing, and notwithstanding the fine work on this subject by Pollin ("Shakespeare in the Works of Edgar Allan Poe") and Fagin, future critics might further explore his imaginative works for theatrical metaphors and allusions, staging devices and twists, and stagy, architecturally detailed settings.

Despite the availability of several good books on Poe's literary criticism (Allen; Alterton; Jacobs; Parks), this area of Poe's canon may offer the richest prospects for future study. Theoretical approaches have rescued for primary attention those aspects of Poe's critical oeuvre once reserved for the margins of critical discourse: his tomahawking style, his comments on originality and plagiarism, and his preparation of periodical filler items for the "Pinakidia" and the "Marginalia." Studying Poe's interest in a fad like cryptography may shed light on his strategies of signification (Rosenheim), or, what is more likely, the process of "decoding" Poe may show how his works resist the theorist's abstract formulations (Hodgson). His topical interests reflect his immersion in the subject matter and practices of the publishing world of his time. The now burgeoning interest in the related fields of literary journalism and the history of publishing (or *l'histoire du livre*) can serve only to reinforce Poe's centrality as a writer confronting a changing, politically charged, and sometimes antagonistic literary marketplace. Sophisticated literary analysis has diverted attention from Poe's literary battles, whether seen as petty individual confrontations or mere personal antagonisms. His mania about plagiarism, for example, merits further study, but not just from the perspective of regional bias or personal animus toward specific figures (e.g., Longfellow). Other areas of future exploration might include Poe's possible debts to John Neal, who shared his obsession with plagiarism; his conception of authorship and literary property; the ideological contexts of copyright debates; and the economics of magazine and book publishing.

In this vein we have had a suggestive study of Poe's ideological affinities with the American Whigs (Long), though more might be said about Poe's relationships with specific Whig figures (e.g., E. P. Whipple, Charles Wilkins Webber). Ever the creature of the periodical milieu, Poe could not help but be knowledgeable about the range and diversity of publishing outlets: the penny daily, the mammoth weekly, the literary magazine, and the collection of fugitive pieces. Able to manipulate

aspects of the periodical on which he was working, Poe used each publishing medium to wield his editorial pen, to function as a patron to
women writers (feminists suggest that he "patronized"), or to engage in
overt promotion of his own work. The author of "Some Secrets of the
Magazine Prison House" and "X-ing a Paragrab," he experienced firsthand the low pay for "poor devil authors," as well as the editorial drudg-
ery of preparing and correcting copy. Poe's subtitles—"An Extrava-
ganza" and "An Allegory"—have been examined, but they may acquire
more specific meaning if read alongside other forms of verbal shorthand
in magazines and newspapers. His manipulation of the language of the
publishing world, for example, surfaced in his creation of a fictional butt
of humor in 1841, a "Mr. Cabbage," who represented one of the mammoth weeklies. The mammoth weeklies, the bulky newspapers that
anticipated the story papers of the latter part of the century, were known
for reprinting original works without permission, and this comic name
comments on that practice: in "X-ing a Paragrab," the printer's devil
discovers that missing letters in a manuscript have been "'cabbaged'"
(i.e., "pilfered" or "stolen") (*Collected Works* 3: 1373). Poe's comic wordplay, especially his verbal manipulations drawn from the world of nineteenth-century periodicals, has yet to receive its authoritative interpreter.

Over the past decade, such well-established periodicals as the Philadelphia *Public Ledger*, the *Philadelphia Saturday News*, the *Boston Notion*,
the *Springfield Republican*, the *New-York Enquirer*, and the *New-York Saturday Emporium* have yielded discoveries relevant to primary or secondary
scholarship on Poe. If outlets mentioned in Poe's own editorial columns
have not yet been exhausted for relevant items, what treasures can be
found in other files of periodicals, specifically in the less studied Mid-
western magazines and newspapers? Pollin speculates that his own
checklist of obituary notices could be doubled if one could more readily
access newspapers in Chicago, Detroit, St. Louis, and other cities. The
story papers of the later nineteenth century offer a rich quarry of material
to be explored for reprintings, adaptations of Poe's works, and reformu-
lations of Poe's popular image.

Even as the literary periodical offered writers a social and aesthetic
medium, the American lyceum offered another outlet by which individual writers and thinkers could alter and shape current taste. *The Poe Log*
contains a good sampling of responses to Poe's lectures, from his presentation on "The Poets and Poetry of America," to his infamous Boston
Lyceum performance, to his disquisition on the nature of the universe in

Eureka. As Pollin has suggested, however, the full story of Poe's ambition to become a lyceum performer has yet to be told. While Melville scholars have access to a monograph on the lyceum in Merton M. Sealts, Jr.'s *Melville as Lecturer* and Thoreauvians have been treated to painstaking reconstructions of several important lectures (Dean), Poe scholars have been provided with limited work. Recent research on the Boston Lyceum fiasco has uncovered previously unknown items in the city's newspapers (Ljungquist, "Poe's 'Al Aaraaf' and the Boston Lyceum"), including reprintings on three successive days of "Al Aaraaf" in its entirety. Work on Poe's lectures can tell us more about the origins and development of his critical ideas and can illuminate textual changes that Poe sanctioned as lecture ideas were transformed into published form. Specific matters that could be scrutinized in close study include J. H. Hopkins's detailed account of Poe's lecture on "The Universe," an account that Poe himself called inaccurate on a number of particulars; what use Poe made in "The Poetic Principle" of his presentations on American poetry in 1843 and 1844—lectures that Silverman sees as responses to Griswold's attempt to establish an American poetic canon in *The Poets and Poetry of America*; what Poe did to reconstruct the lost manuscript of "The Poetic Principle" between his lectures in Lowell, Massachusetts, and Providence, Rhode Island, in 1848; and traces from lectures that find their way into biographically revelatory works such as "Von Kempelen and His Discovery." Study of Poe lectures necessitates consultation of newspapers in the towns and cities where he lectured, and the researcher may encounter, as so many who work on Poe do, incomplete files of relevant periodicals. Holdings in special collections, such as the lecture folders in the Mabbott collection at the University of Iowa, may also yield interesting discoveries. While bringing textual rigor to the study of Poe's lectures, such close examination can shed light on Poe's rhetorical principles. The burlesque that opens *Eureka*, sometimes seen as incongruous in a lofty treatise on the universe, makes more sense if we remember the origins of that work on the lecture platform in 1848, a time when the lyceum system, already two decades old, was inching toward its eventual character as a forum for entertainment as well as edification.

Moreover, Donald Scott's essays on the social history of the lyceum, which examine public lecturing as a medium that bridged the gap between oral and written discourse, can help to illuminate Poe's strategies and methods. Scholars usually date Poe's first encounter with public lecturing as his presentation on "American Poetry" in Philadelphia in

1843. Poe would have agreed with "A Lecture on Lecturing," however, which appeared in Mordecai Noah's *New-York Enquirer* almost fifteen years earlier (1829). In that essay, the pseudonymous author "Jeremy Diddler" defined man as "a lecturing animal," further suggesting that lecturing was an up-to-date way "to raise the wind." Readers familiar with Poe's satires will recognize here a variant on "Raising the Wind," the original title of "Diddling," a text apparently intended for Poe's Folio Club collection. Over two decades before his Boston lyceum hoax, Poe apparently found in "A Lecture on Lecturing" a precedent for his own exercises in self-promotion and confidence games on the lecture platform (Ljungquist, "'Raising More Wind'"). Whatever the case, new research may further illuminate Poe's reception, his sense of audience, and his perspective on the relationship between speaking and writing. In-depth contextual studies may, in fact, clarify connections between lectures and tales: there is evidence that Poe's playful pronouncement that Boston was "waking up" from its slumbers after his lyceum appearance constituted a preview of "The Facts in the Case of M. Valdemar," Poe's tale of mesmeric "sleep-waking," which soon appeared in the *American Whig Review.*

The lectures, of course, constitute materials of biographical significance. Having waited a half century for an authoritative biography to replace Arthur Hobson Quinn's, critics may take some time to digest the implications of Silverman's volume. Though some readers may be impatient with his psychological thrust, they will be grateful that Silverman addresses so many important biographical cruxes, including Poe's relationship to Griswold and the circumstances of Poe's death. Vivid portraits of Poe's contemporaries enhance the value of the volume, though additional work on those individuals who carried the Poe legacy into the second half of the nineteenth century would be most welcome. For example, only a few of Maria Clemm's letters have been published; we know relatively little about Poe's correspondent George Eveleth; and Sarah Helen Whitman, whose best poetry approaches the quality of Emily Dickinson's work, merits modern book-length biographical treatment. We can hope that new material will come to light about specific periods, such as the early years in Baltimore for which the documentary record is faint. Studies of the biographical enterprise, such as the inquiry conducted by the late John Carl Miller on the British Poe enthusiast John Henry Ingram, could show how various versions of Poe's life compete with one another. Miller's *Building Poe Biography* and *Poe's Helen Remembers* constitute portable literary archives, materials to which historically or theoretically minded investigators can gravitate. Studies of other biographers or memoirists—N. P. Willis, William F. Gill, Susan Archer Talley Weiss, Elizabeth Oakes Smith, Anne Lynch Botta, R. H. Stoddard, George Woodberry, Thomas Wentworth Higginson, and Sarah Helen Whitman—would also illuminate the fitful process and progress by which Poe's works entered the American literary canon.

If the study of Poe biography reveals important steps in the shaping of literary taste, the study of Poe and the arts suggests parallel evolutions. John Reilly's dissertation, "Poe in Imaginative Literature," which should have been published in its entirety, has appeared in somewhat piecemeal fashion, testimony to Poe's impact on poetry, fiction, and drama. Other scholars have supplemented and will continue to supplement Reilly's discoveries. Perhaps due to the incantatory power of the poems and tales, Poe's works have been a stimulus to composers in symphonic, operatic, and popular contexts. Scholars will undoubtedly build on Pollin's seminal investigations of Poe and music ("More Music"; "Music and Poe"; "Poe as a Writer of Songs"); likewise they will assist the indefatigable Pollin in investigating paintings and illustrations in which tales and poems have undergone so many unique adaptations. Ronald L. Smith's *Poe in the Media: Screen, Songs, and Spoken Word Recordings* extends the work of Reilly and Pollin into the sphere of popular culture, including film adaptations, musical adaptations, spoken recordings and renderings. A book-length treatment of Poe and a variety of popular forms, including verbal and visual parodies of his works, would contribute to a fuller record of his twentieth-century impact.

As the years 1995–1999 mark a succession of sesquicentennials of important events (e.g., the publication of "The Raven," that of the *Tales*, and that of *The Raven and Other Poems;* the first critical analysis [in a foreign language] by E. D. Forgues of Poe's work; Baudelaire's translation of "Mesmeric Revelation" and subsequent championship of Poe's works), it is a propitious time to take stock of Poe's international renown. An appropriate way to observe these sesquicentennials would be to initiate and coordinate a series of translations of important foreign scholarship, a project performed irregularly by *Poe Studies.* Although French attention to Poe may now have become largely an academic phenomenon (Justin), recent work on Poe and Hispanic authors—Cortazar, Fuentes, Borges, Pessoa, and others—should remind us that John H. Englekirk's *Edgar Allan Poe in Hispanic Literature* (1934) urgently needs updating, especially as regards Poe's impact on imaginative literature in Latin

America. Thomas S. Hansen's research ("Poe's 'German' Source") has rescued the idiosyncratic work of Arno Schmidt from the fringes of German scholarship on Poe and given it wider attention. Reminding comparativists that their critical scrutiny need not stop with Poe's "French face," Hansen, in his work (conducted with Pollin) on the "German Face of Poe," should assist scholars in gauging claims (sometimes inflated or extravagant) about Poe's knowledge of German language, literature, and culture. As scholars continue to debate whether Poe's aesthetic theories derived from British or German sources—or whether his *Blackwood's* formula for the "tale of sensation" (i.e., "tale proper") had roots in the German Novelle (Thompson, "Literary Politics")—Poe's rich global legacy and influence will be unmistakable. Lois Vines's edited collection *Poe Abroad: Influences, Reputation, Affinities*, which is projected for publication in 1997, promises to synthesize much of what we know about Poe's international influence.

From the perspective of the twenty-nine years since Robbins's essay, it is clear that several of his requests for worthwhile scholarly projects (e. g., his calls for a census of Poe dissertations or a listing of Poe manuscripts in private hands) have fallen on deaf ears. Despite obvious gaps in the scholarly record, Poe is no longer a critical orphan, having attracted scrutiny from critics of increasing sophistication. As the sesquicentennial of Poe's death approaches, Joyce Carol Oates's question, articulated in her appropriately titled *Haunted: Tales of the Grotesque*, carries more than strictly rhetorical import and force: "Who has not been influenced by Poe?"

ACKNOWLEDGMENT

I wish to acknowledge the helpful suggestions of Richard Kopley and Joel Brattin.

WORKS CITED

Allen, Michael L. *Poe and the British Magazine Tradition*. New York: Oxford UP, 1969.

Alterton, Margaret. *The Origins of Poe's Critical Theory*. Iowa City: U of Iowa P, 1925.

Bonaparte, Marie. *The Life and Works of Edgar Allan Poe: A Psycho-analytic Interpretation.* Trans. John Rodker. London: Imago, 1949.

Carlson, Eric W. "Poe's Vision of Man." *Papers on Poe.* Ed. Richard P. Veler. Springfield: Chantry Music P, 1972. 7–20.

Casale, Ottavio M. "Poe on Transcendentalism." *ESQ* 50 (1968): 85–97.

Clarke, Graham, ed. *Edgar Allan Poe: Critical Assessments.* 4 vols. New York: Routledge, 1991.

Conron, John J. "Poe and the Theory of the Short Story." Diss. U of Michigan, 1970.

Dameron, J. Lasley, and Irby B. Cauthen, Jr. *Edgar Allan Poe: A Bibliography of Criticism, 1827–1967.* Charlottesville: UP of Virginia, 1974.

Dayan, Joan C. "Amorous Bondage: Poe, Ladies, and Slaves." *American Literature* 66 (1994): 239–73.

———. *Fables of Mind: An Inquiry into Poe's Fiction.* New York: Oxford UP, 1986.

———. "Romance and Race." *The Columbia History of the American Novel.* Ed. Emory Elliott. New York: Columbia UP, 1991. 89–109.

Dean, Bradley P. "Reconstructions of Thoreau's Early 'Life without Principle' Lectures." *Studies in the American Renaissance 1987.* Ed. Joel Myerson. Charlottesville: UP of Virginia, 1989. 285–364.

Englekirk, John H. *Edgar Allan Poe in Hispanic Literature.* New York: Instituto de las Españas en los Estados Unidos, 1934.

Ensley, Helen. "Metrical Ambiguity in the Poetry of Edgar Allan Poe." *No Fairer Land: Studies in Southern Literature before 1900.* Ed. J. Lasley Dameron and James W. Mathews. Troy, NY: Whitston, 1986. 144–58.

———. *Poe's Rhymes.* Baltimore: Edgar Allan Poe Society, 1981.

Fagin, N. Bryllion. *The Histrionic Mr. Poe.* Baltimore: Johns Hopkins UP, 1949.

Fisher, Benjamin Franklin, IV, ed. *Poe at Work: Seven Textual Studies.* Baltimore: Edgar Allan Poe Society, 1978.

———. "Poe in the 1890s: Bibliographical Gleanings." *American Renaissance Literary Report* 8 (1994): 142–68.

———. *The Very Spirit of Cordiality: The Literary Uses of Alcohol and Alcoholism in the Tales of Edgar Allan Poe.* Baltimore: Edgar Allan Poe Society, 1978.

Greenspan, Ezra. "Evert Duyckinck and the History of Wiley and Putnam's Library of American Books, 1845–1847." *American Literature* 64 (1992): 677–93.

Hammond, Alexander. "Further Notes on Poe's Folio Club Tales." *Poe Studies* 8 (1975): 38–42.

———. "A Reconstruction of Poe's Tales of the Folio Club: Preliminary Notes." *Poe Studies* 5 (1972): 25–32.

Hansen, Thomas S. "Poe's 'German' Source for 'The Fall of the House of Usher': The Arno Schmidt Connection." *Southern Humanities Review* 26 (1992): 101–29.

Hansen, Thomas S., with Burton R. Pollin. *The German Face of Edgar Allan Poe: A Study of Literary References in His Works.* Columbia, SC: Camden House, 1995.

Hayes, Kevin J., and Hershel Parker. *Checklist of Melville Reviews.* Evanston, IL: Northwestern UP, 1991.

Hodgson, John. "Decoding Poe: Poe, W. B. Tyler, and Cryptography." *Journal of English and Germanic Philology* 93 (1993): 523–34.

Hull, William Doyle, II. "A Canon of the Critical Works of Edgar Allan Poe with a Study of Poe as Editor and Reviewer." Diss. U of Virginia, 1941.

Hyneman, Esther F. *Edgar Allan Poe: An Annotated Bibliography of Books and Articles in English, 1827–1973.* Boston: G. K. Hall, 1974.

Irwin, John T. *The Mystery to a Solution: Poe, Borges, and the Analytic Detective Story.* Baltimore: Johns Hopkins UP, 1994.

Jackson, David K. "Four of Poe's Critiques in the Baltimore Newspapers." *Modern Language Notes* 50 (1935): 251–56.

Jacobs, Robert D. *Poe: Journalist and Critic.* Baton Rouge: Louisiana UP, 1969.

Jordan, Cynthia S. "Poe's Re-Vision: The Recovery of the Second Story." *American Literature* 59 (1987): 1–19.

Justin, Henri. "Recent Poe Criticism in France: 1983–1987." *Poe Studies* 20 (1987): 27–35.

Kennedy, J. Gerald. *"The Narrative of Arthur Gordon Pym" and the Abyss of Interpretation.* Boston: G. K. Hall, 1995.

Kopley, Richard. *Edgar Allan Poe and "The Philadelphia Saturday News."* Baltimore: Edgar Allan Poe Society, 1991.

———, ed. *Poe's "Pym": Critical Explorations.* Durham, NC: Duke UP, 1992.

Levine, Stuart. "Scholarly Strategy: The Poe Case." *American Quarterly* 17 (1965): 133–34.

Leyda, Jay. *The Melville Log.* New York: Harcourt, 1951.

Ljungquist, Kent. "The Growth of Poe Texts." *Review* 5 (1983): 49–57.

———. "Poe." *American Literary Scholarship: An Annual 1986.* Ed. David J. Nordloh. Durham, NC: Duke UP, 1988. 41–42.

———. "Poe in the Boston Newspapers: Three More Reviews." *English Language Notes* 31 (1993): 43–46.

———. "Poe's 'Al Aaraaf' and the Boston Lyceum: Contributions to Primary and Secondary Bibliography." *Victorian Periodicals Review* 28 (1995): 199–216.

———. "Poe's 'Autography': A New Exchange of Reviews." *American Periodicals* 2 (1991): 51–62.

————. "'Raising More Wind': Another Source for Poe's 'Diddling' and Its Possible Folio Club Context." *Perspectives on Poe.* Ed. D. Ramakrishna. New Delhi: APC Publications, 1996. 53–62.

Long, David A. "Poe's Political Identity: The Mummy Unswathed." *Poe Studies* 23 (1990): 1–22.

"Melville in Review." *Melville Society Extracts* 89 (1992): 1–32.

Meyers, Jeffrey. *Edgar Allan Poe: His Life and Legacy.* New York: Scribners, 1992.

Miller, John Carl. *Building Poe Biography.* Baton Rouge: Louisiana State UP, 1977.

————, ed. *Poe's Helen Remembers.* Charlottesville: UP of Virginia, 1979.

Muller, John P., and William J. Richardson, eds. *The Purloined Poe: Lacan, Derrida, and Psychoanalytic Reading.* Baltimore: Johns Hopkins UP, 1988.

Nelson, Dana D. "Ethnocentrism Decentered: Colonial Motives in *The Narrative of Arthur Gordon Pym.*" *The Word in Black and White: Reading "Race" in American Literature, 1638–1867.* New York: Oxford UP, 1992. 90–108.

Oates, Joyce Carol. *Haunted: Tales of the Grotesque.* New York: Dutton, 1994.

Parks, Edd Winfield. *Edgar Allan Poe as Literary Critic.* Athens: U of Georgia P, 1964.

Poe, Edgar Allan. *Collected Works of Edgar Allan Poe.* Ed. Thomas Ollive Mabbott. 3 vols. Cambridge, MA: Harvard UP, 1969–1978.

————. *Collected Writings of Edgar Allan Poe.* Ed. Burton R. Pollin. 4 vols. Boston: Twayne, 1981; New York: Gordian P, 1985–86. Vol. 5, *Writings from the "Southern Literary Messenger."* Ed. J. V. Ridgely, forthcoming.

————. *The Complete Works of Edgar Allan Poe.* Ed. James A. Harrison. 17 vols. New York: Thomas Y. Crowell, 1902.

————. *Essays and Reviews.* Ed. G. R. Thompson. New York: Library of America, 1984.

————. *The Other Poe: Comedies and Satires.* Ed. David Galloway. New York: Penguin, 1983.

————. *Poems.* Ed. Floyd Stovall. Charlottesville: UP of Virginia, 1965.

————. *The Science Fiction of Edgar Allan Poe.* Ed. Harold Beaver. New York: Penguin, 1977.

Pollin, Burton R. *Images of Poe's Works: A Comprehensive Descriptive Catalogue of Illustrations.* New York: Greenwood P, 1989.

————. "*The Living Writers of America*: A Manuscript by Edgar Allan Poe." *Studies in the American Renaissance.* Ed. Joel Myerson. Charlottesville: UP of Virginia, 1991. 151–212.

————. "More Music to Poe." *Music and Letters* 44 (1973): 391–404.

————. "Music and Edgar Allan Poe: A Second Annotated Checklist." *Poe Studies* 15 (1982): 7–13, 42.

————. "Music and Edgar Allan Poe: A Third Annotated Checklist." *Poe Studies* 26 (1993): 41–58.

————. "A New Englander's Obituary Notice of Poe." *American Periodicals* 4 (1994): 1–11.

————. "Poe as a Writer of Songs." *American Renaissance Literary Report* 6 (1992): 58–66.

————. "Poe 'Viewed and Reviewed': An Annotated Checklist of Contemporaneous Notices." *Poe Studies* 15 (1980): 17–28.

————. "Poe's Authorship of Three Long Critical and Autobiographical Reviews of 1843 Now Authenticated." *American Renaissance Literary Report* 7 (1993): 139–71.

————. "A Posthumous Assessment: The 1849–50 Periodical Press Response to Edgar Allan Poe." *American Periodicals* 2 (1992): 6–50.

————. "Shakespeare in the Works of Edgar Allan Poe." *Studies in the American Renaissance 1985.* Ed. Joel Myerson. Charlottesville: UP of Virginia, 1985. 157–86.

————. "The Temperance Movement and Its Friends Look at Poe." *Insight and Outlooks.* New York: Gordian P, 1986. 147–72.

————. *Word Index to Poe's Fiction.* New York: Gordian P, 1982.

Quinn, Arthur Hobson. *Edgar Allan Poe: A Critical Biography.* New York: Appleton-Century-Crofts, 1941.

Reilly, John E. *The Image of Poe in American Poetry.* Baltimore: Edgar Allan Poe Society, 1976.

————. "Poe in American Drama: Versions of the Man." *Poe and Our Times: Influence and Affinities.* Ed. Benjamin Franklin Fisher IV. Baltimore: Edgar Allan Poe Society, 1986. 18–31.

————. "Poe in Imaginative Literature: A Study of American Drama, Fiction, and Poetry Devoted to Edgar Allan Poe or His Works." Diss. U of Virginia, 1965.

————. "Poe's 'Diddling': Still Another Possible Source and Date of Composition." *Poe Studies* 25 (1992): 6–9.

Richard, Claude. "Poe and the Yankee Hero: An Interpretation of 'Diddling Considered As One of the Exact Sciences.'" *Mississippi Quarterly* 21 (1967–68): 93–109.

Ridgely, J. V. "The Authorship of the 'Paulding-Drayton Review.'" *PSA Newsletter* 20 (1992): 1–3, 6.

Robbins, J. Albert. "The State of Poe Studies." *Poe Newsletter* 1 (1968): 1–2.

Rosenheim, Shawn. "The King of 'Secret Readers': Edgar Poe, Cryptography, and the Origins of the Detective Story." *ELH* 56 (1989): 375–400.

Scharnhorst, Gary. *Henry David Thoreau: An Annotated Bibliography of Comment and Criticism before 1900.* New York: Garland, 1992.

Scott, Donald. "Print and the Public Lecture System, 1840–1860." *Printing and Society in Early America*. Eds. John B. Hench, William L. Joyce, and David Hall. Worcester: American Antiquarian Society, 1983. 278–99.

———. "Public Lectures and the Creation of a Public in Nineteenth-Century America." *Journal of American History* 66 (1980): 791–809.

Sealts, Merton M., Jr. *Melville as Lecturer*. Cambridge, MA: Harvard UP, 1957.

Silverman, Kenneth. *Edgar A. Poe: Mournful and Never-ending Remembrance*. New York: HarperCollins, 1991.

Smith, Geddeth. *The Brief Career of Eliza Poe*. Rutherford, NJ: Fairleigh Dickinson UP, 1988.

Smith, Ronald L. *Poe in the Media: Screen, Songs, and Spoken Word Recordings*. New York: Garland, 1990.

Sorensen, Peter J. "William Morgan, Freemasonry, and 'The Cask of Amontillado.'" *Poe Studies* 22 (1989): 45–47.

Thomas, Dwight R., and David K Jackson. *The Poe Log: A Documentary Life of Edgar Allan Poe 1809–1849*. Boston: G. K. Hall, 1987.

Thompson, G. R. "Literary Politics and the 'Legitimate Sphere': Poe, Hawthorne, and the 'Tale Proper.'" *Nineteenth-Century Literature* 49 (1994): 167–95.

———. "The Poe Case: Scholarship and 'Strategy.'" *Poe Newsletter* 1 (1968): 3.

———. *Poe's Fiction: Romantic Irony in the Gothic Tales*. Madison: U of Wisconsin P, 1973.

———. "Romantic Arabesque, Contemporary Theory, and Postmodernism: The Example of Poe's *Narrative*." *ESQ* 35 (1989): 163–271.

Vines, Lois, ed. *Poe Abroad: Influences, Reputation, Affinities*. Iowa City: U of Iowa P, forthcoming.

Walker, I. M., ed. *Edgar Allan Poe: The Critical Heritage*. London: Routledge & Kegan Paul, 1986.

Whalen, Terence. *Edgar Allan Poe and the Masses*, forthcoming.

Wiley, Elizabeth. *Concordance to the Poetry of Edgar Allan Poe*. Selinsgrove, PA: Susquehanna UP, 1989.

4

Herman Melville

John Bryant

In *A Companion to Melville Studies* (1986), I wrote that the growth of research and criticism had pushed us to the verge of a "Melville Renaissance." No doubt there was more hope than prophecy in that statement, but in looking back over these past eleven years, I see that the prediction (surprisingly) has proven true. Of course, what has happened was not entirely what I anticipated. Then I assumed that the influx of new Melville materials—certain biographical discoveries (the Kring-Carey finding of Melville's faltering marriage), manuscripts (*Typee*), letters (the Augusta papers), and annotations of books (Dante and Milton)—along with the revitalization of the Northwestern-Newberry project and the publication of resource volumes (like the *Companion*) would trigger renewed interest in the writer as a writer. Now, in retrospect, what I find is not a deeper commitment to Melville scholarship (although that has in fact grown) but a more focused use of Melville in larger discussions about culture, politics, sexuality, and race.

In the long run, the renaissance in Melville's critical utility, as opposed to the more scholarly one anticipated, has proven to be the richer, if only because it reaffirms the original vitality of the Melville Revival of the 1920s. There is something compelling about Melville. He gets to us just as he gets into America and into Being. He is political; he is ontological. And this two-step of his pushes us to see the odd but persistent link between America and Being—that is, the way democratic culture threatens as it molds our patterns of self-identity. The urgency to dance that dance is what attracted liberal "Revivalists" in their search for a new pantheon of American writers, and it is the same force that compels today's more radicalized readers in their attempts to expand the canon. What was "new" about Melville before was that, for better or worse, he was taken to be "The Culture." What is "new" about him now is that he represents our "Multiculture."

Also in 1986, I argued for a rapprochement between traditional scholarship and new historicism. The idea was to lessen the dissociation between scholar and critic, between contextualist and hermeneut. Later, in *Melville and Repose* (1993), I proposed a kind of "pluralistic historicism," which might bring together analyses of biography, creative process, culture, and reader response in order to assess Melville's rhetorical condition. The idea is to avoid the error of those who take the end of criticism to be an exclusive focus on either the single author Melville or the single culture America, but to attempt to assess the vital interaction of the two. One furtherance of this critical end is teaching. Often, in essays that take on the "future" of literary study, the discussion is almost exclusively critical and not at all pedagogical. But while in our criticism we speak in new ways of (let's say) Melville's Intertextuality or Rhetorical Strategies, our classroom approach (if the anthologies are any measure) is still to stress the old approach: Sources and Mighty Themes. My hope for the future of Melville studies is that we can also begin to teach Melville as an integral part of how we research him and interpret him. Which brings me to a personal anecdote that may serve as a parable of the problems we face in scholarship, criticism, and pedagogy today.

Last summer, I met a college senior at a picnic. We began to talk Melville. He had sampled Melville two years earlier in a sophomore course: "Didn't he *hate* Indians?" he asked, seeming to doubt his own words. "No, quite the contrary," I responded; and citing various works, I marched professorially through the canon from *Typee* on up, displaying evidence of Melville's liberal cosmopolitanism. And just as my interlocutor's eyes began to roll back under the full force of my picnic disquisition, I reached *The Confidence-Man*, and we both experienced a shock of recognition. The young collegian had read something about "Indian-hating, by Herman Melville," something that had been reprinted in an anthology on the Native American. He could not remember the volume, but as I described to him the Moredock episode in *The Confidence-Man*, he began to recall what he took to be Melville's attack upon the Indian.

I raced through a series of hypotheses in my mind to account for this colossal misinterpretation. Had this collegian misread Melville? Had his professor taught him wrong? Had the anthologizers misrepresented him? Back home, a quick inspection of the anthology in question revealed that Melville had been included as a pro-Indian writer amidst his largely negative contemporaries. What, then, had gone wrong with my collegian? Perhaps he and his instructor had ignored or failed to read the headnote positioning Melville in more favorable light, and, getting caught in the confusing rhetoric, had identified Melville with the Moredock he finally dismantles. Or, perhaps, one hopes, both student and professor became so sensitive to the twists and turns of the Indian-hating section that they engaged in a discourse about Melville's irony, that the student came away—as any reader might—undecided about Melville's final position, and that two years later and the issue still unresolved, he posed his question to me in hopes of getting "a straight answer." A final answer. An answer that does not really exist. While I could assure the student that Melville was no Indian-hater, I am troubled that our collegian had to receive that assurance from an "authority" in the (picnic) field rather than from his own reading experience.

Of course, the cards are stacked against our collegian. Not only was he asked to read Melville out of context, but he was given a radically unstable text to begin with, one that begs to be misread, and even seems designed to suck complacent readers into misreading. He did not stand a chance. And this is my parable of how we study, read, and teach Melville. The student did not stand a chance because he was asked to look in Melville's text for a fully formed ideology that is not there. For Melville does not promote a pro- or anti-Indian ideology; rather, he uses Moredock to engage readers in a process that exercises both belief and doubt about our relation to Indian-hating. Melville's narratorial genius lies in his ability to create moments of "tense repose," where readers are made to walk a thin line between sentiment and awareness. But our collegian's anthology required him to ignore this dance of reasoning and to adopt a one-sided vision, based upon a simplistic either/or pursuit: Melville was either an Indian-Hater or an Indian-Lover.

This is the kind of game a Melville authority might confidently play. As the only available Melville authority at our summer picnic, I was pressed into service to make a stand. I could have con-manishly Socratized the collegian, but my burger was waiting, so I took the authoritarian way and just told him what to think: Melville loved the Indian. But in doing so I sinned—not because I told a lie, as Melville's sympathy for native Americans is biographically indisputable—but because I chose to pronounce an ideology rather than promote the collegian's independent search through meaning, belief, and doubt for that ideology. Thus, last summer, Melville became the iconic "Indian-lover" that he never was and not the questioner that he surely was. And I was complicit in this rigidification.

I know that you will not condemn me for failing to turn that summer picnic into a seminar, but I am not ready to be let off so easily. There is a certain pernicious allegorization of ideas that occurs in any critical endeavor. Our interpretations invariably become frozen symbols, and our vision of Melville's fluidity (lovehatelove) just a frozen portrait (lover or hater). What a disservice to a writer who was more of a doubter than a preacher. To research, read, and teach Melville, we need in some sense to reconstruct his original questioning mode of thought and creativity. Finding the real Melville embedded in the Moredock episode requires a certain pluralism that should discourage a too-confident rigidification of his texts into talismanic emblems of a single ideology. In all, Melville's rhetorical goal was to make readers into intellectual questers. He does not propose to tell us *what to think*, but to show us what it feels like *when we think*, and think deeply, passionately, creatively, daringly, even self-destructively.

If I could relive last summer, I would advise the collegian to return to Melville's text, to place it in its rhetorical context, and to approach it with a sense of history and of irony. I would have him become both a historicist and a rhetorician. The anecdote of the collegian is a parable of misapplied or ignored scholarship, of misreading, and of backfiring pedagogy. But for this prospective essay, it is a touchstone for how we may "do" the scholarship, criticism, and teaching of Melville as we enter the twenty-first century.

Scholarship and Desire

In general, we like to think that the scholar's job is to find facts and the critic's role is to interpret them. It is the classic distinction between objective and subjective modes. But this distinction is as pernicious as it is false. First, scholars presumably assemble *data* not facts: "facts" are bits of information presented in an argument with a certain rhetorical purpose in mind; "data" (one hopes) are just nicely catalogued stuff (handwritten, printed, or reported words, and certain objects). But to suggest that scholars simply discover and publish "stuff" only sharpens a distinction that is, in fact, not there. For, second, a scholar's data are ineluctably shaped by the same agendas that compel critics to write. Scholars interpret at the moment they assemble data, and this obvious point should not only be recognized but also embraced. Similarly, critics would enhance discourse if they built more comprehensive interpretations upon full, not selected, data. The point is twofold: desire shapes scholarship, and scholars should not deny it; moreover, criticism (never having denied desire) should delimit subjectivity as best it can, allowing ideas to grow out of personally researched data, not rhetorical "facts" dressed as data. Overall, we profit when scholars and critics display, even celebrate, their historicist subjectivities.

Melville has attracted some of the best textual and bibliographical scholars and many of the best critics in American literary studies, whose works (both responsible and provocative) have encouraged a unification of scholarship and criticism into one enterprise. And yet, scholar and critic often seem out of touch with one another. The result has been the perpetuation of certain "legends in Melville scholarship," about which more later. But first, a history that one might title "Progress Is Slow."

Progress Is Slow

In 1965, the scholar seeking Melville had few reliable texts and only a handful of scholarly tools with which to conduct research. Editors Harrison Hayford, G. Thomas Tanselle, and Hershel Parker had yet to publish any of their Northwestern-Newberry editions; and only six of the textually unreliable and unevenly annotated Hendricks House editions were in print. At that time, only Hayford and Merton M. Sealts, Jr.'s *Billy Budd* and Walter E. Bezanson's *Clarel* could claim significant textual authority. Merrell Davis and William Gilman's *Letters* and Hugh W. Hetherington's reviews were but five years old. Jay Leyda's *Melville Log* and Leon Howard's biography had been around since 1950, with no one venturing a new major biography. These tools were slim pickings, especially considering the enormous critical appeal Melville had generated since the 1940s, when F. O. Matthiessen made him a central figure and Stanley T. Williams set his graduate students at Yale to do the necessary textual and biographical spadework on Melville. Early students, inspired by Charles Roberts Anderson's *Melville in the South Seas*, contributed useful studies uniting biography and criticism, notably Davis's work on *Mardi* and Gilman's on *Redburn*. Even so, serious scholars well into the 1960s had to root around in journals for the checklists that would later become Sealts's book-length *Melville's Reading,* or in pamphlets for the likes of Leland R. Phelps's *Foreign Reputation* and my *Melville Dissertations,* or in a thesis for Wilson Heflin's work on the sea years (dissertation #46). In 1965, there was no Melville concordance or complete primary bibliography, and, apart from the limited section in Jacob Blanck's *Bibliography of American Literature,* there is still no definitive descriptive bibliography. There was no book-length secondary bibliography such as Brian Higgins's volumes, and the Melville Society *Extracts,* which supplies updates on letters, reviews, and criticism, was only an "occasional newsletter."

The New Criticism of the era seemed little concerned about these lacunae. Historicism in the hands of a Perry Miller or William Charvat was useful in embroidering Melville biography, but it seemed to have little impact on interpretation. With the exception of the "two-*Moby-Dicks*" theory, interest in the creative process had virtually died. Historicist studies tended to offer ways of reading Melville based on specific texts or traditional intellectual topics: Howard P. Vincent on sources in *Moby-Dick,* William Braswell on religion, Nathalia Wright on the Bible, and Henry F. Pommer on Milton. Relatively few critics (Richard Chase being one exception) had ventured to place Melville in the context of his political rather than simply literary culture. Of course, from the beginning Melville always attracted certain over-reaching readers like D. H. Lawrence, Yvor Winters, Charles Olson, William Ellery Sedgwick, Lawrance Thompson, and Newton Arvin, each drawn to Melville's complex darkness. Tamer stuff in the Aristotelian modes eventually supplanted these more idiosyncratic (though, by today's standards, prophetic) approaches. Charles Feidelson's use of Melville as a crucial example in his study of symbolism gave more focus to the writer's aesthetic; Edward H. Rosenberry broadened that focus in a comic vein, even as Harry Levin introduced an existential dimension. Other studies, including those of Merlin Bowen, James E. Miller, Jr., and Warner Berthoff, established the received rhetorical readings of the day as James Baird, Daniel G. Hoffman, Allan Heimert, H. Bruce Franklin, and Leo Marx added social perspectives. And yet Melville criticism was languishing: the New Criticism, never too fond of Melville, had run its course, and the more promising myth-and-symbol approach was ready to fail. Moreover, Melville scholars and critics seemed to be drifting even farther apart.

Since 1965, significant growth in scholarship has occurred, and his-toricism has made a comeback with the engrossing critical perspectives of the "new historicism." But with these advances have come more prob-lems. Many critics still have less than a full understanding of the critical nature of textual studies, and new historicism too often resembles mere thematics in its allegorized readings of culture that ignore the individual artist. It is perhaps no wonder that the collegian of my summer picnic seemed confused: his teachers seem becalmed, or rather, caught in a period of transition in which, as in any renaissance, a wealth of new material, new ideas, and new approaches struggle to mingle and find direction.

The watershed year of 1965 saw more Melville dissertations (sixteen) accepted than in any other previous year; indeed, the average yearly out-put of theses would double in the 1970s. Six of the Northwestern-New-berry editions, as well as Hayford and Parker's Norton edition of *Moby-Dick*, appeared by 1971. However, the editors, hampered by fund-ing problems, delayed release of the later volumes until 1982 with the publication of *Israel Potter*. Now all that remains are two volumes: the published poems (ed. Robert C. Ryan), and *Billy Budd* and other late manuscripts (ed. Hayford and Ryan). A full descriptive bibliography (projected by Tanselle) would fill another volume. But as the Northwest-ern-Newberry project winds down, it must prepare to wind up again, for the 1984 discovery of the *Typee* manuscript fragment (three full chapters in working draft) warrants a new edition of Melville's first book. (I am presently preparing a genetic transcription and reading text of the MS.) If the need now for an expanded Northwestern-Newberry *Typee* suggests that the work of textual scholars is never done, it should also reinforce the idea that textual scholarship must be as fluid as the author's initial creative process.

Scholarly tools also burgeoned after 1965 with Wilson Walker Cowen on the marginalia (dissertation #134) and Sealts on Melville's reading. Leyda's 1969 update of the *Log* is now in serious need of further expan-sion. (According to Hershel Parker, a new *Log* will fill three more volumes.) Attention to Melville's reputation grew with the reprinting of reviews in Parker's *Recognition* and Watson G. Branch's *Critical Heritage*. Reprints and a record of newly uncovered reviews (several quite interest-ing) are now published periodically in *Extracts;* and a *Checklist of Melville Reviews,* compiled by Kevin Hayes and Hershel Parker, appeared in 1991. Higgins's impressive two-volume bibliography of secondary works up to

1960 awaits the projected third volume listing criticism to the present, but no one has yet volunteered to take on the job. Given the continued discovery of new reviews, a second edition of Higgins will become necessary soon enough. In 1983, I annotated six decades' worth of Melville dissertations, and Phelps contributed his bibliography of foreign studies. In 1986, I edited the *Companion*, which brought together twenty-five essays on Melville's texts, life, thought, art, and modern reputation. After ten years, it remains useful for its scholarly and critical focus, but the need for bibliographical updating is inevitable.

The dearth of tools relating to Melville's sources and language that plagued the first decades of research has been addressed, but only recently. Mary K. Bercaw's *Sources* is an indispensable listing, with additional directives on who identified what source and when. Gail H. Coffler's compilation of *Classical Allusions* and Kathleen E. Kier's *Melville Encyclopedia: The Novels* supply useful annotations. Without doubt, Melville deserves a full concordance, but that honor is still far from realized. Early concordances of *Moby-Dick* (Hennig Cohen and James Cahalan, and Eugene F. Irey) were not based on the then as-yet-unpublished Northwestern-Newberry text. Individual concordances of *Clarel* and *Billy Budd* have appeared as dissertations (#487 and #505, respectively). But only Larry Edward Wegener has mounted a unified and reliable project. To date, his *Clarel, Mardi, The Confidence-Man,* and *Pierre* concordances have appeared. The need for a reliable electronic concordance has yet to be addressed.

Who is doing the electronic Melville? In 1994, the Melville Society, with the support of Hofstra University, established the Internet discussion group ISHMAIL. (I'm not proud of that pun, but someone had to make it.) And in 1995 Melville enthusiast Jim Madden designed the first Melville "web-site" on the World Wide Web with the idea of providing users brief samples of texts, criticism, and biography; other web-sites are bound to emerge. Various electronic texts, none too reliable—one version of *Moby-Dick* appears without chapter 73 or etymology—appear on the Web, but these materials are more reliably accessed in something called a book. Yet to be digitized are the less accessible Augusta Papers and manuscripts, the hard-to-acquire secondary critical materials, and such scholarly tools as the *Log*, marginalia, and Wegener's concordances. Once again, we are caught between fertility and stagnation in this Melville Renaissance. The good news, however, is that the Melville Society has charged its newly established Committee for the Electronic

Melville to design and create a comprehensive Melville web-site that will give users reliable access to all primary and secondary materials.

Finally, the discovery in the past twenty years of remarkable biographical and manuscript materials has seeded the clouds of Melville studies, but thus far we hear only dry thunder. In 1975, Walter D. Kring and Jonathan S. Carey unearthed letters involving Melville's wife and Unitarian minister Henry Whitney Bellows that not only established an unknown church affiliation but also startlingly revealed marital problems between Herman and Elizabeth in 1867, the year in which their son Malcolm later killed himself. Not until 1981, with Donald Yannella and Parker's pamphlet *The Endless Winding Way*, did these materials finally reach a larger Melvillean readership, but even then the news failed to penetrate critical circles. After almost two decades of dormancy, these scant but certain data of Melville's faltering marriage have found a recent resurrection in Elizabeth Renker's problematic but provocative claim that Herman may have beaten Elizabeth.

In 1984, along with the *Typee* manuscript were found some five hundred family letters known as the Augusta Papers, named after Melville's sister Augusta, who collected most of the material. Several letters are from Augusta and Herman's mother, and about one-third of the entire collection mentions Herman. Although only one letter is by Melville—a "crowing" announcement to brother Allan of Malcolm's birth in 1850 (analyzed in Cohen and Yannella)—the Augusta Papers provide heretofore unrecorded insights into decades of Melville family life. Thus far, aside from Cohen and Yannella, only a few have explored these materials for their biographical and critical revelations, most notably Neal L. Tolchin on mourning and Stanton Garner on the Civil War years. Why have so few turned to the new Melville finds? Progress is indeed slow. But more: current criticism does not encourage biographical analysis; the *Typee* manuscript and Augusta Papers have not been reproduced; and our graduate schools do not show students the ways of bringing creative process and hermeneutics together.

One hopes that the publication in 1996 of volume 1 of Parker's *Herman Melville: A Biography* (to be followed in a year by volume 2) will stimulate a new era of analysis that can more effectively explore the most meaningful intersections of a life and text. This magisterial production supplies a deeply textured carpet of culture and familial details so thick that certain paragraphs bear re-reading if only for one to recalculate and fine-tune one's sense of Melville's treading of history and society. There is no doubt that Parker's work will be the definitive biography for decades to come. Weighing in at half the poundage is Laurie Robertson-Lorant's necessarily less textured (and at times less precise) *Melville: A Biography*, which is, however, no less stimulating for its direct and measured characterization of Melville's darker traits. Just as Leon Howard's still important biography attempted to balance the too darkly Byronic image of a thwarted Melville propagated by his predecessors, so, too, have Parker and Robertson-Lorant, in quite different but equally engaging modes, put forth new Melvilles that counter Howard's own too dispassionate figure. As always, the pendulum swings, but with these new biographies we are becoming better informed and better situated to understand what counts: the creative Melville, bright side and dark.

Certainly, the study of Melville's creativity has been ably conducted in past decades. James Barbour expanded Howard's early notion of "two *Moby-Dicks*" to three, and Higgins and Parker speculated on how Melville "wrecked" *Pierre*. But surely, Sealts ("Emerson's Rainbow" and "Platonic Tradition") and Hayford ("Unnecessary Duplicates") have offered the most artful studies of how an artist works. Nevertheless, these models of sleuthing out what Sealts calls "the ways of creativity" seem to have done little to encourage the study of Melville's creative process. The sad truth is that criticism, which has come to devalue such analysis, trivializes finds such as the Kring-Carey letters and the *Typee* manuscript. Add to this the lingering tendency to marginalize Melville's years after *Moby-Dick*, and we gain a fair reckoning of why the hoped-for synthesis of scholarship, criticism, and pedagogy has been slow in coming. Thus, the accomplishments of Howard, Hayford, Sealts, and others seem like "dry thunder," not because of a lack of richness, but because of their slight penetration into critical fields notoriously uninterested in creative process.

Legends in Scholarship

Another impediment to the study of Melville's creative process may be due to certain habits of mind. I mean the tendency to reduce the complex interrelationships of life and text (creativity and reader response) to "legends of scholarship." If biographical *data* are the "stuff" of a writer's existence, and *facts* are data tendentiously assembled to support a hypothesis, then a *legend* is a hypothesis somehow elevated to the region of truth. Come the millennium when all critical truth shall be revealed, we shall watch with pleasure or dismay as these cherished legends prove gold or dross. But I am just a rationalist doomed to doubt, and until Revelation arrives, I prefer to play the skeptic.

What are these legends? For many they will sound like established "fact," and that, sadly enough, is the problem. It is not, for instance, proven that Melville revised *Moby-Dick* after meeting Hawthorne in 1850, and yet many teach the "two *Moby-Dicks*" theory as a matter of record, even though the evidence is inferential and utterly "soft." Part of the problem, of course, is that "hard" evidence is hard to come by in Melville studies, and scholars as well as critics too often convert hypotheses into facts to fill the gaps. A striking case in point is Henry Murray's argument that, as an adolescent, Melville's father Allan sired a daughter out of wedlock and that Melville's depiction of Isabel in *Pierre* is based on the family secret of his illegitimate half-sister. Working on the hunch that *Pierre*'s plot was essentially true, Murray set out to find evidence of "Allan's by-blow," and found it, he thought, in a letter that suggested that family members had bought off two women, presumably Allan's former teen lover and their daughter (identified only by their initials). But in a 1991 Melville Centennial address, Hayford displayed Murray's evidence and showed that the Melvilles were not paying off the women but that the women were paying a debt to the Melvilles. This little detail deflates Murray's thesis, just a bit. Even so, the thesis persists as another Melville legend.

Most often legends in Melville scholarship are cartoonish flattenings of the biography used as a kind of stereotyping to support a particular critical reading. Melville was crazy, a violent husband, an abusive father, an alcoholic, a latent homosexual whose advances on Hawthorne drove the older author out of the Berkshires. None of these characterizations is based on hard data, or even in some cases on any evidence at all. These are at best fractional portraits of a complex creative figure whose intense psychological life spanned seventy years with serious ups and downs, and even stretches of normalcy. The so-called split with Hawthorne, for instance, seems hard to accept when we find the two a few years later linking up in Liverpool, and no hint of former improprieties recorded by either individual. The romance of the two, however, is a persistent legend that continually bleeds into our reading. The poem "Monody," for instance, is assumed to be about Hawthorne, although legend-buster Hayford has shown that there is no substantial evidence for this view;

indeed, it is just as compelling to read that late poem as a bewildered lament for Malcolm.

I do not believe that Melville legends are purposefully concocted to delimit understanding, but that is their general intellectual effect. The legend makers, though, are not those who hypothesize, but rather those readers who allow the hypothesis to become a certainty of mind. Scratch a Melville legend, and you will find a mirror of your own desire, a portrait of Melville that looks suspiciously like some part of ourselves seeking expression: believer, disbeliever, authoritarian, recluse, angry hetero, repressed homo, racist, egalitarian. While it is impossible to disavow our desires and achieve critical objectivity, we can be more honest with ourselves and our students about the "truths" we derive. Just as Gerald Graff urges us in treating ideology in the classroom to "teach the conflict," we must go deeper and teach our relation to the past and our desire to mold "facts" to fit our needs. I doubt that we can ever eradicate all legends, but we can investigate their cause, and if there is any true prevention of their spreading, it is through doubt and discourse.

It helps to know how legends are perpetuated if only to see that they do not always last. It was generally agreed, up until the 1970s, for instance, that Melville peaked with *Moby-Dick*, that he fell apart in *Pierre*, and that his subsequent fictions show his collapse. "Benito Cereno" was considered an embarrassment; *The Confidence-Man* the product of burnout. Now, with a sharper discourse on narrative and rhetoric, the critical community applauds these works as masterpieces dramatizing the futility of racism and belief. But the legend of Melville's artistic "failure" persists, putting a lid on some of the more important questions relating to Melville's development as an artist. Few critics, for instance, seem at all interested in the crucial issue of why one of our culture's greatest writers simply gave up fiction writing for poetry, or why in his final years he returned to the narrative of *Billy Budd*. Garner's study of *Battle-Pieces* should direct more to the poetry, and John Wenke's study of how Melville purposefully crafted ambiguity into his text of *Billy Budd* should inspire more genetic analysis of that late work.

But as we bid adieu to the legend of Melville's "peaking" in midcareer, we stand ready to greet new legends in the making. In 1978 Higgins and Parker offered the theory that, angered over adverse reviews of *Moby-Dick*, Melville "wrecked" *Pierre* by adding satiric chapters on the literary establishment. It is an intriguing hypothesis based upon inference and indirect evidence. HarperCollins has now issued a trade edition of

Pierre, edited by Parker and marvellously illustrated by Maurice Sendak, that removes the offending chapters. Suddenly, we have a genetic theory put to use and a legend in the making. Some have erupted with indignation over Parker's presumption; others argue that he is doing only what editors do: he is creating a "more perfect" text. For my part, it is a striking instance in which one of Melville's most stable works (textually) has become a "fluid text," that is, a text shaped as much by readers as by the writer. Truth be told, all texts are fluid in one way or another; Parker's "new *Pierre*" demonstrates how editors physically construct texts to fit historical interpretation. Is this critical intervention into textual scholarship the end of civilization? Let's not rush to that judgment. Rather, it behooves us to pick up the discourse on text and meaning that this edition has provoked and to use that discourse as a means of teaching ourselves how to discern historical fact (the publishing of a work called *Pierre* in 1852) and critical judgment (the problematic editing of said work in 1995).

And another legend is brewing on the heels of Renker's essay, "Herman Melville, Wife Beating, and the Written Page." It seems almost inevitable that readers would respond emotionally to the hypothesis that Elizabeth Melville came to her Unitarian minister in 1867 to enlist support for a scheme to separate from Herman because he beat her. Drawing upon a thin line of rumor—that Herman came home drunk one night and pushed Elizabeth down the stairs—rooted in hearsay perpetuated by poet Charles Olson (who had quarrels with the alleged source of the rumor, Melville granddaughter Eleanor Melville Metcalf, herself only a child when Melville died, years after the alleged incident), Renker goes on to draw connections between Melville's alleged anger against women and his creative process. The good news is that Renker has offered a stimulating way of looking at Melville's creativity; the bad news is that apparently few people have read past her (I think highly problematic, but nevertheless valid) assumptions about a rumored instance of spousal abuse. One result is that one student at a major university has reported on the Internet that a professor has removed *Moby-Dick* from a course syllabus. Whether this bit of hearsay is itself true, I cannot say, but it suggests a climate ripe for legends.

And next summer, when my picnic is interrupted by my collegian friend, this time inquiring not about Melville the Indian-hater but about Melville the Wife-beater, I think that I shall let the burger cool and rather than deliver a "No! in thunder" lecture, will initiate some skepticism and discourse on how critical theses are constructed out of historical materials. I will attempt to display evidence pro and con, if only to counter the student's natural inclination to place too much confidence in the authority of one particular expert. Better that readers be given the tools to derive their own complex relation to Melville than to insist that their reading experience be reduced to the legends and cartoon portraits we academics allow ourselves to perpetuate.

Doing Melville

Aesthetics and Rhetoric

Even during the drought of the New Critical years when it seemed enough to demonstrate that Melville's texts were ambiguous—never mind what the psychological cause or cultural meaning or present-day social construction of that ambiguity—there seemed to be few willing to promote purely aesthetic readings, perhaps because Melville never managed to fabricate a well-wrought urn, or even cared to. His best fictions break down in one place or another and for one reason or another. Thus, aesthetic analyses invariably turn toward historicism, if only in search of the causes of Melville's peculiar artistry, or what his perfectly imperfect texts may mean in their social context. Even so, the search for a Melville aesthetic, based more perhaps on breakdown than coherence, persists. Admirable works focusing on text and mind alone may serve as models for future aesthetic analysis, especially as it bears upon the inevitable turn toward the historicism of rhetorical and narratological concerns prominent today. Bezanson's classic "*Moby-Dick* as Work of Art" reminds us that Melville's masterpiece is voiced primarily by Ishmael, not Ahab, and that to the extent that Ahab is a projection of Ishmael, we must look to the sailor as much as to the captain for the novel's final vision. Paul Brodtkorb, Jr., also remains a vibrant extension of Bezanson's line into the phenomenology of mind, and Robert Zoellner grounds Melville more firmly in metaphysics.

Given the instability of many Melville texts, there seems to be a natural affinity between Melville's romantic irony and the basic tenet of deconstruction that language falls apart. But surprisingly few studies in this field—Barbara Johnson on *Billy Budd* being the most stimulating—

have made a significant impact. I cannot speculate why this is so except to say that in so many Melville texts there is such an insistence upon an authorial presence that one is tempted to attribute formal collapse not to the nature of language but to the author's personality. A close study of the *Typee* manuscript reveals actual, physical, not metaphysical, aporia in Melville's texts, and it would be a welcome sight to find a deconstructionist reading of Melville that begins with the way his creative process operates from easy flow to sudden breakdown. Of course, critics have argued before deconstruction became a trend that Melville's texts fall apart. But their focus has been on the problems of Melville's development as a writer, as well as his metaphysics. For them, the author is a necessary presence. Finally, a Melville aesthetic must be rooted in personality.

But equally present are Melville's audiences; thus, the most compelling approach to Melville in recent years has been the growing interest in rhetoric. Earlier rhetorical analyses such as those by Rosenberry, Berthoff, and John Seelye analyzed tropes, styles, and genres in solid Aristotelian fashion, and Bryan C. Short's *Cast by Means of Figures* is an elegant extension of that primarily noncontextual branch of rhetorical study. But as Edgar A. Dryden so memorably demonstrated, the shape of a narrative itself projects a worldview, even as it fails to hold on to an aesthetic center. Just as he found meaning in rhetorical breakdown, Nina Baym (playing upon the title of Thompson's 1952 book) argued that Melville was not constitutionally suited to the forms of fiction; hence, his "quarrel with fiction" suggests the artistic futility of his problematic transcendentalism. Still, the more visible critical impulse is to stress the ways in which Melville's texts hold together—as in Milton Stern's social analysis, William B. Dillingham's trilogy, and Richard Brodhead's genre study— or, even better, how they fall apart in regenerative ways. Carolyn Porter's "Call Me Ishmael" shows how Melville gives authority to his socially marginalized narrator. Equally strong, although more rooted in style and structure than cultural fact, is Lawrence Buell's "*Moby-Dick* as Sacred Text," which demonstrates the novel's ability to create language that exposes us to the experiences of religious mystery. John Samson studies Melville's early unreliable narrators more in terms of their manipulations within certain cultural ideologies. And I argue, in *Melville and Repose*, for a rhetoric based on an aesthetics of repose in which narrative reliability and comic deception constitute a form of experimental "essaying" of literary structure and ideas.

The work before us in rhetorical analysis is to continue to root ourselves more firmly in historicism in two directions: we need to know more from available data just how much we can ascertain about Melville's evolving personality and about the audiences projected and actually endured, including family, friends, and closeted or underground admirers, as well as reviewers.

Few see Melville's manuscripts as a body of evidence waiting to reveal its biographical and rhetorical secrets, but the newly discovered *Typee* fragment is a gold mine of physical evidence that reveals the ceaseless revising Melville performed in order to find himself and promote certain rhetorical strategies. Generally speaking, historicists tend to look beyond the print-text to find social context, but in fact the most compelling historical evidence (compelling because it is physical) lies "beneath" the text in the process of revision. My forthcoming genetic transcription of the manuscript will include explanations (or "revision narratives") of Melville's numerous alterations, as well as comparisons to the "final" print version, so that readers may explore the raw data of this creative moment. Also due to be published are Hayford's and Ryan's Northwestern-Newberry volumes of the poems and the late manuscripts, including transcriptions of all manuscript poems and *Billy Budd*. One hopes that these projected publications will inspire more interest in genetic criticism and textual fluidity, especially as they pertain to reader response. Wenke's aforementioned study of *Billy Budd*, P. Marc Bousquet's analysis of the *Mosses* review, and Renker's treatment of the *The Confidence-Man* fragments in her essay (also appearing in her book *Strike through the Mask*) are significant steps taken in divergent directions. Whatever the direction, scholars and critics need to develop their understanding of the boon to cultural analysis inherent in the study of revision and manuscript.

Equally relevant are historical readerships. The more we understand about Melville's most immediate readers, including their expectations and ways of responding, the more sensitive we shall become to the way Melville put his words together to address or move them. Recently published are two separate studies of Melville and the city (by Hans Bergmann and Wyn Kelley) that will illuminate Melville's urban readers. Also new are Sheila Post-Lauria's cogent and cagey studies of audience manipulations in Melville's magazine pieces. James Creech's study of *Pierre*, while it is primarily about Melville's sexuality, provides important insights into the "winks" that historical and present-day readers might find in a Melville text. What texts have special meaning to other mariginalized audiences? C. L. R. James, while incarcerated during the McCarthy era, found solace in Melville and the will to resist authoritarianism, and Toni Morrison speaks for many African American readers when she finds Melville's assessment of whiteness to be an attack on racism. What other underground and underclass audiences of Melville are waiting discovery?

Although the Age of Deconstruction made us closer readers, it did little to encourage the articulation of a Melville Aesthetics or a Melville Rhetoric. While deconstruction helps clarify a sense of the failure of language that Melville surely understood, it does not provide the tools to understand the more complex operations of Melville's self as it interacts with art and readers. And there is again the fact of the author's indomitable creativity. Possessing a never fully eradicated Platonism, Melville simply refused to allow the metaphysical impossibility of self-expression and communication (which he acknowledged) to impede his will to write. He operated with an aesthetic that transcended nihilism, even though he knew transcendence was impossible. He could not keep from writing and is best characterized as a pragmatic Platonist, always pushing for earthly expressions of fatally unreachable ideality. ("How," he asks in *Pierre*, "can a man get a Voice out of Silence?" [NN *Pierre*, 208]). Shirley Dettlaff's impressively comprehensive overview of "Melville's Aesthetics" in the *Companion* supplies the background on the aesthetic principles that Melville knew, and Samson's Bakhtinian approach strikes me as a productive means for illuminating the mutually resilient rhetorical poses inherent in a "Melville Aesthetic." Wenke's *Melville's Muse* takes important strides in showing how the author's Platonism, variously derived from ancient and contemporary sources (including Plato, Montaigne, Coleridge, and Emerson), shaped the evolution of Melville's "philosophical fiction." In doing so, Wenke does not tie Melville to genre but watches the author work through and beyond genre to a formless formalism that engages self, idea, word, and reader. To articulate Melville's aesthetics and rhetoric fully, we also need a vision of art that combines the psychological and political, both the Yea and Nay, one that acknowledges the power of geniality and despair, even sentiment as well as tragedy, one that can account for the development throughout the canon and for the fluidity of individual texts, and one that reunites personality and language, as well as race, sexuality, and gender.

This is a tall order, but we have time. One important complementary development that will surely advance the cause has been the focus in the past few years on Melville and the fine arts. Melville collected over three hundred prints throughout his life, toured galleries, attended plays and concerts, and wrote major poetic works on art and artists. Defining the picturesque, for instance, is the announced goal of the long poem "At the Hostelry," and it would make me most happy if anyone were to mount a lifetime project to illustrate and annotate that work. Christopher Sten performed a momentous feat by collecting, editing, and introducing the essays found in *Savage Eye,* an impressive array of pieces ranging from source studies in the arts and genre studies to speculations on aesthetics. Robert Wallace's *Melville and Turner,* which speculates upon Melville's connection to Britain's most brilliant Romantic painter, is nevertheless a model of controlled scholarly insight. Similarly impressive, although focused more on Melville's influence on artists than on his sources in art, is Elizabeth A. Schultz's *Unpainted to the Last,* the most beautiful Melville book to date, and a thorough study of the impact of *Moby-Dick* on painting and sculpture in modern art. Both Wallace and Schultz should serve as inspirations for scholarship in other related fields spanning the past two centuries. Still needed is a study of Melville's connection to nineteenth-century theatricals and other popular art forms (both Lawrence Levine's work and David S. Reynolds's work supply significant theoretical and content grounding for such study). Along these lines, a comprehensive study of Melville's use of Shakespeare, as text, aesthetic model, and popular icon for the young Republic, is needed to stitch together and move beyond the numerous takes on the two that have proliferated from Melville's own statement in his review of Hawthorne to Matthiessen and Olson to Julian Markels's most recent semi-Marxist, semi-New Critical paralleling of *Moby-Dick* and *Lear.* Finally, what Schultz has done with Melville and modern art should be done with Melville and modern writing, or with Melville and modern poetry in particular.

Historicism: Allegory and Process

The advent of the new historicism has given us ample opportunity to rejoice that text and context may yet be reunited, but also ample reason to reflect more upon what historicism can and cannot do. Since historicizing Melville can mean making him relevant to present-day ideologies or rooting him in the past, it makes sense to distinguish at least two kinds of historicism: the allegorical and the processual.

Allegorical historicism has the advantage of being visionary but is often reductive and given to presentism (a flaw in criticism, according to many traditionalists, but an inevitability nonetheless that gives criticism social functionality). Here, patterns of social behavior are perceived to operate as a kind of metaphor or symbol of the workings of culture itself, and the author's text is seen to operate (largely unconsciously) in compliance. Thus, the text has meaning as it is a fulfillment of certain cultural principles, and it becomes therefore a synecdoche or allegory of culture. In allegorical historicism, the author is less important than what Fredric Jameson calls (somewhat mystically) "the political unconscious." But historicism that stresses process illuminates the mechanisms of artistic production and reflects the tensions that arise when an individual attempts to express a self and a culture through writing. The focus of processual historicism is on the various interactions of an author with collaborators, editors, readers, and a range of internal personal and external social forces. Like the study of ritual (at least as given to us by Clifford Geertz), this mode of historicism asks us to weigh not a cultural phenomenon in the abstract but the individual artist as he or she *enacts the culture*. Ritual is neither the Dance nor the Dancer, but the dancer dancing. While this form of historicism has the advantage of building reliably upon historical particulars, it can become too mired in detail so as to neglect the larger critical obligation of showing how the past (or rather an artist's interactions in the past) speak to our present condition.

Rather than draw lines in the sand between these two historicisms, I think it safe to say that most historicists do a little of both, finding a significant moment in literary production and linking it to a broader cultural movement. The best of the lot dramatize as well as allegorize culture; they particularize authorial acts rather than fetishistically deny the impact of individual consciousness. With Emerson in mind, who calls for "creative readers" as well as creative writers, I pick up a piece of criticism hoping to find myself in the hands of a "creative historicist." This is not one who makes up the past (although all histories are fundamentally fictions), but rather one who engages, or reads, the past out of his or her own experience of past records, documents, materials. What is forever disappointing (and here I feel the mantle of Emerson's cold scorn for our little lives too much on my shoulders) is the work of historicism that slaps together a theory of America in vague proximity to a theory of

Melville. More satisfying, and convincing, is to read how the oddly perceived odd particular in a text and in a life bobs oddly in the flowing
river of culture, itself oddly perceived. Let me get free of the Emersonian-
isms to say simply that we learn more about what the past meant and
means by analyzing the idiosyncratic in the context of the expected or
representative. This is not to argue for American or Melvillean excep-
tionalism, but rather to suggest that we can find significant cultural patterns even in the unique, highly particularized twists and turns of literary
production, and that cultural allegories have credibility and social utility
largely to the degree that they are built up from individually researched
historical particulars.

Michael Paul Rogin's political and biographical contextualizing of
Melville, even though it too often seems merely to paste received readings of American history beside received readings of Melville, is nevertheless a landmark in recent historicist writing, projecting a highly
particularized Melville shaped by familial pressures that reflect the
nation's instability. *Subversive Genealogy* remains a rich study, and yet the
Typee manuscript and Augusta Papers, as well as arguments for strains of
conservatism in Melville by James Duban, Larry Reynolds, and Garner,
make this 1983 book in need of an update. Still, Rogin provides an
inspiringly pluralistic integration of biography, rhetoric, and ideology.
We find in it more process than allegory. An equally comprehensive
political analysis of Melville's relation to the legal culture of the day, one
that also brings together the best of traditional and new historicism, is
Brook Thomas's *Cross-examinations*.

Equally thoughtful is Wai-chee Dimock's *Empire for Liberty*, which also
brings rhetorical process and cultural allegory to bear on the issue of
individualism and "the Other." Her Melville is at times imperialistic, at
times submissive, and she correlates the author's textual interactions
with paradigmatic cultural poses toward Manifest Destiny. But since
Dimock adheres to a notion of the political unconscious that obviates any
study of the author as agent, Melville's shifting rhetorical poses are
attributed more to America's affair with Manifest Destiny and less to the
necessities of his personal engagement with readers. Dimock's new
historical approach leaves unexplored the problem of how and why
Melville's rhetorical poses vary from one text to the next. "New Americanist" Donald Pease offers a more particularized rhetorical analysis of
Ahab's Quarter-deck speech to situate our understanding of Melville in
the context of the post-war era's Cold War canonization of *Moby-Dick*. In

so doing, he manages to demonstrate how history is always about the present, without making his own historicist approach sink uselessly into mere presentism. William Spanos adds a Heideggerian dimension to Pease's thesis in an attempt to show that what Cold War canonizers did unto *Moby-Dick* critically (i.e., read it as an anti-authoritarian tract despite its "errant" text, which dances around the issue) is part and parcel of the culture's self-induced amnesia over Vietnam. Unfortunately, Spanos's inept and impenetrable prose—nested abstractions perform abstract acts upon other nested abstractions—thwarts his ability to make this interesting idea come alive.

More lucid and most useful of all is T. Walter Herbert's approach in *Marquesan Encounters*, one that places Melville's discernments about imperialism and race in *Typee* in the context of other Polynesian sojourners (the provocateur David Porter and missionary Charles Stewart). Here Melville's heavily "varnished" rhetoric can be seen at play with these sources in a kind of spur-of-the-moment ritualistic dance of ideology and language. Herbert's work is a model for both traditional and new historicists, one that would be all the more imitable if (again) the *Typee* manuscript materials, with their evidence of ideological shiftings, had been available to Herbert for analysis.

Probably the most fruitful area for historicists seeking out the relation of text and ideology, and one still waiting to be fully explored, is the field of Melville and Race. Of course, this is already a well-enough-plowed field with early and significant historical retrievals supplied by Sidney Kaplan, a valuable and comprehensive analysis in Carolyn L. Karcher's *Shadow over the Promised Land,* and the close political sleuthing in Franklin's "Slavery and Empire," among other valuable studies, many of which focus largely upon "Benito Cereno" as Melville's highly complicated statement on American slavery, freedom, and race. Happily, the resurgence of interest in this tale in the past decade has corrected the earliest critical view that it is "about evil," with the unfortunate use of a black man as the ultimate repository of that evil, a view that stains even the best of the 1950s attempts to show how Melville is in fact dramatizing the absurdities of American slaveholder mentality. Babo, critics have long since come to see, is not "evil"; he is human, and a political reality. Current analysis recognizes that this tale's meaning is located in its narrative strategies. Eric J. Sundquist's *To Wake the Nations* brings rhetorical and cultural analysis together to show that the nation's ambivalence over the brutality of slavery and the savagery of revolt earmarked a prewar cultural paralysis that Melville's tale (and Martin Delany's *Blake*) aptly epitomized with its equally paralytic rhetorical stance. This study demonstrates not only how historicism can effectively combine rhetorical and biographical process with cultural allegory, but also that Melville remains a crucial figure in the still-unfolding story of America and Race.

Despite these advances, problems in the field need to be confronted. The strong focus on "Benito Cereno" seems to have pushed other relevant texts aside. Let's not forget that Ahab's famous Quarter-deck speech eventuates in a little race riot on ship, one that bumps Ishmael back into his narrative voice, or that Pip (Ishmael's alter ego) is the only figure who has any possibility of retrieving Ahab. Earlier works as well—*Typee*, in particular, but also *Omoo*, *Mardi*, and *White-Jacket*—contribute enormously to the fabric of Melville's richly textured discourse on the politics and ontology of race. But not since Karcher's 1980 book, or Joyce Sparer Adler's useful *War in Melville's Imagination*, has anyone attempted a book-length treatment of the entire canon regarding this issue. We are ready now for new treatments that will liven up an already lively discussion, and we are long overdue for treatments by African American scholars.

This problem is itself a reflection of America's racial condition; the academy no less than any other sector of the nation is stunted by the paucity of African American literary scholars. The numbers are changing, but change is glacial, and most young black scholars are busy establishing the African American canon, not writing about Melville. Toni Morrison has written in her 1988 Tanner Lecture that "to this day no novelist has so wrestled with the subject of race [as Herman Melville]." Who will take up the implicit call to Melville that Morrison makes? As part of its Melville centennial celebration in 1991, the Melville Society sponsored a symposium on Melville and Race at the Schomburg Center in New York City, an event featuring Henry Louis Gates, Jr., Arnold Rampersad, David Bradley, and H. Bruce Franklin. One hopes that the varied approaches found in the centennial collection, *Evermoving Dawn*, will light some fires.

Another area that is exasperatingly underexplored is Melville's relation to women. Ann Douglas's treatment of Melville's masculinity in her insightful but dated *Feminization of American Culture* has not been fully expanded or supplemented. Readers have long characterized Melville as a "man's writer," but that tired legend made by those who have read only *Moby-Dick* (and probably skipped such feminist chapters as "Loose Fish" or the "Grand Armada") is about as accurate as the early notion that Melville is just for "boys." Female characterizations in *Typee, Mardi, Moby-Dick, Pierre,* such tales as "The Encantadas" and "Tartarus of Maids," the epic *Clarel,* and numerous later poems including the Rose Poems in *Weeds and Wildings* are enough material for a significant feminist study of Melville. But the major analysis of Melville and gender, one that can bring together the author's sense of manhood (beset or not) and his feminine side (let's not forget "queenly" Ahab), has yet to emerge. Althought Parker's biography draws heavily upon the Augusta papers to clarify the writer's life in a gynocentric home, it does not address the issues of feminism. However, Laurie Robertson-Lorant's biography, the first by a woman since Eleanor Melville Metcalf's biography and Jean Gould's children's biography, does provide this important perspective. Even so, few critical works have attempted to extend the line first cast by Douglas. An exception is David Leverenz's study of masculinity, which develops the intriguing idea that male writers wrestle inwardly with their fear of humiliation stemming from the dynamics of family (i.e. father-son) tensions. While this idea comes close to becoming an allegory of American Manhood, Leverenz's exhilaratingly fresh readings help him cultivate his forest with amply particularized trees. Unfortunately, only one chapter is devoted to Melville, Ahab, and Ishmael.

Would that critical writing on Melville, race, and gender were as fully launched as recent gay studies. Was Melville homosexual? Was he heterosexual? The answer is an emphatic Yes. There is his homosexual squeeze of a hand; there is his heterosexual union of sky and sea. As a writer Herman Melville embraced a range of sexualities. He was pan-sexual: auto, hetero, homo. My frustration with Edwin Haviland Miller's 1975 biography is that the homosexuality he discovers is too pathological. Based upon unprovable (and I think unlikely) encounters between Melville and Hawthorne, the book depends too heavily upon a dated Freudian model of homosexual infantilism. Robert K. Martin's *Hero, Captain, and Stranger* is far more illuminating, flexible, and useful. Here homosexuality is a creative alternative to heterosexual aggression. Martin's ideologies are clear but supple. His humor is engaging and provides a significant means of reevaluating Melville's own comic sensibility. This important work has inspired further thinking, as is evident in Creech's more problematic study of *Pierre.* Creech actually has two closets to dust out of: he is gay; he is a deconstructionist. The two approaches, he reminds us, are inimical to one another, and the value of his work lies largely in Creech's coming to terms with this conflict and with how Melville's "winking" rhetoric (in *Redburn* too) signals deeper homosexual meanings. And Caleb Crain's "Lovers of Human Flesh" draws a connection between homosexuality and cannibalism that helps us resolve issues concerning Tommo's sexuality and fear in *Typee*. The more such readings we have, the more we shall begin to understand the appeal of Melville to the underclass of gay readers, as well as the link between sexuality and being. Equally so, we shall become less involved with legends of scholarship that play upon facile sexual stereotyping and more directed toward a comprehensive notion of the interpenetration of varying sexualities.

As I have been arguing, we need in the future to incorporate more of Melville's creative process into our historicist approaches. For it is in the hard data of Melville's manuscript, his endless revisions, his tinkerings after going to print, that we can discern both his habits of writing, which bear directly upon his personal needs, and the cultural meaning of the forces that impelled his revisions. Geneticism helps expose Melville's rhetorical strategies, and it helps ground our allegories of cultural power in the solid facts of creation and publication. To develop a fuller sense of Melville's composing and its cultural context, we must begin to broaden our notion of Melville's text, not simply to embrace several discrete print-texts from *Typee* to *Billy Budd*, but also to acknowledge the full range of creative processes that eventuated in these print-texts, the range of creativity Tanselle refers to as the "work" of an author, and what I call Melville's "Fluid Text." *Typee*, certainly Melville's most unstable text, is a case in point that is likely to become the fluid text most worth returning to for scholars and critics in the years to come. Here we have a book that exists for us in partial manuscript, a first edition, an expurgated edition, and several posthumous editings. Each text represents a phase in Melville's interactions with himself, his projected audiences, and his real audiences. It reveals in its shimmering variants clear evidence of shifting intentions and ideologies, which in themselves have cultural meaning. If we are to make historicist allegories of literary production, let us begin not so much with single print-texts, which show only a frozen fraction of Melville's creativity, but with the textual fluidities that manifest his full process.

Typee, the late poetry in manuscript, and *Billy Budd* (our most complete manuscript, which itself sprang out of a poem) are the deepest wells for delving into Melville's fluid text. For instance, the poem "Art," as printed, is a frozen statement on aesthetics. But in manuscript we find that statement working its way through varying modulations; those modulations are a set of meanings in themselves, waiting to be assessed. Similarly, in *Typee* (one of the smartest and most complex of freshman endeavors in the English language), we find a print-text that allows us to confront an incredible range of issues: the difference between autobiography and fiction; the power of colonial politics; the awakening of male sexuality; the growth of an artist; the nature and fate of cosmopolitan multiculturalism. These issues can be raised to a higher degree when we consider them in the context of Melville's manuscript revisions, or his submission to editorial expurgation, or his latter-day second thoughts, or even the fact that British and American readers read separate versions of *Typee* throughout the nineteenth century. If we are to historicize Melville fully and bring creative process and cultural allegory in harmony, we need first of all to bring geneticism and rhetoric together.

Scholars and Teachers

Scholarship and writing are the ruling passions, and teaching is our bread and butter. Even so, passions ignite in the classroom; thus, teaching can be a testing ground for ideas, even a fertile ground of discovery. For the scholar-teacher-writer, teaching, as well as scholarship and writing, is a defining strand in the tapestry of intellectual discourse, and yet pedagogy is often our last concern. Because Melville has always been so eminently teachable, the issue of how we teach Melville ought to be raised to the highest level of academic discourse. A good start on this road is Martin Bickman's collection, but little has been done to augment that work, and impediments to teaching linger.

When I say that Melville is teachable, for instance, I most surely hear groans of disbelief. Melville is tough, and students are often resistant. Melville's position as a classic in the canon and his role in the development of modern academe are matters of acrimony that create more hurdles to teaching. One source of bitterness lies in the argument that Melville appears on the syllabus because our male academic forebears have insisted that he be there, and this assumption has created wells of resentment among those who discount the works of "dead white males." Recent studies provide insights that might illuminate the causes of this "miso-melvillainy." Clare Spark questions the male authoritarianism of the early Melville Revivalists and today's "Melville establishment" scholars in Paul Metcalf's *Enter Isabel*. But more germane although over-simplified is Paul Lauter's claim that Melville entered the academy in the 1920s as the darling of those who would "masculinize" the American canon and those equating obscurantism with modernism. Lauter is surely right on both counts, although these are only a portion of the full story. Sealts's compilation of the early Melville biographies records that Melville's reputation was growing even among academics as early as the 1890s. Moreover, he became useful to a variety of special interest readerships: Jeffersonian liberals, British gays, Harlem Renaissance blacks, McCarthy era refugees, and artists from expressionism to realism. For Lauter, the disdain for Melville among his students—he polled his classes on gender and found that no one listed Melville as a "must read" writer—is one canon-busting generation's inevitable negative response to an earlier, exclusionary canon-forming group of academics. That is, Melville may be rejected not for his writing but for his talismanic status in a fading male academe. It is a case of the sins of the sons (and we do mean sons) being visited upon the father. Miso-melvillainy seems to be a pendular reaction to Melville hagiography. Neither pathology is particularly enlightening.

Another source of anxiety comes from students who, culturally conditioned to believe that Melville is Grand and they are but small, feel that they are not worthy of Melville and accordingly hate him. Everyone encounters "mobydickophobia." Its symptoms are a reticence with symbol, a failure to see humor in Ishmael, a dumbfoundedness over deeply textured lines leading to a paralysis in reading that sends students to the nearest Cliffs Notes rack. The result is a debilitating "hermanangst" that, if not confronted, can cripple even the most committed of readers. The question for teachers of Melville today is how we can demystify Melville so that readers and students may be free to experience him in fresh and original ways. How we might do this connects directly with our individual critical approaches.

Gone, one hopes, is the presumption of angry classroom authoritarians who make the reading of *Moby-Dick* a rite of passage into culture or intellectual "manhood." Melville should not be used as a weapon of exclusion, but as an opening to experience the ways of creativity, the logic of symbol, the risk of self-knowledge, and more. We need to make students aware of their cultural restraints and help them find their own means of entry into the novel. Whether they are Ishmaeleans circling about a symbol, or Ahabians breaking through in search of a plot, they need to be empowered to plunge here or skim there, to break down (as Melville did) in places and wonder why—in short, to experience in some personal way (but also in the midst of a community of other readers) the confrontation with ideas, language, and being that shaped Melville's intellectual and artistic life.

These are some of the strategies I try to develop. They may not be yours. But whatever strategies you or I may devise, they need to be experiential. And this thought recalls my collegian of last summer, seeking out an "authority" in the field when what he needed were the skills of discourse that would enable him to doubt myths, legends, and cartoons, and achieve an individual, vital relation to both text and culture. Whether the issue is a particular passage in Melville, or the larger concerns of rhetoric, narrative, history, aesthetics, textuality, and ideology, the goals of our teaching, as well as of our critical and scholarly endeavor, should be to engage fellow readers in the passionate experience of thought. Only with this in mind can we begin to discuss the future of Melville studies.

WORKS CITED

Segments of this essay were first delivered in a paper to the Melville Society at its annual meeting at MLA in December, 1991. The full text of that address was also reproduced in *Extracts* 88 (1992): 10–14.

Adler, Joyce Sparer. *War in Melville's Imagination*. New York: New York UP, 1981.

Anderson, Charles Roberts. *Melville in the South Seas*. New York: Columbia UP, 1939.

Arvin, Newton. *Herman Melville*. New York: Sloane Associates, 1950.

Baird, James. *Ishmael: A Study of the Symbolic Mode in Primitivism*. Baltimore: Johns Hopkins UP, 1958.

Barbour, James. "The Composition of *Moby-Dick*." *American Literature* 47 (1975): 343–60.

Baym, Nina. "Melville's Quarrel with Fiction." *PMLA* 94 (1979): 909–23.

Bergmann, Hans. *God in the Street: New York Writing from the Penny Press to Melville*. Philadelphia: Temple UP, 1995.

Bercaw, Mary K. *Melville's Sources*. Evanston, IL: Northwestern UP, 1987.

Berthoff, Warner. *The Example of Melville*. Princeton, NJ: Princeton UP, 1962.

Bezanson, Walter E. "*Moby-Dick* as Work of Art." *Moby-Dick Centennial Essays*. Ed. Tyrus Hillway and Luther S. Mansfield. Dallas, TX: Southern Methodist UP, 1953. 30–58.

Bickman, Martin. *Approaches to Teaching Melville's "Moby-Dick."* New York: Modern Language Association, 1985.

Blanck, Jacob. "Herman Melville." *Bibliography of American Literature*, vol. 6. New Haven, CT: Yale UP, 1973. 152–81.

Bousquet, P. Marc. "Mathews's Mosses? Fair Papers and Foul: A Note on the Northwestern-Newberry Edition of Melville's 'Hawthorne and His Mosses.'" *New England Quarterly* 67 (1994): 622–49.

Bowen, Merlin. *The Long Encounter: Self and Experience in the Writings of Herman Melville.* Chicago: U of Chicago P, 1960.

Branch, Watson G., ed. *Melville: The Critical Heritage.* Boston: Routledge & Kegan Paul, 1974.

Braswell, William. *Melville's Religious Thought.* Durham, NC: Duke UP, 1943.

Brodhead, Richard H. *Hawthorne, Melville, and the Novel.* Chicago: U of Chicago P, 1976.

———, ed. *New Essays on "Moby-Dick."* New York: Cambridge UP, 1986.

Brodtkorb, Paul, Jr. *Ishmael's White World: A Phenomenological Reading of "Moby-Dick."* New Haven, CT: Yale UP, 1965.

Bryant, John. *Melville and Repose: The Rhetoric of Humor in the American Renaissance.* New York: Oxford UP, 1993.

———. *Melville's Typee Manuscript.* Forthcoming.

———, ed. *A Companion to Melville Studies.* Westport, CT: Greenwood P, 1986.

———, ed. *Melville Dissertations, 1924–1980.* Westport, CT: Greenwood P, 1983.

Bryant, John, and Robert Milder, eds. *Evermoving Dawn: Essays in Celebration of the Melville Centennial, 1991.* Kent, OH: Kent State UP, 1997.

Buell, Lawrence. "*Moby-Dick* as Sacred Text." Brodhead, *New Essays* 53–72.

Chase, Richard. *Herman Melville: A Critical Study.* New York: Macmillan, 1949.

Coffler, Gail H. *Melville's Classical Allusions: A Comprehensive Index and Glossary.* Westport, CT: Greenwood P, 1985.

Cohen, Hennig, and Donald Yannella. *Herman Melville's Malcolm Letter: "Man's Final Lore."* New York: Fordham UP, 1992.

Cohen, Hennig, and James Cahalan, eds. *A Concordance to Melville's "Moby-Dick."* 3 vols. Ann Arbor, MI: U Microfilms International, 1978.

Cowen, Wilson Walker. "Melville's Marginalia." Diss. Harvard U, 1965. [Melville Dissertation #134]

Crain, Caleb. "Lovers of Human Flesh: Homosexuality and Cannibalism in Melville's Novels." *American Literature* 66 (1994): 25–53.

Creech, James. *Closet Writing/Gay Reading: The Case of Melville's Pierre.* Chicago: U of Chicago, 1993.

Davis, Merrell R. *Melville's "Mardi": A Chartless Voyage.* New Haven, CT: Yale UP, 1952.

Davis, Merrell R., and William H. Gilman, eds. *The Letters of Herman Melville.* New Haven, CT: Yale UP, 1960.

Dettlaff, Shirley M. "Melville's Aesthetics." Bryant, *Companion* 625–68.

Dillingham, William B. *An Artist in the Rigging: The Early Works of Herman Melville.* Athens: U of Georgia P, 1972.

———. *Melville's Later Novels.* Athens: U of Georgia P, 1986.

———. *Melville's Short Fiction, 1853–1856.* Athens: U of Georgia P, 1977.

Dimock, Wai-chee. *Empire for Liberty: Melville and the Poetics of Individualism.* Princeton, NJ: Princeton UP, 1989.

Douglas, Ann. *The Feminization of American Culture.* New York: Knopf, 1977.

Dryden, Edgar A. *Melville's Thematics of Form: The Great Art of Telling the Truth.* Baltimore: Johns Hopkins UP, 1968.

Duban, James. *Melville's Major Fiction: Politics, Theology, and Imagination.* DeKalb, IL: Northern Illinois UP, 1983.

Feidelson, Charles. *Symbolism and American Literature.* Chicago: U of Chicago P, 1953.

Franklin, H. Bruce. *In the Wake of the Gods: Melville's Mythology.* Stanford: Stanford UP, 1963.

———. "Slavery and Empire." Bryant and Milder.

Garner, Stanton. *The Civil War World of Herman Melville.* Lawrence: UP of Kansas, 1993.

Geertz, Clifford. "Ethos, World View, and the Analysis of Sacred Symbols." *The Interpretation of Cultures.* New York: Basic Books, 1973. 126–41.

Gilman, William H. *Melville's Early Life and "Redburn."* New York: New York UP, 1951.

Gould, Jean. *Young Mariner Melville.* Illus. Donald McKay. New York: Dodd, Mead, 1956.

Graff, Gerald. *Beyond the Culture Wars.* New York: Norton, 1992.

Hayes, Kevin J., and Hershel Parker. *Checklist of Melville Reviews.* Evanston, IL: Northwestern UP, 1991.

Hayford, Harrison. *Melville's "Monody": Really for Hawthorne?* Evanston, IL: Northwestern UP, 1990.

———. "Unnecessary Duplicates: A Key to the Writing of *Moby-Dick*." Pullin 128–61.

Hayford, Harrison, and Merton M. Sealts, Jr., eds. *"Billy Budd, Sailor (An Inside Narrative)": Reading Text and Genetic Text.* Chicago: U of Chicago P, 1962.

Heflin, Wilson Lumpkin. "Herman Melville's Whaling Years." Diss. Vanderbilt U, 1952.

Heimert, Allan. "*Moby-Dick* and American Political Symbolism." *American Quarterly* 15 (1963): 495–534.

Herbert, T. Walter. *Marquesan Encounters: Melville and the Meaning of Civilization.* Cambridge, MA: Harvard UP, 1980.

Hetherington, Hugh W. *Melville's Reviewers: British and American, 1846–1891.* Chapel Hill: U of North Carolina P, 1961.

Higgins, Brian. *Herman Melville: An Annotated Bibliography.* Vol. 1 (1846–1930) and Vol. 2 (1931–1960). Boston: G. K. Hall, 1979 and 1987.

Higgins, Brian, and Hershel Parker. "The Flawed Grandeur of Melville's *Pierre.*" Pullin 162–96.

Hoffman, Daniel G. *Form and Fable in American Fiction.* New York: Oxford UP, 1961.

Howard, Leon. *Herman Melville: A Biography.* Berkeley: U of California P, 1951.

Irey, Eugene F., ed. *"Moby-Dick" Index Concordance.* New York: Hendricks House, 1978.

James, C. L. R. *Mariners, Renegades, and Castaways: The Story of Herman Melville and the World We Live In.* London: Allison & Busby, 1953.

Jameson, Fredric. *The Political Unconscious: Narrative as a Socially Symbolic Act.* Ithaca, NY: Cornell UP, 1981.

Johnson, Barbara. "Melville's Fist: The Execution of *Billy Budd.*" *Studies in Romanticism* 18 (1979): 567–99.

Kaplan, Sidney. *American Studies in Black and White: Selected Essays, 1949–1989.* Ed. Allan D. Austin. Amherst: U of Massachusetts P, 1991.

Karcher, Carolyn L. *Shadow over the Promised Land: Slavery, Race, and Violence in Melville's America.* Baton Rouge: Louisiana State UP, 1980.

Kelley, Wyn. *Melville's City: Literary and Urban Form in Nineteenth-Century New York.* New York: Cambridge UP, 1996.

Kier, Kathleen E. *A Melville Encyclopedia: The Novels.* New York: Whitston Publishing, 1990.

Lauter, Paul. "Melville Climbs the Canon." *American Literature* 66 (1994): 1–24.

Lawrence, D. H. *Studies in Classic American Literature.* New York: Thomas Seltzer, 1923.

Leverenz, David. *Manhood and the American Renaissance.* Ithaca, NY: Cornell UP, 1989.

Levin, Harry. *The Power of Blackness.* New York: Knopf, 1958.

Levine, Lawrence W. *Highbrow/Lowbrow: The Emergence of Cultural Hierarchy in America.* Cambridge, MA: Harvard UP, 1988.

Leyda, Jay, ed. *The Melville Log: A Documentary Life of Herman Melville, 1819–1891*. New York: Harcourt, Brace, 1951; rpt. with supplement New York: Gordian P, 1969.

Markels, Julian. *Melville and the Politics of Identity: From "King Lear" to "Moby-Dick."* Champaign: U of Illinois P, 1993.

Martin, Robert K. *Hero, Captain, and Stranger: Male Friendship, Social Critique, and Literary Form in the Sea Novels of Herman Melville*. Chapel Hill: U of North Carolina P, 1986.

Marx, Leo. *The Machine in the Garden: Technology and the Pastoral Ideal in America*. New York: Oxford UP, 1964.

Melville, Herman. *The Writings of Herman Melville*. Ed. Harrison Hayford, Alma A. MacDougall, Hershel Parker, and G. Thomas Tanselle. Evanston, IL, and Chicago: Northwestern UP and The Newberry Library, 1967–. [Forthcoming are *Poems*, ed. Robert C. Ryan, and *"Billy Budd" and Other Later Manuscripts*, ed. Ryan and Harrison Hayford.]

———. *Pierre or the Ambiguities*. The Kraken Edition. Ed. Hershel Parker. Illus. Maurice Sendak. New York: HarperCollins, 1995.

Metcalf, Eleanor Melville. *Herman Melville: Cycle and Epicycle*. Cambridge, MA: Harvard UP, 1953.

Metcalf, Paul, ed. *Enter Isabel: The Herman Melville Correspondence of Clare Spark and Paul Metcalf*. Albuquerque: U of New Mexico P, 1991.

Miller, Edwin Haviland. *Herman Melville: A Biography*. New York: Braziller, 1975.

Miller, James E., Jr. *A Reader's Guide to Herman Melville*. New York: Noonday, 1962.

Morrison, Toni. "Unspeakable Things Unspoken: The Afro-American Presence in American Literature." *Michigan Quarterly Review* 28 (1989): 1–34.

Murray, Charles Joseph. "A Concordance to *Billy Budd*." Diss. Miami U, 1979.

Murray, Henry, Harvey Myerson, and Eugene Taylor. "Allan Melvill's By-Blow." *Melville Society Extracts* 61 (1985): 1–6.

Olson, Charles. *Call Me Ishmael*. New York: Reynall & Hitchcock, 1947.

Parker, Hershel. *Herman Melville: A Biography, Volume 1, 1819–1851*. Baltimore: Johns Hopkins UP, 1996.

———. "Why *Pierre* Went Wrong." *Studies in the Novel* 8 (1976): 7–23.

———, ed. *The Recognition of Herman Melville: Selected Criticism since 1846*. Ann Arbor: U of Michigan P, 1967.

Pease, Donald. *Visionary Compacts: American Renaissance Writings in Cultural Context*. Madison: U of Wisconsin P, 1987.

Phelps, Leland R. *Herman Melville's Foreign Reputation: A Research Guide*. Boston: G. K. Hall, 1983.

Pommer, Henry F. *Milton and Melville*. Pittsburgh: U of Pittsburgh P, 1943.

Porter, Carolyn. "Call Me Ishmael, or How to Make Double-Talk Speak." Brodhead, *New Essays* 73–108.

Post-Lauria, Sheila. *Correspondent Colorings: Melville in the Marketplace*. Amherst: U of Massachusetts P, 1996.

Pullin, Faith, ed. *New Perspectives on Melville*. Kent, OH: Kent State UP, 1978.

Renker, Elizabeth. "Herman Melville, Wife Beating, and the Written Page." *American Literature* 66 (1994): 123–50.

———. *Strike through the Mask: Herman Melville and the Scene of Writing*. Baltimore: Johns Hopkins UP, 1996.

Reynolds, David S. *Beneath the American Renaissance: The Subversive Imagination in the Age of Emerson and Melville*. New York: Knopf, 1988.

Reynolds, Larry J. *European Revolutions and the American Literary Renaissance*. New Haven, CT: Yale UP, 1988.

Robertson-Lorant, Laurie. *Melville: A Biography*. New York: Clarkson Potter, 1996.

Rogin, Michael Paul. *Subversive Genealogy: The Politics and Art of Herman Melville*. New York: Knopf, 1983.

Rosenberry, Edward H. *Melville and the Comic Spirit*. Cambridge, MA: Harvard UP, 1955.

Samson, John. *White Lies: Melville's Narratives of Facts*. Ithaca, NY: Cornell UP, 1989.

Schultz, Elizabeth A. *Unpainted to the Last: "Moby-Dick" and Twentieth-century American Art*. Lawrence: UP of Kansas, 1995.

Sealts, Merton M., Jr. *The Early Lives of Melville: Nineteenth-Century Biographical Sketches and Their Authors*. Madison: U of Wisconsin P, 1974.

———. "Melville and Emerson's Rainbow" and "Melville and the Platonic Tradition." *Pursuing Melville, 1940–1980: Chapters and Essays*. Madison: U of Wisconsin P, 1982. 250–77 and 278–336, respectively.

———. *Melville's Reading*. Rev. and enlarged. Columbia: U of South Carolina P, 1988.

Sedgwick, William Ellery. *Herman Melville: The Tragedy of Mind*. Cambridge, MA: Harvard UP, 1944.

Seelye, John. *Melville: The Ironic Diagram*. Evanston, IL: Northwestern UP, 1970.

Short, Bryan C. *Cast by Means of Figures: Herman Melville's Rhetorical Development*. Amherst: U of Massachusetts P, 1992.

Spanos, William. *The Errant Art of "Moby-Dick": The Canon, the Cold War, and the Struggle for American Studies*. Durham, NC: Duke UP, 1995

Sten, Christopher, ed. *Savage Eye: Melville and the Visual Arts*. Kent, OH: Kent State UP, 1991.

Stern, Milton. *The Fine-Hammered Steel of Herman Melville*. Urbana and Chicago, IL: U of Illinois P, 1957.

Sundquist, Eric J. *To Wake the Nations: Race in the Making of American Literature*. Cambridge, MA: Harvard UP, 1993.

Thomas, Brook. *Cross-examinations of Law and Literature: Cooper, Hawthorne, Stowe, and Melville*. Cambridge, England: Cambridge UP, 1987.

Thompson, Lawrance. *Melville's Quarrel with God*. Princeton, NJ: Princeton UP, 1952.

Tolchin, Neal L. *Mourning, Gender, and Creativity in the Art of Herman Melville*. New Haven, CT: Yale UP, 1988.

Vincent, Howard P. *The Trying-out of "Moby-Dick."* Boston: Houghton Mifflin, 1949.

Wallace, Robert. *Melville and Turner: Spheres of Love and Fright*. Athens: U of Georgia P, 1992.

Wegener, Larry Edward. *A Concordance to "Clarel."* Glassboro, NJ: Melville Society, 1979; *"Mardi."* New York: Garland, 1991; *"Pierre."* New York: Garland, 1985; and *"The Confidence-Man: His Masquerade."* New York: Garland, 1987.

———. "A Concordance to Herman Melville's *Clarel: A Poem and Pilgrimage to the Holy Land*." Diss. U of Nebraska, Lincoln, 1978.

Wenke, John. "The Author's Hand: *Billy Budd*, the Genetic Text, and 'the deadly space between.'" *New Essays on "Billy Budd."* Ed. Donald Yannella. Cambridge, England: Cambridge UP, forthcoming.

———. *Melville's Muse: Literary Creation and the Forms of Philosophical Fiction*. Kent, OH: Kent State UP, 1995.

Winters, Yvor. *Maule's Curse: Seven Studies in the History of American Obscurantism*. Norfolk, CT: New Directions, 1938.

Wright, Nathalia. *Melville's Use of the Bible*. Durham, NC: Duke UP, 1949.

Yannella, Donald, and Hershel Parker, eds. *The Endless Winding Way*. Glassboro, NJ: Melville Society, 1981.

Zoellner, Robert. *The Salt-Sea Mastodon: A Reading of "Moby-Dick."* Berkeley: U of California P, 1973.

5

Frederick Douglass

Wilson J. Moses

The most logical place to begin an essay of this sort is perhaps with the pressing need for a comprehensive, annotated bibliography of the writings of Frederick Douglass. The most extensive listing of Douglass materials is *The Papers of Frederick Douglass in the Library of Congress*, which is available on fifty-two microfilm reels. The listing is accompanied by a guide, *Frederick Douglass, a Register and Index of His Papers in the Library of Congress*. To date there is no comprehensive catalogue of Douglass's published and unpublished works, and there is no standard guide to the archival collections containing Douglass manuscripts. *The Frederick Douglass Papers* editorial project, begun in the early 1970s under the editorship of John W. Blassingame, has assembled a large number of Douglass's writings, which are being published, some for the first time, by Yale University Press. The introductions to the Yale volumes provide a useful guide to archival collections. One should also check the manuscripts listed in the scholarly biographies below. A number of well-informed short articles serve as an introduction to the life and literary accomplishments of Frederick Douglass. Among the most interesting and most highly recommended for use in both graduate and undergraduate seminars are those by W. E. B. Du Bois in the *Dictionary of American Biography*, Benjamin Quarles in the *Dictionary of American Negro Biography*, David Blight in the *Encyclopedia Americana*, and Waldo Martin in *Encyclopedia of African-American Culture and History*.

William S. McFeely's *Frederick Douglass*, the most comprehensive biography to date, contributes an admiring, yet realistic appraisal of its subject and a good bibliography. Benjamin Quarles's *Frederick Douglass*, the first scholarly biography of Douglass, is still indispensable. Of historical interest is Booker T. Washington's *Frederick Douglass*, which was mostly ghost-written by S. Laing Williams, a black Chicago lawyer. Charles W. Chesnutt, the African American novelist, published his *Frederick Douglass* in 1899. I commented on similarities between the philosophies of Douglass and Washington in "Industrial Education, From Frederick Douglass to Booker T. Washington." Dickson J. Preston made substantial contributions to our knowledge of Douglass's formative years in his *Young Frederick Douglass*. Waldo Martin's *The Mind of Frederick Douglass* is an excellent study of Douglass's intellectual milieu. Thoughtful and well researched is David Blight's *Frederick Douglass' Civil War*. Between 1950 and 1955, the Marxist historian Philip S. Foner published *The Life and Writings of Frederick Douglass*, selections from Douglass's published and unpublished papers. The introductions to these volumes were compiled and republished as *Frederick Douglass: A Biography*. Foner published a supplementary compilation as *The Life and Writings of Frederick Douglass* in 1975. As of this writing, Foner's compilation retains its position as the best compendium of Douglass's non-autobiographical writings, and it has the advantage of being available in paperback.

Douglass's three autobiographies became widely available in reprint editions during the black studies revival of the late 1960s. More recently, all three have been republished in a new collection by the Library of America as *Autobiographies: "Narrative of the Life of Frederick Douglass"; "My Bondage and My Freedom"; "Life and Times of Frederick Douglass."* The annotations by Henry Louis Gates, Jr., are of unequaled quality. In the appended "Note on the Texts," Gates provides a thoughtful discussion of some of the problems of establishing a definitive listing of the numerous editions of Douglass's autobiographical works. The strength of the Gates edition is that it brings all the autobiographies together with excellent notes, chronology, and index.

Of the abundant reprints of *The Narrative of the Life of Frederick Douglass*, David Blight's edition is among the best. Not only has Blight provided helpful notes, a scholarly introduction, a chronology, and an excellent index, but also he has included a selection of supporting documents that helps to place the narrative in historical context. Literary and intellectual historians will find Blight's thematic organization particularly useful. Michael Meyer's *Frederick Douglass: "The Narrative" and Selected Writings* conveniently provides the complete *Narrative* of 1845, as well as excerpts from both *My Bondage and My Freedom* and *Life and Times*. Meyer also includes some 163 pages of selections from other writings. His thoughtful introduction points up stylistic differences and other differences in the three versions of the autobiography. Both the Blight and the Meyer introductions should be helpful to first-year graduate students, who often find it difficult to identify topics for seminar papers.

Future researchers and interpreters of Douglass will be obliged to mention what William McFeely calls the "unidentical" quality of Douglass's three autobiographies. McFeely observes that, in the *Narrative* of 1845, Douglass states as a matter of fact, "My father was a white man." Douglass softens this somewhat in *My Bondage and My Freedom*, saying, "My father was a white man or nearly white. It was sometimes whispered that my master was my father." Yet he says, in *The Life and Times of Frederick Douglass*, "Of my father I know nothing." Douglass shifts from an assertion that his father was a white man, possibly his master, to the speculation that his father was perhaps white or nearly white, to the admission that he knows nothing of his father. McFeely notes that no one has solved the question of whom Douglass referred to when he repeated the "whisper" that his father was his master, for Douglass referred to several persons as his master, including Aaron Anthony, Thomas Auld, and Edward Lloyd, any of whom might conceivably have been Douglass's father (McFeely 7, 8, 12, 14).

Some scholars have been perplexed by Douglass's recounting of his youthful struggle with Covey, the slave breaker, whom he physically resisted when Covey tried to beat him. The story's veracity is not in question here since Douglass had no reason to create any fictions regarding his physical courage. This he ably demonstrated in clashes with proslavery mobs on the antislavery lecture circuit, where he was said to have handled himself like a professional pugilist. Covey's failure to punish Douglass admits of more than one interpretation, however, as Douglass concedes. Why, in fact, did Covey allow a sixteen-year-old to defy him, and why did he allow the other slaves to refuse to assist him in administering the beating? The Covey story is an inspirational starting point for fruitful discussion, but it successfully skirts discussion of Douglass's family connections, which may have been the basis for Covey's behavior. Clever undergraduates may wonder if Douglass's experiences with Covey, ugly though they were, really represented the worst aspects of slavery.

The need for further study of the reception of Frederick Douglass is suggested by the fact that so many treatments of him teeter embarrassingly on the brink of hero-worship. The short biography of Frederick Douglass in the *Norton Anthology of American Literature* is a typical example of the hagiographic mode in Frederick Douglass studies, as it asserts that "His life . . . has become the heroic paradigm for all oppressed people" (1867). In William L. Andrews's fine preface to *My Bondage and My Freedom*, an edition whose usefulness is unfortunately limited by its lack of an index, the accolade of Douglass's African American contemporary James McCune Smith is accepted: Douglass is viewed as a "representative American man" (xxiii). My own "Where Honor Is Due: Frederick Douglass as Representative Black Man" does not contradict this view, but it does raise some questions as to what Douglass represented, and how well.

Andrews, in his preface to *My Bondage and My Freedom*, with a few deft strokes relates Douglass's ties to his "Romantic literary" contemporaries of the New England Renaissance, particularly Henry David Thoreau and Margaret Fuller (xxv). In recent years, the transcendental sainthood of Douglass has been questioned by authors who are informed by feminist sensibilities, typically David Van Leer and Jenny Franchot. Douglass's self-projection as "The Heroic Slave" has come to be perceived as masculinist. Mary Helen Washington concurs with Valerie Smith's observation that the angle of vision in Douglass's *Narrative* is disturbingly biased and places it in the category of documents that "by mythologizing rugged individuality, physical strength, and geographical mobility . . . , enshrine cultural definitions of masculinity" (8). At the same time, one must acknowledge the activism on behalf of women's rights that is documented in Philip Foner's *Frederick Douglass on Women's Rights*.

Others who have been troubled by this masculinist perspective in the writings of Douglass include Deborah McDowell and Henry Louis Gates, Jr., who notes with dismay that Douglass's election "as the 'father' of the tradition is central to the construction of an image of the black canon as both male engendered and male dominated" ("Wheatley to Douglass" 47). Future scholars will certainly wish to consider these charges seriously and reflect on the cultural and historical factors that have shaped Douglass's literary reputation and have led to his canonization and continuing dominance within the pantheon of African American heroes and heroines.

As a principal beneficiary of black bourgeois boosterism, Douglass has been adulated almost uncritically. Lerone Bennett's treatment of him in *Pioneers in Protest* typifies this tradition, which is concerned, as is much American historical writing, with the creation of a pantheon of heroes, presumably for the edification of young people. Such writing fails to problematize historical figures, avoids discussion of their human depth and complexity, and divests their thought of its vigor and poignancy. Douglass was a man of two souls—he was torn between his conception of universal humanity and his loyalty to a more specifically conceived racial ideal. His ambivalence removed him from the group of his contemporaries who identified dogmatically with a black nationalist conception of racial pride.

We should never assume that every black American was completely taken in by Frederick Douglass's showmanship. Many of his peers found his ideological instability and perpetual self-magnification annoying. Douglass was a brilliant and courageous man, but his ego was enormous, an observation made by John Mercer Langston, one of Douglass's mulatto contemporaries, although some twelve years younger. Langston, an accomplished intellectual in his own right, who later founded the Howard University Law School, advised Douglass against assuming the presidency of the ill-fated Freedman's Bank in 1874, which closed under Douglass's leadership that same year. Researchers on Douglass will find it profitable to peruse biographies and autobiographies of other favored mulatto slaves who were or may have been closely related to their owners. Much insight is to be gained from the autobiography of John Mercer Langston, and from the excellent biography by William and Aimee Lee Cheek, *John Mercer Langston and the Fight for Black Freedom, 1829–65.*

Although Douglass was never comfortable with black American chauvinism, he occasionally—and perhaps even to his own surprise—expressed himself in a rhetoric harmonious with that of black nationalism. As an independent black newspaper publisher, he became a sometime supporter of African American institutional separatism. He accommodated pragmatically to the idea of separate black trade schools at a time when alternative opportunities for black industrial training were practically nonexistent. On the eve of the Civil War, he flirted with the idea of African American emigration to Haiti. He supported the black chauvinist tradition, which identified Pharaonic Egypt with the rest of Africa, and claimed that the ancient Egyptians were racially identical to nineteenth-century African Americans. Nevertheless, he opposed the "Back to Africa Movement" of the 1850s, and he never accepted the idea that black Americans were a "peculiar people" with a separate and independent destiny apart from other Americans. In fact, in his later years, Douglass denounced the ideas of racial pride and ethnic solidarity.

Douglass's life and writings in some respects typify African American experience before the Civil War, but it should be borne in mind that his life is not representative of the experiences of the majority of his black male contemporaries. It is more the experience of an extremely lucky and atypical mulatto than he ever cared to admit. Douglass was a particularly clever and attractive child, who appealed to white adults and often received special treatment because of his personal charm and good looks. His autobiographies therefore represent the experiences of a privileged individual who received much special treatment, presumably because of white family connections. It has been noted that his experiences were different from those of black females, but it should also be noted that they differed from those of black males born into less favorable circumstances.

Future Douglass researchers should also bear in mind that Douglass interacted with and was influenced by the "Free African" community of Baltimore. In 1837 he became a member of a small group styling itself the East Baltimore Mental Improvement Society, "notwithstanding it was intended that only free persons should attach themselves, and was, several times, assigned a prominent part in its debates" (Douglass, *Autobiographies* 334, 336, 633). If, in fact, Douglass's experiences were a paradigm for a larger pattern of American experience, it would be profitable to understand his activities in connection with those of African American literary and debating societies, such as the one in East Baltimore with which he interacted.

Douglass's usefulness as a paradigm, while questionable, is not necessarily wrong, but it should be discussed within the context of the specific classes in American society with which he occasionally sought to identify. Like many people in a society as fluid as that of nineteenth-century America, Douglass found it convenient to exploit more than one social identity. For example, we might seek to learn more about Douglass's position as a representative of the mulatto or "multi-racial" category. Much is to be gained by studying the biography of Douglass in connection with the biographies of other mulattoes, such as the more privileged John Mercer Langston, who was mentioned earlier. William Wells Brown, whose experiences more closely resemble those of Douglass, is the subject of a biography by William Edward Farrison. Brown's autobiographical writings are also of interest, especially his curiously overlooked *Three Years in Europe; or Places I Have Seen and People I Have Met.*

The presence of a group of persons in nineteenth-century America who were highly conscious of their mixed-racial ancestry is incontestable, despite the passionate refusal of some academics and politicians to acknowledge the historical and cultural importance of mulattoes in American life.

Douglass regarded the fact that he was both a slave and a mulatto as the important elements of his early life, but few scholars seem to investigate carefully what is meant by the peculiar circumstances of Douglass's birth; in general, scholars have shown little interest in discussing how Douglass's birth status can be differentiated from the amorphously generalized status of slavery. Much of the purpose of Douglass's writing was to render the status of slavery as amorphous as possible and to blur the distinctions between his experience and that of less fortunate brethren. The precisely different nature of his position, within the broad sociological category of slavery, affected the specific features of his early mental growth and his later career as a writer.

Generally speaking, there were advantages for a slave to being in Maryland, rather than in one of the frontier territories. There were also advantages to being light-skinned, good-looking, and a favorite with the owners of the plantation. The *Norton Anthology* tells us that Douglass taught himself to read, but Douglass's narratives reveal a more complex story. Douglass himself reveals that he learned to read the alphabet and a few simple words from his mistress in Baltimore, Sophia Auld. Perhaps the story of Douglass's literacy begins even earlier. Historian Rayford Logan, in noting that "Douglass learned to speak well, to read and write early in life" (Douglass, *Life and Times* 54), seems to suggest that his acculturation was never entirely that of a plantation slave. Douglass attributed the fact that his speech contained few traces of slave accent to his early association with Daniel Lloyd, the son of wealthy planter Colonel Edward Lloyd, whom Douglass sometimes implied may have been his own father. It is not at all unlikely that Douglass acquired his first inclinations toward literacy on the plantation. Eric J. Sundquist notes in his introduction to *Frederick Douglass: New Literary and Historical Essays* that Douglass's mother was able to read (5). His association with Daniel Lloyd may have contributed to his nascent yearning, for as Douglass noted, "While this lad could not associate with ignorance without sharing its shade, he could not give his black playmates his company without giving them his superior intelligence as well" (*Autobiographies* 492). All

Douglass's narratives reveal something of his early exposure to the culture of the white upper class, whose manners he came to emulate.

The debate as to whether "mass culture" or "high culture" was a more effective vehicle for the expression of militancy is a perennial one in African American studies. Douglass reveals in the *Narrative* an appreciation for both. On the one hand, he was grateful for the assistance of the African magician, Sandy, in resisting Covey; on the other, he recognized that his exposure to the Lloyds, his special relationship to Lucretia Anthony Auld, and his residency with the Aulds in Baltimore were influences that brought him into contact with a wider world of culture and led to his developing literacy and his expectations of eventual freedom. Douglass poignantly associated his rising expectations with a recollection of a plantation ditty.

> I am going away to the Great House Farm!
> O, Yea! O, Yea! O, Yea! (Douglass, *Life and Times* 54)

Future work on Frederick Douglass will benefit greatly from the efforts of scholars to understand the extent to which his background differed from that of the more typical African American. It should also lead us to envision the ways in which he was, paradoxically, a representative man. Douglass's writings, like those of every writer, become more interesting when viewed within their social and historical context and in comparison with those of his contemporaries. It is surprising, given the fact that Douglass was primarily an orator, that his speeches have seldom been placed within the context of nineteenth-century oratory. The first book that Douglass purchased and owned was Caleb Bingham's compilation, *The Columbian Orator*, which was, according to Douglass's own testimony, a primary influence on his youthful thinking and his developing literary style.

It will be useful, moreover, to view Douglass in connection with major white American orators, many of whom have been curiously neglected in American literary studies. Douglass frequently alluded to the speeches of such figures as Daniel Webster, Henry Clay, and John C. Calhoun, who, although considerably older, were at the height of their influence during Douglass's young manhood. The styles developed by these men represented mainstream patterns of American rhetoric in Douglass's intellectual environment. American literary scholars must cease to marginalize political rhetoric of the nineteenth century and begin to stress more emphatically its relationship to other forms of literary expression.

Webster's speech in an 1830 debate with Robert V. Hayne has been described by historian William W. Freehling as a "thrilling peroration" (62), but present-day readers may be inclined to agree with John C. Calhoun that the speech was pure bombast—despite their disinclination to tolerate Hayne's and Calhoun's pro-slavery and disunion stances.

In connection with Douglass's position within American intellectual history, scholars will certainly wish to explore his relation to the idea of Progress. Kenneth Warren tantalizes us with his allusions to Douglass's "Progressive Rhetoric" (253), and Waldo Martin calls our attention to Douglass's observations on "the history of progress" ("Images" 277). Douglass was, in fact, a progressive, in the sense that he followed in the traditions of Condorcet's Enlightenment perfectionism and Comte's "scientific" optimism. Douglass's theory of human progress is outlined in a most interesting address inspired by the trial of Galileo, "'It Moves,' or the Philosophy of Reform."

Recent scholarship has attempted to enlist Douglass in the debate over multiculturalism. Howard Brotz, in *African-American Social and Political Thought, 1850–1920*, has argued that Douglass rejected multiculturalism, an observation that is not entirely false, despite its obvious "presentism." The term "multiculturalism" was not current in the 1880s, and the discourse of twentieth-century "multiculturalism" should not be carelessly interjected into nineteenth-century debates. What Douglass specifically rejected was the withholding of literate culture from the black population. This is something quite different from a rejection of multiculturalism, and it cannot be separated from the tendency of the times to confuse cultural difference with racial inferiority. Viewed within context, Douglass's beliefs cannot be separated from the Lamarckian beliefs that dominated his oft-cited work, *The Claims of the Negro Ethnologically Considered*. Douglass's later interest in Darwin led to some revision of his raciology, serving at the same time to buttress his progressivist views. The influences of Darwin and Lamarck on Douglass should be of interest to scholars who seek to understand his evolving theory of human progress.

It will be useful to bear in mind that Douglass's infrequent references to African American culture included insightful commentary on slave songs and a strikingly respectful discussion of magical practices. The discussion of magic occurs in his recollection of his frequently celebrated physical contest with Covey, the slave breaker. Shortly before his decision to resist Covey's final attempt to whip him, Douglass paid a visit to an older slave in the neighborhood named Sandy, who is described as "a genuine African [who] had inherited some of the so-called magical powers said to be possessed by the eastern nations." Sandy advised Douglass to carry the root of a certain herb on his right side and promised that "with this root about my person, no white man could whip me." Douglass, as is well known, employed Sandy's witchcraft with success, for he "saw in Sandy, with all his superstition, too deep an insight into human nature not to have some respect for his advice" (*Autobiographies* 280, 281).

The foregoing passage, present in all Douglass autobiographies, expresses more than tolerance; it shows an outright sympathy for Afrocentric folk practices and would seem to be an unusual example of nineteenth-century "multiculturalism." Scholars should be interested in investigating this sympathy within the context of Douglass's perennial hostility to superstition, especially since he believed superstition to occur in the religious traditions of the black masses. Sterling Stuckey, in *Slave Culture*, has noted this hostility among other black leaders, most notably in the African Methodist Bishop Daniel Alexander Payne. Kenneth W. Warren has observed that "Douglass's disapproval of black Protestant oratory is well known" (259). Douglass admitted to some alienation from the Southern style of mass leadership. He was infected with the somewhat condescending spirit of what Kevin Gaines has called "uplift ideology" (3). Douglass gives evidence of this missionary spirit in the *Life and Times*, saying, "In my communication with colored people I have endeavored to deliver them from the power of superstition, bigotry, and priestcraft."

William L. Andrews has written on Douglass's relationship to the African Methodist Episcopal Zion (AMEZ) Church. David E. Swift has noted the hostility of Rev. Henry Highland Garnet, who commented in 1849 on Douglass's sometime status as deacon within that denomination, accusing him of apostasy: "Being matchless in mimicry and unrivaled in buffoonery, he amuses scoffers and infidels by imitating their religious exercises" (255). Fellow abolitionist Sojourner Truth once publicly confronted him with the question, "Frederick, is God dead?" (Bennett 126). This public embarrassment may have been the source of continuing resentment that later occasioned his deprecation of Truth's speaking style (*Life and Writings* 507). Douglass was accused of heresy by the Reverend Walter Henderson Brooks when, in 1882, he critiqued the biblical account of Creation and asserted that it was man, and not God, who brought about progressive change in the world (*Papers* 2:284). Future scholars may wish to investigate the changes in Douglass's uses of the Bible in his autobiographies and other writings.

Douglass's complex and ambivalent feelings about religion must be the subject of further investigation and explication. Among the best existing treatments of his religious rhetoric is that of David Blight in *Frederick Douglass' Civil War*. Blight's work pays homage to James Moorhead's *American Apocalypse*, a treatment of religion during the Civil War with which all American literary scholars ought to be familiar. Blight sees Douglass as a clever manipulator of religious rhetoric. To this, I would add the observation that Douglass was not above employing emotional Christian fundamentalism in his 1854 attack on scientific racism. Contemporary ethnologists were obviously wrong in their demarcation of Africans as a subhuman species, he argued, because their theories were in conflict with the Bible. This employment of a fundamentalist rhetoric is particularly interesting in view of the frequent apostasy and infidelity charges.

For the past thirty years, much scholarship in African American literary and cultural history has elaborated on the theme of the "internal dialectic" between the black nationalist ideologies and the integrationist ideologies that Harold Cruse outlined in his path-breaking *The Crisis of the Negro Intellectual*. Howard Brotz contrasted the assimilationist tradition, represented by Frederick Douglass, with a nationalist or emigrationist tradition, represented by Martin Delany, Alexander Crummell, and Edward Wilmot Blyden, *inter alia*, in the still useful introduction to the 1966 edition of his *Negro Social and Political Thought*. Sterling Stuckey's *The Ideological Origins of Black Nationalism* similarly contrasts black nationalism with integrationism (19). I have accepted in my own work, *The Golden Age of Black Nationalism*, the nationalist/integrationist distinction, but I have offered two caveats. Integrationists, such as Douglass, have frequently engaged in black nationalist rhetoric, and black nationalists, such as Crummell, have stressed cultural assimilation, even while advocating geopolitical and institutional separatism.

In fact, Douglass claimed to have flirted with the idea of emigrating from the United States. With the fall of Fort Sumter, Frederick Douglass claimed that he was on the brink of an exploratory mission to the black republic of Haiti, long a focus of black nationalist and emigrationist plans. Sure enough, if one takes a look at a facsimile of *Douglass' Monthly* for May 1861, one will see a front-page article in which Douglass describes a planned trip to Haiti, followed by another article in which he postpones the expedition. One wonders if his attention to a tentative trip is not a somewhat dramatic exploitation of a journalistic situation, albeit the newspaper had been carrying a series of articles on Haiti for several months.

Anthony Appiah has recently discussed, as I once did, the European cognates and analogues of nineteenth-century African American ideology. Otey Scruggs, in a brilliant article, "Two Black Patriarchs: Frederick Douglass and Alexander Crummell," has taken issue with this perspective and stressed an American "ideological provenance," correctly emphasizing the conflict between Jeffersonian liberal and Federalist conservative influences in the thought and writings of Douglass and Crummell. One cannot overstress the necessity of studying the formative influences on Douglass and his black contemporaries within the social and political and, most importantly, for those who are reading this essay, the literary contexts of their times.

Douglass was primarily concerned with the African American struggle for abolitionism, which was perhaps the only arena of public intellectualism from which he and his contemporaries were not summarily barred. Like all abolitionists and black nationalists, however, he frequently employed a rhetorical strategy that aligned the struggle for black freedom with a universal humanism and the struggle for the rights of all oppressed peoples. Douglass was in a tradition of African American leaders, including W. E. B. Du Bois and Marcus Garvey, who saw parallels between the contest for Irish independence and the African American freedom struggle. Douglass's courageous attacks on British anti-Catholicism may be seen as a form of nineteenth-century multiculturalism. His defense of the struggles of Irish Catholics is particularly impressive at a time when hostilities between African Americans and Irish Catholic immigrants were bitter and violent. Douglass also supported the struggles of the Hungarian people (*Papers* 2:292).

I have argued in "Writing Freely" that Douglass's intellectual potential was tragically confined by the African American antislavery struggle. I pursue the same theme in "Where Honor Is Due." I have argued in "From Frederick Douglass to Booker T. Washington" that at times Douglass's ideology seemed conservative by the standards of the late nineteenth century. Kenneth Warren has made similar observations concerning Douglass's "Progressive Rhetoric" and his problems of consistency. Douglass's attitudes toward the black masses are most confusing in that he sought to derive his authenticity from identification with those masses while at the same time stressing his alienation from the "great unwashed," whether in Rome, Cairo, or the American South (Warren 266). In the post–Civil War years, he contradicted himself endlessly, calling one day for a color-blind society, but asserting racial pride on the next. On one occasion he chided Alexander Crummell for cautioning against the constant recollection of slavery; on another, he rebuked African Americans for excessively pleading their special grievances.

Crummell was correct to criticize him for his continued reliance on anti-slavery rhetoric, which reflected a persistent and unhealthy nostalgia for the great days of the abolitionist movement. It was on the petard of slavery that Douglass had hoisted himself into the position of principal black spokesman, and in the aftermath of the Civil War, Douglass's rhetorical platform began to slip from beneath him. With the demise of slavery, he was unable to construct a public role that spoke adequately to the problems of Reconstruction. During the reign of terror, following the collapse of Reconstruction, new social and economic problems of staggering scope required leadership in a different mold—not the cringing accommodationism of Booker T. Washington, whom Crummell despised, but certainly a leadership with something more to offer than powerless moralizing.

Scholars have avoided, with embarrassment, certain obvious points of sensitivity in Douglass's rhetoric. I refer to his tendency to distinguish between blacks and mulattoes in a number of his writings. In 1886, he wrote:

> "It is only prejudice against the Negro which calls everyone, however nearly connected with the white race, and however remotely connected with the Negro race, a Negro. The motive is not a desire to elevate the Negro, but to humiliate and degrade those of mixed blood; not a desire to bring the Negro up, but to cast the mulatto and the quadroon down by forcing him below an arbitrary and hated color line" (Brotz 310).

Douglass also had a disturbing tendency to use the image of blackness as a metaphor for evil. Such phrases as "hell black crime of slavery" (*Autobiographies* 932) "hell black enactment" (*Douglass Papers* 2:269), and "heathen darkness" (*Douglass Papers* 2:269), and his descriptions of the Fugitive Slave Law as a "hell black enactment" (*Douglass Papers* 2:375) and again as a "hell black law" (*Douglass Papers* 2:421) seem to have elicited little commentary from students of language. Douglass once described slavery as a "dark and ugly hag," an unfortunate metaphor to be employed by a black leader who eventually married a white woman.

The greatest honor that we can bestow on Frederick Douglass or any other black thinker is to demonstrate that we take him seriously enough to submit his life and writing to the same critical scrutiny that we apply to other authors. Major historical figures of such prominence as Jefferson, Clay, Lincoln, Darwin, Marx, and Wagner have been the subjects of criticism as well as praise. Their faults, as well as their strengths, have been subjects of endless discussion. Douglass, if we consider him comparable to such figures, must be studied with the same degree of critical scrutiny, and with a careful consideration of those attacks that were launched against him by ideological fellow travelers such as Crummell, Garrison, and Garnet. This important area of research remains to be undertaken.

In my opinion, Douglass unquestionably deserves his reputation as a major American literary and intellectual figure. According to all evidence, he was among the brightest lights among nineteenth-century orators, and his speeches display a timeless brilliance, a universal statesmanship, and a forceful logic, unfortunately lacking in much of the output of Daniel Webster, John C. Calhoun, and Stephen A. Douglas. Frederick Douglass requires no special pleading and should receive none. His greatness is undeniable—and so are his flaws. I refer to his egocentric interpretation of history, which led him to confuse his own progress with that of his race.

The most significant contributions in Douglass scholarship to date have come from historical scholarship rather than from literary scholarship. The major editions of Douglass's works, cited above, have resulted from the efforts of historians or teams of historians. Henry Louis Gates, Jr.'s edition of the autobiographical writings would have been impossible were it not for the results of the Yale editorial project, under the direction of his one-time mentor, the historian John W. Blassingame. The most impressive work on Douglass in recent years is in the area of investigative research, analytic bibliography, and the tracing of intellectual influences. Literary historians and biographers in all areas of African American studies should be encouraged to follow the example set by Arnold Rampersad in his *Life of Langston Hughes* and to engage in some of the more vigorous aspects of investigative research, rather than confining themselves to purely critical and interpretative enterprises.

Gates himself admits to the dominance of historians in Frederick Douglass studies, at least until 1978, although Charles H. Nichols's pioneering 1963 work, *Many Thousand Gone: The Ex-Slaves' Account of Their Bondage and Their Bondage and Their Freedom*, is an important interdisciplinary study by a literary scholar, in which Douglass's narrative is used to illustrate broader aspects of African American life and culture. As Gates observes, "The recovery of Douglass by contemporary literary theorists who have analyzed his 1845 *Narrative* extensively, and with satisfying results, is one of the most important signs of the shift of African American studies away from the dominance of historians, whose work held sway . . . until . . . Robert Stepto and Dexter Fisher published *Afro-American Literature: The Reconstruction of Instruction*, a book that included three important readings of Douglass's text" (Gates, "Wheatley to Douglass" 48). Gates refers to Robert Stepto's "Narration, Authentication and Authorial Control," Henry Louis Gates, Jr.'s "Binary Oppositions in Chapter One of the Narrative of Frederick Douglass," and Robert O'Meally's "Douglass' 1845 *Narrative*: The Text Was Meant to Be Preached." O'Meally's emphasis on the *Narrative*'s hortatory character places him in opposition to Houston Baker, who would divorce the *Narrative* from the declamatory tradition (*Long Black Song* 79).

Among the more useful collections of critical essays are Harold Bloom's *Modern Critical Interpretations: Frederick Douglass's "Narrative of the Life of Frederick Douglass"* and William L. Andrews's *Critical Essays on Frederick Douglass*. Andrews is also the author of *To Tell a Free Story: The First Century of Afro-American Autobiography, 1760–1865*. A more interdisciplinary approach is represented by Eric J. Sundquist's *Frederick Douglass: New Literary and Historical Essays*. Sundquist's introduction provides an accurate observation that ought to guide future study and research in all disciplines: "Although his autobiographies are of greater literary interest, Douglass's journalism and his oratory provide the fullest record of his achievements as an abolitionist and black political leader" (9).

Literary scholars must abandon the practice of continually submitting to scholarly journals purely interpretive articles focusing almost exclusively on the *Narrative* of 1845. Changing times and emerging public issues will perpetually generate the necessity for new interpretive readings of old "classics." In order to make the best contributions, however, literary scholars must avoid guild complacency, and we must continually familiarize ourselves with the contributions of other disciplines.

The seminal insights of psychologist Allison Davis, and of philosopher Bernard Boxill, for example, can be of much usefulness to us, but works such as theirs are disturbingly omitted from literary studies of Douglass while irrelevant and frequently useless works by well-placed academic Beckmessers are invariably listed in bibliographies.

Far too much work in African American literary studies has been purely exegetical. This has been true not only of work on Frederick Douglass, but also of studies on the Harlem Renaissance, where the most useful works include Nathan Huggins's *Harlem Renaissance* and David Lewis's *When Harlem Was in Vogue*. The only work on the Harlem Renaissance that can be mentioned in such company is Arnold Rampersad's monumental *The Life of Langston Hughes*. Houston Baker's *Modernism and the Harlem Renaissance* is a pretentious exercise in solipsism and an *ad hominem* attack on the far superior work of Huggins and Lewis; it offers little in the way of evidence, argument, or original research. Literary scholarship benefits tremendously from the sort of basic research evidenced in Henry Louis Gates, Jr.'s introduction to Harriet Wilson's *Our Nig* and Jean Fagan Yellin's introduction to Harriet Jacobs's *Incidents in the Life of a Slave Girl*. Other excellent examples of real literary scholarship are Frances Smith Foster's well-edited compilation *Three Rediscovered Novels of Frances E. W. Harper* and Miriam De Costa Willis's *The Memphis Diary of Ida B. Wells*. Claudia Tate's brilliant *Domestic Allegories of Political Desire* is another example of research-based scholarship; it contains excellent insights into the cultural symbolism of the Douglass myth.

A great deal of work remains to be done on Frederick Douglass, and much of this will appropriately be accomplished by literary scholars. Future authors will provide their most useful insights when they leaven their interpretive efforts with evidence of solid study. This does not mean that all literary scholarship can or should be based on historical detective work. Erudite readings of familiar texts will always provide intellectual and aesthetic pleasure to thoughtful readers. Interpretive essays will be most successful, however, when they reflect responsible efforts to master the existing documentary history. For many years, the speeches and letters of Douglass have been accessible in the Foner edition, and these are now supplemented by the ongoing Yale Project. The Library of Congress microfilms and the compilations of C. Peter Ripley and his associates in *The Black Abolitionist Papers* should be consulted in the complete microfilm edition. The five-volume printed edition, an abridgement, amounts to only 10 percent of the total collection, although its ready availability makes it a splendid teaching tool. It is works such as these that should dominate the footnotes and bibliographies of future work on Frederick Douglass and his contemporaries.

WORKS CITED

Andrews, William L. "Frederick Douglass, Preacher." *American Literature* 54 (1982): 592–97.

———. *To Tell a Free Story: The First Century of Afro-American Autobiography, 1760–1865.* Urbana: U of Illinois P, 1986.

———, ed. *Critical Essays on Frederick Douglass.* Boston: G. K. Hall, 1991.

Appiah, Anthony. *In My Father's House.* New York: Oxford UP, 1992.

Baker, Houston A., Jr. *Long Black Song: Essays in Black American Literature and Culture.* Charlottesville: UP of Virginia, 1972.

———. *Modernism and the Harlem Renaissance.* Chicago: U of Chicago P, 1987.

Bennett, Lerone. *Pioneers in Protest.* New York: Penguin, 1968.

Bingham, Caleb. *The Columbian Orator: Containing a Variety of Original and Selected Pieces Together with Rules Calculated to Improve Youth and Others in the Ornamental and Useful Art of Eloquence.* Boston: Manning and Loving, 1797.

Blight, David. "Frederick Douglass." *Encyclopedia Americana.* Danbury, CT: Grolier, 1991.

———. *Frederick Douglass' Civil War.* Baton Rouge: Louisiana State UP, 1989.

Bloom, Harold, ed. *Modern Critical Interpretations: Frederick Douglass's "Narrative of the Life of Frederick Douglass."* New York: Chelsea House, 1988.

Boxill, Bernard. "Fear and Shame as Forms of Moral Suasion in the Thought of Frederick Douglass." *Transactions of the Charles Pierce Society* 31 (1995): 713–44.

Brotz, Howard. *African-American Social and Political Thought, 1850–1920.* New Brunswick, NJ: Transaction, 1992.

Brown, William Wells. *Three Years in Europe; or Places I Have Seen and People I Have Met.* London: C. Gilprin, 1852.

Cheek, William, and Aimee Lee. *John Mercer Langston and the Fight for Black Freedom, 1829–65.* Urbana: U of Illinois P, 1989.

Chesnutt, Charles W. *Frederick Douglass.* Boston: Small, Maynard, 1899.

Cruse, Harold. *The Crisis of the Negro Intellectual.* New York: William Morrow, 1967.

Davis, Allison. *Leadership, Love and Aggression*. New York: Harcourt Brace Jovanovich, 1983.

Douglass, Frederick. *Autobiographies: "Narrative of the Life of Frederick Douglass"; "My Bondage and My Freedom"; "Life and Times of Frederick Douglass."* Ed. Henry Louis Gates, Jr. New York: Library of America, 1994.

———. *The Claims of the Negro Ethnologically Considered: An Address in Hudson Ohio, on July 12, 1854.* Rochester, NY, 1854. Reprinted in *The Frederick Douglass Papers*. Ed. John W. Blassingame. Vol. 2. 497–525.

———. *The Frederick Douglass Papers, Series One, Speeches, Debates, and Interviews.* 5 vols. Ed. John W. Blassingame, John R. McKivigan et al. New Haven: Yale UP, 1979.

———. *"'It Moves,' or the Philosophy of Reform: An Address Delivered in Washington D.C. on 20 November 1883."* Reprinted in *The Frederick Douglass Papers*. Ed. John W. Blassingame. Vol. 5. 124–44.

———. *Life and Times of Frederick Douglass.* 1892. Ed. Rayford Logan. New York: Collier, 1962.

———. *The Life and Writings of Frederick Douglass.* 4 vol. Ed. Philip S. Foner. New York: International Publishers, 1950–55. Supplementary vol. 5, 1974.

———. *My Bondage and My Freedom.* 1855. Ed. William L. Andrews. Urbana: U of Illinois P, 1987.

———. *The Narrative of the Life of Frederick Douglass.* 1845. Ed. David Blight. Boston: Bedford Books, 1993.

———. *Papers in the Library of Congress*, Microfilm.

———. *A Register and Index of His Papers in the Library of Congress.* Washington: Library of Congress, 1976.

Douglass' Monthly. Vol. 1–3, 1859–61 and vol. 4–5, 1861–63. Facsimile ed. Westport, CT: Negro UP, 1969.

Du Bois, W. E. B. "Frederick Douglass." *Dictionary of American Biography.* Ed. Allen Johnson and Dumas Malone. Vol. 5. New York: Scribners, 1930. 406-7

Farrison, William Edward. *William Wells Brown: Author and Reformer.* Chicago: U of Chicago P, 1969.

Fisher, Dexter, and Robert Stepto. *Afro-American Literature: The Reconstruction of Instruction.* New York: Modern Language Association, 1979.

Foner, Philip S. *Frederick Douglass: A Biography.* New York: Citadel P, 1964.

———, ed. *Frederick Douglass on Women's Rights.* Westport, CT: Greenwood P, 1976.

Franchot, Jenny. "The Punishment of Esther: Frederick Douglass and the Construction of the Feminine." Sundquist, *Frederick Douglass* 141–65.

"Frederick Douglass." *Norton Anthology of American Literature.* 2d ed. Ed. Nina Baym et al. New York: W. W. Norton, 1985. Vol. 1, 1866–67.

Freehling, William W. *The Nullification Era: A Documentary Record.* New York: Harper Torchbooks, 1967.

Gaines, Kevin. *Uplifting the Race: Black Leadership, Politics, and Culture in the Twentieth Century.* Chapel Hill: U of North Carolina P, 1996.

Gates, Henry Louis, Jr. "Binary Oppositions in Chapter One of the *Narrative of the Life of Frederick Douglass an American Slave Written by Himself.*" Fisher and Stepto, *Afro-American Literature: The Reconstruction of Instruction.* 212–32.

——. "From Wheatley to Douglass: The Politics of Displacement." Sundquist, *Frederick Douglass* 47–65.

Harper, Frances Ellen Watkins. *Three Rediscovered Novels of Frances E. W. Harper.* Ed. Frances Smith Foster. Boston: Beacon P, 1994.

Huggins, Nathan. *Harlem Renaissance.* New York: Oxford UP, 1971.

Jacobs, Harriet. *Incidents in the Life of a Slave Girl.* Ed. Jean Fagan Yellin. Cambridge, MA: Harvard UP, 1987.

Langston, John Mercer. *From the Virginia Plantation to the National Capitol; or, The First and Only Negro Representative in Congress from the Old Dominion.* Hartford, 1894. Repr. New York: Johnson Reprint, 1968.

Lewis, David. *When Harlem Was in Vogue.* New York: Knopf, 1981.

Martin, Waldo E., Jr. "Frederick Douglass." *Encyclopedia of African-American Culture and History.* New York: Macmillan, 1996.

——. "Images of Frederick Douglass in the Afro-American Mind: The Recent Black Freedom Struggle." Sundquist, *Frederick Douglass* 271–85.

——. *The Mind of Frederick Douglass.* Chapel Hill: U of North Carolina P, 1984.

McDowell, Deborah. "In the First Place: Making Frederick Douglass and the Afro-American Tradition." Andrews, *Critical Essays on Frederick Douglass* 192–214.

McFeely, William S. *Frederick Douglass.* New York: W. W. Norton, 1990.

Meyer, Michael. "Introduction." *Frederick Douglass: The Narrative and Selected Writings.* New York: Modern Library, 1984. x–xxx.

Moorhead, James. *American Apocalypse: Yankee Protestants and the American Civil War, 1860–1869.* New Haven, CT: Yale UP, 1978.

Moses, Wilson J. *The Golden Age of Black Nationalism.* Hamden, CT: Archon Books, 1978.

——. "Industrial Education, From Frederick Douglass to Booker T. Washington." *Review of Black Political Economy* 4 (1974): 39–46.

——. "Where Honor Is Due: Frederick Douglass as Representative Black Man." *Prospects: An Annual of American Cultural Studies* 17 (1992): 177–89.

——. "Writing Freely? Frederick Douglass and the Constraints of Racialized Writing." Sundquist, *Frederick Douglass* 66–83.

Nichols, Charles H. *Many Thousand Gone: The Ex-Slaves' Account of Their Bondage and Their Bondage and Their Freedom*. Leiden: Brill, 1963.

O'Meally, Robert G. "Douglass' 1845 *Narrative*: The Text Was Meant to Be Preached." Fisher and Stepto, *Afro-American Literature* 192–211.

Preston, Dickson J. *Young Frederick Douglass*. Baltimore, MD: Johns Hopkins UP, 1980.

Quarles, Benjamin. *Frederick Douglass*. Washington, DC: Associated Publishers, 1948.

———. "Frederick Douglass." *Dictionary of American Negro Biography*. Ed. Rayford W. Logan and Michael R. Winston. New York: Norton, 1982.

Rampersad, Arnold. *The Life of Langston Hughes*. 2 vols. New York: Oxford UP, 1986–88.

Ripley, C. Peter et al., eds. *The Black Abolitionist Papers*. New York: Microfilm Corporation of America, 1981–83; Ann Arbor: U Microfilms International, 1984–.

———, eds. *The Black Abolitionist Papers*. 5 vols. Chapel Hill: U of North Carolina P, 1985–92.

Scruggs, Otey. "Two Black Patriarchs: Frederick Douglass and Alexander Crummell." *Afro-Americans in New York Life and History* 6 (1982): 17–30.

Smith, Valerie. *Self Discovery and Authority in Afro-American Narrative*. Cambridge, MA: Harvard UP, 1987.

Stepto, Robert. "Narration, Authentication, and Authorial Control in Frederick Douglass' *Narrative* of 1845." Fisher and Stepto, *Afro-American Literature* 178–91.

Stuckey, Sterling. *The Ideological Origins of Black Nationalism*. Boston: Beacon P, 1972.

———. *Slave Culture: Nationalist Theory and the Foundations of Black America*. New York: Oxford UP, 1987.

Sundquist, Eric J. ed. *Frederick Douglass: New Literary and Historical Essays*. New York and Cambridge, England: Cambridge UP, 1990.

Swift, David E. *Black Prophets of Justice: Activist Clergy before the Civil War*. Baton Rouge: Louisiana State UP, 1989.

Tate, Claudia. *Domestic Allegories of Political Desire: The Black Heroine's Text at the Turn of the Century*. New York: Oxford UP, 1992.

Van Leer, David. "Reading Slavery: The Anxiety of Ethnicity in Douglass's *Narrative*." Sundquist, *Frederick Douglass* 118–40.

Warren, Kenneth W. "Frederick Douglass's *Life and Times*: Progressive Rhetoric and the Problem of Constituency." Sundquist, *Frederick Douglass* 253–70.

Washington, Booker T. [with the assistance of Samuel Laing Williams]. *Frederick Douglass*. Philadelphia: G. W. Jacobs, 1907.

Washington, Mary Helen, ed. *Invented Lives: Narratives of Black Women.* Garden City, NY: Anchor Books, 1987.

Wells-Barnett, Ida B. *The Memphis Diary of Ida B. Wells.* Ed. Miriam DeCosta-Willis. Boston: Beacon P, 1995.

Wilson, Harriet E. *Our Nig: or, Sketches from the Life of a Free Black, in a Two-Story White House: Showing that Slavery's Shadows Fall Even There.* Ed. Henry Louis Gates, Jr. New York: Vintage Books, 1983.

6

Harriet Beecher Stowe

Joan D. Hedrick

After a long period of neglect, Harriet Beecher Stowe, one of the most controversial writers the United States has produced, has reentered the canon of American literature. Scholarship on Stowe has dramatically increased in the last fifteen years as *Uncle Tom's Cabin* has become a staple of many undergraduate course offerings in History, American Studies, Women's Studies, and English. A Harriet Beecher Stowe Society has recently been formed. Yet much of the scholarly work on Stowe remains ahead of us. To my knowledge, there are no previous attempts to assess the research required in Stowe scholarship. This essay can only broadly outline where we are and what needs to be done.

Uncle Tom's Cabin remains the touchstone of response, both positive and negative. James Baldwin's famous 1949 dismissal of Stowe's sentimental blockbuster shaped popular and academic responses to *Uncle Tom's Cabin* for many twentieth-century readers who would never crack its pages. The power of Baldwin's critique lingers on in the pages of the prize-winning *American Heritage Dictionary*, where under the word "novel" the following quotation illustrates proper usage: "'*Uncle Tom's Cabin* is *a very bad novel*' (James Baldwin)." In 1956 a white man, J. C. Furnas, in a Book-of-the-Month-Club selection titled *Goodbye to Uncle Tom*, continued Baldwin's attack on Stowe's "Sunday school superficiality" and blamed her for the country's failure to resolve "the Negro problem": "In my view Mrs. Stowe's book had more to do than any other single factor with this moral disgrace" (10). Once the conscience that moved the nation against the sin of slavery, Stowe had become a well of misconceptions, distortions, and "wishful thinkings about Negroes" that "have made her titular hero a hissing and a byword" (8). Philip Fisher undertook to explain in *Hard Facts* how books like *Uncle Tom's Cabin* "become themselves political targets of every later mind privileged to look out through the structure that would never have existed without those very elements that now seem so offensive" (7). The full story of Stowe's fall from grace and the parallel story of the many lives of her characters have yet to be written. For someone attuned to historiography, the development of American literature as a profession, and the politics of race and gender, an excellent project would be the history of the reception, cultural appropriation, and revision of *Uncle Tom's Cabin*. Thomas F. Gossett's *"Uncle Tom's Cabin" and American Culture*, which surveys the nineteenth-century response, makes an excellent starting point for such a study, especially if supplemented by suggestive essays by Laura Donaldson, Thomas P. Riggio, and Patricia A. Turner.

The timeliness of such a critical study is underscored by the numerous theatrical re-creations and reinterpretations of *Uncle Tom's Cabin* that have appeared in recent years. These include Robert Alexander's *I Ain't Yo' Uncle*, commissioned for the San Francisco Mime Troupe and the Lorraine Hansberry Theatre; Rick Rankin's *Unkle Tomm's Kabin*, performed by Seattle's Empty Space and Alice B. Theatre; and the Bill T. Jones/Arnie Zane Dance Company's dance-theatre piece, *Last Supper at Uncle Tom's Cabin/The Promised Land*. The Alexander and Rankin plays openly talk back to Harriet Beecher Stowe and try to educate her. In Alexander's *I Ain't Yo' Uncle*, a revisionist version of George Aiken's nineteenth-century stage version of *Uncle Tom's Cabin*, Topsy is an in-your-face urban rapper whom Tom educates about Africa. *Unkle Tomm's Kabin*, performed by a gay theatre company, plays havoc with racial and sexual identities: "[T]he whites play blacks, the blacks play whites, and in one scene a white performer teaches a black performer how to 'play black'" (Berson 73). These revivals of *Uncle Tom's Cabin* open up new pathways to old topics, including Stowe's use of mulatto and mulatta characters, with their ambiguous racial identities. A stimulating framework here is Eric Lott's *Love and Theft: Blackface Minstrelsy and the American Working Class*, which explores what playwright Rankin calls the lure of the "taboo." Hazel V. Carby's *Reconstructing Womanhood* is another important context for this work on racial and gender stereotypes, and Harry Birdoff's *The World's Greatest Hit* is still the most comprehensive survey of the many stage versions of *Uncle Tom's Cabin*.

Toni Morrison's novel *Beloved* revisits Stowe's nineteenth-century material from a late-twentieth-century African-American standpoint; similarities between *Beloved* and *Uncle Tom's Cabin* have stimulated numerous scholarly essays, including those by Lori Askeland, Eileen Bender, and Cynthia Griffin Wolff ("Masculinity"). What does it say about the cultural moment that American artists and scholars are willing to engage in dialogue with Stowe's vision, stereotypes and all? It is time for a synthetic essay that examines the most recent cultural appropriations and reinterpretations of Stowe's heavily freighted drama.

In the 1950s and 1960s, Charles H. Foster and Alice Crozier produced excellent studies of Stowe's novels, and Edward Wagenknecht and John R. Adams looked at her life and work, but it was not until the women's movement and the establishment of Women's Studies in the 1970s that the groundwork was laid for the scholarly revival. While bibliographies by Margaret Holbrook Hildreth and Jean W. Ashton built the scaffolding, Ann Douglas's *The Feminization of American Culture* fired the first shot in the recent culture wars over Stowe's sentimentality. Douglas treated Stowe in the context of a larger argument about the effect of the emerging consumer culture with its split of literature into high and low forms, focusing on the conservative New York novels. What Douglas argued about these late works had a broad symmetry, however, with what Baldwin and Furnas had argued in their influential dismissals of *Uncle Tom's Cabin*. All assumed that Stowe had sold out the cause of art and engaged in a lower form; just as Furnas had blamed her for "the Negro problem," Douglas appeared to blame Stowe for the triumph of consumer capitalism. Essays by Elizabeth Ammons, Dorothy Berkson, Laurie Crumpacker, and Jane Tompkins ("Sentimental Power") led the feminist revision of Stowe's reputation, and all contributed to a more radical understanding of her politics. They also attempted to see the author's message in the millennial, Christian context in which Stowe had written it. In 1980, Ammons's *Critical Essays on Harriet Beecher Stowe* usefully brought together key essays in the two-century debate. Since then, essays by Gillian Brown, Rachel Bowlby, Richard Yarborough, Arthur Riss, Cynthia Griffin Wolff, and numerous others have continued the vigorous exploration of the racial and sexual politics of *Uncle Tom's Cabin*. Many such may be found in Eric J. Sundquist's excellent collection, *New Essays on "Uncle Tom's Cabin."* Unlike the first wave of feminist recovery, which tended to valorize what had been spurned as sentimental, the most recent interpretations of Stowe's politics are more nuanced: often drawing on new historicist assumptions, they are open to the complexities of Stowe's involvement with her own culture without unequivocally praising or condemning. Jane Tompkins's influential

"Sentimental Power" showed how much could be revealed by a rhetorical analysis of a book meant to persuade, and two recent volumes follow her lead: Gladys Sherman Lewis's book on Puritan sermonic forms in *Uncle Tom's Cabin* and *The Stowe Debate: Rhetorical Strategies in "Uncle Tom's Cabin,"* edited by Mason I. Lowance, Jr., Ellen E. Westbrook, and R. C. De Prospo, a work that includes Catharine O'Connell's splendid analysis of the contradictions of sentimental rhetoric. Josephine Donovan's monograph on the problem of evil, affliction, and redemptive love is another recent addition.

The literary and cultural importance of *Uncle Tom's Cabin* is beyond dispute, and discussion of this key text will continue to evolve in the United States, if only because, as playwright Rankin observed, it "distilled so many things in the American psyche" (Berson 73). How about *Uncle Tom's Cabin* abroad? Translated into sixty-three languages, appearing in hundreds of editions in France and Germany, the book has not been sufficiently written about in terms of its international career. We need to know more about the book's reception and cultural appropriation in other countries. Nineteenth-century readers compared *Uncle Tom's Cabin* to Tolstoy's *War and Peace*, and twentieth-century readers in China and other lands have seen Stowe's novel in the context of epic stories of liberation. It is time to recapture the context of world-wide revolutionary ferment that was part of its incubation. Michael Hanne's inclusion of Stowe in *The Power of the Story: Fiction and Political Change* is a step in this direction.

When one turns from *Uncle Tom* to Stowe's other thirty volumes, almost everything remains to be done. A number of areas in this uncharted critical terrain may be defined: early stories; other antislavery writing; the New England novels; the New York novels; journalistic writing; travel writing; religious writing. No one has analyzed Stowe's first book, *The Mayflower*; a careful look at the stories in this volume and in the magazines and giftbooks in which they appeared would tell us a great deal about Stowe's literary apprenticeship. A comparison of this book with her late collection, *Oldtown Fireside Stories*, could illustrate her changing artistry and purposes. Her use of the framing device of a genteel narrator who meets characters who speak in dialect could be compared to Twain's use of the same device.

Of Stowe's other antislavery writings, *A Key to "Uncle Tom's Cabin"* and *Dred* are the most significant. Written in 1856 as the country plunged toward civil war, *Dred*, Stowe's second antislavery novel, reflects the troubled tenor of the times. The titular character, based on Nat Turner, has often been recognized as providing a strong foil to Uncle Tom, and Theodore R. Hovet and Lisa Whitney consider the book with *Uncle Tom's Cabin*. Their work and recent articles by Lynn Veech Sadler (on the Samson figure) and Richard Boyd (on models of power) add to the handful of earlier essays and discussions in longer works that comprise the sum of scholarship on this complex text; clearly we need more discussions of *Dred*'s characters, politics, and literary achievement. Similarly, *A Key to "Uncle Tom's Cabin"* has been little analyzed. It deserves study in its own right as a polemic, and its effect on the slavery debate should be assessed.

Stowe's importance as a regional or "local color" writer has often been noted (e.g., in Lawrence Buell's *New England Literary Culture* and Josephine Donovan's *New England Local Color Literature*). While one can question whether an author whose canvas included the North, the South, the East, and the West should be considered "regional" rather than "national," certainly Stowe's sensitivity to geography and regional types deserves study, as does her use of the village sketch as a genre. Stowe's New England novels, her most sustained literary contribution, are receiving increased attention, but they have yet to attract the book-length investigations they deserve. *The Minister's Wooing*, probably Stowe's best after *Uncle Tom's Cabin*, initially drew attention for Stowe's critique of Calvinism (Berkson, Buell ["Calvinism Romanticized"], Crozier, Foster, Hedrick ["'Peaceable Fruits'"]); more recent studies (Harris, Schultz, Christopher P. Wilson) deepen our understanding of the complexity and artistry of this text by examining Stowe's domestic imagery and the secondary plot involving Virginie de Frontignac. *Oldtown Folks* has received attention for its theology and vision of New England (Buell [*New England*], Crumpacker, Foster, May, among others), and a handful of essays on *The Pearl of Orr's Island* (Fetterley on Stowe's critique of the romance plot, Baker on Puritan providences, Kirkham's introduction) have begun the exploration of that troubled novel. Work has hardly begun on *Poganuc People*, Stowe's novel of her life in Litchfield. Sandra Zagarell is at work on a book-length study of narratives of community that will include discussions of Stowe's early village sketches as well as *The Minister's Wooing*, *The Pearl of Orr's Island*, and *Oldtown Folks*. Someone should undertake to study Stowe's New England novels as the coherent cultural project that Stowe clearly took them to be.

Stowe was a pioneer in the use of dialect, beginning with her prize-winning sketch, "Uncle Lot," which captured New England speech rhythms, and extending to her use of the multicultural accents of the American West and South. A series of questions deserve attention in this regard. What are the felicities and pitfalls of Stowe's use of dialect? What exaggerations and distortions emerged as she listened to fresh accents with a New England ear? Who and what were her sources? How did she achieve distinctive voices in her fiction? How are these voices like or unlike what had been recorded on stage and in print? How did they influence later writers such as George Washington Cable, Mary Wilkins Freeman, and Mark Twain? How did translators of *Uncle Tom's Cabin* handle its range of regional, racial, and class dialects?

Stowe's use of dialect and dialogue is part of a larger topic: her use of voice and personae. Almost none of the rhetorical analysis lavished on *Uncle Tom's Cabin* has been applied to Stowe's other work. Stowe's conversational, intimate narrative voice is one of her most distinctive literary contributions (Hedrick, "Parlor Literature," Warhol), and we need more careful attention to its modulation and variety. In *Poganuc People*, for example, Stowe uses at least three voices (the first two of which are characteristic): the voice of the chimney-corner gossip, relaying local eccentricities; the voice of the syndicated columnist, commenting with relish on national trends; and an aging version of this second voice, the voice of the cranky grandmother, complaining about new fads. Stowe's use of male personae such as Christopher Crowfield (*House and Home Papers*) and Harry Henderson (*My Wife and I*) deserves study. A study of Stowe's debt to eighteenth-century rhetoric texts and prose stylists—whom she mentions during her literary apprenticeship—would be a new way to approach rhetorical issues. Stowe was an architect of Victorian sentiment—a culture that did not exist when she was born. Like the romanticism of which it is a part, it emerged in a complex reaction against deism and eighteenth-century rationalism. A study of eighteenth-century influences on Stowe could tell us much about this historical process. How did her early reading shape her sense of style? How did she transform eighteenth-century rhetoric to make it fit her nineteenth-century agenda?

The New York novels (*My Wife and I; Pink and White Tyranny; We and Our Neighbors*) are much neglected; Lisa MacFarlane has taken the first serious look at them since Douglas. Registering responses to burning social issues of the 1870s such as the woman question, free love, and the

Beecher/Tilton trial, these volumes need to be understood as *Uncle Tom's Cabin* has long been understood, as attempts to shape public opinion. (The way in which Boydston et al. introduce a chapter from *My Wife and I* makes this point.) Careful analysis of the social and political contexts of these novels will illuminate the conservative reaction against what was arguably one of the most radical moments in nineteenth-century American culture: the Reconstruction push for woman's rights. Work on all these novels needs to be developed much further, exploring Stowe's purposes, characters, style, and audience. In particular, the domestic politics of these novels should be compared to that of other writings in which Stowe elaborates her ideal notions of home and domesticity: *The Chimney Corner, House and Home Papers,* and *The American Woman's Home.*

Similarly, Stowe's journalistic writings for the *Independent,* the *Atlantic Monthly,* and *Hearth and Home* should be studied for their purposes, style, and cultural agendas. Her Chimney Corner columns for the *Atlantic Monthly* contain some very interesting essays on domestic topics, but they have not been much written about. (Patricia Hill's "Writing Out the War" discusses them, along with other pieces that Stowe wrote during the Civil War.) The essays published as *Little Foxes* would repay attention for their psychological insight and literary expression.

Stowe's travel writings—*Sunny Memories of Foreign Lands* and *Palmetto Leaves*—have hardly been touched; as insight into Victorian travel writing continues to develop, they will be a rich resource. Stowe's voice and purposes could be compared to Twain's in his extensive travel writings. Stowe's Italian novel, *Agnes of Sorrento,* is treated in Charles H. Foster, Nathalia Wright, and recently in Jenny Franchot's study of antebellum Protestantism's encounter with Catholicism. Someone should look at Stowe's Italian travel diary (at the Harriet Beecher Stowe Center) in which Stowe began *Agnes of Sorrento* to see what it tells about Stowe's materials and method of composition. Her use of that diary might be compared to Hawthorne's use of his *Italian Notebooks* for the construction of *The Marble Faun.* In some ways, *The Minister's Wooing* is Stowe's French novel; written between her second and third trips to Europe, it reflects Stowe's growing cosmopolitanism, before the free love battles made all things "French" suspect. It should be studied in the context of her other travel writings.

Stowe did her best religious writing in her novels, but she also wrote sermons and reflections on biblical topics for the *New York Evangelist* during the 1830s and 1840s, a volume of *Religious Poems,* and two book-length studies, *Woman in Sacred History* and *Footsteps of the Master*. Mary De Jong and Eileen Razzari Elrod are among the few to look at Stowe's nonfiction religious writings.

When she was a schoolgirl, Harriet Beecher studied drawing and painting and aspired to become an artist and teacher. Her imagination was vividly pictorial, and she relied on "graphic sketches" to carry her points: "My vocation is simply that of a painter," Stowe wrote to the editor of the *National Era* as she launched the sketches that became *Uncle Tom's Cabin* (Hedrick [*Harriet Beecher Stowe* 208]). The visual character of her prose is also what lends itself to dramatization in "scenes." A study of Stowe's pictorial method of composition could unlock the building blocks of Stowe's seemingly artless style. How did the serialization of her novels shape her style and pictorial artistry? Comparisons with Charles Dickens in this regard might be illuminating. An accomplished amateur artist, Stowe also left many excellent examples of her talent in oil paintings of flowers, designs for tea cups (both may be seen at the Harriet Beecher Stowe House in Hartford), and sketches for book illustrations. What might a systematic evaluation of her amateur art work tell us about her aesthetic?

Susan Geary has underscored how the modern marketing techniques of J. P. Jewett boosted *Uncle Tom's Cabin* to unprecedented sales. Further study of the marketing of Stowe's works is in order. Careful research could reveal more about sales and earnings for specific works. *The Cost Books of Ticknor and Fields*, edited by William Charvat and W. S. Tryon, covers the period prior to Stowe's publications; for information on Stowe, one must turn to the manuscript business records of Ticknor and Fields held by the Houghton Library. These documents, supplemented by Stowe's correspondence and by publishers' book advertisements, could tell us much about the development of authorship in America during a time of transition.

As the study of Stowe matures, the monographs on her will likely expand to studies that place her in the context of nineteenth-century literary culture. Recent dissertations put Stowe in the company of Sarah Orne Jewett, Willa Cather, and Elizabeth Stuart Phelps, as well as Caroline Lee Hentz, Harriet Jacobs, Harriet Wilson, Augusta Evans, Sarah Grimke, Fanny Fern, Kate Chopin, Louisa May Alcott, Jane Addams, Elizabeth Cady Stanton, George Eliot, Mary Chesnut, Anna Katharine Green, Victor Metta, Mary Roberts Rinehart, Constance Fenimore Woolson, and finally, Nathaniel Hawthorne, Mark Twain, and

Leo Tolstoy. Even if the best of these dissertations are published, the work on Stowe largely stands apart from what has been the "mainstream" since the middle of this century: the hundreds of studies of Emerson, Poe, Hawthorne, Melville, Twain, Howells, and James. What would American literary history look like if Stowe were integrated into that canon? Inclusion of Stowe would entail bridging the gap between the evangelical culture that sustained Stowe and the more secular, modernist mentality into which the male writers have been cast. It would mean questioning what Richard Chase defined as "the" American novel—the "romance" that eschews social and political concerns for what Nina Baym has dubbed "Melodramas of Beset Manhood." Jane Tompkins in her work on the politics of Hawthorne's literary reputation has shown how similar, in fact, Hawthorne's sketches of village life were to sketches by women writers. The scholarship on Stowe that preceded the women's movement not surprisingly put Stowe in the company of male writers; her connections with these writers should be recovered and synthesized with the new frameworks from feminist scholarship. We need studies of Stowe that situate her against Hawthorne, Poe, Melville, and Emerson, as well as against Kirkland, Harper, Davis, Jewett, and others. Lawrence Buell's excellent study of New England literary culture begins this work. We need to understand in what terms and through what literary, editorial, and political processes the dominance of women writers such as Stowe in mid-nineteenth-century America gave way to the male literary establishment. An institutional study of the *Atlantic Monthly*, with particular reference to Stowe and other women writers (Gail Hamilton, Rebecca Harding Davis, Lucy Larcom, Celia Thaxter, Julia Ward Howe), could illuminate this process. A literary history of the nineteenth century that took as its two poles Harriet Beecher Stowe and Henry James, comparing their careers, styles, editorial strategies, and politics, would provide an essential link between the earlier and later period.

In order to situate Stowe in a reconstructed literary history, we need to understand the history of criticism itself. As Baym's work on "romance" demonstrates, the terms of literary history are historically specific, not immediately transparent, and subject to politically important shifts in meaning. A history of central terms ("sentimentalism," "realism," "naturalism," "idealism"), one that includes male and female writers in equal proportions, would provide an important frame for reassessing Stowe. The work of Kaplan on sentimentality and Howard on naturalism provides excellent conceptual starting points for such a study. Relatively little has been done with Stowe's realism beyond Ellen Moers's pioneering studies; Mary Kelley's *Private Woman, Public Stage* touches suggestively on the real-life biographical contexts and financial needs that drove women to write, and I look at the realism of women's letters as a source for women's novels in my "Parlor Literature." Stowe, Davis, and Kirkland receive only passing mentions in David Shi's synthetic study of American realism—a rather outrageous slighting when one considers the willingness of these writers to look at the realities of slavery, industrial capitalism, and western migration. Has realism been defined as the modernist's detached gaze? An examination of the interplay of idealism and realism—what Crozier termed the "alternation between the sentimental and anti-sentimental modes"(87) in Stowe's works—could prove illuminating. The Lady Byron case, in regard to which Stowe's Christian and Victorian ideals did battle with the seamy reality of incest, is a natural vehicle for such research. A study of Poe and Stowe with regard to what Byron meant to these two very different nineteenth-century magazine writers could reveal much about their impulses and the literary marketplace in which they exercised them. The work of Nicole Tonkovich, Lynette Carpenter, and myself on the Semi-Colon Club ("Parlor Literature") illuminates Stowe's literary apprenticeship, but we need to know more about literary clubs in the nineteenth century in order to place this material in a larger context. How common were mixed-sex literary clubs in the 1830s and 40s? Did they become segregated by sex as the century proceeded? When and how? Through what processes? The work of Karen Blair, Anne Ruggles Gere, Theodoro Penny Martin, and Catherine Hobbs on women's groups, study clubs, and literacy provide useful frameworks in which to explore these questions.

For a writer so immersed in her time, Stowe has been the subject of surprisingly few studies of influences and sources. E. Bruce Kirkham's *The Building of "Uncle Tom's Cabin"* and Buell's and Foster's studies of Stowe's debt to Hopkinsian and Edwardsean theology in *The Minister's Wooing* are the most prominent examples; Stowe mentions Grace Greenwood's letters in the *National Era* as one inspiration for *Uncle Tom's Cabin*, but these have not been investigated. Someone should explore in detail the influence of Edgeworth and Scott on Stowe's style. An essay on Stowe's reading—of Edgeworth, Scott, Dickens, Brontë, Eliot, as well as of the evangelical and political newspapers and periodicals—would surely turn up productive connections between this material and her writing. Clearly she was reading and influenced by Hawthorne, as Foster mentions, but no one has elaborated upon this fact. The many reactions to and revisions of *Uncle Tom's Cabin* are well known, but in other ways Stowe's dialogue with her contemporaries remains to be written. As Judith Fetterley has pointed out, what we need is "an intertextual approach—for example, Sigourney, Sedgwick, Harper, Stowe in relation to each other, to their male contemporaries, to British and continental contemporaries" ("Commentary" 604).

Forrest Wilson's *Crusader in Crinoline*, which won the 1942 Pulitzer Prize for biography, reigned for over fifty years as the definitive life of Harriet Beecher Stowe. My *Harriet Beecher Stowe: A Life*, which won the 1995 Pulitzer Prize, has succeeded to its place. It puts Stowe in the context of the social history of the nineteenth century and argues that her career marked the flowering and passing of amateur "parlor literature" and the emergence of American literature as a profession. Patricia Hill is completing a biographical study that focuses on Stowe's sibling relationships and the culture of evangelical gentility in nineteenth-century America. We need also more focused studies of particular periods in her life. Stowe's literary apprenticeship could be the subject of a book-length study, as could her career as a professional writer during the 1860s, when she was a regular contributor to the *Atlantic Monthly*. A study of Stowe's three trips to Europe and the attitudes and writings that emanated from them is another natural, for which the publication of Van Why and French's *Harriet Beecher Stowe in Europe* provides a good starting point. We would benefit from knowing more about Stowe's work with black schools in Florida during Reconstruction. Local sources and other people's papers could be used to supplement what we know from her correspondence, and all of this could be put in a larger context. The same is true for her support of African American causes throughout her life, such as her patronage of black artists, including Emily Greenfield. Stowe's self-presentation as a creative person also deserves study; much can be learned from looking at how Stowe and other women writers saw themselves and shaped their public personae. Were these different from the personae adopted by male writers? In the 1870s Stowe wrote many pieces for Henry Ward Beecher's *Christian Union*, including, in all likelihood, a number of unsigned editorials. Tracking these down, placing them in the context of current social, political, and religious debates, and analyzing their import is all work that remains to be done. Analysis of Stowe's role as coeditor of *House and Home* in 1868–69 might make a useful essay. Her correspondence reveals some of her uses of this agricultural and domestic journal; the papers of coeditor Donald G. Mitchell (Ik Marvel), if they exist, may add other information, and careful scrutiny of Stowe's columns will yield still further insights. Finally, someone should analyze the structure of opportunity that supported Stowe's career. Because of her influential father and well-connected brothers, she had many venues in which to address the public. What can we learn from this fact about the role of family, siblings, and networks in determining what and how much a woman can publish?

Biographical treatments of the large Beecher clan provide useful contexts for Stowe. Milton Rugoff's readable and well-researched book on the Beecher family provides an overview of those members who had a public life. Kathryn Kish Sklar's biographical and cultural treatment of Catharine Beecher has remained definitive for almost twenty-five years and will not easily be excelled. Robert Merideth's study of Edward Beecher, which he describes as "something less and something more" than a biography, focuses on the cultural meaning of Edward's abolitionist response to the murder of Elijah Lovejoy, but no full biography exists. Myra Glenn's full-scale biography of Thomas K. Beecher was published in 1996. The obvious needs are for biographies of the other two Beechers who had the most public lives: Henry Ward Beecher and Isabella Beecher Hooker. Considering the latter's family ties, prominence in the women's rights movement, and interesting psychology, it is surprising that no one has written a biography of Isabella, whose involvement with women's suffrage drew Harriet into short-lived but significant alliances in the period 1868–72. Clifford E. Clark, Jr.'s and William G. McLoughlin's book-length interpretations of Henry Ward usefully situate him in American culture, but the only biographies of him are nineteenth-century compilations done soon after his death and Paxton Hibben's *Henry Ward Beecher* and Jane Shaffer Elsmere's *Henry Ward Beecher: The Indiana Years, 1837–1847*. Alice Scoville Barry, a descendant of Henry Ward Beecher, has been working for some years on a biography, and it is to be hoped that she publishes this. Richard Wightman Fox is at work on a book on the Beecher-Tilton scandal, a volume that promises to illuminate both Henry Ward Beecher and late Victorian American culture. Edward Beecher's wife, Katherine, is credited with urging Stowe to write what became *Uncle Tom's Cabin*, but nothing has been written on her. Beyond the immediate family circle, biographies on related figures such as James T. and Annie Fields provide important contexts for Stowe and other women writers. Judith A. Roman's monograph on Annie Fields is a good start, but we need a more analytic and interpretive biography; Rita K. Gollin's work-in-progress may provide this. Susan Coultrap-McQuin treats James T. Fields in her monograph on nineteenth-century publishers and their relationship to women writers, but there has been no modern biography of this influential publisher and editor since W. S. Tryon's *Parnassus Corner*.

In his review of my *Harriet Beecher Stowe*, E. L. Doctorow called for a collection of Stowe's letters "because it is in her letters Stowe's genius is most apparent" (33). Almost none of her letters are in print. Annie Fields's *Life and Letters of Harriet Beecher Stowe* takes great license with the originals, as does Charles Stowe to a lesser degree in his *Harriet Beecher Stowe*. Jeanne Boydston, Mary Kelley, and Anne Margolis bring together letters and other writings on women's issues by Catharine, Isabella, and Harriet in their splendid collection, *The Limits of Sisterhood*, but these represent a tiny fraction of the literary record. A few other letters appear in Cynthia Reik's *Harriet Beecher Stowe Reader*. E. Bruce Kirkham has been working for many years to compile a complete collection of Stowe's letters, from which he is now shaping an edition of selected letters. This will be an invaluable resource for Stowe scholars and will surely spur Stowe studies in many fruitful directions, for the epistolary record is both unusually rich and unusually in need of the ordering, dating, and contextualizing that a scholarly edition will provide. More focused collections of letters would also make attractive volumes: the extensive, humorous, and often moving correspondence between Harriet and husband Calvin Stowe would make an excellent publishing project, one that could provide resources for the study of the Victorian family and nineteenth-century social history. The same is true for the circular letters that members of the Beecher family wrote when they were scattered from Hartford to the farthest reaches of the Western Reserve. A collection of Beecher sibling letters is another possibility.

The sixteen-volume 1896 Riverside edition of Stowe's *Writings* remains the standard edition of Stowe's works. Still uncollected are some early stories, "sermons" written for the *New York Evangelist*, and journalistic pieces such as letters to the *Independent* during the Civil War and writings for *Hearth and Home*. Some of these will appear in my Stowe reader, forthcoming from Oxford University Press. *Uncle Tom's Cabin* has long been available in paperback editions for teaching, and Elizabeth Ammons's Norton Critical Edition of *Uncle Tom's Cabin* recently joined earlier editions by Douglas and others. Kathryn Kish Sklar's edition of that novel and *The Minister's Wooing* and *Oldtown Folks* in the Library of America series makes Stowe's major novels handily available. However, none of the New York novels are in print, and all deserve to be. All of Stowe's other novels are in print, but there are few editions, sometimes only one edition, as in the case of *Poganuc People*, so that individual volumes are sometimes out of print for brief periods between print runs. A volume that deserves to be made more accessible is *Little Foxes*, comprising domestic advice columns that Stowe wrote for the *Atlantic Monthly*. The quality of the writing is more textured and psychologically interesting than is that of much of the practical advice in *The American Woman's Home*, coauthored with Catharine Beecher. Stowe's *Mayflower* stories deserve reprinting in an accessible volume for classroom use, perhaps with some of her later stories.

So the work ahead is prodigious. The riches of Stowe's multivolumed career need to be mined and nineteenth-century literary history needs to be reconstructed so that the realities of women's lives and writings can be apprehended. We need textual, biographical, and critical studies; publication of her letters and out-of-print works; and synthetic studies that place Stowe against her contemporaries, male and female, American and European.

Henry James's description of *Uncle Tom's Cabin* as a "'leaping' fish" (Ammons, *Critical Essays* 286) could as well be applied to Stowe herself. The range of her writing, the responses it evoked among national and international audiences, the complexities of her life and her career, the volatility of the racial and sexual types that she dramatized, and the continuing cultural debates over her aesthetics, politics, and religion make her a key figure in American literary and cultural history. Our critical and scholarly frameworks must catch up to this leaping fish.

ACKNOWLEDGMENT

I am grateful to Jo Blatti, Director of the Harriet Beecher Stowe Center, for her useful suggestions and comments on this essay.

WORKS CITED

Adams, John R. *Harriet Beecher Stowe*. New York: Twayne, 1963.

Aiken, George L. *Uncle Tom's Cabin, or, Life Among the Lowly: A Domestic Drama, in Six Acts.* New York: Samuel French, n.d.

Alexander, Robert. *I Ain't Yo' Uncle: The New Jack Revisionist "Uncle Tom's Cabin."* Woodstock, IL: Dramatic P, 1996

Ammons, Elizabeth. "Heroines in *Uncle Tom's Cabin.*" *Critical Essays* 152–65.

———, ed. *Critical Essays on Harriet Beecher Stowe.* Boston: G. K. Hall, 1980.

Ashton, Jean W., comp. *Harriet Beecher Stowe: A Reference Guide.* Boston: G. K. Hall, 1977.

Askeland, Lori. "Remodeling the Model Home in *Uncle Tom's Cabin* and *Beloved.*" *American Literature* 64 (1992): 785–805.

Baker, Dorothy Z. "Puritan Providences in Stowe's *The Pearl of Orr's Island*: The Legacy of Cotton Mather." *Studies in American Fiction* 22 (1994): 61–79.

Baldwin, James. "Everybody's Protest Novel." *Partisan Review* 16 (1949): 578–85.

Baym, Nina. "Concepts of the Romance in Hawthorne's America." *Feminism* 57–70.

———. *Feminism and American Literary History: Essays.* New Brunswick, NJ: Rutgers UP, 1992.

———. "Melodramas of Beset Manhood." *Feminism* 3–18.

Bender, Eileen. "Repossessing *Uncle Tom's Cabin*: Toni Morrison's *Beloved.*" *Cultural Power/Cultural Literacy.* Ed. Bonnie Braendlin. Gainesville: UP of Florida, 1991. 129–42.

Berkson, Dorothy. "Millennial Politics and the Feminine Fiction of Harriet Beecher Stowe." Ammons, *Critical Essays* 244–58.

Berson, Misha. "Cabin Fever." *American Theatre* (1991): 16–23, 71–73.

Birdoff, Harry. *The World's Greatest Hit: "Uncle Tom's Cabin."* New York: Vanni, 1947.

Blair, Karen. *The Clubwoman as Feminist: True Womanhood Redefined, 1868–1914.* New York: Holmes & Meier, 1980.

Bowlby, Rachel. "Breakfast in America—*Uncle Tom's* Cultural Histories." *Nation and Narration.* Ed. Homi K. Bhabha. London: Routledge, 1990. 197–212.

Boyd, Richard. "Models of Power in Harriet Beecher Stowe's *Dred.*" *Studies in American Fiction* 19 (1991): 15–30.

Boydston, Jeanne, Mary Kelley, and Anne Margolis, eds. *The Limits of Sisterhood: The Beecher Sisters on Women's Rights and Woman's Sphere.* Chapel Hill: U of North Carolina P, 1988.

Brown, Gillian. "Getting in the Kitchen with Dinah: Domestic Politics in *Uncle Tom's Cabin.*" *American Quarterly* 36 (1984): 503–23.

Buell, Lawrence. "Calvinism Romanticized: Harriet Beecher Stowe, Samuel Hopkins, and *The Minister's Wooing*." *ESQ: A Journal of the American Renaissance* 23 (1978): 119–32. Reprinted in Ammons, *Critical Essays* 259–75.

———. *New England Literary Culture: From Revolution through Renaissance.* Cambridge, England: Cambridge UP, 1986.

Carby, Hazel V. *Reconstructing Womanhood: The Emergence of the Afro-American Woman Novelist.* New York: Oxford UP, 1987.

Carpenter, Lynette. "S/he Who Discover a New Pleasure: Cincinnati's Semi-Colon Club and the Woman Intellectual." Paper presented at the National Women's Studies Association, Minneapolis, 1987.

Charvat, William, and W. S. Tryon. *The Cost Books of Ticknor and Fields.* New York: Bibliographic Society of America, 1949.

Chase, Richard. *The American Novel and Its Tradition.* Garden City, NY: Doubleday, 1957.

Clark, Clifford E., Jr., *Henry Ward Beecher: Spokesman for a Middle-Class America.* Urbana: U of Illinois P, 1978.

Coultrap-McQuin, Susan. *Doing Literary Business: American Women Writers in the Nineteenth Century.* Chapel Hill: U of North Carolina P, 1990.

Crozier, Alice. *The Novels of Harriet Beecher Stowe.* New York: Oxford UP, 1969.

Crumpacker, Laurie. "Four Novels of Harriet Beecher Stowe: A Study in Nineteenth-Century Androgyny." *American Novelists Revisited: Essays in Feminist Criticism.* Ed. Fritz Fleischmann. Boston: G. K. Hall, 1982.

De Jong, Mary. "Dark-Eyed Daughters: Nineteenth-Century Popular Portrayals of Biblical Women." *Women's Studies: An Interdisciplinary Journal* 19 (1991): 283–308.

———. "'I Want to Be Like Jesus': The Self-Defining Power of Evangelical Hymnody." *Journal of the American Academy of Religion* 54 (1986): 461–93.

Doctorow, E. L. Review of *Harriet Beecher Stowe: A Life,* by Joan D. Hedrick. *New York Times Book Review* (13 February 1994): 3, 33.

Donaldson, Laura. "*The King and I* in Uncle Tom's Cabin, or on the Border of the Women's Room." *Cinema Journal* 29 (1990): 53–68.

Donovan, Josephine. *New England Local Color Literature: A Women's Tradition.* New York: Ungar, 1983.

———. *Uncle Tom's Cabin: Evil, Affliction, and Redemptive Love.* Boston: Twayne, 1991.

Douglas, Ann. *The Feminization of American Culture.* New York: Knopf, 1977.

Elrod, Eileen Razzari. "'Exactly Like My Father': Feminist Hermeneutics in Harriet Beecher Stowe's Non-fiction." *Journal of the American Academy of Religion* 63 (1995): 695–719.

Elsmere, Jane Shaffer. *Henry Ward Beecher: The Indiana Years, 1837–1847.* Indianapolis: Indiana Historical Society, 1973.

Fetterley, Judith. "Commentary: Nineteenth Century American Women Writers and the Politics of Recovery." *American Literary History* 6 (1994): 600–611.

———. "Only a Story, Not a Romance: Harriet Beecher Stowe's *The Pearl of Orr's Island.*" *The (Other) American Traditions: Nineteenth-Century Women Writers.* Ed. Joyce Warren. New Brunswick, NJ: Rutgers UP, 1993. 108–25.

Fields, Annie Adams. *Life and Letters of Harriet Beecher Stowe.* Boston: Houghton Mifflin, 1897.

Fisher, Philip. *Hard Facts: Setting and Form in the American Novel.* New York: Oxford UP, 1985.

Foster, Charles H. *The Rungless Ladder: Harriet Beecher Stowe and New England Puritanism.* Durham, NC: Duke UP, 1954.

Franchot, Jenny. *Roads to Rome: The Antebellum Protestant Encounter with Catholicism.* Berkeley: U of California P, 1994.

Furnas, J. C. *Goodbye to Uncle Tom.* New York: William Sloane, 1956.

Geary, Susan. "The Domestic Novel as a Commercial Commodity: Making a Best Seller in the 1850s." *Papers of the Bibliographical Society of America* 70 (1976): 365–93.

Gere, Anne Ruggles. *Writing Groups: History, Theory, Implications.* Carbondale: Southern Illinois UP, 1987.

Glenn, Myra C. *Thomas K. Beecher: Minister to a Changing America, 1824–1900.* Westport, CT: Greenwood P, 1996.

Gossett, Thomas F. *"Uncle Tom's Cabin" and American Culture.* Dallas, TX: Southern Methodist UP, 1985.

Hanne, Michael. *The Power of the Story: Fiction and Political Change.* Providence, RI: Berhahn Books, 1994.

Harris, Susan K. "The Female Imaginary in Harriet Beecher Stowe's *The Minister's Woong.*" *New England Quarterly* 66 (1993): 179–98.

Hedrick, Joan D. *Harriet Beecher Stowe: A Life.* New York: Oxford UP, 1994.

———. *The Harriet Beecher Stowe Reader.* New York: Oxford UP, forthcoming.

———. "Parlor Literature: Harriet Beecher Stowe and the Question of 'Great Women Artists.'" *Signs: Journal of Women in Culture and Society* 17 (1992): 275–303.

———. "'Peaceable Fruits': The Ministry of Harriet Beecher Stowe." *American Quarterly* 40 (1988): 307–32.

Hibben, Paxton. *Henry Ward Beecher: An American Portrait.* New York: The Press of the Readers Club, 1942.

Hildreth, Margaret Holbrook, comp. *Harriet Beecher Stowe: A Bibliography.* Hamden, CT: Shoestring Press, 1976.

Hill, Patricia R. "Writing Out the War: Harriet Beecher Stowe's Averted Gaze." *Divided Houses: Gender and the Civil War.* Ed. Catherine Clinton and Nina Silber. New York: Oxford UP, 1992. 260–78.

Hobbs, Catherine. *Nineteenth-Century Women Learn to Write*. Charlottesville: UP of Virginia, 1995.

Hovet, Theodore R. *The Master Narrative: Harriet Beecher Stowe's Subversive Story of Master and Slave in "Uncle Tom's Cabin" and "Dred."* New York: UP of America, 1989.

Howard, June. *Form and History in American Literary Naturalism*. Chapel Hill: U of North Carolina P, 1985.

James, Henry. Reflection on *Uncle Tom's Cabin*. Ammons, *Critical Essays* 286–87.

Jones, Bill T., and Arnie Zane Dance Company. *Last Supper at Uncle Tom's Cabin/The Promised Land*.

Kaplan, Fred. *Sacred Tears: Sentimentality in Victorian Literature*. Princeton, NJ: Princeton UP, 1987.

Kelley, Mary. *Private Woman, Public Stage: Literary Domesticity in Nineteenth-Century America*. New York: Oxford UP, 1984.

Kirkham, E. Bruce. *The Building of "Uncle Tom's Cabin."* Knoxville: U of Tennessee P, 1977.

———. Introduction. *The Pearl of Orr's Island*. Hartford: Stowe-Day Foundation, 1979.

Lewis, Gladys Sherman. *Message, Messenger, and Response: Puritan Forms and Cultural Reformation in Harriet Beecher Stowe's "Uncle Tom's Cabin."* Lanham, MD: UP of America, 1994.

Lott, Eric. *Love and Theft: Blackface Minstrelsy and the American Working Class*. New York: Oxford UP, 1993.

Lowance, M. I., Jr., Ellen E. Westbrook, and R. C. De Prospo. *The Stowe Debate: Rhetorical Strategies in "Uncle Tom's Cabin."* Amherst: U of Massachusetts P, 1994.

MacFarlane, Lisa. "The New England Kitchen Goes Uptown: Domestic Displacements in Harriet Beecher Stowe's New York." *New England Quarterly* 64 (1991): 272–91.

Martin, Theodoro Penny. *The Sound of Our Own Voices: Women's Study Clubs, 1860–1910*. Boston: Beacon P, 1987.

May, Henry. Introduction. *Oldtown Folks*. By Harriet Beecher Stowe. Cambridge, MA: Harvard UP, 1966. 3–43.

McLoughlin, William G. *The Meaning of Henry Ward Beecher*. New York: Knopf, 1970.

Merideth, Robert. *The Politics of the Universe: Edward Beecher, Abolition, and Orthodoxy*. Nashville, TN: Vanderbilt UP, 1968.

Moers, Ellen. *Harriet Beecher Stowe and American Literature*. Hartford: The Stowe Day Foundation, 1978.

———. "Money, the Job, and Little Women: Female Realism." *Literary Women*. New York: Doubleday, 1977. 101–35.

Morrison, Toni. *Beloved: A Novel.* New York: Knopf, 1987.

O'Connell, Catharine E. "'The Magic of the Real Presence of Distress': Sentimentality and Competing Rhetorics of Authority." Lowance et al., *The Stowe Debate* 13–36.

Rankin, Rick. *Unkle Tomm's Kabin.*

Reik, Cynthia. *Harriet Beecher Stowe Reader.* Hartford: Stowe-Day Foundation, 1993.

Riggio, Thomas P. "*Uncle Tom* Reconstructed: A Neglected Chapter in the History of a Book." *American Quarterly* 28 (1976): 56–70. Also Ammons, *Critical Essays* 139–51.

Riss, Arthur. "Racial Essentialism and Family Values in *Uncle Tom's Cabin.*" *American Quarterly* 46 (1994): 513–44.

Roman, Judith A. *Annie Adams Fields: The Spirit of Charles Street.* Bloomington: U of Indiana P, 1990.

Rugoff, Milton. *The Beechers: An American Family in the Nineteenth Century.* New York: Harper & Row, 1981.

Sadler, Lynn Veech. "The Samson Figure in Milton's *Samson Agonistes* and Stowe's *Dred.*" *New England Quarterly* 56 (1983): 440–48.

Schultz, Nancy Lusignan. "The Artist's Craftiness: Miss Prissy in *The Minister's Wooing.*" *Studies in American Fiction* 20 (1992): 33–45.

Shi, David E. *Facing Facts: Realism in American Thought and Culture, 1850–1920.* New York: Oxford UP, 1995.

Sklar, Kathryn Kish. *Catharine Beecher: A Study in American Domesticity.* New York: W. W. Norton, 1976.

Stowe, Charles Edward, and Lyman Beecher Stowe. *Harriet Beecher Stowe: The Story of Her Life.* Boston: Houghton Mifflin, 1911.

Stowe, Harriet Beecher. *Agnes of Sorrento.* Boston: J. R. Osgood, 1862.

———. *The American Woman's Home; or, Principles of Domestic Science. Being a Guide to the Formation and Maintenance of Economical, Healthful, Beautiful, and Christian Homes.* By Catharine Esther Beecher and Harriet Beecher Stowe. New York: J. B. Ford, 1869.

———. *The Chimney-Corner.* Boston: Ticknor & Fields, 1868.

———. *Dred: A Tale of the Great Dismal Swamp.* 2 vols. Boston: Phillips, Sampson, 1856.

———. *Footsteps of the Master.* New York: J. B. Ford, 1877.

———. *House and Home Papers.* Boston: Ticknor & Fields, 1865.

———. *A Key to "Uncle Tom's Cabin"; presenting the original facts and document upon which the story is founded. Together with corroborative statements verifying the truth of the work.* Boston: John P. Jewett, 1853.

———. *Lady Byron Vindicated: A History of the Byron Controversy, from its Beginnings in 1816 to the Present Time.* Boston: Fields, Osgood, 1870.

———. *Little Foxes.* Boston: Ticknor & Fields, 1866.

————. *The Mayflower; or, Sketches of Scenes and Characters among the Descendants of the Pilgrims.* New York: Harper, 1843.

————. *The Minister's Wooing.* New York: Derby & Jackson, 1859.

————. *My Wife and I; Or, Harry Henderson's History.* Boston: Houghton Mifflin, 1896/1871

————. "A New England Sketch." *Western Monthly* 3 (April 1834): 169–92.

————. *Oldtown Fireside Stories.* Boston: J. R. Osgood, 1872.

————. *Oldtown Folks.* Boston: Fields, Osgood, 1869.

————. *Palmetto Leaves.* Boston: J. R. Osgood, 1873.

————. *The Pearl of Orr's Island: A Story of the Coast of Maine.* Boston: Ticknor & Fields, 1862.

————. *Pink and White Tyranny: A Society Novel.* Boston: Roberts Brothers, 1871.

————. *Poganuc People: Their Loves and Lives.* New York: Ford, Howard & Hulbert, 1878.

————. *Religious Poems.* Boston: Ticknor & Fields, 1867.

————. *Sunny Memories of Foreign Lands.* 2 vols. Boston: Phillips, Sampson, 1854.

————. "Uncle Lot." See "A New England Sketch."

————. *Uncle Tom's Cabin; Or, Life Among the Lowly.* Boston: J. P. Jewett, 1852.

————. *Uncle Tom's Cabin; Or. Life Among the Lowly.* Ed. Elizabeth Ammons. Critical Editions Series. New York: Norton, 1994.

————. *Uncle Tom's Cabin; Or, Life Among the Lowly.* Ed. Ann Douglas. New York and Middlesex, England: Penguin, 1981.

————. *Uncle Tom's Cabin, The Minister's Wooing,* and *Oldtown Folks.* Ed. Katherine Sklar. New York: The Library of America, 1982.

————. *We and Our Neighbors.* New York: J. B. Ford, 1875.

————. *Women in Sacred History: A Series of Sketches Drawn from Scriptural, Historical, and Legendary Sources.* New York: J. B. Ford, 1874.

————. *The Writings of Harriet Beecher Stowe.* 16 vols. Boston: Houghton Mifflin, 1896.

Sundquist, Eric J. *New Essays on "Uncle Tom's Cabin."* Cambridge, England: Cambridge UP, 1986.

Tompkins, Jane. "Masterpiece Theatre: The Politics of Hawthorne's Literary Reputation." *Sensational Designs* 3–39.

————. *Sensational Designs: The Cultural Work of American Fiction, 1790-1850.* New York: Oxford UP, 1985.

————. "Sentimental Power: *Uncle Tom's Cabin* and the Politics of Literary History." *Sensational Designs* 122–46.

Tonkovich, Nicole. "Writing in Circles: Harriet Beecher Stowe, The Semi-Colon Club, and the Construction of Women's Authorship." Hobbs, *Nineteenth-Century Women* 145–75.

Tryon, W. S. *Parnassus Corner: A Life of James T. Fields, Publisher to the Victorians.* Boston: Houghton Mifflin, 1963.

Turner, Patricia A. *Ceramic Uncles and Celluloid Mammies: Black Images and Their Influence on Culture.* New York: Anchor Books, 1994.

Van Why, Joseph S., and Earl French, eds. *Harriet Beecher Stowe in Europe: The Journal of Charles Beecher.* Hartford: The Stowe-Day Foundation, 1986.

Wagenknecht, Edward. *Harriet Beecher Stowe: The Known and the Unknown.* New York: Oxford UP, 1965.

Warhol, Robyn. "Toward a Theory of the Engaging Narrator: Earnest Intervention in Gaskell, Stowe and Eliot." *PMLA* 101 (1986): 811–18.

Whitney. Lisa. "In the Shadow of *Uncle Tom's Cabin*: Stowe's Vision of Slavery from the Great Dismal Swamp." *New England Quarterly* 66 (1993): 552–69.

Wilson, Christopher P. "Tempests and Teapots: Harriet Beecher Stowe's *The Minister's Wooing.*" *New England Quarterly* 58 (1985): 554–77.

Wilson, Forrest. *Crusader in Crinoline: The Life of Harriet Beecher Stowe.* Philadelphia: J. B. Lippincott, 1941.

Wolff, Cynthia Griffin. "Margaret Garner: A Cincinnati Story." *Massachusetts Review* 32 (1991): 417–40.

———. "Masculinity in *Uncle Tom's Cabin.*" *American Quarterly* 47 (1995): 595–618.

Wright, Nathalia. "Harriet Beecher Stowe." *American Novelists in Italy.* Philadelphia: U of Pennsylvania P, 1965. 86–103.

Yarborough, Richard. "Strategies of Black Characterization in *Uncle Tom's Cabin* and the Early Afro-American Novel." Sundquist, *New Essays* 45–84.

7

Walt Whitman

Ed Folsom

Fifteen years ago, in his survey of the critical work on Whitman from 1940 to 1975, Donald D. Kummings suggested a "few areas left to explore." He specified several possibilities for comparative studies (Whitman's connections to Count Gurowski, Joaquin Miller, Isadora Duncan, Alfred Stieglitz, Jean Toomer, Clarence Darrow, and Emma Goldman). He noted that little had been done on Whitman and the American Indian. Whitman's "humor and diction," he said, remained relatively unexplored. While some of Whitman's poems had gathered voluminous commentary, many others were barely remarked upon, so Kummings announced that the field for close reading was still open. Finally, Whitman's "major prose works" had not received the kind of close attention they deserved (Kummings, *Walt Whitman* x).

How have critics over the past decade and a half responded to these challenges? Countless comparative studies have appeared, and recently the Stieglitz, Toomer, Goldman, and Duncan connections have been investigated (Dougherty; Hutchinson, "The Whitman Legacy"; Adrian; Bohan), though Darrow, at least, remains open. I've dealt with Whitman and American Indians in *Walt Whitman's Native Representations*. Ronald Wallace's *God Be with the Clown* analyzed Whitman's humor in more detail than ever before, finding slapstick and *alazon* backwoods jokes in places no one had looked before. C. Carroll Hollis took on Whitman's diction with a vengeance, showing how his poetic language was an innovative blend of journalism and oratory. Follow-up studies by James Perrin Warren, Mark Bauerlein, and Tenney Nathanson have probed the diction further (while incrementally etherealizing the critical vocabulary we use to discuss Whitman's earthy words), and Erik Thurin has recently subjected Whitman's language to a relentless grammatical analysis. We now have close readings of many of Whitman's less well-known works, though many poems remain without commentary, and the handful of agreed-upon great poems continue to garner extensive commentary: Section 11 of "Song of Myself" and "The Sleepers" have been written about more in the past decade than in the previous fifty years. As for Whitman's prose, *Democratic Vistas* and *Specimen Days* have in the past few years become major works; even Whitman's short stories and his novel *Franklin Evans* have received serious attention in recent years. *The Walt Whitman Encyclopedia* (LeMaster and Kummings), now in preparation, will escalate the explicatory campaign by including commentary by an army of scholars on virtually every one of Whitman's poems and prose pieces.

Critical energies have gone into numerous other areas as well, many of which were unimaginable even ten years ago. Whitman has been deconstructed, rhetorically reconfigured, politicized, newly historicized, postcolonialized, and psychoanalyzed; he has been read in the light of Lacan, Foucault, and Kristeva, attacked as antifeminist and defended as an early feminist, and condemned as a racist and praised as a multiculturalist. He has been transformed from the "good gray poet" to the "good gay poet," his sexual identity now read as a badge of radicalizing marginality instead of as a sign of troubling abnormality.

Since 1980 there have been over seventy-five books published about Whitman. Also appearing have been the final four volumes of Whitman's conversations with his disciple Horace Traubel during the poet's last years, six large volumes of Whitman's notebooks and unpublished prose manuscripts, a second supplemental volume of his correspondence (and a volume of his selected correspondence), three double volumes of facsimiles of his manuscripts, ten special issues of journals devoted to Whitman, four volumes of selected criticism about Whitman from the past hundred years, a giant new descriptive bibliography (Myerson), and countless reprintings and special editions of his works (including at least one politically correct version of the 1855 *Leaves of Grass* that "humanizes" Whitman's language by removing all gender-specific pronouns [Ash]).

Since just 1990, the scholarly output has been huge, generated in part by the various gatherings honoring the centennial of the poet's death; by my count, nearly two hundred centennial essays were written during the 1992–93 centennial year, many of them now collected in books (Camboni, Erkkila and Grossman, Folsom, Villar Rosa), all the result of Whitman symposia in at least eight different countries, with five major events in the United States. Collections of essays focusing on teaching Whitman at the elementary, secondary, college, and graduate level have recently appeared (Padgett, Kummings), along with a collection of essays focusing on Whitman as a gay poet (Martin). Recent critical books have dealt with Whitman's short lyrics (Schwiebert), his religious beliefs (Kuebrich), his shamanistic role (Hutchinson), his artisanal faith (Thomas), his politics (Erkkila), his debt to tradition (Price), his theory of language (Warren), his bodily figures (Moon, Killingsworth), his voice (Nathanson), his homoerotic text (Fone), his absorption of nineteenth-century popular culture (Folsom, Reynolds), and his ways of seeing (Dougherty). More toward the fringe of Whitman studies, other books have presented two decades of ouija board conversations with a posthumous Whitman (Gold) and an updating of Richard Maurice Bucke's "cosmic consciousness" theory of Whitman in light of the Big Bang theory of the origins of the universe (Akers). There's even a new book about all the other books, M. Jimmie Killingsworth's *The Growth of "Leaves of Grass": The Organic Tradition in Whitman Studies*, which ends with a sobering thought about the future of Whitman scholarship: concerned about the new historicist tendencies of recent criticism, evident in the treatment of the author as a cultural construct, Killingsworth suggests that "we must add to the agenda of future critical studies the problem of how to preserve the authority of the poet (or the poetic text) even as we assert our own authority as critics" (141).

Long before theory announced the death of the author, of course, Whitman was already threatening to evaporate back into the culture, to "shake my white locks" and "effuse my flesh in eddies and drift it in lacy jags," to "bequeath myself to the dirt to grow from the grass I love" (Whitman, *Leaves* [1965] 89). Whitman announced his identity with America, and so it isn't surprising that he has turned out to be an author well suited for the recent upsurge of cultural criticism. His poetry absorbed so many elements of his cultural landscape that he has been an easy mark for New Historicists and cultural revisionists. He always was an author happy to be reabsorbed into the culture that gave him identity, and a lot of recent readings have been facilitating that reabsorption, viewing him as the manifestation of the best and worst of nineteenth-century American culture. The most aggressive of these readings is David Reynolds's *Walt Whitman's America*, a book that the author names a "cultural biography." Virtually every page offers some nearly forgotten event in nineteenth-century American culture and shows how it works its way into Whitman's thoughts and usually into his poetry; Reynolds's Whitman emerges as a poet for the New Historical era, so thoroughly enmeshed in the sublime and the ridiculous of his time and place that he cannot help but be the embodiment of a nation.

It is appropriate, then, as we try to locate some sites for future projects in Whitman studies, to begin with the intersection of Whitman's texts and American culture. Even though it has been customary in recent years to talk about the complexity of the publishing history of *Leaves of Grass*, few critics have attempted to tie the exciting discoveries of bibliographic and textual scholars to the resurgence of interest in nineteenth-century culture. Cultural critics have tended to stand back and treat *Leaves of Grass* as a unified whole instead of the shifting and contradictory composite that it demonstrably is. As a result, cultural criticism about Whitman has often been suspect because it generalizes Whitman's text while specifying historical and cultural contexts. So far, only textual scholars have dared enter the morass of Whitman's publishing history. Arthur Golden, for example, in the 1980 variorum *Leaves of Grass* (lvii–lxxv), offered a textual key to the complex history of Whitman's metamorphosing "clusters" of poems in *Leaves*, but few scholars have utilized this important information; no one has begun the work of precisely relating Whitman's intricate decisions about the arrangement of his poems to the events of his life and times.

For over half a century following Whitman's death, critics were generally content to work with the "deathbed edition" of *Leaves*, the final authorized version, the one that Whitman made clear was his choice for all future editions: "As there are now several editions of L. of G.," he wrote on the copyright page of his 1892 printing, "I wish to say that I prefer and recommend this present one complete, for future printing, if there should be any." But, at the same time, he retained a fondness for each of the earlier editions: "They all count," he told Horace Traubel late in his life; "I don't know that I like one better than any other" (Traubel 1: 280). In the past forty years, critics have begun to endorse their preferred editions. Malcolm Cowley's reprinting of the 1855 edition of *Leaves* in 1959—with his spirited introduction claiming that the 1855 version was "the buried masterpiece of American writing" (x)—generated a series of studies of the first edition. Roy Harvey Pearce then offered a reprint of the 1860 edition, claiming its superiority as "an articulated whole, with an argument" (xxv), the most unified of all the editions. Facsimiles of the

1856 edition, of *Drum-Taps,* and of Whitman's short-lived *Passage to India* volume became available, and each of these volumes had a short vogue as the "best" or "most characteristic" Whitman book.

Perhaps, then, it is time for a new generation to claim yet a different edition of *Leaves* as the most revealing and illuminating, the best fit for this era of renewed historical and cultural concern. Betsy Erkkila in *Whitman the Political Poet* has suggested the ways in which each of Whitman's editions might be understood as a response to specific political concerns and historical moments. But much remains to be done in gaining an understanding of just how the various editions responded to their historical moments, how the very forms of the books reflected ideological and philosophical struggles that Whitman was undergoing, not to mention publishing struggles. Each book reifies a moment of political and publishing history, embodying Whitman's decisions on production, marketing, distribution, and readership.

One result of the emerging historical/cultural concern will be more studies of *Leaves* focusing on Whitman's book as a material object; its binding, typeface, paper, illustrations, and mode of printing all point to the fertile interplay between poet, audience, and culture. Now that the known photographs of Whitman have been gathered and catalogued (see Folsom, "Heart's"), for example, critics have begun to track the ways in which Whitman manipulated his visual image and used photographs to create and control his public image (see Folsom, "Appearing in Print" and *Native Representations*; Trachtenberg, *Reading*; and Clarke). Whitman's interaction with photography and photographers—he was the most photographed writer in the nineteenth century—tells us a great deal about his absorption of technology and his developing theories of democratic art. His responses to and uses of other aspects of visual design— from his critiques of the many paintings and drawings of himself to his intriguing use of engraved decorations in his various editions—remain largely unexplored. Work on Whitman's books as physical objects will be greatly facilitated by Joel Myerson's impressive descriptive bibliography, which gives scholars for the first time exquisitely detailed summaries of the features of each issue of each edition of Whitman's work.

The era of nineteenth-century American history receiving the most renewed attention in recent years is the Reconstruction period, increasingly seen as the time that generated questions of race and democracy and civil rights that have occupied the culture ever since. Whitman left us three wonderfully idiosyncratic Reconstruction issues of *Leaves,* and they remain the least studied of his books, beginning with his 1867 version, the most chaotic of all the *Leaves*. That text, in one of its issues, did not contain his Civil War poems, *Drum-Taps*, but for another issue Whitman had the *Drum-Taps* book sewn in with the *Leaves*, his first attempt to absorb the Civil War into his big book—a book bound as tenuously as the reunified North and South. Cheaply printed and not even containing a portrait of the poet (the only version of *Leaves* not to represent Whitman visually), this edition captures Whitman's confusion at the end of the war—both his own uncertainty about his role as representative American poet and his deep ambivalence about how the country should step into its future. The 1870–71 edition of *Leaves* appeared at the heart of Reconstruction and reveals Whitman's feverish attempts to pull everything (his healing nation, his developing book, and his unraveling life) together; *Drum-Taps* had now bled into the entire *Leaves*, disappearing as a separate book and reappearing instead in clusters ("Drum-Taps," "Marches Now the War is Over," "Bathed in War's Perfume") and in poems scattered throughout the text. Then, at the end of Reconstruction, Whitman offered a two-volume matched set, an edition of his work celebrating America's Centennial, consisting of *Leaves of Grass* and the generally ignored *Two Rivulets*. *Two Rivulets* is a fascinating compilation (Whitman calls it a "Melange") that gathers between two covers his prose books *Memoranda during the War* and *Democratic Vistas*, as well as his aborted book of poems called *Passage to India*; the book features also a literary experiment, with prose and poetry appearing on the same page, two separate linguistic rivulets moving toward confluence. Whitman offers this odd mélange as a companion to a reprinting of the 1870–71 *Leaves* and thus alters *Leaves* by balancing it with a book of a very different kind.

These three appearances of *Leaves*—1867, 1870–71, and 1876—form one of the most intriguing correspondences between Whitman's texts and Whitman's times, and they are waiting for innovative cultural critics who have the patience for some complex bibliographic and textual work. There are signs that such work is now just beginning (see Mancuso). The payoff will be an illuminating critique of Whitman's changing book as a dark mirror of one of the most chaotic periods in our country's history.

Further, a focus on Whitman's overall publishing history in relation to political and cultural developments will shift the critical debate away from an exclusive focus on *Leaves of Grass* toward a more inclusive investigation of Whitman's overall project, one that included prose works, poetic supplements to *Leaves,* and experimental works that challenged generic distinctions: the 1876 Centennial matched volumes, with their roiling mixture of texts, can be read as the culminating moment of Whitman's career instead of a sign of decline. Critics often seem to forget that Whitman continued to issue new editions of *Leaves* in conjunction with his prose, not separate from it—thus we have a volume of *Specimen Days and Collect* issued just after and perfectly matched to his 1881 *Leaves,* and we have his 1888 *Complete Poems & Prose,* where he united the poetry and prose in one volume. We also must examine more closely his 1888 *November Boughs* and his 1891 *Good-Bye My Fancy,* both innovative mixtures of poetry and prose, and both often forgotten because Whitman extracted the poetry from these volumes and appended it to the final edition of *Leaves* (an edition, we must remember, that was also issued with a matching volume, *Complete Prose Works*).

Whitman's project, then, clearly involved melding his poetry and prose, but this century's critical emphasis on *Leaves* alone has blurred the nature and significance of Whitman's larger scheme. Thus we have had many reprints of editions of *Leaves,* but few reprints of his prose books and no reprints of his most experimental conjoinings of poetry and prose. Future scholarship on Whitman will have to take into account Whitman's overarching of genres; such investigation will more firmly embed the poetry in nineteenth-century cultural concerns since the prose tends to historicize the poetry. We are still emerging from the legacy of New Criticism, which created a focus on a handful of Whitman's poems; Whitman criticism has now contextualized those poems in the larger poetic project of *Leaves of Grass* and has recognized the complexity of the history of that project, but it has yet to contextualize *Leaves* itself in Whitman's even larger and more complex endeavor to unite prose and poetry in the service of an emerging democratic aesthetics.

The contextualizing of *Leaves of Grass* will be made easier by major accomplishments in Whitman textual studies during the last fifteen years: the variorum edition of *Leaves* appeared in three volumes in 1980; Whitman's daybooks and notebooks (including his invaluable notebooks on language) appeared in three volumes in 1978; and his notebooks and unpublished prose manuscripts appeared in six volumes in 1984. These collections, all part of the still-ongoing New York University Press edition of *The Collected Writings of Walt Whitman,* have made easily available most of the important Whitman materials that reside in major archives.

There is still much to do, however. The long-awaited edition of Whitman's journalism—a cornerstone for any in-depth cultural studies approach to Whitman—was abandoned by the *Collected Writings* project; the fate of Herbert Bergman's multivolume edition of Whitman's newspaper writings is now uncertain, and the work may well have to be redone by others. Scholars still have to depend on the currently available motley assortment of Whitman's selected newspaper pieces. Ezra Greenspan's recent important work on the centrality of Whitman's newspaper and printing experience to his developing poetics has underscored the importance of the journalism, and many fertile projects await those prepared for some deep immersion in newspaper archives. Whitman worked on and wrote for many newspapers before 1860, including the *Long Islander, Aurora, Evening Tattler, Long Island Star*, Brooklyn *Daily Eagle*, New Orleans *Crescent*, Brooklyn *Freeman, Life Illustrated*, and the Brooklyn *Times*. Complete runs of some of these papers no longer exist, and even partial runs may be difficult to find (the only run of the *Aurora* during Whitman's tenure is in the Paterson [New Jersey] Free Library, for example). Future archival discoveries will fill out and contextualize Whitman's journalistic record, illuminating his complex and intense involvement with the social issues of mid-nineteenth-century America.

The incompleteness of scholarly editions of Whitman's journalism is paralleled by the incompleteness of the scholarly edition of *Leaves of Grass*. The variorum edition of *Leaves* covers only the *book* appearances of the poems, leaving the periodical and manuscript variations unexamined. (Arthur Golden is working on a supplemental variorum that will deal with these versions of the poems, but the work is moving very slowly.) One problem with the variorum is that, while it offers easy access to Whitman's changes in wording, it does not give much of a sense of how the editions themselves changed, what they looked like, how they were composed, or how their print and paper and binding altered the way they would have to be read. To clarify such matters, of course, there is no substitute for examining original copies. One project awaiting some enterprising scholar (or group of scholars) with computer facility is a hypertext version of *Leaves of Grass* (and other Whitman books) that will allow computer access to the various editions by scanning color page-by-page photographs of the texts into a database, thus allowing anyone to examine the physical attributes of the various editions on a computer screen: all scholars could then have all the editions (including *Drum-Taps, Specimen Days, Two Rivulets*, etc.) present in state-of-the-art computer realization, complete with cross-referencing, textual annotation, and publishing history. Facsimiles of Whitman's manuscripts and corrected proof sheets could also be included, thus allowing scholars to call up each step in the evolution of Whitman's poems. Such hypertextual scholarship could revolutionize commentary on Whitman. (An electronic concordance of Whitman's work released several years ago had the potential to have a similar impact on the field, but the publisher discontinued it.)

In 1995, Whitman scholars, along with the rest of the world, got a glimpse of the digitized textual future. Ten important Whitman notebooks had been missing from the Library of Congress since World War II; in a stunning development, four of them resurfaced in the winter of 1995 (Birney). More than half a century after their disappearance, they were returned to the Library of Congress, which had the foresight to scan digitally each page of the notebooks while they were disbound for conservation work. The digital images were then immediately put on the World Wide Web (http://LCWEB.LOC.GOV). Within weeks after the notebooks' return, then, Whitman's important manuscripts (including the first jottings for "Song of Myself" and some of his most powerful Civil War hospital writings) were accessible for minute examination around the world, each page in wondrously clear facsimile form on the computer screen, available for downloading and printing. Urgent calls for a facsimile edition of the notebooks abruptly ceased as scholars experienced firsthand just what computer access to archival materials really meant. With new programs like Adobe Photoshop, it is possible to manipulate and explore the virtual Whitman manuscripts in ways that would be impossible with the actual manuscripts (which in any case are in such fragile condition that the Library of Congress is not allowing direct access to them).

At the current point in Whitman textual scholarship, we find ourselves in the paradoxical situation of having easy access to minor scraps of Whitman's prose jottings (thanks to Edward Grier's six volumes of the notebooks and unpublished prose manuscripts and William White's three volumes of daybooks and notebooks on words), but still having no quick access to the manuscript versions of his poems, which still require archival retrieval. The early decisions that generated the structure of the New York University Press *Collected Writings of Walt Whitman* have locked Whitman studies into an artificial demarcation between his poetry and his prose. Much of his prose has been dumped into volumes containing his calendar jottings and address books, while much of his manuscript poetry has been held back from timely publication. Like much of his journalism, many of Whitman's important poetry manuscripts are still available only through visits to library collections and thus are not widely known. Joel Myerson's recent *Walt Whitman Archive* contains facsimiles of many poem manuscripts and corrected proofs and thus helps to correct this problem, though the collection is unfortunately not clearly indexed, not keyed to the variorum edition, and not complete. Confusion still reigns among scholars about just which Whitman poetry manuscripts are available and where. The confusion is compounded by the fact that many Whitman manuscripts and letters are still being discovered. In addition to the return of the four Whitman Library of Congress notebooks, with six more presumably still hidden out there somewhere, fifteen or so letters and manuscript fragments keep appearing each year. Only a few years ago, the important cache of 1840s Whitman letters to his friend Abraham Leech appeared, altering significantly our image of Whitman during his schoolteaching days. Within the last couple of years, important Whitman manuscripts outlining his racial views have surfaced. Such discoveries, of course, take their toll on the "definitive" collections of correspondence and manuscripts, and so the *Collected Writings* project, still not officially complete, is already in need of some major additions. The new manuscripts, along with the thousands that appeared in Grier's volumes of Whitman's notebooks, have yet to be fully absorbed into Whitman scholarship; they will become vital tools as the cultural reconstructions of Whitman continue to take place.

The new manuscripts and new letters alter our biographical knowledge of Whitman, even if only incrementally. But, again, the advances in cultural understanding of the nineteenth century have created some revealing new contexts in which to place Whitman's life and into which his life can be more fully woven. Sean Wilentz's *Chants Democratic*, for example, a study of the rise of the working class in New York City in the first half of the nineteenth century, has been tremendously influential on a number of Whitman scholars as they reopen Whitman's pre–Civil War years and deal with his attitudes toward labor and the dying artisanal culture (see Thomas, "Dreams of Labor" and *Lunar Light*; Trachtenberg, "Politics of Labor"). The enhanced understanding of the way racial and labor issues were intertwined in the nineteenth century is beginning to clarify some of Whitman's more controversial racial views and to explain the shift away from racial issues in editions of *Leaves* after the Civil War.

Never an abolitionist, Whitman held views on slavery that responded to his passionate support of white labor. He was a "Free Soil" advocate, and his developing racial attitudes followed a circuitous route through an array of romantic racialist, colonialist, and racial evolutionist ideas, culminating in a paralyzing ambivalence about the role of free African Americans in America's post–Civil War culture. His shifting notions about race can be tracked most clearly through his journalism (pointing again to the crucial role that thorough study of his newspaper work will play in Whitman studies over the next decade) and through his poetic revisions (African Americans have a diminishing role in *Leaves* following the 1860 edition). As Whitman scholars reopen Whitman's postwar years, Eric Foner's *Reconstruction: America's Unfinished Revolution*, with its detailed tracing of postbellum racial debates, may be the next historical text to have the kind of influence on Whitman scholars that Wilentz's book has had during the past few years.

Whitman studies have been well served by Gay Wilson Allen's *The Solitary Singer*, a biography that has virtually set a record for maintaining the designation "definitive" (it is over forty years old), but there is a great deal of work yet to be done on Whitman biography. While Justin Kaplan and Philip Callow have attempted full biographies since Allen's, we may be at a stage when a truly revisionist comprehensive biography will have to wait for a number of more focused partial ones. Kaplan's biography offered a fresh narrative and some valuable psychological insights, but both his book and Callow's volume are more superficial than Allen's, skimming over key parts of the life. Joseph Rubin and Paul Zweig may have pointed the way to the future of Whitman biography by covering a shorter period of Whitman's life (Rubin only fifteen years, 1840 to 1855, and Zweig from the 1840s to the mid-1860s), but doing so in rich and textured detail. Restricted-time biographies allow for a more capacious contextualization, and after several more narrow periods of Whitman's life have been unfolded more fully in the light of recent developments in historical and cultural studies, then we will be able to return to the overall pattern of the life with fresh insight. There are good books yet to be done about Whitman during the Civil War years (arguably the most fascinating part of Whitman's life, even though the first two years of the war remain the mystery years in Whitman biography) and during the Reconstruction years (for which we have plenty of documentation and endless intrigue, including his complex relationship with Peter Doyle, his declining health, and his stormy relationship with his champion, W. D. O'Connor).

David Reynolds's *Walt Whitman's America* tells Whitman's life against the backdrop of nineteenth-century American culture, but often the culture itself is foregrounded, and Whitman as a distinct individual fades into an identity defined by the ideas, events, and trends that surrounded him. Jerome Loving, meanwhile, has embarked on a different kind of biography (now in progress), one that will seek to do the necessary work of clearing away the accumulated and accumulating layers of Whitman myth and legend, paring the inflated narratives back to what we actually know about the life, and returning us to a factual foundation on which we can construct a reasonable frame for understanding his experience.

Promising related areas of investigation are the lives of Whitman's friends, associates, and family. Their biographies provide another way of exploring separate aspects of Whitman's life in order to construct vital segments of what will eventually become a more complete portrait. In the past dozen years, a biography of his friend and sometime-suitor Anne Gilchrist has appeared (Alcaro), as well as a biography of William Douglas O'Connor (Freedman), and shorter biographies of Peter Doyle (Murray) and Whitman's reformist friend Abby Price (Ceniza). Whitman is in the title of all these studies, a sign of their dual mission—to refocus our attention on a lesser-known figure and to illuminate an important facet of the well-known poet's life. This endeavor can no doubt go too far: recently, for example, a book appeared devoted to an examination of Whitman's brief relationship with one of his physicians, Sir William Osler (Leon). But important work does remain to be done: no biography has yet appeared of any of Whitman's family members, though separate collections of letters by his brothers George Whitman (Loving) and Thomas Jefferson Whitman (Berthold and Price) have been published, along with a collection by his sister-in-law Mattie (Waldron). All of these projects have furnished illuminating insight into Whitman's life, and there are other important family/friend projects yet to be undertaken. Most of Whitman's mother's letters have never been published, even though they offer some surprising insights into the Whitman family, and even though their style (she has often been unjustly described as semiliterate) may in fact furnish some hints toward Whitman's loosened syntax.

Perhaps most surprising is the fact that, except for two early hagiographic studies (Bain, Karsner), no one has written a biography of Horace Traubel, Whitman's most devoted friend and an accomplished writer, publisher, and social activist, who was central to the American Socialist movement and who dedicated his life to the construction of a Walt Whitman consonant with Traubel's own beliefs. The Horace Traubel collection, now at the Library of Congress, has only recently been catalogued; it is the great unexplored treasure trove of Whitman-related materials, filled with surprises. A thorough study of Traubel's life is now possible, and such a study would not only offer fresh insights into Whitman's last years, but also make available for the first time a full history of the early marketing of Whitman, of the creation of Whitman as a major writer, and of the formation of an international association of "Whitmaniacs," at the same time that it would give us an examination of an important social and literary figure in his own right. The model here might well be Jerome Loving's book on Whitman and Emerson, in which the two writers' lives are traced as similar cycles out of sync with each other; the two writers thus always sensed a kinship even as they were keenly aware of their differences. This kind of kinetic influence study would serve both Whitman and Traubel well.

In the Traubel collection are thousands of letters, most of them unexamined. Such letters *about* and *to* Whitman have recently been providing some key insights about his life and work. Charley Shively in the 1980s published the letters written to Whitman by his various young male friends—Peter Doyle, Harry Stafford, and many soldiers whom the poet nursed and befriended during the Civil War. These letters filled in the missing half of the correspondence, the absence that we always sense when we read a collection of letters by an author; Whitman's tonality seems transformed when his letters are read next to the letters he was receiving. Shively professes to hear a clearly gay tone in the letters, and he is convinced that he has proven Whitman's sexual involvement with these young men. Much Whitman criticism in the past five years has assumed that Whitman was not just "homoerotic" (Gay Wilson Allen's term) but actively homosexual (see Shively, Moon, Fone, Martin). This work suggests that, whenever the next full biography of Whitman is written, it will have to be built on the assumption that (not built out of the suspicion that) Whitman was gay.

Previous Whitman scholarship has demonstrated how the facts of Whitman's life, his attitudes, and his poetry are illuminated and obscured by embedding all the evidence in a matrix that assumes he was *not* actively homosexual; it is time now to fit the evidence into a matrix that assumes that he *was*, so that we can see what previously obscured aspects of Whitman's life and writing become clear, and what familiar aspects of Whitman become encrypted in such a reconfiguration of his life. Just as we have learned a great deal in recent years about the Reconstruction period (and can thus imagine reseeing Whitman's life against that backdrop), so have we also observed developments in gay history indicating that a newly contextualized Whitman is bound to appear soon (a Whitman seen against a social backdrop that increasingly appears to have incorporated a gay life-style long before the word "homosexual" was even coined). This biography of a recontextualized Whitman could be reductive if it forced *Leaves* to implode into little more than an expression of gay sexual experience, but it could be revelatory if it illuminated Whitman's homosexuality and examined the ways it related to, resisted, challenged, and expanded Whitman's familiar concepts of democracy, poetry, camaraderie, and the cosmos. His unsanctioned sexual nature might then be viewed as the seed of his unorthodox poetry and as an impetus for his radical democratic demands. The work of critics like Shively, Moon, Fone, and Martin has cleared the ground for such a study.

We are only now beginning to understand the ways in which Whitman has been constructed for us by biographers from Whitman's own time (in whose biographies Whitman often had a hand) on up to ours. Incisive biographies of Whitman's biographers, exploring their motivations, biases, and preconceptions, would help to explain just how and why we have inherited the Whitmans with which we are most familiar. Whitman has seldom attracted biographers who even pretended to be disinterested in their subject, and their enthusiasms and fears have a lot to tell us about Whitman's entrance into the American literary canon. Joann P. Krieg and Jerome Loving have done work on Emory Holloway's insistence on a heterosexual Whitman, and Walter Grünzweig has investigated Eduard Bertz's early formulation of a homosexual Whitman, but there are more aspects to the construction of a biographical Whitman than his sexuality, and filling in the record of Whitman's biographers from John Burroughs and Richard Maurice Bucke on up to contemporary biographers from Allen to Zweig would illuminate the politics of biographical representation.

Biographers are not the only ones who have investments in particular versions of Whitman. American poets over the past century have also created a multitude of Whitmans, finding his poetry an inexhaustible resource. These poets have responded to Whitman more often and more directly than to any other American precursor. Poets from his time to the present have argued with him, praised him, identified with him, rejected him, and revised him. Virtually all American poets have at some point talked back to him, defining themselves in relation to Whitman's goals and his practice (see Folsom, "Talking Back"). The ongoing conversation, now well over a century old, forms a self-sustaining guarantee that influence studies will remain a vital part of Whitman scholarship. In the past few years, several books have investigated poets' responses to Whitman, looking at the ways that poets keep "Discovering Ourselves in Whitman" (to use the title of Thomas Gardner's recent book tracing Whitmanian patterns in six contemporary poets). But each year, new evidence of Whitman's influence is discovered and explored, and as the careers of contemporary poets unfold, previously unexamined aspects of Whitman's writing are revealed. A substantial amount of work has been done on the importance of Whitman to poets like Galway Kinnell, Allen Ginsberg, and Robert Creeley, though much yet remains. One unexplored aspect of Whitman's relationship to contemporary poets involves those writers like Kinnell and Creeley who have actually edited selections of Whitman's work and who thus may reveal in their Whitman collections just how a particular subset of Whitman's poetry helps form a cohesive foundation for the contemporary poet's own work. Major studies have yet to be written about Whitman's effect on the Language poets (a promising field for investigation, given all the recent work on Whitman and language theory), and on the shape of his influence on poets like Gerald Stern and Sharon Olds, who often invoke him by name in their poetry.

Whitman's influence has also been international, and his cross-cultural impact is one of the most promising areas for future study. Huck Gutman has recently demonstrated the potential for the study of American literature worldwide, and Gay Wilson Allen and I edited *Walt Whitman and the World*, which traces the absorption of Whitman into various cultures, from China to Spain to Mexico; this is a proleptic look at the phenomenon, however, and not an exhaustive survey. Betsy Erkkila and Walter Grünzweig have demonstrated the possibilities for full-scale studies of Whitman's absorption in particular cultures; Whitman often enters into foreign literary traditions in surprising political and artistic guises. The history of his reception into many Spanish- and Portuguese-speaking cultures, where his influence has been strongly felt for a century, remains to be written. James Nolan's recent book comparing the "Native American poetics" of Whitman and Pablo Neruda demonstrates that affinities between two major poets can cross language, culture, and time. Several white and black writers from various African nations (writers from Alan Paton to Ngugi Wa Thiong'o) have looked to Whitman for inspiration, but their debt to him has yet to be thoroughly investigated. There have been studies of Whitman's relation to Indian thought and to Vedic scriptures (see Chari, Kanadey, Kumar, and Nambiar), but no one has yet studied the remarkable political history of Whitman's reception into Indian culture. Given the imperialistic undertones of a poem like "Passage to India," and given the current development of postcolonial theory, a study of this subject might clarify the tensions between the controlling and liberating aspects of Whitman's rhetoric. Entering India via British colonial domination, Whitman's work nonetheless contained the seeds of the end of empire, even while it sang the glories of a passage to India. In this context, E. M. Forster's use of Whitman's poem for the title of his novel exploring the fragile emergence of postcolonial relations between Britain and India is particularly telling.

Given the domination of critical theory in graduate curricula during the past decade, it comes as no surprise that many of the doctoral dissertations written on Whitman in recent years are exercises in applied theory: Foucault, Lukács, Lacan, Jameson, and Kristeva are names frequently invoked in such work, which has looked into Whitman and such issues as the mechanization of craft labor, monologic imagination, representation of race, intertextuality, *l'écriture féminine*, and the medical institutionalization of suffering. Many of these projects have produced fine new insights, but often Whitman is merely grist for powerful theoretical mills. He has always been a pliable subject for various theorists, from psychoanalysts to deconstructionists, and his vast body of work will no doubt remain a lure for theories yet to come. But the best dissertations in recent years have been marked by an innovative theoretical approach married to careful textual and bibliographical work, and several of these dissertations have become important books (see Eiselein, Klammer, Mancuso, Sweet, Warren).

The instability of the American canon has led to the discovery of Whitman influences in many unsuspected places, including Asian American writers (see Li), Harlem Renaissance writers (see Hutchinson), and women writers (see Ceniza). Just as he claimed, Whitman seems in fact to be large and contain multitudes, and that is good news for scholars on the lookout for new topics: his influence extends to fiction writers, dramatists, and musicians. (Hundreds of composers have set Whitman's words to music—a greater number than for any other American writer.) Even architects, painters, and sculptors have found that there are lessons to be learned from Whitman, and future studies will no doubt build on cross-disciplinary intertextuality. So much has been suggested in recent years, and so little examined thoroughly. The textual and bibliographic tools—the major work of Whitman studies during the past fifteen years—are now available to allow for the kind of thorough reexamination of virtually everything that has been said about Whitman, and these tools have given us a far vaster Whitman than anyone had access to before. It's a daunting but exciting time to take the plunge into Whitman studies. Just as Whitman knew that the key to creating an endless circuit of meaning in a work of literature was "always to leave the best untold" (*Variorum* 270), so have Whitman's critics responded by piling up words about the poet, but leaving the mysteries of his identity, his aesthetics, his sexuality, his philosophy, and his politics, tantalizingly out of reach, endlessly beckoning.

WORKS CITED

Adrian, Lynne. "Emma Goldman on Whitman." *Walt Whitman Quarterly Review*, forthcoming.

Akers, Philip. *The Principle of Life.* New York: Vantage, 1991.

Alcaro, Marion Walker. *Walt Whitman's Mrs. G.* Rutherford, NJ: Fairleigh Dickinson UP, 1991.

Allen, Gay Wilson. *The Solitary Singer.* 1955. Chicago: U of Chicago P, 1985.

———. *Walt Whitman Abroad.* Syracuse, NY: Syracuse UP, 1955.

Allen, Gay Wilson, and Ed Folsom, eds. *Walt Whitman and the World.* Iowa City: U of Iowa P, 1995.

Ash, A. S., ed. *The Original 1855 Edition of "Leaves of Grass."* Santa Barbara, CA: Bandanna, 1992.

Bain, Mildred. *Horace Traubel.* New York: Albert and Charles Boni, 1913.

Bauerlein, Mark. *Whitman and the American Idiom.* Baton Rouge: Louisiana State UP, 1991.

Berthold, Dennis, and Kenneth Price, eds. *Dear Brother Walt: The Letters of Thomas Jefferson Whitman.* Kent, OH: Kent State UP, 1984.

Birney, Alice L. "Missing Whitman Notebooks Returned to Library of Congress." *Walt Whitman Quarterly Review* 12 (1995): 217–29.

Bohan, Ruth L. "'I Sing the Body Electric': Isadora Duncan, Whitman, and the Dance." Greenspan, *Cambridge Campanion* 166–93.

Bucke, Richard Maurice. *Walt Whitman*. Philadelphia: McKay, 1883.

Burroughs, John. *Notes on Walt Whitman: As Poet and Person*. 2nd ed. New York: Redfield, 1871.

———. *Whitman: A Study*. Boston: Houghton, Mifflin, 1896.

Callow, Philip. *From Noon to Starry Night*. Chicago: Ivan R. Dee, 1992.

Camboni, Marina, ed. *Utopia in the Present Tense: Walt Whitman and the Language of the New World*. Rome: Il Calamo, 1994.

Ceniza, Sherry. "'Being a Woman . . . I Wish to Give My Own View': Some Nineteenth-Century Women's Responses to the 1860 *Leaves of Grass*." Greenspan, *Cambridge Companion* 110–34.

———. "Walt Whitman and Abby Price." *Walt Whitman Quarterly Review* 7 (1989): 49–67.

———. "Whitman and Democratic Women." Kummings, *Approaches to Teaching* 153–58.

Chari, V. K. *Whitman in the Light of Vedantic Mysticism*. Lincoln: U of Nebraska P, 1964.

Clarke, Graham. *Walt Whitman: The Poem as Private History*. New York: St. Martin's, 1991.

Dougherty, James. *Walt Whitman and the Citizen's Eye*. Baton Rouge: Louisiana State UP, 1993.

Eiselein, Gregory. *Literature and Humanitarian Reform in the Civil War Era*. Bloomington: Indiana UP, 1996.

Erkkila, Betsy. *Walt Whitman among the French*. Princeton: Princeton UP, 1980.

———. *Whitman the Political Poet*. New York: Oxford UP, 1989.

Erkkila, Betsy, and Jay Grossman, eds. *Breaking Bounds: Whitman and American Cultural Studies*. New York: Oxford UP, 1995.

Folsom, Ed. "Appearing in Print: Illustrations of the Self in *Leaves of Grass*." Greenspan, *Cambridge Companion* 135–65.

———. "Talking Back to Walt Whitman." *Walt Whitman: The Measure of His Song*. Ed. Jim Perlman, Ed Folsom, and Dan Campion. Minneapolis: Holy Cow!, 1981. xxi–liii.

———. *Walt Whitman's Native Representations*. Cambridge, England: Cambridge UP, 1994.

———, ed. "'This Heart's Geography's Map': The Photographs of Walt Whitman." *Walt Whitman Quarterly Review* 4 (1986–87): 1–76.

———, ed. *Walt Whitman: Centennial Essays*. Iowa City: U of Iowa P, 1994.

Fone, Byrne R. S. *Masculine Landscapes: Walt Whitman and the Homoerotic Text.* Carbondale: Southern Illinois UP, 1992.

Foner, Eric. *Reconstruction: America's Unfinished Revolution.* New York: Harper & Row, 1988.

Forster, E. M. *A Passage to India.* London: E. Arnold, 1924.

Freedman, Florence Bernstein. *William Douglas O'Connor: Walt Whitman's Chosen Knight.* Athens: Ohio UP, 1985.

Gardner, Thomas. *Discovering Ourselves in Whitman.* Urbana: U of Illinois P, 1989.

Gold, Dilys. *A Marriage of True Minds: Walt Whitman to Dora.* London: Regency, 1990.

Greenspan, Ezra. *Walt Whitman and the American Reader.* Cambridge, England: Cambridge UP, 1990.

——, ed. *The Cambridge Companion to "Leaves of Grass."* Cambridge, England: Cambridge UP, 1995.

Grünzweig, Walter. "Adulation and Paranoia: Eduard Bertz's Whitman Correspondence." *The Gissing Journal* 27.3 (1991): 1–20; and 27.4 (1991): 16–35.

——. *Constructing the German Walt Whitman.* Iowa City: U of Iowa P, 1995.

——. *Walt Whitmann* [sic]: *Die deutschsprachige Rezeption als interkulturelles Phänomen.* Munich: Wilhelm Fink, 1991.

Gutman, Huck. *As Others Read Us.* Amherst: U of Massachusetts P, 1991.

Hollis, C. Carroll. *Language and Style in "Leaves of Grass."* Baton Rouge: Louisiana State UP, 1983.

Hutchinson, George. *The Ecstatic Whitman.* Columbus: Ohio State UP, 1985.

——. "Langston Hughes and the 'Other' Whitman." Martin, *Continuing Presence* 16–27.

——. "The Whitman Legacy and the Harlem Renaissance." Folsom, *Centennial Essays* 201–16.

Kanadey. V. R. "Walt Whitman and the Bhagavad Gita." *The Gita in World Literature.* Ed C. D. Verma. New Delhi: Sterling, 1990. 200–213.

Kaplan, Justin. *Walt Whitman: A Life.* New York: Simon & Schuster, 1980.

Karsner, David. *Horace Traubel: His Life and Work.* New York: Arens, 1919.

Killingsworth, M. Jimmie. *The Growth of "Leaves of Grass": The Organic Tradition in Whitman Studies.* Columbia, SC: Camden House, 1993.

——. *Whitman's Poetry of the Body.* Chapel Hill: U of North Carolina P, 1989.

Klammer, Martin. *Whitman, Slavery, and the Emergence of "Leaves of Grass."* University Park: Pennsylvania State UP, 1995.

Krieg, Joann P. "Emory Holloway's Final Word on Whitman's Son." *Walt Whitman Quarterly Review* 10 (1992): 74–80.

Kuebrich, David. *Minor Prophecy.* Bloomington: Indiana UP, 1989.

Kumar, Sudhir. "The *Gita* and Walt Whitman's Mysticism." *India and World Literature.* Ed. Abhai Maurya. New Delhi: Indian Council for Cultural Relations, 1990. 524–34.

Kummings, Donald D., ed. *Approaches to Teaching Whitman's "Leaves of Grass."* New York: Modern Language Association, 1990.

———. *Walt Whitman, 1940–1975: A Reference Guide.* Boston: G. K. Hall, 1982.

LeMaster, J. R., and Donald D. Kummings, eds. *The Walt Whitman Encyclopedia.* New York: Garland, in preparation.

Leon, Philip W. *Walt Whitman and Sir William Osler.* Toronto: ECW, 1995.

Li, Xilao. "Walt Whitman and Asian American Writers." *Walt Whitman Quarterly Review* 10 (1993): 179–94.

Loving, Jerome, ed. *Civil War Letters of George Washington Whitman.* Durham, NC: Duke UP, 1975.

———. *Emerson, Whitman, and the American Muse.* Chapel Hill: U of North Carolina P, 1982.

———. "Emory Holloway and the Quest for Whitman's 'Manhood.'" *Walt Whitman Quarterly Review* 11 (1993): 1–20.

Mancuso, Luke. "'Reconstruction is still in Abeyance': Walt Whitman's *Democratic Vistas* and the Federalizing of National Identity." *ATQ* 8 (1994): 229–50.

———. *The Strange Sad War Revolving: Walt Whitman, Reconstruction, and the Emergence of Black Citizenship.* Columbia, SC: Camden House, 1997.

Martin, Robert K., ed. *The Continuing Presence of Walt Whitman.* Iowa City: U of Iowa P, 1992.

Moon, Michael. *Disseminating Whitman.* Cambridge, MA: Harvard UP, 1991.

Murray, Martin. "'Pete the Great': A Biography of Peter Doyle." *Walt Whitman Quarterly Review* 12 (1994): 1–51.

Myerson, Joel, ed. *The Walt Whitman Archive.* 3 vols. New York: Garland, 1993.

———. *Walt Whitman: A Descriptive Bibliography.* Pittsburgh: U of Pittsburgh P, 1993.

Nambiar, O. K. *Mahayogi Walt Whitman.* Bangalore: Jeevan, 1978.

Nathanson, Tenney. *Whitman's Presence.* New York: New York UP, 1992.

Nolan, James. *Poet-Chief.* Albuquerque: U of New Mexico P, 1994.

Padgett, Ron, ed. *The Teacher & Writers Guide to Walt Whitman.* New York: Teachers & Writers Collaborative, 1991.

Price, Kenneth M. *Whitman and Tradition.* New Haven, CT: Yale UP, 1990.

Reynolds, David S. *Walt Whitman's America.* New York: Knopf, 1995.

Rubin, Joseph Jay. *The Historic Whitman.* University Park: Pennsylvania State UP, 1973.

Schwiebert, John E. *The Frailest Leaves.* New York: Peter Lang, 1992.

Shively, Charley, ed. *Calamus Lovers.* San Francisco: Gay Sunshine, 1987.

———. *Drum Beats*. San Francisco: Gay Sunshine, 1989.

Sweet, Timothy. *Traces of War*. Baltimore: Johns Hopkins UP, 1990.

Thomas, M. Wynn. *The Lunar Light of Whitman's Poetry*. Cambridge, MA: Harvard UP, 1987.

———. "Whitman and the Dreams of Labor." Folsom, *Centennial Essays* 133–52.

Thurin, Erik Ingvar. *Whitman between Impressionism and Expressionism*. Lewisburg, PA: Bucknell UP, 1995.

Trachtenberg, Alan. "The Politics of Labor and the Poet's Work." Folsom, *Centennial Essays* 120–32.

———. *Reading American Photographs*. New York: Hill & Wang, 1989.

Traubel, Horace. *With Walt Whitman in Camden*. Vol. 1. 1905. New York: Rowman & Littlefield, 1961. Vol. 6. Ed. Gertrude Traubel and William White. Carbondale: Southern Illinois UP, 1982. Vol. 7. Ed. Jeanne Chapman and Robert MacIsaac. Carbondale: Southern Illinois UP, 1992. Vols. 8–9. Ed. Jeanne Chapman and Robert MacIsaac. Oregon House, CA: W. L. Bentley, 1996.

Villar Rosa, Manuel, Miguel Martínez López, and Rosa Morillas Sánchez, eds. *Walt Whitman Centennial International Symposium*. Granada: I.C.E., University of Granada, 1992.

Waldron, Randall H., ed. *Mattie: The Letters of Martha Mitchell Whitman*. New York: New York UP, 1977.

Wallace, Ronald. *God Be with the Clown*. Columbia: U of Missouri P, 1984.

Warren, James Perrin. *Walt Whitman's Language Experiment*. University Park: Pennsylvania State UP, 1990.

Whitman, Walt. *Complete Poems & Prose . . . 1855–1888*. Philadelphia: Ferguson Brothers, 1888.

———. *Daybooks and Notebooks*. 3 vols. Ed. William White. New York: New York UP, 1978.

———. *The Early Poems and the Fiction*. Ed. Thomas L. Brasher. New York: New York UP, 1963.

———. *Good-Bye My Fancy*. Philadelphia: David McKay, 1891.

———. *"Leaves of Grass": Comprehensive Reader's Edition*. Ed. Sculley Bradley and Harold W. Blodgett. New York: New York UP, 1965.

———. *"Leaves of Grass": Facsimile Edition of the 1860 Text*. Ed. Roy Harvey Pearce. Ithaca, NY: Cornell UP, 1961.

———. *"Leaves of Grass": The First (1855) Edition*. Ed. Malcolm Cowley. New York: Viking, 1959.

———. *"Leaves of Grass": A Textual Variorum of the Printed Poems*. 3 vols. Ed. Sculley Bradley, Harold W. Blodgett, Arthur Golden, William White. New York: New York UP, 1980.

———. *Notebooks and Unpublished Prose Manuscripts.* 6 vols. Ed. Edward Grier. New York: New York UP, 1984.

———. *November Boughs.* Philadelphia: David McKay, 1888.

———. *Prose Works 1892.* 2 vols. Ed. Floyd Stovall. New York: New York UP, 1963–64.

———. *Two Rivulets.* Camden, NJ: Author's Edition, 1876.

Wilentz, Sean. *Chants Democratic: New York City & the Rise of the American Working Class, 1788–1850.* New York: Oxford UP, 1984.

Zweig, Paul. *Walt Whitman: The Making of the Poet.* New York: Basic Books, 1984.

8

Mark Twain

David E. E. Sloane and Michael J. Kiskis

A number of major efforts verify the power of Mark Twain's canon in 1997; most of these efforts will spark active scholarship and publishing over the next two decades. The most notable of these efforts are two projects to offer Twain's complete works in new editions between 1996 and 2015. Oxford University Press published in the fall of 1996 a twenty-nine-volume edition of the works under the editorship of Shelley Fisher Fishkin, an edition that features introductions by major contemporary writers and thinkers, facsimiles of first editions, and afterwords by prominent Twain scholars. The Mark Twain House in Hartford is tentatively planning to work closely with the edition to produce related educational programs. The massive scholarly undertaking known as the "Mark Twain Project," headquartered at the University of California, Berkeley, under the general editorship of Robert H. Hirst, continues to turn out one of the most ambitious scholarly projects of our era. With annotations and apparatus frequently larger than the texts, the more-than-twenty volumes in print (of a projected seventy-four volumes) offer significant insights into nineteenth-century life; the context and figures involved in Twain's writing; manuscript development, editing, and production; and a variety of related topics. The fourth volume of Twain's *Letters*, the most recent volume to reach print, brings us to only 1871.

Massive amounts of new information will be forthcoming. A volume of newspaper writings from the 1860s and 1870s, edited by Louis Budd, is ready for print but not yet available, and this volume, like a number of other completed volumes now queued for publication, contains material not previously available except to those who actually visited the Mark Twain Project. *Roughing It*, the most recent of Twain's published works to be reprinted, has actually been completely redone from its first appearance as part of this edition in 1972. The 1972 volume, without illustrations, has been replaced by the 1993 facsimile-style volume, with its comic illustrations in place—a change resulting from a courageous but frustrating scholarly decision that reflects the recent shift in American literary scholarship from an emphasis on the text as words alone to an emphasis on the text as a reader-oriented multi-faceted object. The Twain Project's two *Roughing Its*, along with other editions aimed at varied audiences (one thinks of the Rinehart edition, which simply lopped off the eighteen Hawaiian chapters as not integrally related to the American West), could create a cottage industry focusing on changes in an artifact to suit particular audiences, scholarly interpretations, and publishing needs. Space considerations here scarcely allow a full discussion of the unparalleled resources for new study, literary analysis, critical reinterpretation, and source assessment that the remaining fifty volumes will open up to scholars in the next two decades; however, treatments of these and of many other topics in Twain studies, for that matter, appear in the compendious *Mark Twain Encyclopedia* of J. R. LeMaster and James D. Wilson. Related projects such as Louis Budd's two-volume Library of America collection *Mark Twain: Collected Tales, Sketches, Speeches, & Essays* and Tom Quirk's recent anthology *Mark Twain: Tales, Speeches, Essays, and Sketches* will allow for more depth in classroom teaching, response, and analysis of Twain's vitally important shorter works.

The value of more effective intra-disciplinary connections was proven in 1986 when Mark Twain scholars originated the Mark Twain Circle. Of central interest to anyone working in the field, the Circle provides access to major scholars and to new directions in the field. Affiliated publications are the *Mark Twain Circular*, published six times a year from The Citadel under the editorship of James Leonard, and the *Mark Twain Journal*, edited by Tom Tenney, a major source for documentary/biographical scholarship on Twain. Current bibliographies, scholarly notes, notices of new publications, calls for papers, and related matters all flow freely and rapidly through these conduits. In addition, *To Wit* and *Studies in American Humor*, publications of the American Humor Studies Association, bear directly and frequently on Mark Twain studies.

Surfing the Internet also plunges cyberscholars into Twain-related materials. CD-ROM sound/picture/graphic diskettes and various Twain texts accompanied by software finding systems are already available from a number of suppliers. Significant pressure will build to apply hypertext capabilities and multimedia research to the production of

Twain resources; the alternative is to leave both the task and its profitability to nonscholarly producers who may take less care than scholars would. The "Mark Twain Forum," an electronic bulletin board for Twain scholars, has already proven its value: the forum was originated in 1992 by Taylor Roberts at the University of British Columbia, Vancouver, Canada (ROBERTST@UNIXG.UBC.CA). Articles and book reviews are already appearing either exclusively through this medium or in advance of paper publication, and the trend will continue.

A final, yet significant, element in the mix of popular and academic efforts that will increase demands for scholarly work aimed at public presentation is the activity of four separate and independent house museums. The Mark Twain House, at 351 Farmington Avenue in Hartford, Connecticut (John V. Boyer, director) completed during the summer of 1994 a major NEH study of its direction for the twenty-first century—a study that emphasizes interpretation of life, work, and deeds and that allows for a full representation of Twain's effort to rectify racial injustice. Publishing projects, public forums, scholarly readings, and round tables will all be part of the mix. Serving the needs of scholars, secondary school teachers, and the general public, the educational programs of the Mark Twain House will continue the demand for fresh, lively research. Issues of class will be addressed through tighter focus on the Twain family servants, and cultural and technological innovations will be addressed through the study of the mechanics of the house itself. Another major site of scholarly Mark Twain activity is the Center for Mark Twain Studies at Elmira College, Elmira, New York (Gretchen Sharlow, director). The Center for Mark Twain Studies publishes scholarly monographs on Twain's life and family in the crucial 1870–90 period, as well as critical evaluations and major scholarly research on Twain's backgrounds, such as the Washoe experience. Six "Quarry Farm Papers" have been published to date. Summer symposia have treated *Connecticut Yankee* (1989) and "The State of Mark Twain Studies" (1993); a third symposium is being planned for 1997 in honor of the centennial of *Following the Equator*. Finally, the Mark Twain Birthplace in Florida, Missouri, and the Mark Twain Boyhood Home in Hannibal, Missouri, draw large popular audiences. The periodical *The Twainian*, with a fifty-year history, has become a project of the Birthplace Historic Site and the Mark Twain Research Foundation, in company with Hannibal La Grange College. While the Birthplace Historic Site and the Boyhood Home have not as yet involved themselves in major scholarly undertakings, their existence underscores a special obligation of Twain scholars to present Twain to a wide constituency of readers who are not academics but who have a strong interest in Twain and in their own feelings about their encounters with his works.

Popular connections notwithstanding, in the next two decades literary scholarship will become increasingly technical in many interpretive aspects, and Twain scholarship will accommodate itself to this trend, as it has done over the past 120 years with its critical judgments, which, decade by decade, mirror American self-awareness. Mark Twain remains a central figure. In a country where literary figures can take on mythic importance—as did the Fireside Poets Longfellow, Lowell, Whittier, and Holmes in the nineteenth century and Hemingway and Faulkner in the twentieth—perhaps no literary figure but Twain has so come to represent American cultural aspirations and American national identity. He continues to be tugged in so many directions by contending forces arguing belletristic concerns, sexuality/abnormality, and racism as social issues of the later half of the twentieth century. As the twenty-first century dawns, the retrieved *Adventures of Huckleberry Finn* will have been decoded by Vic Doyno, and a host of scholars will explore yet again Twain's stylistics and failure of style, his position as a regionalist-male-white-middle-class-Victorian-repressed-decultured-profit-driven-capital-ist-moral-humorist-author, and the issues of personality and culture that are raised naturally by the extent of his life, works, and self-projection. Because his works directly involve themselves with American foreign policy, Twain will be subject to radical new interpretations as our own critical lens changes; likewise, his personal stance related to the exportation of culture and his moral stance on bankruptcy (financial and moral) will continue to be important. Critics will also continue to critique American experience by mistaking Twain's literary realism for lack of cultural and social insight and by chronicling battles fought to maintain his works in high school curricula. As Brander Matthews wrote of Twain in 1896, such is "The Penalty of Humor": it is always subject to reinterpretation, offense, and misunderstanding.

In coming years, major studies will likely focus on challenging long-held myths about the relationship between Twain and his readers, Twain and his culture, and Mark Twain and Samuel Clemens. Yet, textual studies, biography and autobiography, psychology, and new critical and new historical modes, powered by poststructuralist theories and new biographical and psychological modes of inquiry, may validate traditional ideas. Scholars will struggle with the tendency of myth to influence their studies and run the risk of perpetuating misunderstandings of Twain's canon. Their concerns can be our entryway into how we might "Reset the Context" of textual, biographical, humor, culture, theoretical, and thematic studies. Considerations of such broad interests need to come down to specific critical categories: Twain and Textual Studies, Twain Biography, Twain and Humor, Twain and Cultural Influences, Twain and Literary Theory, and Twain's Values and Thematics. We will take up the six topics in order.

Resetting the Context: Mark Twain and Textual Studies

The biggest news of recent years in Twain circles, in terms of the work that is the leading focus of college English courses and scholarship, was the discovery of the first half of the original manuscript of *Adventures of Huckleberry Finn* in California in 1991, just as Vic Doyno was publishing his intensive work on the manuscript based on the available second half. The discovery was unexpected but not unhoped for; a murder mystery, Julie Smith's *Huckleberry Fiend* (1987), had even been constructed around the possibility. Returned to its intended home at the Buffalo and Erie County Public Library, the manuscript is available for analysis, and Vic Doyno is now following up on his research on the second half of the manuscript in *Writing Huck Finn* (1991) to include the entire document (a brief portion of the manuscript was published in the 3 July 1995 issue of the *New Yorker,* and Random House plans to publish a revised version of the novel that will include Twain's excisions). Walter Blair, the dean of American humor scholars, was, according to our information, saddened at the end of his life by a sense that his work on the California edition of *Huck Finn* had been compromised by the discovery of the new manuscript—as if such a seminal presence as Blair's in American humor and Mark Twain studies could ever be diminished. But his response suggests how much importance Twain scholars attach to the meticulous examination of Twain's language in this most representative of American classics. Happily, Doyno's earlier analysis is being borne out by his later discoveries, and although some of the details of the California *Huck Finn* will require reworking at some future time, the value of Blair's contribution will not be lessened. As the various changes and alterations come into focus, it is clear that Twain did indeed push a less ambitious work toward its major motifs, and Doyno's future work will document this "push" fully. Logically, it follows that new analyses of the text in whole and part will be called for, both in response to Doyno's work and in response to the textual variants. Some of the current discussions that hinge on close interpretations of style at key points will also have to be rethought, and the role and place of Jim in the text will undergo renewed scrutiny. Also, some major rethinking will have to be done on Twain's capability as a stylist, his own pretense to being a "jackleg" novelist now made less tenable by the sheer weight of documentary evidence.

Another force in textual studies is increasing consideration of works that Twain composed during the last two decades of his life, works now reaching their centennials. *Pudd'nhead Wilson* has already benefitted with Gillman and Robinson's *Mark Twain's "Pudd'nhead Wilson": Race, Conflict, and Culture*, published with foresight in 1990; another projected volume of essays awaits publication as *One Hundred Years of "Pudd'nhead Wilson,"* possibly retitled *One Hundred and One Years of "Pudd'nhead Wilson,"* since it has yet to appear. *Huck Finn* studies were boosted by Sattelmeyer and Crowley's *One Hundred Years of "Huckleberry Finn,"* and the centennial impulse will bring us to focus appropriately on *Joan of Arc* (1896), as feminist studies are increasingly brought to bear on Twain, and on *Following the Equator* (1897), at a time of increasing concern with international relations, and so on well into the twenty-first century. The test of the coming twenty years will be to discover new modes of addressing what have previously been dismissed as minor works. Fortunately, Howard Baetzhold and Joseph McCullough's *The Bible According to Mark Twain: Writings on Heaven, Eden, and the Flood,* and related earlier studies of "The Autobiography of Eve" and "Extracts from Adam's Diary," demonstrate that exciting prospects for new research and analysis lie ahead. Considering Twain's wide array of subjects, modes, and genres, study of his short works will clearly be an extraordinarily fruitful ground for cultivation.

Just when the presumption is made that no new news on Mark Twain texts can possibly come forth, Jim Zwick appears with *Mark Twain's Weapons of Satire: Anti-Imperialist Writings on the Philippine-American War* and Shelley Fisher Fishkin asks *Was Huck Black?* Fishkin's work is based on an examination of the influence of African American oral tradition and narrative form on Twain's approach to storytelling, in which "Sociable Jimmy," as portrayed in a previously ignored Twain newspaper account, provides an intriguing cross-cultural link to initiate a wide-ranging study. Zwick offers a truly fresh and imposing collection of

Twain's strongly stated antiwar writings, an important part of Twain's oeuvre at the turn of the last century. (John Kendrick Bangs attacked Twain's "To the Person Sitting in Darkness" as traitorous at that time, and Hal Holbrook brought a shiver rippling down the spines of viewers when he offered a program including Twain's antiwar material during the Vietnam era on CBS.) For Twain, the texts themselves will always speak to Americans of our central issues. With all due apologies to Eugene Angert, who asked if Mark Twain were dead in 1909, new students of the works generated in a supposedly "dead" period of creativity will amaze us as they bring forth this material in new and timely ways. Furthermore, it is highly promising that attention to the Nevada newspaper writing and the early letters is being facilitated by the Mark Twain Project's publication schedule. Personal correspondence had a still unacknowledged infuence on Twain's storytelling. We have not yet begun to explore Twain's use of private writing as rehearsal; the letters, journals, and notebooks deserve a deeper look. Of special interest to composition and literary studies will be the recursiveness of the writing process and the symbiotic relationship between audience and author and between personal and public writing. Further work in reader response criticism and statistical work in reading-related topics in schools could spread outside of English studies into the field of education as well.

Resetting the Context: Mark Twain Biography

Complicity in setting personal, academic, and public perceptions of Mark Twain is an important issue for Twain biography. In the future, scholars are likely to step back from the icon that is Mark Twain—unless they intend to advance the study of it as icon, as Louis Budd did, for example, in *Our Mark Twain*. Albert Bigelow Paine, Van Wyck Brooks, and Bernard DeVoto established adversarial positions that nobly attempted to present an "American" character, not without self-interested bias, especially in Paine's case, where Twain's reputation was viewed as a commercial property. Twain himself was not above a sort of complicity with his critics: his pretense to being a "jackleg" in the preface to *Those Extraordinary Twins* actually downplayed a remarkable literary exercise in construction and imagination that has yet to be fully understood in its relation to *Pudd'nhead Wilson* in the 1894 first edition, or in relation to our own contemporary debates regarding so-called "political correctness" (in this case, it is not race that is at issue, but, rather, deformity and human abnormality). A better understanding of how Twain creates images and ideologies would do much to help us elucidate how scholarship, public policy, social movements, and interest groups reinforce and break traditions. New historicism, among other theoretical impulses militating in this direction, argues for careful study of the ideological underpinnings of literature and other cultural forces. As a matter of American iconography, too, Twain and his readers maintained a kind of complicity in visualizing American agendas. Scholars including James Zwick and Peter Messent have recently begun nibbling at related questions in informative ways. Recent analyses of Twain's psychology from Freudian, Jungian, and existential positions likewise show him in a tortured relationship with himself, a view that will continue to provoke. As critical paradigms shift, Twain and his canon will probably come into clearer focus. The great danger, of course, is that new critical templates will merely proliferate doctrinal positions that misapply ideology to Twain's protean personality and vision.

Biographical studies of Mark Twain, and of his works through his life, have always been driven by the critics' cultural agendas, from the landmark studies of Brooks's *The Ordeal of Mark Twain* through Justin Kaplan's Pulitzer Prize–winning *Mr. Clemens and Mark Twain*, passing to a more somber note in Hamlin Hill's *Mark Twain: God's Fool*. The early 1990s have seen an explosion of biographical work. Jeffrey Steinbrink's *Getting to Be Mark Twain* explores microscopically the formative period of 1869 to 1872, giving us more opportunity to speculate on the early development of Twain's career just as the Poe and Melville *Log* books allow us to regard the early development of those authors' careers. The Kiskis revision of *Mark Twain's Own Autobiography*, a reproduction of the *North American Review* 1906–7 chapters, brings some clarity to that tortuous construction project of self-discovery. Laura Skandera-Trombley's examination of the feminist, familial, and local influences on Twain, *Mark Twain in the Company of Women*, introduces a balanced feminist approach to the paradoxes of Twain as a male author. What remains? Virtually all major Twain scholars, and especially the most thoughtful of the recent biographers, see major opportunities for examining periods of Twain's life. Two full-length biographies are in process, by Andrew Hoffman and Fred Kaplan, even while the focus of biographical studies seems to be shifting toward concentrated explorations of limited facets and periods.

To the works by Steinbrink and Skandera-Trombley might be added works by Miriam Shillingsburg, Carl Dolmetsch, and John Cooley.

Bringing forth the available documents coherently will throw more light on Twain himself, on his works, on the culture in which he lived, and on American expectations for self and society. No *Twain Log* exists, but the California edition footnotes represent one, and the Mark Twain House and other interpreters of Twain have assembled as many day-by-day records as possible, but this item is an isolated lacuna. As a role-player of awesome proportions, Twain projected himself beyond normal boundaries, but had an array of needs and perspectives that deserve far more thoughtful examination than has been possible to the present. Gonzo scholarship is potentially dangerous in this area, with a variety of specialized distortions waiting to be put forth by advocates of special causes: the brief flap over the possibility of Twain having homoerotic experiences and the more wide-ranging claims of Twain's "cultural racism" are the most obvious examples. However, documentary developments will ultimately enforce critical accuracy. As volumes of newspaper clippings and unrepublished work appear in the California edition, scholars will be better able to look at Twain as a popular writer drawn to topics of his day and one who sometimes complicates his portrait by seeming inconsistent. For example, analysts will have to come to grips with his capacity for expressing the irony of allowing women only low-paying jobs as schoolteachers—a practice that he clearly recognized as sexual discrimination, even though he was unenthusiastic about female suffrage and began a series of comic newspaper items in St. Louis in 1867 by attacking the suffrage movement. Properly understood in the context of Victorian ideality, such a contradiction will illuminate a complex set of desires of the era that new scholarship is approaching gingerly but with increasing insistence. The publication of other Twain material, including letters often unseen because they lie in individual hands, will further enhance scholarly understanding.

Resetting the Context: Mark Twain and Humor

It was not so long ago that literary scholars preferred, oddly enough, to distance themselves from Mark Twain the comedian and joke maker—David Sloane's *Mark Twain as a Literary Comedian* was reviewed by one scholar as focusing a good deal on Artemus Ward, whom many would prefer to minimize as a minor literary indiscretion in Twain's life rather than acknowledge as a major influence. Pascal Covici's admirable *Mark Twain's Humor* blazed a valuable trail that was not to be obliterated. Yet studies that see major comparatist possibilities between Twain and other humorists and literary comedians are still needed, and few scholars seem to be carrying out such enterprises. These efforts require an immersion in nineteenth-century American popular culture, including newspaper sources and periodical texts that are frequently not easy to locate and are often in brittle, large-binding files that resist skimming and hamper note-taking; frankly, the ease of using already-identified research materials provided in neat folders of rare manuscripts may have discouraged a full and fair analysis of how Twain differs from other practitioners of his era. Doesticks (Mortimer Thomson), whom Twain knew, and who was a major presence in the late 1850s, wrote and published extensively in New York newspapers until his death in 1873: what a rich comparatist opportunity for humor studies he presents. But who will go through the files of the *New York Weekly* and the *New York Mercury* and do the other research on such a minor figure to make such a study possible? Josh Billings wrote aphorisms and published *Allminax*, which Twain once thought of mimicking, but only several short articles have compared the two writers and their careers. A major comparison of Twain and Marrietta Holley, a most obvious female humorist counterpart, would be useful (though, frankly, the level of analysis on Holley will have to rise to the task). At several recent conferences, scholars have argued that we must not overlook Twain's status as a humorist and popular writer, and that a failure to include this component in serious analyses was skewing the findings in critical ways. Studies of Twain run the risk always, of course, of falling too far in the direction of seriousness (losing the crucial importance of Twain as a popular humorist) or too far in the direction of the disingenuous "jackleg" interpretation that has successfully muddied scholarship otherwise more capable of detecting Twain's irony. Harry Wonham's useful discussion of the major works via the American tall tale in *Mark Twain and the Art of the Tall Tale* exemplifies one recent approach to Twain's humor. Bruce Michelson's *Mark Twain on the Loose: A Comic Writer and the American Self* opens up another path for exploration.

Increasingly, scholars will be pushed to place themselves in a comparatist framework with regard to previous scholarship. A major book on Twain as humorous social critic could offer a serious critical analysis by reviewing the array of criticism, now available in a double handful of critical anthologies, several specifically on *Huck Finn*, some more generally on Mark Twain as writer and humorist, and chronologically listed in Thomas Tenney's *Mark Twain: A Reference Guide* (now updated regularly in the *Mark Twain Circular*). A sense of the development of a scholarly tradition, however, would be more than welcome. The possibilities for comparative studies, though, remain daunting. A single brief article comparing Twain and Trowbridge constitutes the entire analytic attention to two major presences in children's literature—a serious book-length study of the parallel careers would throw light not only on their literature but also on their positions as representatives of caste, class, and culture in Victorian America; an important scholarly task begs for proper completion here. Extremely important, as well, is the need to compare foreign perceptions of Twain's humor with our own. James Papp recently presented a discussion of translations of *Adventures of Huckleberry Finn* at the American Humor Studies Association/Mark Twain Circle Conference on American Humor (Cancun, 1994) and showed that the distortions of the text had reached alarming proportions. Should Huck and Jim's dialect, for example, be presented for European readers in Gypsy argot? Comparing texts and cultures, can we see a real danger in the world's perception of Americans? Furthermore, given the limited language training now available in American education at any level, where will scholars be found who are competent to bring us the news of distortion and to correct the record nationally and internationally? For the right scholar, a lifelong task exists here. Or, perhaps, only a widely based consortium of international scholars could bring about such an elaborate undertaking with success. An increasing number of American Studies programs at major and minor international universities will add impetus to this study and its relative importance in the hierarchy of Mark Twain scholarship.

Alita Kelley, at the same conference, made a further point that came as thought-provoking news to Twainiacs and humor scholars. Kelley, whose work has focused on translating foreign humorists like Bryce Echenique into accurate American English texts, pointed out that although Twain was freely discussed as a humorist abroad and although his standing as a comic writer had always been recognized internationally, a writer like Cervantes is not similarly recognized as a humorist in Spanish scholarship. The task remains for us to find out how Twain represents humor as a specialized American response to the world. Implications for cross-cultural studies of humor are, it seems, wide-ranging, and present scholars with genuine opportunities.

Resetting the Context: Mark Twain and Cultural Influences

If we are to look more closely at the critical traditions informing work on Twain, we might also explore a variety of collaborative relationships. Over the past seventy years, a valuable array of individual source studies has related Twain to other authors, but many of these source studies ought to be reviewed and restated. Pertinently, Horst Kruse and David Ketterer in two closely related articles in the *Mark Twain Journal* reviewed and updated charges of plagiarism against Twain regarding *A Connecticut Yankee*—charges made by literary comedian Max Adeler and initially documented as evidence of a source influence by Edward F. Foster. Lawrence Berkove's *Ethical Records of Twain and His Circle of Sagebrush Journalists* added to and reinterpreted the history of Twain, Dan DeQuille, and others of the Washoe years, 1862–64, broadening the range of characters/participants. Ethical and social insights of increasing sophistication come out of such work, and detailed historical study has matured since the original researchers identified characters and described biographical relations in a supposedly objective narrative. Over the next twenty years, many pockets of Twain's life will be further explored in this fashion, from Hartford socializing and intellectualizing to Elmira summers to New York literati and club life and foreign lionizing.

Mark Twain was a natural collaborator—as perhaps are more writers than we presume—and he used many sources and persons for inspiration. To accomplish his work, he used people around him, such as "Mother" Fairbanks, who was employed to help confirm his direction in his Quaker City letters. He used groups; Laura Skandera-Trombley argues that his use of the women in his family during the Quarry Farm summer writing campaigns brought them almost to the level of co-authors. Studies of Twain's "product" are sure to touch on collaboration, and a measurement of their success will lie in the degree of sophistication they bring to the discussion; we can hope that the argument over Mark Twain's repression or self-suppression will be modified from absolute judgments to a more complex understanding of the interplay of the human mind and emotions. "Corn Pone Opinions" tells us that Twain recognized the problem, and it should answer those critics who think he did not do "enough" to fight racism, when, in fact, he was consummately effective in establishing and helping to realize expectations regarding equality of race. More will certainly need to be done with Twain's relations with Howells, Twichell very definitely, H. H. Rogers, and others. We need a more careful consideration of the careers of Twain and Warner and, especially, of Twain and Harte. Good short essays have been done, but major cultural-biographical inquiries would be valuable; certainly H. S. Canby's work on James and Twain shows that such studies can be of lasting value. The beginning stages of extended work on Twain's family and its influence on his writing is evident in two or three scholarly books of the last two years, notably Steinbrink's and Skandera-Trombley's, and discovering how various separations and deaths pushed Twain into new creative pathways will supply analysts with a challenge. At the same time, literary source analysts benefitting from Alan Gribben's *Mark Twain's Library: A Reconstruction* and its projected supplement have a universe of almost untouched secondary material to review in relation to special topics and selected works.

On such a broad stage, recent work by Peter Stonely, J. D. Stahl, and Randall Knopper demonstrates the movement toward understanding Twain more fully within the context of United States and European culture. Gregg Camfield has entered by the portico of the Scottish School of philosophy (prominent in America in the 1840–60 period), and it seems highly likely that similar good studies can come out of other perspectives. The work now integrating Twain within the broad study of sentimentalism, gender definition, women's rights, and oral-literary performance really appears to be at the beginning rather than the concluding stages of exploration. Critical demands on Twain to be our "greatest" writer tend to place him outside of the dynamics and constraints of real cultural boundaries, and critics must work earnestly to restore balance. As a writer, Twain proclaimed, "Training is everything," yet our scholarship—to an unprecedented extent—has treated him as immune from his own background. Readers who notice and read Louis Budd's "Chronology," at the end of the Library of America collected tales volume, however, will be impressed with the solidity of detail showing a "life" in progress. American egalitarianism as an influence could be nicely revisited using further background documentation from the period in light of new historical principles. Carl Dolmetsch in *"Our Famous Guest": Mark Twain in Vienna* explores another of those rich but relatively unknown pockets of Twain's life to bring insights into the possible influences on his late "pessimism," underscoring how much biographical commonplaces about Twain have limited our thinking about the cultural motivations influencing his thinking as a "sterner realist" or naturalist author.

Another area where new thinking is called for is in Twain's attitudes toward class, race, and related issues. Louis Budd, in *Mark Twain, Social Philosopher*, and Philip Foner, in *Mark Twain, Social Critic*, explored political and class beliefs intelligently and informatively, but a new generation of scholars will want to revisit these concerns in light of changing social concepts. They will find the earlier work excellently done, but they will also find different terminologies that they may wish to apply. The specter of class hung solidly over Twain throughout his career as a writer. He was concerned with authority; with establishing himself in the literary elite; and with literacy, social and economic inadequacy, sexual differentiation, memories of his father and childhood poverty, and themes basic to the human condition, but in ways that sometimes openly and sometimes covertly deepened or darkened his canon. Along with Twain's attitudes toward Native Americans, his attitudes toward class remain obscure. Twain's writings on race are likely to continue to generate a subindustry in the field. We hope that the obvious racial compassion in Twain will come to figure more strongly in the thinking of those who seek to use Twain as a whipping boy for the very ills he sought to mitigate. Fishkin's *Was Huck Black?* and Leonard, Tenney, and Davis's *Satire or Evasion? Black Perspectives on "Huckleberry Finn"* certainly provide a base for further work. The most fearsome challenge here is likely to come from racists outside the academy who would like to kill the messenger—Twain—for the message he brings—that racism is endemic in American and world experience.

Resetting the Context: Mark Twain and Literary Theory

Literary theory has been applied to Twain scholarship in relatively fewer instances than it has been for some other authors, although approaches like Susan Gillman's immediately come to mind. Bakhtin and others, however, have been applied in article-length studies such as Peter Messent's "The Clash of Language: Bakhtin and *Huckleberry Finn*" with interesting results. Still, the number of Twain studies explicitly employing literary theory remains small. The explanation is partly that humor theory has been around for a much longer time, partly that Twain's canon is extraordinarily varied, and partly that a lot of what has been derived from theoretical approaches has been said in some form by a wide array of critics who have already worked over parts of the Twain canon, most notably *Huck Finn.*

We should also remember that humor studies as a generic field has been interested in theoretical issues from its beginnings. We have Hobbes on laughter, and Freud, Meredith, and Bergson, all providing frameworks for study that sometimes overlap with postmodern approaches. To a modest extent, where theorists now wish to go, many students of humor have already been. Budd and Foner were contextualizing in the 1960s; Blair, Gerber, Hill, Rogers, and Henry Nash Smith were discussing (although not with the oppressive nomenclature that renders so much modern critical writing stilted and impenetrable) festival disunity, psychosocial archetypes, and cultural projection, building on work begun well before them. Maria Ornella Marotti's *The Duplicating Imagination* ought to be a good place to begin thinking, with its fresh look at previously unpublished manuscripts of the late period.

Much of the genuinely new in theoretical approaches will still find arresting parallels with critical discourse from the period of Twain's original authorship. New Historicist and Postcolonialist studies, in conjunction with psycho-intellectual studies, offer new windows on old material; however, the labeling of Twain as a boor or a carpetbagger by British and Southern romantic critics in the 1870–90 period presaged some more recent viewpoints. Articles approaching Twain and feminist issues appeared as early as the 1920s. Mythic and historical approaches in Twain studies began with the Mississippi River—deified by Lionel Trilling as the "great brown god" of *Huck Finn.* In his own period, Twain's name was regularly mapped along the Mississippi and along the mountain ranges of the Western Slope, the Washoe motherload country that he immortalized in *Roughing It.* As a regionalist, he was thus identified with the American frontier mythos. The frontier myth, though, has been questioned in contemporary approaches: Huck Finn has been assessed as a child of alcoholic parents and psychoanalyzed as a patient; Twain's "nigger wench" dream has been treated to Freudian and Jungian interpretations; the social novels centered in his own era and in the South have been analyzed as representations of linguistic complexity and the determinacy and indeterminacy of language. As much dynamism exists in the theoretical approaches to Twain as in any other area of Twain studies. Twain's view of American Indians, of course, was jaundiced, and postcolonialist critics note his wavering in *Following the Equator,* though

Cameron Nickels recently presented to the American Humor/Mark Twain Conference remarkable notes on Congo reformer Diedwo Twei's seeking Twain's help circa 1906–10 (the notes were derived from the folk archives of the Library of Congress rather than from a Twain source). Domestic and community perspectives on Twain will draw more interest because they fuse American Studies issues with literary analysis and biography. Twain's home was a model of Victorian domestic life; the doings of his family, servants, children, cousins, sister and brother-in-law are significant topics driven by The Mark Twain House in Hartford and the Center for Mark Twain Studies at Elmira.

Anniversary studies of various Twain dates and works occur naturally, climaxing, one would think, with Twain's death in 1910. Anniversary studies might be extended to secondary works or editions, especially those like Paine's 1912 biography and Paine and Duneka's fraudulent 1916 *Mysterious Stranger*. This last text, as a false construction, is a feast for deconstructionists of all sorts. *Following the Equator*, already mentioned as a piece of colonialist discourse, is both a failed work and a problem in confused perspectives. This book will command more attention from analysts of the "fluid text," where the artifact is in a process of becoming, moderated by the writer's experience, his writing, his publisher's intention, and his public's response. *Following the Equator* has the potential of becoming a study of importance when examined with these multiple concerns in view. Furthermore, a variety of hotly contended shorter works was published in the 1895–1910 period: strongly stated visionary positions about American racism and colonialism need to be moved to the forefront of the study of this period. These works call out for vigorous discussion, analysis of public response, and broadly intelligent discussion and revision.

Resetting the Context: Mark Twain's Values and Thematics

Definitions of community have always been a vital part of Twain scholarship, in terms of both his own personal circle and the projection of the image of communities of people in his writings. The notion of community as an image is spread through Twain's writing from the "boys" of *Innocents Abroad* to the stagedrivers and miners of *Roughing It* to the pilots in *Life on the Mississippi*: "By the Shadow of Death, but he's a lightning pilot" represents in its elliptical grandeur an entire professional ethic underpinning our civilization. Huck and Jim's raft, Hank Morgan's final pleas across time to Sandy and Hello Central, Stormfield's attempt to understand heaven and Scotty Briggs's attempt to understand the preacher, even the ramble of the *Autobiography* are all inquiries into and representations of the communal undertakings that provide individuals with the real benefits of human congress and civilization. As much as America is the land of the individual and Twain is a spokesman for the isolated hero like Huck or Hank or Pudd'nhead Wilson, Twain's writings show a deep-seated human longing for involvement at the communal level. The socially oriented criticism of the 1950s and 1960s caused us to see Twain as a sharp critic of communities, and so he clearly is in "Hadleyburg" and other stories, but it will be immensely useful to explore the values Twain wished for and hoped to find, and expressed in various ways in the matter of Hannibal and slavery—considerations readily available in *Mark Twain's Hannibal, Huck & Tom*—or in the suppressed chapter of *Life on the Mississippi* on the North and the South. Community might be seen in visionary, literary, political, and personal terms; it might involve the notion of the "professional" in America— pilot, newspaperman, doctor, clergyman, lawyer. With each new dimension, we may add new opportunities for thorough literary and contextual analysis, and the way has been prepared by earlier topical studies. Community might be interpreted as positive, negative, or ambiguous. Ultimately, community leads us to compassion because, at its most effective, intimate, and personal, it is evident in the community of two, Huck and Jim.

At the end of all our studies must lie the recognition that both the positive and negative sides of Twain were mobilized by intense compassion for the plight of suffering humanity; his humor and his visionary writing enabled him to state his compassion in popular literature, irrespective of or despite his personal faults and failings. The image of the irascible misanthrope that the later writings suggest—and which their publication at the chronological front-end of the California edition of Twain's works has furthered to some extent—should not obscure the central role of compassion in his stories and novels, let alone its explicit presentation in early essays, like the one on Vanderbilt (*Packard's Monthly*, 1869) or his later writing on King Leopold after the turn of the century. Edgar Branch's collections of Twain's very earliest cub reporting show evidence of a motivating compassion in Twain's intellectual makeup. Twain's heroes are more interested in the bonds of relation than in open-ended freedom, though the latter has been seen as their defining characteristic during the past fifty years. Twain's compassionate humanity is involved in his concept of American democracy as it was developed in the 1850s and 1860s, and more studies can investigate from our current perspective how American culture might have influenced him. Twain's nonfiction aims at expanding the circle of human interest and caring as the author expresses political ideals and objectives in his anti-imperialist writings and his autobiography; his compassion for the victims of injustice—racial and social alike—motivated his canon. All of this may lead us to a more accurate and complicated image of the man behind Mark Twain, an image that eludes specialists and casual readers alike—and certainly eluded those minority students at Greater Hartford (Connecticut) Community College in 1994 who objected to renaming their college after Twain because he "did not speak to them," a tragic commentary on the failure of American education to reach a growing proportion of our citizenry.

WORKS CITED

Angert, Eugene. "Is Mark Twain Dead?" *North American Review* (September 1909): 319–29.

Baetzhold, Howard, and Joseph McCullough. *The Bible According to Mark Twain: Writings on Heaven, Eden, and the Flood.* Athens: U of Georgia P, 1995.

Baetzhold, Howard, Joseph McCullough, and Donald Malcolm. "Mark Twain's Eden/Flood Parable: 'The Autobiography of Eve.'" *American Literary Realism* 24 (1991): 23–38.

Bangs, John Kendrick. "Is the Philippine Policy of the Administration Just?—Yes." *Harper's Weekly* (9 Feb. 1901): 155. Rpt. in Sloane, *Mark Twain's Humor* 496–503.

Berkove, Lawrence. *Ethical Records of Twain and His Circle of Sagebrush Journalists* (Quarry Farm Papers #5). Elmira, NY: Center for Mark Twain Studies, 1994.

Branch, Edgar M. *The Literary Apprenticeship of Mark Twain.* Urbana: U of Illinois P, 1950.

Brooks, Van Wyck. *The Ordeal of Mark Twain.* New York: E. P. Dutton, 1920.

Budd, Louis J. *Mark Twain, Social Philosopher.* Bloomington: Indiana UP, 1962
———. *Our Mark Twain: The Making of His Public Personality.* Philadelphia: U of Pennsylvania P, 1983.

————, ed. *Mark Twain: Collected Tales, Sketches, Speeches, and Essays*. 2 vols. New York: Library of America, 1992.

Camfield, Gregg. *Sentimental Twain: Samuel Clemens in the Maze of Moral Philosophy*. Philadelphia: U of Pennsylvania P, 1994.

Canby, Henry S. *Turn West, Turn East: Mark Twain and Henry James*. Boston: Houghton Mifflin, 1951.

Coleman, Rufus A. "Trowbridge and Clemens." *Modern Language Quarterly* 9 (1948): 216–23.

Cooley, John, ed. *Mark Twain's Aquarium: The Samuel Clemens Angelfish Correspondence, 1905–1910*. Athens: U of Georgia P, 1991.

Covici, Pascal. *Mark Twain's Humor*. Dallas, TX: Southern Methodist UP, 1962.

DeVoto, Bernard. *Mark Twain's America*. Boston: Little, Brown, 1932.

Dolmetsch, Carl. *"Our Famous Guest": Mark Twain in Vienna*. Athens: U of Georgia P, 1992.

Doyno, Victor. *Writing Huck Finn*. Philadelphia: U of Pennsylvania P, 1991.

Fishkin, Shelley Fisher. *Was Huck Black?* New York: Oxford UP, 1993.

Foner, Philip S. *Mark Twain: Social Critic*. New York: International Pubs., 1958.

Foster, Edward F. *"A Connecticut Yankee* Anticipated: Max Adeler's *Fortunate Island*." *Ball State University Forum* 9 (1968): 73–76. Rpt. in Sloane, *Mark Twain's Humor* 265–70.

Gillman, Susan. *Dark Twins: Imposture and Identity in Mark Twain's America*. Chicago: U of Chicago P, 1989.

Gillman, Susan, and Forrest Robinson, eds. *Mark Twain's "Pudd'nhead Wilson": Race, Conflict, and Culture*. Durham, NC: Duke UP, 1990.

Gribben, Alan. *Mark Twain's Library: A Reconstruction*. Boston: G. K. Hall, 1980.

Hill, Hamlin. *Mark Twain: God's Fool*. New York: Harper & Row, 1973.

Holbrook, Hal. *Mark Twain Tonight*, CBS New York: 6 March 1967.

Jones, Joseph. "Josh Billings: Some Yankee Notions of Humor." *University of Texas Studies in English* 43 (1943): 148–61.

Kaplan, Justin. *Mr. Clemens and Mark Twain*. New York: Simon & Schuster, 1966.

Kelley, Alita. "Linguistic Affinities: Translating Bryce Echenique's Humor for the Reader in English." Paper presented at the American Literature Association/Mark Twain Circle Conference on American Humor. Cancun, Mexico. 10 December 1994.

Kesterson, David B. "The Mark Twain-Josh Billings Friendship." *Mark Twain Journal* 18 (1975–76): 5–9.

Ketterer, David. "'The Fortunate Island' by Max Adeler: Its Publication History and *A Connecticut Yankee*." *Mark Twain Journal* 29 (1991): 28–32.

Knopper, Randall. *Acting Naturally: Mark Twain in the Culture of Performance.* Berkeley: U of California P, 1995.

Kruse, Horst. "Literary Old Offenders: Mark Twain, John Quill, Max Adeler and Their Plagiarism Duels." *Mark Twain Journal* 29 (1991): 10–27.

LeMaster, J. R., and James D. Wilson, eds. *The Mark Twain Encyclopedia.* New York: Garland, 1993.

Leonard, James S., Thomas Tenney, and Thadious M. Davis. *Satire or Evasion? Black Perspectives on "Huckleberry Finn."* Durham, NC: Duke UP, 1992.

Marotti, Maria Ornella. *The Duplicating Imagination: Twain and the Twain Papers.* University Park: Pennsylvania State UP, 1990.

Matthews, Brander. "The Penalty of Humor." *Harpers Monthly* (May 1896): 897–900.

McCullough, Joseph. "Mark Twain's First Chestnut: Revisions in 'Extracts from Adam's Diary.'" *Essays in Arts and Sciences* 23 (1994): 49–58.

Messent, Peter. "The Clash of Language: Bakhtin and *Huckleberry Finn.*" *New Readings of the American Novel: Narrative Theory and Its Applications.* Ed. Peter Messent. New York: St. Martin's, 1990. 204–42; 310–15.

Michelson, Bruce. *Mark Twain on the Loose: A Comic Writer and the American Self.* Amherst: U of Massachusetts P, 1995.

Nickels, Cameron. "Mark Twain: An Offbeat International Interview." American Humor Studies Association/ Mark Twain Circle Conference on American Humor. Cancun, Mexico. 10 December 1994.

Paine, Albert Bigelow. *Mark Twain: A Biography.* 3 vols. New York: Harper & Bros., 1912.

Papp, James. "*Huck Finn*: From Communist to Post-Communist in Central Europe." American Humor Studies Association/ Mark Twain Circle Conference on American Humor. Cancun, Mexico. 10 December 1994.

Quirk, Thomas, ed. *Mark Twain: Tales, Speeches, Essays, and Sketches.* New York: Penguin, 1994.

Sattelmeyer, Robert, and J. Donald Crowley. *One Hundred Years of "Huckleberry Finn": The Boy, His Book, and American Cuture.* Columbia: U of Missouri P, 1985.

Shillingsburg, Miriam Jones. *At Home Abroad: Mark Twain in Australasia.* Jackson: U of Mississippi P, 1988.

Skandera-Trombley, Laura E. *Mark Twain in the Company of Women.* Philadelphia: U of Pennsylvania P, 1994.

Sloane, David E. E. *Mark Twain as a Literary Comedian.* Baton Rouge: Louisiana State UP, 1979.

———, ed. *Mark Twain's Humor: Critical Essays.* New York: Garland, 1993.

Smith, Julie. *Huckleberry Fiend.* New York: The Mysterious Press, 1987.

Stahl, J. D. *Mark Twain, Culture and Gender: Envisioning America through Europe.* Athens: U of Georgia P, 1994.

Steinbrink, Jeffrey. *Getting to Be Mark Twain.* Berkeley: U of California P, 1991.

Stoneley, Peter. *Mark Twain and the Feminine Aesthetic.* New York: Cambridge UP, 1992.

Tenney, Thomas, ed. *Mark Twain: A Reference Guide.* Boston: G. K. Hall, 1976.

Twain, Mark (Samuel L. Clemens). *Adventures of Huckleberry Finn.* Ed. Walter Blair and Victor Fischer. Berkeley: U of California P, 1988.

———. *A Connecticut Yankee in King Arthur's Court.* Ed. Bernard L. Stein. Berkeley: U of California P, 1979.

———. "Corn Pone Opinions." *Europe and Elsewhere.* Ed. A. B. Paine. Vol. 20. Authorized Edition of *The Complete Works of Mark Twain.* New York: Harper & Bros., 1923, 399–406. Rpt. in Budd, *Collected Tales, Sketches, Speeches, and Essays 1891–1910.* 507–11.

———. *Following the Equator.* Hartford: American Publishing Co., 1897.

———. *Innocents Abroad.* Hartford: American Publishing Co., 1869.

———. "Jim and the Dead Man." *New Yorker* (3 July 1995): 129–30.

———. "King Leopold's Soliloquy: A Defense of his Congo Rule." Boston: P. R. Warren Co., 1905. Rpt. in Budd, *Collected Tales, Sketches, Speeches, and Essays 1891–1910.* 661–85.

———. *Life on the Mississippi.* Boston: James R. Osgood, 1883.

———. "The Man That Corrupted Hadleyburg." *Harpers New Monthly Magazine* (December 1899). Rpt. in Budd, *Collected Tales, Sketches, Speeches, & Essays 1891–1910.* 390–438.

———. *Mark Twain's Autobiography.* Ed. A. B. Paine. New York: Harper & Bros., 1924.

———. *Mark Twain's Hannibal, Huck & Tom.* Ed. Walter Blair. Berkeley: U of California P, 1969.

———. *Mark Twain's Letters, Volume 1: 1853–1866.* Ed. Edgar Marques Branch, Michael B. Frank, and Kenneth M. Sanderson. Berkeley: U of California Press, 1988.

———. *Mark Twain's Letters, Volume 2: 1867–1868.* Ed. Harriet Elinor Smith and Richard Bucci. Berkeley: U of California Press, 1990.

———. *Mark Twain's Letters, Volume 3: 1869.* Ed. Victor Fischer and Michael B. Frank. Berkeley: U of California Press, 1992.

———. *Mark Twain's Letters, Volume 4: 1870–1871.* Ed. Victor Fischer, Michael B. Frank, and Lin Salamo. Berkeley: U of California P, 1995.

———. *Mark Twain's "Mysterious Stranger" Manuscripts.* Ed. William M. Gibson. Berkeley: U of California P, 1969.

———. *Mark Twain's Own Autobiography: The Chapters from the "North American Review."* Ed. Michael J. Kiskis. Madison: U of Wisconsin P, 1990.

————. *The Mysterious Stranger. A Romance.* Ed. Albert Bigelow Paine and Frederick Duneka. New York and London: Harper & Bros., 1916.

————. "Open Letter of Commodore Vanderbilt." *Packard's Monthly* (March 1869). Rpt. in Budd, *Collected Tales, Sketches, Speeches, & Essays 1852–1890.* 285–90.

————. *The Oxford Mark Twain.* Ed. Shelley Fisher Fishkin. 29 vols. New York: Oxford UP, 1996.

————. *Personal Recollections of Joan of Arc.* New York: Harper & Bros., 1896.

————. *Roughing It.* Ed. Rodman W. Paul. New York: Holt, Rinehart & Winston, 1953.

————. *Roughing It.* 1972. Ed. Harriet Elinor Smith and Edgar Margues Branch. Berkeley: U of California P, 1993.

————. "The Suppressed Passages." *Life on the Mississippi.* New York: Heritage Press, 1944. 383–418.

————. *The Tragedy of Pudd'nhead Wilson and the Comedy of Those Extraordinary Twins.* Hartford: American Publishing Co., 1894.

Wonham, Harry. *Mark Twain and the Art of the Tall Tale.* New York: Oxford UP, 1993.

Zwick, James. *Mark Twain's Weapons of Satire: Anti-Imperialist Writings on the Philippine-American War.* Syracuse, NY: Syracuse UP, 1992.

9

Henry James

Daniel Mark Fogel

Nearly four years ago, in an introduction to a volume of original essays on Henry James by many hands, I observed that the sixties, seventies, and eighties had witnessed a spectacular avalanche of critical and scholarly work on James. While noting that the best of this work ran the gamut from traditional literary scholarship to dazzling poststructuralist criticism, I would at the time have judged that the most important and enduring recent work on James was critical and heavily theoretical as opposed to scholarly and preponderantly empirical. Six months after the publication of *A Companion to Henry James Studies*, however, students of Henry James from around the world gathered in New York City for two sesquicentennial conferences commemorating the novelist's birth there 150 years before, and the consensus among the extraordinarily diverse community convened for the occasion would perhaps have tilted the balance the other way, at least prospectively. The prospects that most intensively engaged participants in the Henry James Sesquicentennial were, first, the pursuit of a long-awaited, long-deferred complete edition of James's correspondence, and, second, the scholarship—principally, though to be sure not exclusively, biographical—that might follow on the publication of a complete letters.

Some 150 years after James's birth, and some 80 years after his death, there is still a great deal of work to be done in textual editing and in providing for the availability of basic primary documents. This particular prospect and need will no doubt astonish some readers, for James has been a high canonical author almost since his anointment as a "great" writer by William Dean Howells before James's long career was two decades old. But while his novels and tales are available in a variety of celebrated editions—his own New York Edition of the *Novels and Tales of*

Henry James, Percy Lubbock's 35-volume edition, Leon Edel's editions of the *Complete Plays of Henry James* and of *The Complete Tales of Henry James*, and the ongoing publication of James's works in the Library of America—it must be noted that, with the exception of Maqbool Aziz's slowly appearing edition of the tales, there are no variorum editions of James's works, not even of such important and famously revised texts as *The American* and *The Portrait of a Lady*. The equivalent, for Henry James, of the variorum Yeats or of the volumes of the Arden variorum Shakespeare would constitute, to be sure, a monumental undertaking, and yet it is one that would greatly benefit all students of Henry James.

Electronic media may not only facilitate the creation of such scholarly resources, but also constitute the preferred form of publication for variorum editions, concordances, and collections of correspondence. It may well be, for example, that publication of all of Henry James's fiction in CD format, including variant texts (e.g., for *The Portrait of a Lady*, the serial version of 1880–81, both the English and American book publications of 1881, and the New York Edition revision), would be the most economical and useful way of accomplishing the aims of both a variorum edition and a concordance to all of James's fiction. Such a CD publication would have to be equipped with a text-comparison program so that one could quickly locate variants in different editions of the same title; an indispensable utility would allow one to view the variant texts simultaneously (each variant in its own window) and to print them in a multi-column format. If the CD also had a program to locate words, perhaps with boolean operators as well, it would outstrip in value any conventional concordance, for one could search not only for every occurrence of a given word in James's fiction—"opera," say, or "Palladian," or "scientific"—but also for combinations or proximities of terms within a given region of text. For example, one might want to find every occurrence of the words "love" and "death" within two hundred words of each other, or every proximate occurrence of "knowledge" and "power." In the latter half of the 1980s, Todd and Claire Bender, D. Leon Higdon, and Erika Hulpke brought out concordances to a few of James's novels, very useful volumes that would nevertheless be rendered obsolete by the CD publication I have been envisioning.

The first edition of Henry James's letters was published in 1920 in two volumes under the editorship of one of the novelist's acolytes, Percy Lubbock. Highly selective, heavily weighted toward correspondence of Henry James's later years, and protectively expurgated within letters,

Lubbock's edition remained the standard for more than half a century, supplemented by such specialized volumes as Elizabeth Robins's *Theatre and Friendship*, which contains some of James's letters to Robins (the actress who first played Ibsen's major female roles in London in the late 1880s and 1890s), and Leon Edel's slender *Selected Letters of Henry James* (1955). From the mid-1970s through the early 1980s, Edel then brought out the four-volume collection *Henry James Letters*. With the Edel imprimatur upon them, the volumes of *Henry James Letters* seemed to lay claim to being the definitive collection, but immediate and widespread criticism focused on the quality of the textual editing of the letters themselves (particularly in the first volume) and, more importantly perhaps, on the still highly selective nature of the epistolarium they presented. Depending on varying estimates of the number of letters in Henry James's extant correspondence, Edel's four-volume collection contains only 6, 10, or at most 15 percent of the letters of Henry James.

In the 1980s and the first half of the 1990s, therefore, scholars sought to fill some of the gaps by bringing out more specialized editions of James's letters—for example, his correspondence with Henry Adams, with Edmund Gosse, with Frederick Macmillan, and with Edith Wharton. A signal event in the early 1990s was the publication of the first three volumes of *The Correspondence of William James*, each of which was subtitled *William and Henry*. Containing the brothers' letters to each other throughout their lives, these volumes added significantly to the published corpus of Henry James's letters. Even so, at the Henry James Sesquicentennial in 1993, there was, as we have already noted, a broad consensus that the most pressing agenda item for Henry James scholarship was the creation of a complete correspondence of Henry James. Perhaps the single most important impetus behind this consensus was a feeling that a new phase was opening up in the history of biographical studies of Henry James and of the James family generally and that a complete correspondence was one of the essential foundational requirements for scholars engaged in the biographical enterprise.

As a result, an advisory committee has been formed to pursue a complete edition of the correspondence under the editorship of Greg Zacharias and Pierre A. Walker, and discussions are actively under way—the most recent at the annual MLA meeting in December of 1995— on editorial procedures and on the extent to which the letters should be made available in electronic media and on whether their publication should be divided between book and electronic form, with some letters available only in the latter version. Early in 1996, Bay James, who succeeded the novelist's great nephew Alexander James as Henry James's literary executor, granted permission for the complete correspondence project and joined its editorial board. The edition is likely to take at least two decades to complete; if none of the material is reserved for publication in electronic media, it is likely to require at least two dozen volumes. As the project proceeds, moreover, additional letters, some held in private collections, are likely to come to light. Fortunately, the ground has been prepared in some significant measure by two daunting works of scholarship completed by Stephen H. Jobe: the first is Jobe's calendar of Henry James's published correspondence, which identifies for each letter the place of publication, the correspondent, the date, and the current location; the second is Jobe's much longer (and thus far unpublished) calendar of all known extant letters of Henry James, a project supported by the National Endowment for the Humanities. An indispensable trove of material for James scholars, incidentally, lies in the one hundred or so notebooks recently donated by Leon Edel to the library at his alma mater, McGill University—mentioned at this juncture in the present essay because the notebooks include Edel's transcripts of a number of James letters that were destroyed during World War II and that now exist only among Edel's notes on his nearly century-long research on Henry James. Stephen Jobe has recently identified some one hundred James letters unknown to him before his examination of the Edel notebooks at McGill.

Biographers and would-be biographers of Henry James have for nearly half a century pursued their scholarly agendas in the shadow of Leon Edel, whose five-volume *Life of Henry James*, winner of Pulitzer Prizes and National Book Awards, presents an account of James's life that, however hotly disputed in its psychobiographical readings of its subject, tells a formidably detailed, coherent, and imaginatively engaging story. Edel's *Life*, in my view, remains by far the most important single scholarly document on Henry James. Yet in the 1980s and 1990s, important new biographical work has appeared, including an ambitious and valuable full-scale biography of James by Fred Kaplan, a critical biography by Kenneth Graham, R. W. B. Lewis's group portrait of the James family, an iconoclastic and ground-breaking biography of Henry James's father by Alfred Habegger, Jean Strouse's biography of Henry James's sister, and studies of the James family by Howard Feinstein, by Jane Maher, and, most recently, by Carol Holly. Feinstein, a psychiatrist and intellectual historian, and Holly bring to their investigations the insights and methods of family systems therapy. Significant new pieces of information emerge in many of these books, and in journal articles as well, including a recent essay that established for the first time that Henry James was in fact drafted for military service during the Civil War and not merely exempted outright in connection with the disability that James himself called his "obscure hurt." With new materials becoming available in the form of letters and other documents, and with unabating interest in such issues as Henry James's own sexuality and the construction of gender in his fiction (about which more shortly), it seems certain that biographical scholarship will continue to be an area of considerable activity.

A specialized area of biographical work treats James's work as a writer, particularly with respect to his practice as an inveterate reviser of his work, to his construction of the New York Edition of the *Novels and Tales of Henry James*, and to the writing of his autobiographies. Major contributors to these lines of investigation in recent years have been Michael Anesko, Philip Horne, Hershel Parker, Thomas Leitch, Priscilla Gibson Hicks, and David McWhirter, as well as some of the commentators already mentioned, notably Carol Holly. Horne's work in particular is a remarkably detailed and powerfully argued study of James's revisionary practice, though some of Horne's findings and interpretations are usefully challenged by both Parker and Hicks. Horne's general view is that James's revisions were masterful improvements over the originals, even in such cases as *The American* and *Daisy Miller*, on which there has been considerable opinion to the contrary (see, for example, the discussion of the revisions to *Daisy Miller* in my *"Daisy Miller": A Dark Comedy of Manners*). Parker offers a redating of the order of composition of the New York Edition prefaces. Careful study of Horne, Parker, and Hicks suggests that, despite the admirable contributions of these scholars, we do not yet have a definitive chronology of James's work on the New York Edition and of the relation of his work on the edition to other projects in which the novelist was engaged at the same time. The important task of precisely dating James's literary labors is therefore another key agenda item for James studies in the years ahead. Holly focuses on the autobiographies rather than the New York Edition, concentrating on the act of writing the autobiographies as, in and of itself, a key episode in the writer's life. Other important recent work on the autobiographies has been done by Donna Przybylowicz, Paul John Eakin (in both *Fictions* and *Touching the World*), Ross Posnock (*The Trial of Curiosity*), James M. Cox, and Paul S. Nielsen. Holly offers an indispensable survey of this area of James studies in her "The Autobiographies: A History of Readings." A fascinating new study, heavily inflected with literary theory and expressing the author's penetrating investigation of modernism and postmodernism, is Charles Caramello's *Henry James, Gertrude Stein, and the Biographical Act.*

McWhirter's collection of new essays on the New York Edition by many hands is less concerned with textual scholarship than with deconstructing the traditional view of Henry James as having created in the edition a monument to his own literary mastery. The authors in the McWhirter collection are very diverse in their approaches to James, but they have in common an emphasis on James's uncertainty, his ambivalences, and the ways in which his work may be read less as an inscription of literary authority than as a challenge to it. As John Carlos Rowe puts the matter in a brief preface, "the vulnerable, sexually anxious, and lonely writer struggling with the new modern art and the new age he had helped to make possible" is, far more than "the pompous figure of James as Master of the Novel," "full of life and interest." The new Henry James of whom Rowe speaks is not one James, a monolithic figure, but many alternative Jameses: "The Jameses we discover in his place [that of Henry James the Master] are anxious, conflicted, even ashamed of themselves, utterly at odds it would seem with the royal 'we' that James assumed in his deathbed dictations" (xxiv–xxv).

The new Henry Jameses, in contrast to the masterful figure created by a long line of influential commentators from Percy Lubbock and R. P. Blackmur to Leon Edel, have been emerging in James studies at least since the mid-1970s. However, it is convenient to turn back to a moment more than a dozen years ago when two signal books by John Carlos Rowe and Mark Seltzer pointed toward the extremely pluralistic and increasingly political ways of reading James that have energized James studies in the last half of the 1980s and first half of the 1990s. Rowe's 1984 study *The Theoretical Dimensions of Henry James* presents James as a radical international modernist in a tightly woven series of chapters, each of them devoted to demonstrating the rewards and limitations of subjecting James's texts to a particular theoretical praxis: first, influence theory à la Harold Bloom, then feminist theory, then psychological criticism, then Marxism, then phenomenology and reader response criticism. Rowe demonstrates how each successive approach compensates for shortcomings of the preceding one even as he deconstructs the new approach in its turn. This brilliant and engaging book is an excellent starting place for advanced undergraduates and graduate students.

Mark Seltzer's *Henry James and the Art of Power* may be seen in retrospect as the harbinger of an array of new historicist approaches to James. Exploring the relation between art and power in James, Seltzer draws on Bakhtin and, especially, Foucault to demonstrate in fascinating treatments of three texts—*The Princess Casamassima, The Golden Bowl,* and *The American Scene*—that far from being first and foremost (or simply) a genteel novelist of manners, Henry James was a political novelist who was deeply, though often covertly, implicated in the power structures and power relations of his place and time. Although vastly different from Seltzer's work in many respects, the work of a significant number of subsequent commentators on James may be seen to participate in the new historicizing movement that *Henry James and the Art of Power* represents. Particularly notable in the later 1980s was Susan L. Mizruchi's *The Power of Historical Knowledge: Narrating the Past in Hawthorne, James, and Dreiser* and, in the early 1990s, Ian F. A. Bell's *Henry James and the Past: Readings into Time* and Roslyn Jolly's *Henry James: History, Narrative, Fiction.*

In recent years, more and more attention has been given to Henry James's relation to the emerging social sciences of the late nineteenth century, a topic explored by Seltzer in his consideration of connections between *The Princess Casamassima,* for example, and the new sciences of criminology, penology, and sociology. Recent excursions in this vein have included Nancy Bentley's discussion of James's use of anthropology in the treatment of English kinship practices in *The Spoils of Poynton* and James Buzard's discussion of James's travel writings and modern ethnography. These studies bear on an important dimension of Henry James that has come to prominence in recent years, the increasing recognition that Henry James was a high-powered intellectual, very much abreast of current developments in the sciences and social sciences outside of the belle lettristic universe to which traditional views of the novelist have often confined him. The portrait of James as engaged intellectual, well and widely read, is an important aspect of Fred Kaplan's biography, and it has also been promoted, in varying degrees, in studies by Jonathan Freedman, Alwyn Berland, Ross Posnock, and Strother Purdy, among others. The publication of *The Library of Henry James,* a list of all books known to have been owned by James, compiled by Leon Edel and Adeline Tintner, has played a considerable role in the enterprise of placing James intellectually in his time, as has the publication of all of

James's extant literary criticism and book reviews (including about one thousand pages not hitherto reprinted) in two volumes of the Library of America. Undoubtedly, the continuing publication of James's correspondence will also extend investigations along these lines.

Gender, race, and class have long been hot keys in literary and cultural studies, and many of the most vital and provocative contributions to Henry James studies in the last two decades have revolved around these issues. James's treatment of women has always been of special interest, and, from Judith Fetterley to Alfred Habegger, the 1970s, 1980s, and 1990s have seen numerous excellent commentaries devoted in whole or in part to this seemingly inexhaustible topic, including not only Fetterley's *The Resisting Reader* and Habegger's two critical studies *Gender, Fantasy, and Realism* and *Henry James and "the Woman Business,"* but also Mary Doyle Springer's *A Rhetoric of Literary Character: Some Women of Henry James*, Elizabeth Allen's *A Woman's Place in the Novels of Henry James*, Priscilla Walton's *The Disruption of the Feminine in Henry James*, Virginia C. Fowler's *Henry James's American Girl*, and Carren Osna Kaston's *Imagination and Desire in the Novels of Henry James*. One of the most fascinating discussions of James's representation of gendered consciousness is Philip M. Weinstein's "A Round of Visits: James among Some European Peers," in which Weinstein compares and contrasts, first, scenes of adultery in *The Golden Bowl*, *Madame Bovary*, and *Anna Karenina*, and, second, scenes in which gendered subjects encounter the social world in *The Golden Bowl* (again), *The Brothers Karamazov*, and *À la recherche du temps perdu*.

Questions about Henry James's sexuality seem to have haunted discourse about James almost from the moment of the novelist's death. Edmund Wilson's reading of *The Turn of the Screw* in his famous essay "The Ambiguity of Henry James" foreshadowed Saul Rosenzweig's early Freudian analysis of James's castration anxiety, which in turn was one of the fertile germs for Leon Edel's biography, with its sensational focus in volume 5 on what Edel presented as Henry James's unconsummated "homo-eroticism," relating in the last two decades of James's life to a series of beguiling young men—Jocelyn Persse, Hugh Walpole, and, above all, the sculptor Hendrik Christen Andersen. In the 1980s and 1990s, a consensus has emerged that Henry James was, however discreetly and perhaps, indeed, celibately, homosexual. This thesis has been pursued by Howard Feinstein and Richard Hall, both of whom see Henry as having had a deep erotic attachment to his older brother William; by

Fred Kaplan in *Henry James: The Imagination of Genius*; and by a variety of practitioners of queer theory—most powerfully and imaginatively by Eve Kosofsky Sedgwick, but also by Michael Moon, Kelly Cannon, Eric Savoy, Hugh Stevens, Michael Wilson, Leland Person, Cheryl Torsney, and others. Sedgwick's notorious English Institute paper "The Beast in the Closet," reprinted from a volume of English Institute essays in her book *The Epistemology of the Closet*, is a *tour de force*, compellingly reading John Marcher's account of his relation with May Server in "The Beast in the Jungle" as a palimpsest for homosexual panic. Leland Person's recent essays on James, notably his *PMLA* essay on James and George Sand (exploring the gender of James's literary persona and the tensions and predilections evident in his consideration of the gender identity of Sand) and his 1993 essay on "James's Homo-Aesthetics" are among the valuable exemplars of this critical trend.

As intriguing and refreshing as much of the work on James and women and on James and homosexuality is, there is a great deal yet to be done. On the biographical side, James so assiduously cleared the approaches to his privacy that it is doubtful whether there will ever be incontrovertible evidence of his active homosexuality; since, however, new biographical material is still coming to light, there may be future revelations on this score. In any case, a deep division exists in the way James is read on issues of gender, either as a progressive with deep sympathy and insight into women and gays or as a profoundly reactionary and repressive figure. James may well have been of two minds (or indeed of many minds) on a variety of issues—exemplifying in this regard his own aspiration as a writer to "look all round" every subject, that is, to see all its facets, from all sides—but to have James as both protofeminist and antifeminist, as apostle of freedom and agent of repression, would seem to be a misuse of language as conspicuous as that of the art critics in George Orwell's "Politics and the English Language," one of whom says of an artist's work that its outstanding feature "is its living quality," while a second says of the same artist that "the immediately striking thing" about his work is its "peculiar deadness" (2264). These issues will remain lively topics of discussion among students of Henry James.

Discussions of race in James have until recently revolved in large measure around James's expressions, in *The American Scene*, of distaste for the immigrant communities he encountered in New York City on his return to America in 1904–1905 after two decades of absence and also around his accounts of the African Americans he encountered in the

South during the same visit. Many of the most prominent commentators on James have been Jewish—a fact commented on very interestingly by Jonathan Freedman in a recent essay—and yet by and large these critics, notably Leon Edel and Irving Howe, have acted the part of apologists for the apparent anti-Semitism of some oft-remarked passages in *The American Scene*. In a very fine recent essay, however, Charles Caramello provides an unvarnished review of the racist elements in James's *American Scene* accounts of Jewish Americans, Italian Americans, and African Americans; apologists will be able to read Caramello's trenchant remarks only with considerable discomfort ("Duality"). Even more recently, participating in the new historicist trend in criticism remarked on earlier, several recent books bring to the broad topic of race in James a consideration of late nineteenth- and early twentieth-century race theory, ethnography, anthropology, and nativist politics: Sara Blair's *Henry James and the Writing of Race and Nation*, Kenneth Warren's *Black and White Strangers: Race and American Literary Realism*, and Bryan R. Washington's *The Politics of Exile: Ideology in Henry James, F. Scott Fitzgerald, and James Baldwin*. The whole issue of the construction of race and nationality, like questions about the construction of gender, is virtually certain to generate continuing interest in Henry James studies, as indicated by the special forum on race in a recent issue (Fall 1995) of the *Henry James Review*.

Issues of race, gender, and class tend to intersect, but discussions of class in Henry James have by and large received less attention than questions of gender and race, perhaps primarily because there is often very little class differentiation among the inhabitants of James's fictional world. Discussions of social class, therefore, have tended to focus on the small number of works in which servants, lower-class, and lower-middle-class characters appear: for example, *The Princess Casamassima* (Hyacinth Robinson, Millicent Henning, Mr. Vetch, Miss Pynsent, and the Poupins), *The Turn of the Screw* (the governess and Mrs. Grose), *In the Cage* (the telegraphist, Mrs. Jordan, and Mr. Mudge), *What Maisie Knew* (Mrs. Wix), and "Brooksmith" (Brooksmith). The governess in *The Turn of the Screw* has increasingly become a focal point for discussions of class and gender in James's fiction. See, for example, Bruce Robbins's "Shooting Off James's Blanks: Theory, Politics, and *The Turn of the Screw*," Terry Heller's "*The Turn of the Screw*: Bewildered Vision*, and John Carlos Rowe's "Henry James and Critical Theory." At the Henry James sesquicentennial conferences in New York City in 1993, *In the Cage* emerged as the hot James title of the meetings, discussed in paper after paper, including talks by Rowe,

William Veeder (subsequently published), and Eric Savoy. Each of these commentators approached *In the Cage* from a distinctive angle (Rowe through the lens of Marxism, deconstruction, and critical theory in the Althusserian sense of the term; Veeder from the perspective of post-Freudian psychoanalysis; and Savoy within the frame of queer theory), but each focused in large measure on the class relations operative in the world of James's telegraphist, a considerable distance from commentaries on the same work published in the eighties such as those by Naomi Schor and Ross Chambers, which dealt primarily with the telegraphist as "a figure of the act of reading" (Chambers 36). As recent work by Nancy Bentley and others demonstrates, ethnographic/anthropological approaches to the question of social class in Henry James (and in other authors as well) are very productive of challenging new readings, and such approaches do not depend on the presence of characters belonging to different social classes but may be applied to the generally homogeneous world of the novel of manners (as Bentley's title *Ethnography of Manners* suggests).

There are many other strains of James studies that have been extremely vital in the 1980s and 1990s. Important new views of James as dramatist have been developed by Susan Carlson, Anne Margolis, and Brenda Murphy, and yet James's comparatively neglected plays remain fertile ground for new work. James's relation to popular culture has been explored by Adeline Tintner in *The Pop World of Henry James* and by Martha Banta in her wonderfully witty and wonderfully illustrated "'Harry Jim' to 'St. James.'" Many of the other books in Tintner's "world series"—*The Museum World of Henry James*, *The Book World of Henry James*, and *The Cosmopolitan World of Henry James*, as well as her more recent *Henry James and The Lust of the Eye*—participate in another broad current in James studies, analyses of James's relation to other writers and to a variety of literary and artistic movements: examples of works in this vein include two very different books on James's relation to Impressionism, one by H. Peter Stowell, the other by James Kirschke; Robert Emmet Long's *The Great Succession: Henry James and the Legacy of Hawthorne*, Richard Brodhead's *The School of Hawthorne*, and Elissa Greenwald's *Realism and Romance: Nathaniel Hawthorne, Henry James, and American Fiction*; Robert Dawidoff's *The Genteel Tradition and the Sacred Rage: High Culture vs. Democracy in Adams, James, and Santayana*; Edwin Sill Fussell's *The French Side of Henry James* and Pierre A. Walker's *Reading Henry James in French Cultural Contexts*; and Jonathan Freedman's *Professions of Taste:*

Henry James, British Aestheticism, and Commodity Cultural, William Stowe's *Balzac, James, and the Realistic Novel,* John Auchard's *Silence in Henry James: The Heritage of Symbolism and Decadence,* Stephen Donadio's *Nietzsche, Henry James, and the Artistic Will,* Sergio Perosa's *Henry James and the Experimental Novel,* and many others, including my own *Covert Relations: James Joyce, Virginia Woolf, and Henry James.*

Three other broad currents in James studies that deserve special mention are the stylistic and narratological, the psychological, and the philosophical. Major studies of James's style and narratology include Seymour Chatman's *The Later Style of Henry James,* William Veeder's *Henry James— The Lessons of the Master: Popular Fiction and Personal Style in the Nineteenth Century,* David Smit's *The Language of the Master: Theories of Style and the Late Writing of Henry James,* Sheila Teahan's *The Rhetorical Logic of Henry James,* and Paul Beidler's *Frames in James: "The Tragic Muse," "The Turn of the Screw," "What Maisie Knew," and "The Ambassadors."* Psychological approaches to reading Henry James are not always easy to distinguish from philosophical studies, but among those that fall more heavily on the psychological side I would cite as especially notable among recent works Beth Sharon Ash's "Frail Vessels and Vast Designs: A Psychoanalytic Portrait of Isabel Archer" and also her "Narcissism and the Gilded Image: A Psychoanalytic Reading of *The Golden Bowl,*" William Veeder's "The Portrait of a Lack," his "Feminine Orphan and the Emergent Master," and also his "Toxic Mothers, Cultural Criticism: 'In the Cage' and Elsewhere," Donna Przybylowicz's Lacanian-Marxist critique of James in her *Desire and Repression: The Dialectic of Self and Other in the Late Works of Henry James,* Carol Holly's *Intensely Family: The Inheritance of Family Shame and the Autobiographies of Henry James,* Susan Winnett's *Terrible Sociability: The Text of Manners in Laclos, Goethe, and James,* and Suzi Naiburg's "Archaic Depths in Henry James's 'The Last of the Valerii.'"

Philosophical readings of Henry James represent one of the richest strains in James studies. The headwaters of contemporary philosophical approaches to James lie in the early 1960s in two extraordinarily influential volumes, Dorothea Krook's *The Ordeal of Consciousness in Henry James* and Laurence Bedwell Holland's *The Expense of Vision: Essays on the Craft of Henry James.* The trend that I am very broadly labeling "philosophical" is extremely broad and heterogeneous. It includes Coleridgean readings of James by J. A. Ward (*The Search for Form*), Richard A. Hocks (*Henry James and Pragmatistic Thought*), and by the present author (*Henry James and the Structure of the Romantic Imagination*). Phenomenological and epistemological investigations have been particularly rich and stimulating, notably two books by Paul Armstrong, *The Phenomenology of Henry James* and *The Challenge of Bewilderment*, Ruth Bernard Yeazell's *Language and Knowledge in the Late Novels of Henry James*, John Carlos Rowe's *Henry Adams and Henry James: The Emergence of a Modern Consciousness*, J. Hillis Miller's *The Ethics of Reading*, Sharon Cameron's *Thinking in Henry James*, Shoshana Felman's "Turning the Screw of Interpretation," Susan M. Griffin's *The Historical Eye: The Texture of the Visual in Late James*, Merle A. Williams's *Henry James and the Philosophical Novel: Being and Seeing*, Millicent Bell's *Meaning in Henry James*, Ross Posnock's *The Trial of Curiosity: Henry James, William James, and the Challenge of Modernity*, and Garry Hagberg's *Meaning & Interpretation: Wittgenstein, Henry James, and Literary Knowledge*. James's famously ambiguous texts invite continuing investigation of the grounds of knowledge in his fictional world, and this subject will surely remain a lively area of inquiry, with perhaps more and more dialogue between philosophers and literary scholars as the two scholarly communities converge.

James's ambiguity itself has been the topic of some very valuable books, among which I would draw special attention to Jean Frantz Blackall's *Jamesian Ambiguity and "The Sacred Fount,"* Shlomith Rimmon's *The Concept of Ambiguity: The Example of James*, and Ralf Norrman's *The Insecure World of Henry James's Fiction: Intensity and Ambiguity*. Another steady current in the field has explored James's professional career, his relation to the publishing industry and its markets, and the commodification of his art; this current includes significant books by Marcia Jacobson, Michael Anesko, and Jennifer Wicke. It remains to be said that there is in James studies an often fascinating, steady, but in no way predictable current of specialized studies, many of them one of a kind. Among the most intriguing and useful in the first half of the 1990s have been Edwin Sill Fussell's *The Catholic Side of Henry James* and Mary J. Joseph's *Suicide in Henry James's Fiction*.

Elsewhere in the present volume, Michael S. Reynolds observes that there have been more than thirty scholarly books and twelve collections of essays on Ernest Hemingway since 1980. For Henry James, the tally is roughly three times greater, and the outpouring of articles that treat James in whole or in part is enormous. There are many plausible explanations for this plenitude. Richard Hocks suggests that "more than any other American writer, poet, or novelist, James has become the receptacle for all the divergent, interlocking strands of postmodern critical theory" and that James is "the lifeblood of the academy itself" ("From Literary Analysis to Postmodern Theory" 14, 18). Similarly, David McWhirter calls recent James criticism "a virtual encyclopedia of the pluralistic universe of contemporary literary theory" (1). But traditional literary scholarship such as Adeline Tintner's also abounds, and, as I noted at the outset of this chapter, major tasks in James scholarship at present include vast textual projects such as the complete edition of James's letters. To explain the unabating floodtide of work on Henry James, one might best have recourse to the observation that he left an astonishing variety of texts, fiction and nonfiction: short stories, novellas, novels, and plays; art, literary, and cultural criticism; and travel writing, autobiographies, and letters—all characterized by an utterly distinctive discourse that by and large combines astonishing verbal texture and felicity with thematic complexity, perspectival subtlety, and intellectual power of an order rarely matched in the annals of literature. As long as his works continue to reward attention, attention will be paid, and the end is nowhere in sight.

For the scholar and critic—particularly for the younger scholar and critic—it is daunting to attempt to find one's place in the busy, crowded, and yet very large universe of Henry James studies, let alone to gauge the prospects for new work. Richard Hocks provides a good starting point in his narrative history of James studies, the opening essay in a volume I edited four years ago, *A Companion to Henry James Studies*. The *Companion* aimed to provide both advanced students and scholars with a reference guide to the field in all of its dimensions. The *Companion* was also intended to supplement Robert L. Gale's indispensable *Henry James Encyclopedia*. Good secondary bibliographies on Henry James are essential for anyone trying to map the terrain: Beatrice Ricks, Linda J. Taylor, John Budd, Nicola Bradbury, Dorothy Scura, and Judith Funston have all provided helpful bibliographical volumes. The James chapters in the annual volume *American Literary Scholarship* are always intelligent and helpful, though the editors must restrict the length of the *ALS* essays so tightly that it is no longer possible to garner from them a thorough survey of the year's work on Henry James. As the founding editor of the journal devoted to James, I hope I am not immodest in concurring with Hocks that "Any student or fledgling scholar who wishes to obtain a flavor of James criticism would do well to begin with the *Henry James Review*" ("From Literary Analysis to Postmodern Theory" 22), now under the editorship of Susan M. Griffin at the University of Louisville. I would also recommend Ruth Bernard Yeazell's James chapter in the *Columbia Literary History of the United States.*

I would be remiss if I did not also caution those contemplating writing about Henry James that they should become familiar with the scholarship and criticism of earlier decades, for while I have focused on the last two decades (with some minor glances at the early 1970s and the 1960s), some of the most important contributions to our understanding of Henry James lie in the twenties, thirties, forties, and fifties. No one should venture into the field without a firm grasp of the foundational work of commentators like Leon Edel, Edmund Wilson, Lionel Trilling, F. O. Matthiessen, Richard Poirier, and Wayne Booth, not to mention T. S. Eliot, Ezra Pound, Stephen Spender, Graham Greene, and Virginia Woolf, all of whom produced important work on James. Although the first volume of Leon Edel's biography of James was published more than forty years ago, *The Life of Henry James* remains (as I observed earlier) the single most important work of scholarship on Henry James. As a long-time editor of a learned journal, I have often advised authors and would-be authors that nothing is a tell-tale for editorial rejection of a new manuscript so much as an author's letting one see that he or she does not know the history of commentary to date on the topic at hand, that the author does not have a clear sense of what new contribution he or she is making, and that the author cannot convey where his or her work fits into existing knowledge. For an old-fashioned but still superb exposition of what is required to prepare scholarly work for publication, I recommend to everyone, and commend to students of Henry James and of all American authors, R. B. McKerrow's "Form and Matter in the Publication of Scholarly Research."

Where are we going in Henry James studies? Given the great multiplicity and diversity of the field, the answer, undoubtedly, is that we are heading toward many different destinations, by many forms of locomotion. I predict that the recent surge in attention to James's nonfiction—*The American Scene*, the autobiographies, and the art, literary, and cultural criticism—will continue unabated, and that commentary on the fiction, though it will focus with some regularity on comparatively neglected works (witness the turn in the early 1990s to *In the Cage*), will dwell most frequently on the novels denominated as "major," though that grouping will change from time to time. In various eras, *The Portrait of a Lady*, *The Ambassadors*, and *The Golden Bowl* have each in its turn been *the* book for James studies; surely, in the years ahead, *The Wings of the Dove*, *What Maisie Knew*, *The Princess Casamassima*, and *The Bostonians* will each have its day. Our ways of reading and thinking about all of James's work will evolve not only as new critical approaches emerge, but also as electronic media allow us new ways to navigate within and among the texts. And, if all goes according to plan, in the twenty-first century the first generation of biographers free to labor without acute anxiety of influence vis-à-vis Leon Edel will have an unprecedented scholarly resource with which to work in the form of the complete letters. O brave new world!

WORKS CITED

Allen, Elizabeth. *A Woman's Place in the Novels of Henry James*. London: Macmillan, 1984.

Anesko, Michael. *"Friction with the Market": Henry James and the Profession of Authorship*. New York: Oxford UP, 1986.

Armstrong, Paul B. *The Challenge of Bewilderment: Understanding and Representation in James, Conrad, and Ford*.

———. *The Phenomenology of Henry James*. Chapel Hill: U of North Carolina P, 1983.

Ash, Beth Sharon. "Frail Vessels and Vast Designs: A Psychoanalytic Portrait of Isabel Archer." Porte 123–62.

———. "Narcissism and the Gilded Image: A Psychoanalytic Reading of *The Golden Bowl*." *Henry James Review* 15 (1994): 55–90.

Auchard, John. *Silence in Henry James: The Heritage of Symbolism and Decadence*. University Park: Pennsylvania State UP, 1986.

Banta, Martha. "From 'Harry Jim' to 'St. James' in *Life Magazine* (1883–1916): Twitting the Author; Prompting the Public." *Henry James Review* 14 (1993): 237–56.

Beidler, Paul G. *Frames in James: "The Tragic Muse," "The Turn of the Screw," "What Maisie Knew," and "The Ambassadors."* Victoria, BC: English Literary Studies, University of Victoria, 1993.

Bell, Ian F. A. *Henry James and the Past: Readings into Time*. New York: St. Martin's P, 1991.

Bell, Millicent. *Meaning in Henry James*. Cambridge, MA: Harvard UP, 1991.

Bender, Claire E., and Todd K. Bender. *A Concordance to Henry James's "The Turn of the Screw."* New York: Garland, 1988.

Bender, Todd K. *A Concordance to Henry James's "The Awkward Age."* New York: Garland, 1989.

———. *A Concordance to Henry James's "Daisy Miller."* New York: Garland, 1987.

Bender, Todd K., and D. Leon Higden. *A Concordance to Henry James's "The Spoils of Poynton."* New York: Garland, 1988.

Bentley, Nancy. *The Ethnography of Manners: Hawthorne, James, Wharton.* Cambridge, England: Cambridge UP, 1995.

———. "James and the Tribal Discipline of English Kinship." *Henry James Review* 15 (1994): 127–40.

Berland, Alwyn. *Culture and Conduct in the Novels of Henry James.* Cambridge, England: Cambridge UP, 1981.

Blackall, Jean Frantz. *Jamesian Ambiguity and "The Sacred Fount."* Ithaca, NY: Cornell UP, 1965.

Blair, Sara. *Henry James and the Writing of Race and Nation.* Cambridge, England: Cambridge UP, 1996.

Booth, Wayne C. *The Rhetoric of Fiction.* Chicago: U of Chicago P, 1961. Rev. ed., 1983, U of Chicago P.

Bradbury, Nicola. *An Annotated Critical Bibliography of Henry James.* New York: St. Martin's P, 1987.

Brodhead, Richard. *The School of Hawthorne.* New York: Oxford UP, 1986.

Budd, John Henry. *Henry James: A Bibliography of Criticism, 1975–1981.* Westport, CT: Greenwood P, 1983.

Buzard, James. "A Continent of Pictures: Reflections on the 'Europe' of Nineteenth-Century Tourists." *PMLA* 108 (1993): 30–44.

Cameron, Sharon. *Thinking in Henry James.* Chicago: U of Chicago P, 1989.

Cannon, Kelly. *Henry James and Masculinity. The Man at the Margins.* New York: St. Martin's P, 1994.

Caramello, Charles. "The Duality of the American Scene." Fogel, *Companion* 447–73.

———. *Henry James, Gertrude Stein, and the Biographical Act.* Chapel Hill: U of North Carolina P, 1996.

Carlson, Susan. *Women of Grace: James's Plays and the Comedy of Manners.* Ann Arbor, MI: UMI Research P, 1985.

Chambers, Ross. "Narrative and Other Triangles." *Journal of Narrative Technique* 19 (1989): 31–48.

Chatman, Seymour. *The Later Style of Henry James.* Oxford: Blackwell, 1972.

Cox, James M. "The Memoirs of Henry James: Self-Interest as Autobiography." *Southern Review,* n.s. 22 (1986): 231–51.

Dawidoff, Robert. *The Genteel Tradition and the Sacred Rage: High Culture vs. Democracy in Adams, James, and Santayana.* Chapel Hill: U of North Carolina P, 1992.

Donadio, Stephen. *Nietzsche, Henry James, and the Artistic Will.* New York: Oxford UP, 1978.

Eakin, Paul John. *Fictions in Autobiography: Studies in the Art of Self-Invention.* Princeton, NJ: Princeton UP, 1985.

———. *Touching the World: Reference in Autobiography.* Princeton, NJ: Princeton UP, 1992.

Edel, Leon. *Henry James: A Life.* New York: Harper & Row, 1985.

———. Introduction to *The American Scene* by Henry James, vii–xxiv. Bloomington: Indiana UP, 1968.

———. Leon Edel Papers. Department of Rare Books and Special Collections. McGill University Libraries. Montréal, Québec.

———. *The Life of Henry James.* 5 vols. Philadelphia: J. B. Lippincott, 1953–72.

Edel, Leon, and Adeline Tintner. *The Library of Henry James.* Ann Arbor, MI: UMI Research P, 1987.

Eliot, T. S. "In Memory" and "The Hawthorne Aspect." *Little Review* 5 (1918): 44–53.

Feinstein, Howard. *Becoming William James.* Ithaca, NY: Cornell UP, 1984.

Felman, Shoshana. "Turning the Screw of Interpretation." *Yale French Studies* 55/56 (1977): 94–207.

Fetterley, Judith. *The Resisting Reader: A Feminist Approach to American Fiction.* Bloomington: Indiana UP, 1978.

Fogel, Daniel Mark. *A Companion to Henry James Studies.* Westport, CT: Greenwood P, 1993.

———. *Covert Relations: James Joyce, Virginia Woolf, and Henry James.* Charlottesville: UP of Virginia, 1990.

———. *"Daisy Miller": A Dark Comedy of Manners.* Boston: Twayne, 1990.

———. *Henry James and the Structure of the Romantic Imagination.* Baton Rouge: Louisiana State UP, 1981.

Fowler, Virginia C. *Henry James's American Girl: The Embroidery on the Canvas.* Madison: U of Wisconsin P, 1984.

Freedman, Jonathan. *Professions of Taste: Henry James, British Aestheticism, and Commodity Culture.* Stanford: Stanford UP, 1990.

———. "Trilling, James, and the Uses of Cultural Criticism." *Henry James Review* 14 (1993): 141–50.

Funston, Judith. *Henry James: A Reference Guide, 1975–1987.* Boston: G. K. Hall, 1991.

Fussell, Edwin Sill. *The Catholic Side of Henry James.* Cambridge, England: Cambridge UP, 1993.

———. *The French Side of Henry James.* New York: Columbia UP, 1990.

Gale, Robert L. *A Henry James Encyclopedia.* Westport, CT: Greenwood P, 1989.

Graham, Kenneth. *Henry James: A Literary Life.* New York: St. Martin's P, 1995.

Greene, Graham. *The Lost Childhood and Other Essays.* New York: Viking P, 1951.

Greenwald, Elissa. *Realism and Romance: Nathaniel Hawthorne, Henry James, and American Fiction.* Ann Arbor, MI: UMI Research P, 1989.

Griffin, Susan M. *The Historical Eye: The Texture of the Visual in Late James.* Boston: Northeastern UP, 1991.

Habegger, Alfred. *The Father: A Life of Henry James, Sr.* New York: Farrar, Straus & Giroux, 1994.

———. *Gender, Fantasy, and Realism in American Literature.* New York: Columbia UP, 1982.

———. *Henry James and the "Woman Business."* New York: Cambridge UP, 1989.

Hagberg, Garry. *Meaning & Interpretation: Wittgenstein, Henry James, and Literary Knowledge.* Ithaca, NY: Cornell UP, 1994.

Hall, Richard. "An Obscure Hurt: The Sexuality of Henry James." *New Republic,* 28 April 1979, 25–31; 5 May 1979, 25–29.

Heller, Terry. *"The Turn of the Screw": Bewildered Vision.* Boston: Twayne, 1989.

Hicks, Priscilla Gibson. "A Turn in the Formation of James's New York Edition: Criticism, the Historical Record, and the Siting of *The Awkward Age.*" *Henry James Review* 16 (1995): 195–221.

Higdon, David Leon, and Todd K. Bender. *A Concordance to Henry James's "The American."* New York: Garland, 1985.

Hocks, Richard A. "From Literary Analysis to Postmodern Theory: A Historical Narrative of James Criticism." Fogel, *Companion* 3–24.

———. *Henry James and Pragmatistic Thought: A Study in the Relationship between the Philosophy of William James and the Literary Art of Henry James.* Chapel Hill: U of North Carolina P, 1974.

Holland, Laurence Bedwell. *The Expense of Vision: Essays on the Craft of Henry James.* Princeton, NJ: Princeton UP, 1964.

Holly, Carol. "The Autobiographies: A History of Readings." Fogel, *Companion* 427–46.

———. *Intensely Family: The Inheritance of Family Shame and the Autobiographies of Henry James.* Madison: U of Wisconsin P, 1995.

Horne, Philip. *Henry James and Revision: The New York Edition.* New York: Oxford UP, 1990.

Howe, Irving. Introduction to *The American Scene,* by Henry James, v–xvi. New York: Horizon P, 1967.

Hulpke, Erika. *A Concordance to Henry James's "What Maisie Knew."* New York: Garland, 1989.

Jacobson, Marcia. *Henry James and the Mass Market.* University: U of Alabama P, 1983.

James, Henry. *Complete Plays of Henry James.* Ed. Leon Edel. Philadelphia: Lippincott, 1949.

———. *Complete Tales of Henry James.* Ed. Leon Edel. 12 vols. London: Rupert Hart-Davis, 1962–64.

———. *The Correspondence of Henry James and Henry Adams, 1877–1914.* Ed. George Monteiro. Baton Rouge: Louisiana State UP, 1992.

———. *The Correspondence of Henry James and the House of Macmillan, 1877–1914.* Ed. Rayburn S. Moore. Baton Rouge: Louisiana State UP, 1993.

———. *Henry James and Edith Wharton: Letters, 1900–1915.* Ed. Lyall H. Powers. New York: Scribners, 1990.

———. *Henry James Letters.* Ed. Leon Edel. 4 vols. Cambridge, MA: Harvard UP, 1975–84.

———. *The Letters of Henry James.* Ed. Percy Lubbock. 2 vols. New York: Scribners, 1920.

———. *Literary Criticism: Essays on Literature, American Writers, English Writers.* Ed. Leon Edel. New York: Library of America, 1984.

———. *Literary Criticism: French Writers, Other European Writers, the Prefaces to the New York Edition.* Ed. Leon Edel. New York: Library of America, 1984.

———. *The Novels and Stories of Henry James.* Ed. Percy Lubbock. 35 vols. London: Macmillan, 1921–23.

———. *The Novels and Tales of Henry James.* New York Edition. 26 vols. New York: Scribners, 1907–17.

———. *Selected Letters of Henry James.* Ed. Leon Edel. London: Rupert Hart-Davis, 1955.

———. *Selected Letters of Henry James to Edmund Gosse, 1882–1915: A Literary Friendship.* Ed. Rayburn S. Moore. Baton Rouge: Louisiana State UP, 1988.

———. *The Tales of Henry James.* Ed. Maqbool Aziz. 3 vols. to date. Oxford, England: Clarendon P, 1973–.

———. *Theatre and Friendship: Some Henry James Letters.* Ed. Elizabeth Robins. New York: G. P. Putnam's Sons, 1932.

James, William. *The Correspondence of William James: William and Henry.* Vols. 1–3 of *The Correspondence of William James.* Ed. Ignas K. Skupskelis and Elizabeth M. Berkeley. Charlottesville: UP of Virginia, 1992–94.

Jobe, Stephen H. "A Calendar of the Published Letters of Henry James." Parts 1, 2. *Henry James Review* 11 (1990): 1–29, 77–100.

Joseph, Mary J. *Suicide in Henry James's Fiction,* New York: Peter Lang, 1994.

Jolly, Roslyn. *Henry James: History, Narrative, Fiction.* Oxford, England: Clarendon P, 1993.

Kaplan, Fred. *Henry James: The Imagination of Genius.* New York: William Morrow, 1992.

Kaston, Carren Osna. *Imagination and Desire in the Novels of Henry James.* New Brunswick, NJ: Rutgers UP, 1984.

Kirschke, James. *Henry James and Impressionism.* Troy, NY: Whitston P, 1981.

Krook, Dorothea. *The Ordeal of Consciousness in Henry James.* New York: Cambridge UP, 1962.

Leitch, Thomas M. "The Prefaces." Fogel, *Companion* 55–72.

Lewis, R. W. B. *The Jameses.* New York: Farrar, Straus & Giroux, 1991.

Long, Robert Emmet. *The Great Succession: Henry James and the Legacy of Hawthorne.* Pittsburgh: U of Pittsburgh P, 1979.

Maher, Jane. *Biography of Broken Fortunes: Wilkie and Bob, Brothers of William, Henry, and Alice James.* Hamden, CT: Archon Books, 1986.

Margolis, Anne T. *Henry James and the Problem of Audience.* Ann Arbor, MI: UMI Research P, 1985.

Matthiessen, F. O. *Henry James: The Major Phase.* New York: Oxford UP, 1944.

McKerrow, R. B. "Form and Matter in the Publication of Scholarly Research." *Review of English Studies* 16 (1940): 116–21. Rpt. in Lester A. Beaurline, ed., *A Mirror for Modern Scholars.* New York: Odyssey P, 1966. 383–89.

McWhirter, David B., ed. *Henry James's New York Edition: The Construction of Authorship.* Stanford: Stanford UP, 1995.

Miller, J. Hillis. *The Ethics of Reading: Kant, de Man, Eliot, Trollope, James, and Benjamin.* New York: Columbia UP, 1987.

Mizruchi, Susan L. *The Power of Historical Knowledge: Narrating the Past in Hawthorne, James, and Dreiser.* Princeton, NJ: Princeton UP, 1988.

Moon, Michael. "Sexuality and Visual Terrorism in *The Wings of the Dove.*" *Criticism* 28 (1986): 427–43.

———. "*A Small Boy and Others:* Sexual Disorientation in Henry James, Kenneth Anger, and David Lynch." *Comparative American Sexual Identities: Race, Sex, and Nationality in the Modern Text.* Ed. Hortense Spillers. New York: Routledge, 1991. 151–56.

Murphy, Brenda. *American Realism and American Drama: 1880–1940.* Cambridge, England: Cambridge UP, 1987.

———. "James's Later Plays: A Reconsideration." *Modern Language Studies* 13 (1983): 86–95.

Naiburg, Suzi. "Archaic Depths in Henry James's 'The Last of the Valerii.'" *Henry James Review* 14 (1993): 151–65.

Nielsen, Paul S. "Henry James and the Process of Autobiography." Diss. Louisiana State U, 1995. UMI Number: 9538752.

Norrman, Ralf. *The Insecure World of Henry James's Fiction: Intensity and Ambiguity.* London: Macmillan, 1982.

Orwell, George. "Politics and the English Language." *The Norton Anthology of English Literature.* Ed. M. H. Abrams et al. 5th ed. New York: Norton, 1986. 2:2260–70.

Parker, Hershel. "The Authority of the Revised Text and the Disappearance of the Author: What Critics of Henry James Did with Textual Evidence in the Heyday of the New Criticism." *Flawed Texts and Verbal Icons: Literary*

Authority in American Fiction. Evanston, IL: Northwestern UP, 1984. 85–144.

———. "Deconstructing *The Art of the Novel* and Liberating James's Prefaces." *Henry James Review* 14 (1993): 284–307.

———. "Henry James 'In the Wood': Sequence and Significance of his Literary Labors, 1905–1907." *Nineteenth-Century Fiction* 38 (1984): 429–513.

Perosa, Sergio. *Henry James and the Experimental Novel*. Charlottesville: UP of Virginia, 1978.

Person, Leland S., Jr. "Henry James, George Sand, and the Suspense of Masculinity." *PMLA* 106 (1991): 515–28.

———. "James's Homo-Aesthetics: Deploying Desire in the Tales of Writers and Artists." *Henry James Review* 14 (1993): 188–203.

Poirier, Richard. *The Comic Sense of Henry James: A Study of the Early Novels*. New York: Oxford UP, 1960.

Porte, Joel. *New Essays on "The Portrait of a Lady."* New York: Cambridge UP, 1990.

Posnock, Ross. *Henry James and the Problem of Robert Browning*. Athens: U of Georgia P, 1985.

———. *The Trial of Curiosity: Henry James, William James, and the Challenge of Modernity*. New York: Oxford UP, 1991.

Pound, Ezra. "Brief Note." *Little Review* 5 (1918): 6–9.

———. "Henry James." *Literary Essays of Ezra Pound*. Ed. T. S. Eliot. New York: New Directions, 1968. 295–338.

Przybylowicz, Donna. *Desire and Represssion: The Dialectic of Self and Other in the Late Works of Henry James*. Tuscaloosa: U of Alabama P, 1986.

Purdy, Strother B. *The Hole in the Fabric: Science, Contemporary Literature, and Henry James*. Pittsburgh: U of Pittsburgh P, 1977.

Ricks, Beatrice. *Henry James: A Bibiliography of Secondary Works*. Metuchen, NJ: Scarecrow P, 1975.

Rimmon, Shlomith. *The Concept of Ambiguity: The Example of James*. Chicago: U of Chicago P, 1977.

Robbins, Bruce. "Shooting Off James's Blanks: Theory, Politics, and *The Turn of the Screw*." *Henry James Review* 5 (1983–84): 192–99.

Rosenzweig, Saul. "The Ghost of Henry James." *Partisan Review* 11 (1944): 436–55.

Rowe, John Carlos. Foreword. McWhirter xxiii–xxvi.

———. *Henry Adams and Henry James: The Emergence of a Modern Consciousness*. Ithaca, NY: Cornell UP, 1976.

———. "Henry James and Critical Theory." Fogel, *Companion* 73–93.

———. *The Theoretical Dimensions of Henry James*. Madison: U of Wisconsin P, 1984.

Savoy, Eric. "*Hypocrite Lecteur*: Walter Pater, Henry James, and Homotextual Politics." *Dalhousie Review* 72 (1993): 12–36.

Schor, Naomi. "Fiction as Interpretation/Interpretation as Fiction." *The Reader in the Text: Essays on Audience and Interpretation*. Ed. Susan R. Suleiman and Inge Crosman. Princeton, NJ: Princeton UP, 1980. 165–82.

Scura, Dorothy. *Henry James, 1960–1974: A Reference Guide*. Boston: G. K. Hall, 1979.

Sedgwick, Eve Kosofsky. "The Beast in the Closet: James and the Writing of Homosexual Panic." *Sex, Politics, and Science in the Nineteenth-Century Novel*. Selected Papers from the English Institute, 1983–84. Ed. Ruth Bernard Yeazell. Baltimore: Johns Hopkins UP, 1986. 148–86.

———. *Epistemology of the Closet*. Berkeley: U of California P, 1990.

Seltzer, Mark. *Henry James and the Art of Power*. Ithaca, NY: Cornell UP, 1984.

Smit, David. *The Language of the Master: Theories of Style and the Late Writing of Henry James*. Carbondale: Southern Illinois UP, 1988.

Spender, Stephen. *The Destructive Element: A Study of Modern Writers and Beliefs*. London: Jonathan Cape, 1935.

Springer, Mary Doyle. *A Rhetoric of Literary Character: Some Women of Henry James*. Chicago: U of Chicago P, 1978.

Stevens, Hugh. "Sexuality and the Aesthetic in *The Golden Bowl*." *Henry James Review* 14 (1993): 55–71.

Stowe, William W. *Balzac, James, and the Realistic Novel*. Princeton, NJ: Princeton UP, 1983.

Stowell, H. Peter. *Literary Impressionism: James and Chekhov*. Athens: U of Georgia P, 1980.

Strouse, Jean. *Alice James: A Biography*. Boston: Houghton Mifflin, 1980.

Taylor, Linda J. *Henry James, 1866–1916: A Reference Guide*. Boston: G. K. Hall, 1982.

Teahan, Sheila. *The Rhetorical Logic of Henry James*. Baton Rouge: Louisiana State UP, 1995.

Tintner, Adeline R. *The Book World of Henry James: Appropriating the Classics*. Ann Arbor, MI: UMI Research P, 1987.

———. *The Cosmopolitan World of Henry James*. Baton Rouge: Louisiana State UP, 1991.

———. *Henry James and The Lust of the Eye: Thirteen Artists in His Work*. Baton Rouge: Louisiana State UP, 1993.

———. *The Museum World of Henry James*. Ann Arbor, MI: UMI Research P, 1986.

———. *The Pop World of Henry James: From Fairy Tales to Science Fiction*. Ann Arbor, MI: UMI Research P, 1989.

Torsney, Cheryl B. "Henry James, Charles Sanders Pierce, and the Fat Capon: Homoerotic Desire in *The American.*" *Henry James Review* 14 (1993): 166–78.

Trilling, Lionel. *The Liberal Imagination.* New York: Macmillan, 1948.

Veeder, William. "The Feminine Orphan and the Emergent Master." *Henry James Review* 12 (1991): 20–54.

———. *Henry James—The Lessons of the Master: Popular Fiction and Personal Style in the Nineteenth Century.* Chicago: U of Chicago P, 1975.

———. "The Portrait of a Lack." Porte 95–121.

———. "Toxic Mothers, Cultural Criticism: 'In the Cage' and Elsewhere." *Henry James Review* 14 (1993): 264–72.

Walker, Pierre A. *Reading Henry James in French Cultural Contexts.* DeKalb: Northern Illinois UP, 1995.

Walton, Priscilla. *The Disruption of the Feminine in Henry James.* Toronto: U of Toronto P, 1992.

Ward, J. A. *The Search for Form: Studies in the Structure of James's Fiction.* Chapel Hill: U of North Carolina P, 1967.

Warren, Kenneth W. *Black and White Strangers: Race and American Literary Realism.* Chicago: Chicago UP, 1993.

Washington, Bryan R. *The Politics of Exile: Ideology in Henry James, F. Scott Fitzgerald, and James Baldwin.* Boston: Northeastern UP, 1995.

Weinstein, Philip. "A Round of Visits: James among Some European Peers." Fogel, *Companion* 235–64.

Wicke, Jennifer. *Advertising Fictions: Literature, Advertisement & Social Reading.* New York: Columbia UP, 1988.

Williams, Merle A. *Henry James and the Philosophical Novel: Being and Seeing.* New York: Cambridge UP, 1993.

Wilson, Edmund. "The Ambiguity of Henry James." *Hound and Horn* 7 (1934): 385–406.

Wilson, Michael. "Lessons of the Master: The Artist and Sexual Identity in Henry James." *Henry James Review* 14 (1993): 257–63.

Winnett, Susan. *Terrible Sociability: The Text of Manners in Laclos, Goethe, and James.* Stanford: Stanford UP, 1993.

Woolf, Virginia. *Collected Essays.* Ed. Leonard Woolf. 4 vols. New York: Harcourt, Brace and World, 1967.

Yeazell, Ruth Bernard. "Henry James." *Columbia Literary History of the United States.* Ed. Emory Elliott et al. New York: Columbia UP, 1988. 668–89.

———. *Language and Knowledge in the Late Novels of Henry James.* Chicago: U of Chicago P, 1976.

10

Edith Wharton

Linda Wagner-Martin

To assert that serious criticism of the writing of Edith Wharton began with R. W. B. Lewis's 1975 *Edith Wharton: A Biography* would be an exaggeration. Yet for many readers and scholars of the 1980s and the 1990s, this single book—and its attendant publicity and awards—led to waves of reevaluation. In the long run, the attention meant that Wharton's work would be assessed in the context of the later twentieth century, rather than the earlier, a shift that has been healthy in a number of ways.

Following the Lewis biography by just two years was Cynthia Griffin Wolff's *A Feast of Words: The Triumph of Edith Wharton*, a more psychologically based study of not only Wharton's life and writing but also the integral relationship between the two. The acclaim for Wolff's book signaled both a wide popular market for scholarship on Wharton and a hunger for information about the supposedly remote and austere "Mrs. Wharton" among women scholars who thought of themselves as feminist. In the project of the 1970s and 1980s, to reclaim and—in Adrienne Rich's term—to revision writing by women, reading Wharton's novels and short stories was truly a "feast."

In the early 1980s, the now-flourishing Edith Wharton Society was formed. Its leadership arranged panels on Wharton's work at existing professional conferences and at several important meetings devoted entirely to discussions of Wharton (in Lenox, Massachusetts; New York; Paris; and, most recently, New Haven, Connecticut). Part of the society's work was to institute a journal—first known as *The Edith Wharton Newsletter* but now titled *The Edith Wharton Review*. Included regularly in the journal, which was often edited by Annette Zilversmit, was a comprehensive bibliography prepared by Alfred Bendixen. The excellent leadership in Wharton studies continues, providing both information and support to scholars interested in her work.

I emphasize the society and its publication because Wharton studies had previously been marked by an air of dutifulness. Good and generous work had been done by many critics, among them E. K. Brown, Percy Lubbock, Vernon L. Parrington, Edmund Wilson, Blake Nevius, and Irving Howe. However, their writings so obviously championed Wharton, aimed so apparently at creating a solid, scholarly reputation for her, that some readers were skeptical. Was Wharton being placed in the canon because professors of American literature taught no other women fiction writers? One might have suggested this when Arthur Mizener wrote a chapter on Wharton's *The Age of Innocence* in his 1967 *Twelve Great American Novels*: Wharton was the only woman writer included.

Graduate students were not rushing to write dissertations on Edith Wharton; undergraduates were not eager to read her fiction. The atmosphere surrounding the study of Wharton—like that surrounding the study of Ellen Glasgow—was one of nostalgia. Yes, Wharton was a novelist of manners and, yes, she had been one of the best of the local color writers. Yes, those of us interested in the New York scene in the 1870s and 1880s—particularly those of us interested in the narratives of the social elite—would continue to read her novels. Nonetheless, there was little passion attached to the study of her writing. The person who "did Wharton" in most English departments was probably the aging woman teacher whose publications were counted but seldom read. The assumption, even as late as the 1970s, was that women writers were of little interest to those faculty members who taught Wordsworth, Chaucer, and Hemingway—writers whose work formed the real business of English departments.

This is not to say that James Tuttleton's 1972 *The Novel of Manners in America* was obsolete, but rather that new ways of viewing the written text had begun to eclipse those based on existing literary classifications. A knowledge of history became less important a consideration for even Wharton's most-acclaimed novel, *The Age of Innocence*, winner of the Pulitzer Prize for Fiction in 1921. In addition, the usual way of establishing that Wharton belonged among the great American writers—because, in E. K. Brown's words, she was "at ease in a man's world" and was, therefore, a gentlemanly novelist rather than a woman writer—had fallen into disrepute. No matter how often she had been labeled "Mrs. Wharton," Edith Newbold Jones was coming into her rightful place in

American letters as a great woman writer. During the late 1970s, readers focused more intently on Wharton as woman writer—traveling widely, living abroad in France, and succeeding as a best-selling author until her death in 1937.

The figuration of Edith Wharton as a striking and powerful woman, a woman who accrued power both because of her ability to create memorable, sympathetic protagonists and because of the clear financial success of her fiction, appeared on the horizon of Wharton studies in ways that embarrassed some literary critics. Better that Wharton remain the dignified upper-class woman whose personal energy terrified the more leisurely Henry James. (Even though Millicent Bell had clarified the relationship between James and Wharton in her 1965 study, the tendency to reduce Wharton to James's apprentice lingered.) Better that readers continue to negate the fiery intelligence and feeling that made Wharton's writing more forceful than many other turn-of-the-century and modernist fictions.

The past twenty years of criticism, drawing partially on the biographies, have created a new sense of Edith Wharton as woman writer. They have brought innovative critical perspectives to some of her fiction, although a great deal of her extensive oeuvre remains neglected. Even though Alfred Bendixen claims in his 1993 bibliographic essay that Wharton's place as a major novelist is firmly established ("New Directions" 20), a great quantity of work remains to be done. In this essay, I will suggest only a few of the kinds of explorations that would be fruitful.

All Americanists recognize that criticism of Edith Wharton is at a far different place than that of Walt Whitman or Ernest Hemingway—that is, truly canonized writers. For them, the scaffolding of good bibliographies, good biographies, and good collections of essays and letters has long been in place. The tools so necessary to excellent scholarship, then, are already accessible. So far as research on Wharton is concerned, the past decade has brought improvement in such resources. To Marlene Springer's 1976 reference guide to both Wharton and Kate Chopin (the combination of the two writers reflective of the amount of work then being done—as well as of publishers' views of the importance of these writers) came other listings of secondary criticism (Tuttleton, "Edith Wharton"; Springer and Gilson; Bendixen, "A Guide," "New Directions," "Recent Wharton Studies," "Wharton Studies," "The World"; Joslin, "Edith Wharton at 125"; and Lauer and Murray). Vito J. Brenni's 1966 bibliography was followed by Stephen Garrison's 1990 descriptive work, published in the Pittsburgh series. And to help make research for Wharton students somewhat manageable, in 1992 Tuttleton, Lauer, and Murray brought out the useful *Edith Wharton: The Contemporary Reviews* in the Cambridge series. Of all twentieth-century writers, Wharton had amassed a huge, almost undescribed, body of reviews. Because she lived abroad during many of the years she published, she herself had been unable to collect the newspaper and magazine commentaries extant. Tracing these materials and collecting representative reviews has been a valuable project.

What now exists suggests further lacunae that need to be filled. Scholars would benefit from having a volume—or several volumes—of retrospective critical essays, drawing from the quantity of excellent recent work as well as those essays already published in Irving Howe's 1962 collection. Millicent Bell's recent *Cambridge Companion to Edith Wharton*, with essays by Gloria Erlich, Elaine Showalter, William Vance, Elizabeth Ammons, and others, begins to fill that need. Such collections begin the process of making standard Wharton criticism easily available to students. Today, doing research on Wharton remains an arduous library task, and an *Edith Wharton: Six Decades of Criticism* (or perhaps *Seven Decades*) would at least begin to describe some patterns in the commentary.

Even more valuable would be a collection of Wharton's own reviews and occasional essays. Perhaps her 1925 *The Writing of Fiction* could be republished in conjunction with her comments on her art from both reviews and letters; an *Edith Wharton on Writing* would help readers understand the author's pose of modest irony, which she tended to assume whenever she discussed her craft (see Wegener). It goes without saying that publication of Wharton's previously unpublished writings will also be both desirable and, eventually, necessary. The interest provoked by R. W. B. Lewis's inclusion (as an appendix to his biography) of Wharton's "Beatrice Palmato" fragment, a previously unknown fiction about father-daughter incest, suggests the need to publish materials that remain inaccessible. When Cynthia Griffin Wolff found the Palmato fragment in the Yale Wharton collection, she asked Lewis—whose book was to be in print before her own—to make the work available. Many scholars are less generous; to ensure that interested parties have access to materials, we should both publish these materials and catalogue them.

An obvious gap in resources for Wharton scholarship is the absence of either print or on-line catalogues for the largest manuscript and correspondence collections—the Beinecke collection at Yale; the Harry Ransom Humanities Research Center collection at University of Texas, Austin; and the Lilly Library collection at Indiana University. Also of interest are materials in the Firestone Library at Princeton, the Houghton Library and the Pusey Library at Harvard, the Villa I Tatti (Bernard Berenson's former home in Florence, which is now the Harvard Center for Renaissance Studies), and other collections. Access to these materials is now dependent upon actually visiting the site, an expensive and time-consuming process for researchers.

One of the most dramatic illustrations of scholars' lack of awareness of what a collection held was the discovery in the early 1980s that the Harry Ransom Humanities Research Center at Texas had, in 1980, purchased the three hundred letters written by Wharton to her lover Morton Fullerton (Gribben, Colquitt). Presumed to have been destroyed, the cache of poignant, passionate letters had an immense impact both on the biography of the author and on readings of her fiction. Eighty of the letters were published, at least partially, in the Lewises' 1988 *Letters of Edith Wharton*, and Shari Benstock and other recent critics and biographers have made great use of the collection (see Benstock's appendix in *No Gifts from Chance: A Biography of Edith Wharton* on the history of the discovery).

The difficulty of trying to publish a meaningful sample of Edith Wharton's letters is apparent: she wrote hundreds, perhaps thousands, of letters. Lewis recounts that, on one instance in 1924, Wharton returned from a short trip to find sixty-five letters (three days' mail) waiting for her (*Letters* 3). Most of her correspondents were not famous, of course, so many of her letters are simply lost. Of the four thousand pieces of correspondence that the Lewises located, they could print only a tenth, four hundred letters, in their volume. That collection has since been supplemented by Lyall Powers's collection of the James-Wharton letters, but much more of Wharton's correspondence needs to be made available. Literally hundreds of letters from Wharton to Sara Norton, Gaillard Lapsley, Bernard and Mary Berenson, and others exist; it appears that, regrettably, either she or the recipients destroyed her letters to Percy Lubbock and Walter Berry.

The impact made by the discoveries of both the "Beatrice Palmato" fragment and Wharton's letters to Fullerton suggests a pervasive problem within Wharton studies. Perhaps because the earlier critical history of response to Wharton's work followed such predictable patterns, new pieces of information have a great potential to change the existing body of work. The shock value of discoveries, then, depends as much on their effect on the critical givens as on their intrinsic meaning. Accordingly, criticism of Wharton and her work tends to plateau, to halt in pools of agreement, while evidence that supports new information is put forth. This tendency is especially noticeable because publication outlets for criticism about Wharton are relatively few: therefore, when one reads essays in the Society publication, or in *American Literary Realism*, *American Literature*, or *Studies in American Fiction*, the same material is often repeated—or at least alluded to.

Such a pattern suggests another problem within Wharton studies: that even current criticism tends to reify its past history. Discussions of Wharton's various uses of irony, for example, always a significant tactic for this writer, still return to Blake Nevius's excellent early work. Those discussions could be grounded as easily in the more recent work on irony of such critics as Wayne Booth and Linda Hutcheon. In other words, today's scholars might study Wharton's work by using theories of critics who do not treat Wharton's work. One instance of reliance on non-Whartonians is Kathy Miller Hadley's 1993 book, *In the Interstices of the Tale*, which discusses Wharton's narrative achievements from *The Reef* to *The Mother's Recompense* and *The Children*, using such feminist narratological approaches as those given in Rachel Blau DuPlessis's *Writing beyond the Ending* and work by Sandra M. Gilbert and Susan Gubar. Other instances are essays by Ellie Ragland Sullivan (a psychoanalytic reading) and D. Quentin Miller (a language-based narratological reading).

More diverse critical approaches would seem to be particularly useful in dealing with Wharton's women characters, and with themes that must be characterized as women-centered (as in *The Mother's Recompense* or *Twilight Sleep*, for example). Dale M. Bauer's 1994 study, *Edith Wharton's Brave New Politics*, shows the kinds of wide-ranging information provided by a serious look at social, philosophical, and medical issues contemporary with Wharton's fictions from *Summer* through the late 1920s. As useful as Bauer's 1988 Bakhtinian reading of Wharton was (*Female Dialogics*), *Brave New Politics* breaks more—and newer—ground. It places Wharton's late writing in the mainstream of philosophical and biological theories of reproduction and eugenics, as well as in such less often scrutinized currents of popular culture as the self-help movement, the marriage market, and the public obsession with film stars. Bauer here draws Wharton as a novelist keenly aware of the foibles of modernism, an author far different from the aging woman said to be past her peak as a writer.

A different kind of contextualization occurs in Shari Benstock's 1986 *Women of the Left Bank: Paris, 1900–1940.* In this rich study of more than a dozen women's lives, Benstock both describes the existences of expatriate women and shows the way insistent parallels from their lives create a culture that shaped much of twentieth-century modernism. In this context, Wharton was one of the most essential figures of European and American modernity. Similarly, Elizabeth Ammons's 1992 study, *Conflicting Stories: American Women Writers at the Turn into the Twentieth Century,* juxtaposes what might appear to be singular, even unique, lives into parallel patterns. Her sometimes harsh criticism of privileged white culture, represented in part by Wharton, is a long-overdue corrective to critical views of what is normative about modernist writing.

While *Women of the Left Bank* and *Conflicting Stories* have been immensely important in helping readers place Wharton and her work, two books by Susan Goodman have had as their aim the further surrounding of Wharton with her own immediate cultural context. In her 1990 *Edith Wharton's Women: Friends and Rivals,* Goodman explores key relationships between Wharton and other women, pointing out that many of her most intimate letters were written to women correspondents. In her 1994 study of the men who comprised what she termed *Edith Wharton's Inner Circle,* Goodman again provides a quantity of previously uncollected information to show Wharton's deep interest in aspiring artists, and her genuine gift for friendship with achieving people (many of them, given the cultural climate of her time, male).

For all this attention to the context of Wharton's life as a writer, however, much criticism of the work itself remains myopic. It is as if readers find Wharton's characters so fascinating, her plots so involving, that many are unwilling to discuss more than one text, or more than one character, at a time. Yet some of the best earlier studies of Wharton's works (McDowell; Lawson; Ammons, *Edith Wharton's Argument*; Wershoven; Gimbel) surveyed most of her novels. Much recent criticism of Wharton tends, in contrast, to be New Critical. At their best, as in essays by Sherrie A. Inness, D. Quentin Miller, and Jean Frantz Blackall, or the book by Catherine M. Rae, close readings of texts are never outdated. Some publishers' formats call for readings of single texts (Springer on *Ethan Frome,* Wagner-Martin on *The House of Mirth* and *The Age of*

Innocence). For students trained in various kinds of criticism, however, the close-reading approach makes Wharton's work seem less interesting than works by her peers—Virginia Woolf, Willa Cather, Djuna Barnes, Katherine Mansfield—who have received attention from scholars whose critical practices are more diverse.

Partly because of the reification of past criticism, coupled with an emphasis on close-reading techniques, the ways in which Wharton's best-known texts are read have been difficult to change—or even modify. Male characters still occupy the center of critical attention, for example. (An index of the power of the male-focused interpretations of the novels was the kind of attention Judith Sensibar's 1988 essay in *American Literature*—questioning Wharton's view of "the bachelor type"—received [and see Holbrook].) Readings are still dominated by the view that Wharton was as good a writer as she was largely because she *was* one of the boys, voiced in studies by Percy Lubbock and others through Lewis's biography, although countered by Goodman in her book on Wharton's male circle. This view discounts the issue of whether or not she was influenced by Henry James by contending that in some ways she *was* Henry James—or at least Walter Berry.

A corollary to the problem that Wharton is consistently identified with male writers is that earlier criticism often identified her with her male protagonists. Such identification causes immense problems for today's readers, who are accustomed to having women writers, like writers of color, identify themselves proudly rather than disguise their gender and race. The logical autobiographical correspondence in *The Reef*, for example, is between Wharton and some composite of Sophy Viner and Anna Leath—just as in *The Age of Innocence* the logical correspondence is between Wharton and Ellen Olenska. The traditional reading of the latter novel, however, is to identify the author with Newland Archer (Mizener, Parrington, Lewis, but see Benstock, *No Gifts*, and Wagner-Martin, "Introduction"). Any attempt to rescue Wharton's work from long-entrenched perspectives will require serious investigation of her treatment of gender roles and new kinds of analyses of both female and male characters.

The impulse to give Edith Wharton as writer the characteristics and attributes of a male author is understandable: "raising" women writers into the largely male canon was most often accomplished in this way. Nonetheless, a 1995 book by Carol J. Singley proves just how weak a strategy this division of writers' traits into male and female is. *Edith*

Wharton: Matters of Mind and Spirit establishes Wharton's crucial involvement in the compelling intellectual, philosophical, and religious debates of her times (i.e., Wharton assumes an intellectual—and perhaps "male"—role in her culture). Singley combines biography, cultural history, and focused readings of a number of texts—short stories as well as such novels as *The Reef, Summer, The Age of Innocence, Hudson River Bracketed*, and others.

Singley treats this body of work in conjunction with wide-ranging discussions of Wharton's knowledge of, and responses to, Darwinian science, aestheticism, rationalism, and such religious movements as Calvinism, Catholicism, and transcendentalism. She often presents the more abstract contextualizations through her readings of Wharton's texts; through her discussion of "The Angel at the Grave," for example, the reader comes to understand why Wharton preferred rationalism to William James's pragmatism. Similarly, in Singley's reading, *Ethan Frome* illustrates not realism so much as Calvinism, showing "both a personal and cultural defeat" (122) while *The Reef* posits a kind of feminine wisdom and power, *Summer* evokes Emersonian beliefs, and *Hudson River Bracketed* and *The Gods Arrive* explore Catholicism.

Singley deals with a myriad of ideas in *Edith Wharton: Matters of Mind and Spirit*—information about Wharton's affinity with George Eliot, discussion of the scientists and philosophers Wharton called her "Awakeners" (Henry Coppee, William Hamilton, Blaise Pascal, and Charles Darwin), the pervasive New York Episcopalian social (if not religious) forms. She has written a comprehensive study of Wharton and her intellectual times, and I would group this book with Dale Bauer's 1994 study of Wharton and politics and Kathy Fedorko's 1995 *Gender and the Gothic in the Fiction of Edith Wharton* to create an impressive paradigm for future directions in Wharton criticism. Each book gives an immense amount of new factual information, providing contexts that few Wharton critics have ever associated with her work. Because each scholar has written widely not just on Wharton but also on other American writers, the systematic application of the factual material to Wharton's writing is managed with balance and acumen. This is not to say that these three studies avoid the controversial; sometimes large claims are made, but they are palatable because the reader has confidence in the scholarship. These three books are filled with the evidence of diligent work; no one has taken short cuts. Even more to the point, Singley, Bauer, and Fedorko are keenly imaginative, so that the quantities of facts are put to expert use.

Such a triumvirate implicitly answers a somewhat petulant 1989 essay by a dedicated Wharton scholar. James Tuttleton's *New Criterion* defense of R. W. B. Lewis's work on Wharton—the ostensible purpose for his publishing "The Feminist Takeover of Edith Wharton"—met with much less opposition than did his assumption that only women scholars could be feminist, and that all women scholars, by virtue of biology, were feminist. That a great amount of the best criticism on Wharton's work is currently being done by women scholars is apparent, but the critical persuasion of at least some of these scholars is far from feminist, or it is feminist in so broad a sense as to be comparatively meaningless. If one defines "feminist" to mean using a methodology dependent on the work of the French feminist critics Kristeva and Cixous, or British or American scholars influenced by them, then very little current criticism on Wharton's work is feminist.

In surveying significant publications during the 1980s and the 1990s, however, I have noted (with some initial surprise) that women scholars have written a number of these works (what follows is a very limited list; for more inclusion, see Bendixen's bibliographic essays). One explanation for this phenomenon is that women scholars are likely to be pushed to try newer methodologies—perhaps because they are looking for strategies that allow their text-based readings more sophistication. It also appears that some of the most interesting criticism on Wharton's works in the 1980s was economically grounded: Wai-chee Dimock's "Debasing Exchange: Edith Wharton's *The House of Mirth*" in *PMLA* for 1985 became an instant reference point (and see Dubow, Kaplan, and Robinson). Much more study of Wharton and the literary marketplace could be undertaken.

A quantity of criticism in the 1980s and 1990s insists that Wharton's writing be read as a woman's text (Gilbert and Gubar, Herndl), while one approach to that kind of reading is the mythic (Donovan's 1989 *After the Fall*; Waid's 1991 *Edith Wharton's Letters from the Underworld*). Other interesting attempts to fuse the diverse elements of Wharton's oeuvre are made from the perspective of the author's use of space (Fryer's 1986 *Felicitous Space*) and of the domestic trope of the house (Chandler's 1992 *Dwelling in the Text*).

Excellent work on Wharton as a local color writer (Donovan, *Local Color*), or the opposite of that classification (Campbell), has set the pace for what may prove to be one of the most helpful ways of reading Wharton—as a practitioner of the Gothic. Martha Banta's 1994 essay "The Ghostly Gothic of Wharton's Everyday World" extends work done by Lynette Carpenter and Kathy Fedorko into the field of anthropology. Fedorko's 1995 book, a consummate and convincing study of the way the trope of horror/suspense informs a great deal of Wharton's writing, not merely her apparent ghost stories, provides yet another point of departure for critics who question the finality of existing readings. In *Gender and the Gothic in the Fiction of Edith Wharton*, Fedorko uses feminist archetypal theory to explore the ways in which Wharton adopts Gothic elements as a means of describing the nature of feminine and masculine ways of knowing and being, thereby dramatizing the tension between them. Fedorko's reading of six novels and sixteen stories, written in four different periods of Wharton's career, provides the reader with plausible and, in many cases, new interpretations.

The apparent genre study, in the case of Wharton's writing, provides a workable format to delineate freshly observed patterns in the work. Much more extensive investigation needs to be done on Wharton's memoirs and travel writing (excellent models are the 1987 essay by Mary Suzanne Schriber and the 1990 book by Janet Goodwyn). Barbara A. White's careful work on Wharton's short stories (*Edith Wharton*) revisits her important two-part essay on incest in Wharton's writing and perhaps her life ("Neglected Areas"). More attention needs to be given to Wharton's novellas and short stories. Like James, Wharton wrote consistently and well in shorter forms, yet most critical attention has gone to her novels. Evelyn E. Fracasso's 1994 study reads many of the short stories from Wharton's dominant trope of imprisonment; it also deals with the figurative imprisonment of fear, often that of the supernatural. Useful in this connection would be studies of Wharton's reading, particularly her reading of the Gothic tale.

Recent book-length studies of Wharton's work have helped to change the direction of future critical investigation. Incorporating psychoanalytic methodologies, both Gloria Erlich and Lev Raphael assume somewhat atypical stances toward Wharton and her work. Raphael's *Edith Wharton's Prisoners of Shame: A New Perspective on Her Neglected Fiction* scrutinizes such texts as *The Touchstone, Sanctuary, The Glimpses of the Moon*, her war writing, and the later fiction, discerning the pattern of shame (in affect theory) that marks so many of her characters' behaviors. While Raphael does not make what might seem logical biographical extensions,

Erlich, in her 1992 *Sexual Education of Edith Wharton*, continues various interrogations about not only incest but also the full extent of Wharton's relationship—or lack of relationship—with Fullerton.

Much of the impetus for excellent criticism seems, in Wharton's case, to remain biographical. In 1994, publishers marked the twentieth anniversary of the R. W. B. Lewis biography of Edith Wharton with a reissue of his study, and, in 1995, the Radcliffe Biography Series brought out a new edition of Cynthia Griffin Wolff's *A Feast of Words: The Triumph of Edith Wharton*, a book that includes a new introduction and several of Wolff's previously uncollected essays. Also useful as treatments of Wharton's life and work are Katherine Joslin's clearly written and always accurate *Edith Wharton*, Margaret B. McDowell's much-revised edition of her earlier *Edith Wharton*, and Eleanor Dwight's *Edith Wharton: An Extraordinary Life*, the best illustrated of the recent biographies. Superior even to these is Shari Benstock's *No Gifts from Chance: A Biography of Edith Wharton*.

An assiduously drawn portrait of Wharton as woman writer, Benstock's creation pulls together strands of aesthetics, biography, cultural history, and feminist insight into the problems of Wharton's dilemma. Plagued by issues of class, race, and sexuality, the writer led a life more often disguised than transparent. In a period when being unlettered was fashionable, Wharton was truly well educated; when being poor was not onerous, Wharton was wealthy; when being sexually adventurous was fashionable, Wharton had little opportunity for any kind of sensual exploration. Benstock's achievement is not in adding to the chorus of lament for Edith Wharton, but in showing how her writing became her joy, and how she conceived of herself and her life, her strength. The immense amount of new material, the calmly evocative style, and the obvious clarity of judgment make *No Gifts from Chance* the starting point for the next twenty years of Wharton criticism.

In conclusion, I would remind readers that much work remains to be done. We would all benefit from more attention to manuscripts. There is also the fact that Wharton's novels were often serialized before they were published entire; criticism that deals with the history of the publication of her work, as well as criticism that deals with manuscript revision, such as Alan Price's essay on *The Age of Innocence*, would be useful. Recent collections of essays (see Bell, Bendixen and Zilversmit, Joslin and Price), as well as past special issues of *College Literature* and *Women's Studies*, provide a number of insights into the critical health of the Wharton project; more such collections would continue to build a body of solid Wharton criticism (see Werlock). The various film versions of Wharton's texts also interest many readers, and much could be learned about cultural history and the perceptions of women characters in women's fiction through further study in that area. The 1993 publication of Wharton's early novella, *Fast and Loose*, in conjunction with her unfinished last work, *The Buccaneers*, edited by Viola Hopkins Winner (or in its somewhat bastardized 1993 form, completed by Marion Mainwaring), also suggests the keen interest in whatever material remains unpublished (plays, translations, essays, fiction). It seems clear that—sixty years after her death—Edith Wharton has once again become an American author to be reckoned with.

WORKS CITED

Ammons, Elizabeth. *Conflicting Stories: American Women Writers at the Turn into the Twentieth Century.* New York: Oxford UP, 1992.

———. *Edith Wharton's Argument with America.* Athens: U of Georgia P, 1980.

Banta, Martha. "The Ghostly Gothic of Wharton's Everyday World." *American Literary Realism* 27 (1994): 1–10.

Bauer, Dale M. *Edith Wharton's Brave New Politics.* Madison: U of Wisconsin P, 1994.

———. *Female Dialogics: A Theory of Failed Community.* Albany: State U of New York P, 1988.

Bell, Millicent, *Edith Wharton and Henry James: The Story of Their Friendship.* New York: George Braziller, 1965.

———, ed. *The Cambridge Companion to Edith Wharton.* New York: Cambridge UP, 1995.

Bendixen, Alfred. "A Guide to Wharton Criticism, 1976–1983." *Edith Wharton Newsletter* 2 (1985): 1–8. [Comments also by others]

———. "New Directions in Wharton Criticism: A Bibliographic Essay." *Edith Wharton Review* 10 (1993): 20–24.

———. "Recent Wharton Studies: A Bibliographic Essay." *Edith Wharton Newsletter* 3 (1986): 5, 8–9.

———. "Wharton Studies, 1986–1987: A Bibliographic Essay." *Edith Wharton Newsletter* 5 (1988): 5–8, 10.

———. "The World of Wharton Criticism: A Bibliographic Essay." *Edith Wharton Review* 7 (1990): 118–21.

Bendixen, Alfred, and Annette Zilversmit, eds. *Edith Wharton: New Critical Essays.* New York: Garland, 1992.

Benstock, Shari. *No Gifts from Chance: A Biography of Edith Wharton.* New York: Scribners, 1994.

———. *Women of the Left Bank: Paris, 1900–1940.* Austin: U of Texas P, 1986.

———, ed. *Case Studies in Contemporary Criticism: "The House of Mirth."* New York: St. Martin's P, Bedford Books, 1994.

Blackall, Jean Frantz. "Edith Wharton's Art of Ellipsis." *Journal of Narrative Technique* 17 (1987): 145–61.

Booth, Wayne C. *A Rhetoric of Irony.* Chicago: U of Chicago P, 1974.

Brenni, Vito J. *Edith Wharton: A Bibliography.* Morgantown, VA: McClain Printing, 1966.

Brown, E. K. "Edith Wharton: The Art of the Novel." *The Art of the Novel: From 1700 to the Present Time.* Ed. Pelham Edgar. New York: Macmillan, 1933: 196–205.

Campbell, Donna M. "Edith Wharton and the 'Authoresses': The Critique of Local Color in Wharton's Early Fiction." *Studies in American Fiction* 22 (1994): 169–83.

Carpenter, Lynette. "Deadly Letters, Sexual Politics, and the Dilemma of the Woman Writer: Edith Wharton's 'The House of the Dead Hand.'" *American Literary Realism* 24 (1992): 55–69.

Chandler, Marilyn. *Dwelling in the Text: Houses in American Fiction.* Berkeley: U of California P, 1992.

Colquitt, Clare. "Unpacking Her Treasures: Edith Wharton's 'Mysterious Correspondence' with Morton Fullerton." *Library Chronicle of the University of Texas at Austin* 2 (1985): 73–107.

Dimock, Wai-chee. "Debasing Exchange: Edith Wharton's *The House of Mirth.*" *PMLA* 100 (1985): 783–92.

Donovan, Josephine. *After the Fall: The Demeter-Persephone Myth in Wharton, Cather, and Glasgow.* University Park: Pennsylvania State UP, 1989.

———. *Local Color: A Woman's Tradition.* New York: Ungar, 1983.

Dubow, Wendy M. "The Businesswoman in Edith Wharton." *Edith Wharton Review* 8 (1991): 11–18.

DuPlessis, Rachel Blau. *Writing beyond the Ending: Narrative Strategies of Twentieth-Century Women Writers.* Bloomington: Indiana UP, 1985.

Dwight, Eleanor. *Edith Wharton: An Extraordinary Life.* New York: Henry A. Abrams, 1994.

Erlich, Gloria C. *The Sexual Education of Edith Wharton.* Berkeley: U of California P, 1992.

Fedorko, Kathy A. *Gender and the Gothic in the Fiction of Edith Wharton.* Tuscaloosa: U of Alabama P, 1995.

Fracasso, Evelyn E. *Edith Wharton's Prisoners of Consciousness.* New York: Greenwood, 1994.

Fryer, Judith. *Felicitous Space: The Imaginative Structures of Edith Wharton and Willa Cather.* Chapel Hill: U of North Carolina P, 1986.

Garrison, Stephen, ed. *Edith Wharton: A Descriptive Bibliography.* Pittsburgh: U of Pittsburgh P, 1990.

Gilbert, Sandra M., and Susan Gubar. *No Man's Land.* Vol. 2 of *Sexchanges.* New Haven, CT: Yale UP, 1989.

Gimbel, Wendy. *Edith Wharton: Orphancy and Survival.* New York: Praeger, 1984.

Goodman, Susan. *Edith Wharton's Inner Circle.* Austin: U of Texas P, 1994.

———. *Edith Wharton's Women: Friends and Rivals.* Hanover, NH: UP of New England, 1990.

Goodwyn, Janet. *Edith Wharton: Traveller in the Land of Letters.* London: Macmillan, 1990.

Gribben, Alan. "'The Heart Is Insatiable': A Selection from Edith Wharton's Letters to Morton Fullerton, 1907–1915." *Library Chronicle of the University of Texas at Austin* 2 (1985): 7–18.

Hadley, Kathy Miller. *In the Interstices of the Tale: Edith Wharton's Narrative Strategies.* New York: Peter Lang, 1993.

Herndl, Diane Price. *Invalid Women: Figuring Feminine Illness in American Fiction and Culture 1840–1940.* Chapel Hill: U of North Carolina P, 1993.

Holbrook, David. *Edith Wharton and the Unsatisfactory Man.* New York: St. Martin's, 1991.

Howe, Irving, ed. *Edith Wharton: A Collection of Critical Essays.* Englewood Cliffs, NJ: Prentice-Hall, 1962.

Hutcheon, Linda. *Irony's Edge: The Theory and Politics of Irony.* New York: Routledge, 1995.

Inness, Sherrie A. "Nature, Culture, and Sexual Economics in Edith Wharton's *The Reef.*" *American Literary Realism* 26 (1993): 76–90.

Joslin, Katherine. *Edith Wharton.* New York: St. Martin's, 1991.

———. "Edith Wharton at 125." *College Literature* 14 (1987): 193–206.

Joslin, Katherine, and Alan Price, eds. *"Wretched Exotic": Essays on Edith Wharton in Europe.* New York: Peter Lang, 1993.

Kaplan, Amy. *The Social Construction of American Realism.* Chicago: U of Chicago P, 1988.

Lauer, Kristin O., and Margaret P. Murray, eds. *Edith Wharton: An Annotated Secondary Bibiography.* New York: Garland, 1990.

Lawson, Richard H. *Edith Wharton.* New York: Ungar, 1976.

Lewis, R. W. B. *Edith Wharton: A Biography.* New York: Harper & Row, 1975.

Lubbock, Percy. *Portrait of Edith Wharton.* New York: Appleton-Century-Crofts, 1947.

McDowell, Margaret B. *Edith Wharton.* Boston: Twayne, 1976; revised, 1990.

Miller, D. Quentin. "'A Barrier of Words': The Tension between Narrative Voice and Vision in the Writings of Edith Wharton." *American Literary Realism* 27 (1994): 11–22.

Mizener, Arthur. *Twelve Great American Novels.* New York: New American Library, 1967.

Nevius, Blake. *Edith Wharton: A Study of Her Fiction.* Berkeley: U of California P, 1961.

Parrington, Vernon L. "Our Literary Aristocrat." *Pacific Review* 2 (1921): 157–60.

Powers, Lyall H., ed. *Henry James and Edith Wharton, Letters: 1900–1915.* New York: Scribners, 1990.

Price, Alan. "The Composition of Edith Wharton's *The Age of Innocence.*" *Yale University Library Gazette* 55 (1980): 22–30.

Rae, Catherine M. *Edith Wharton's New York Quartet.* Lanham, MD: UP of America, 1984.

Raphael, Lev. *Edith Wharton's Prisoners of Shame: A New Perspective on Her Neglected Fiction.* New York: St. Martin's, 1991.

Robinson, Lillian S. "The Traffic in Women: A Cultural Critique of *The House of Mirth.*" Benstock, *Case Studies* 340–58.

Schriber, Mary Suzanne. "Edith Wharton and Travel Writing as Self-Discovery." *American Literature* 59 (1987): 257–67.

Sensibar, Judith. "Edith Wharton Reads the Bachelor Type: Her Critique of Modernism's Representative Man." *American Literature* 60 (1988): 575–90.

Singley, Carol J. *Edith Wharton: Matters of Mind and Spirit.* New York: Cambridge UP, 1995.

Springer, Marlene, ed. *Edith Wharton and Kate Chopin: A Reference Guide.* Boston: G. K. Hall, 1976.

———. *Ethan Frome: A Nightmare of Need.* New York: Twayne, 1993.

Springer, Marlene, and Joan Gilson, eds. "Edith Wharton: A Reference Guide Updated." *Resources for American Literary Study* 14 (1984): 85–111.

Sullivan, Ellie Ragland. "The Daughter's Dilemma: Psychoanalytic Interpretation and Edith Wharton's *The House of Mirth.*" Benstock, *Case Studies* 464–81.

Tuttleton, James W. "Edith Wharton." *American Women Writers: Bibliographical Essays.* Ed. Maurice Duke, Jackson R. Bryer, and M. Thomas Inge. Westport, CT: Greenwood, 1983. 71–107.

———. "The Feminist Takeover of Edith Wharton." *New Criterion* 7 (1989): 6–14.

———. *The Novel of Manners in America.* Chapel Hill: U of North Carolina P, 1972.

Tuttleton, James W., Kristin O. Lauer, and Margaret P. Murray, eds. *Edith Wharton: The Contemporary Reviews.* New York: Cambridge UP, 1992.

Wagner-Martin, Linda. *"The Age of Innocence": A Novel of Ironic Nostalgia.* New York: Twayne, 1996.

———. *"The House of Mirth": A Novel of Admonition.* Boston: Twayne, 1990.

———. Introduction. *The Age of Innocence.* New York: Washington Square P, 1995.

Waid, Candace. *Edith Wharton's Letters from the Underworld.* Chapel Hill: U of North Carolina P, 1991.

Wegener, Frederick. "Edith Wharton and the Difficult Writing of *The Writing of Fiction.*" *Modern Language Studies* 25 (1995): 60–79.

Werlock, Abby H. P. "Whitman, Wharton, and the Sexuality in *Summer.*" *Speaking the Other Self: New Essays on American Women Writers.* Ed. Jeanne Campbell Reesman. Athens: U of Georgia P, forthcoming.

Wershoven, Carol. *The Female Intruder in the Novels of Edith Wharton.* Rutherford, NJ: Fairleigh Dickinson UP, 1982.

Wharton, Edith. *The Age of Innocence.* New York: Appleton, 1920.

———. "The Angel at the Grave." *The Best Short Stories of Edith Wharton.* Ed. Wayne Andrews. New York: Scribners, 1958. 117–32.

———. *"The Buccaneers": A Novel by Edith Wharton.* Completed by Marion Mainwaring. New York: Penguin, 1993.

———. *The Children.* New York: Appleton, 1928.

———. *The Collected Short Stories.* 2 vols. Ed. R. W. B. Lewis. New York: Scribners, 1968.

———. *Ethan Frome.* New York: Scribners, 1911.

———. *"Fast and Loose" & "The Buccaneers."* Ed. Viola Hopkins Winner. Charlottesville: UP of Virginia, 1993.

———. *The Glimpses of the Moon.* New York: Appleton, 1922.

———. *The Gods Arrive.* New York: Appleton, 1932.

———. *The House of Mirth.* New York: Scribners, 1905.

———. *Hudson River Bracketed.* New York: Appleton, 1929.

———. *The Letters of Edith Wharton.* Ed. R. W. B. Lewis and Nancy Lewis. New York: Scribners, 1988.

———. *The Mother's Recompense.* New York: Appleton, 1925.

———. *The Reef.* New York: Appleton, 1912.

———. *Sanctuary.* New York: Scribners, 1903.

———. *Summer.* New York: Appleton, 1917.

———. *The Touchstone.* New York: Scribners, 1900.

———. *Twilight Sleep.* New York: Appleton, 1927.

———. *The Writing of Fiction.* New York: Scribners, 1925.

White, Barbara A. *Edith Wharton: A Study of the Short Fiction.* Boston: Twayne, 1991.

———. "Neglected Areas: Wharton's Short Stories and Incest." *Edith Wharton Review* 8.1 (1991): 3–12; and 8. 2 (1991): 3–10, 32.

Wilson, Edmund. "Justice to Edith Wharton." *The Wound and the Bow*. New York: Oxford UP, 1947. 195–213.

Wolff, Cynthia Griffin. *A Feast of Words: The Triumph of Edith Wharton*. New York: Oxford UP, 1977. Reissued (expanded), New York: Addison-Wesley, 1995.

11

Willa Cather

Susan J. Rosowski

Recent decades have witnessed a dramatic rise in Willa Cather's standing among academics. During the late 1960s and early 1970s, fewer than twenty essays on Cather appeared annually and a book only occasionally; now upward of eighty essays and a score of books concerning Cather appear each year, and there is now a hardback series devoted to scholarship on her (*Cather Studies*). These years have seen Cather move from marginalized to canonical status; indeed, she is one of only four women writers, and the only American woman, represented on the *Encyclopaedia Britannica*'s 1990 update of its list, "Great Books of the Western World." Not surprisingly, perhaps, Cather's newly acquired status is signaled by her becoming territory over which lit crit battles are waged. Cather's books are now called texts and treated as interpretive sites to be problematized, and whereas only twenty years ago Cather scholars were arguing that she was a major writer, last year the *New Yorker* emblazoned its newsstand cover with the question, "What have the academics done to Willa Cather?" While territorial skirmishes of the moment play out, a fundamental shift is occurring within Cather studies that signals another notion of canonicity, by which (as Barbara Herrnstein Smith has argued) a writer is important, not because she represents transcendent values or universal truths, but because she is inscribed into a culture. Whereas critics once wrote *about* Cather and her life, they are now beginning to write *through* Cather in addressing ideas and concerns important to us today.

It is no accident that the recent explosion of academic interest in Cather corresponds with the so-called age of criticism and theory within the American academy. Methods of formalism, ill-suited to a writer who introduced her best-known work with the disclaimer that it "has n't any form" (*My Ántonia* xiii), have been supplemented by approaches that respond well to the challenges offered by her writing: those of feminism and gender studies, narratology, cultural studies, new historicism, and the like. But the vitality of Cather studies within the academy comprises only part of the story of what lies ahead; the other part has to do with her ongoing appeal to the community at large. As I shall argue in the following essay, prospects for Cather studies include returning scholarship to criticism, engaging more substantially with theory and then leavening theory with common sense, and, most importantly, broadening the discourse.

Whereas the past decade has demonstrated the responsiveness of Cather's work to theory, the challenge for the upcoming decade is to provide the materials that will support the more substantial theoretical engagements and the full range of inquiry that Cather's texts invite. Thus I begin by considering the texts themselves, which in the past decade have become both problematic and promising. Until the late 1980s, copyright protection meant that persons working on Cather used the Houghton Mifflin editions of *O Pioneers!*, *The Song of the Lark*, and *My Ántonia*, and the Knopf editions of *One of Ours* through *Sapphira and the Slave Girl*. [That's "Sa FEAR ah," not "Sa FIRE ah," by the way.] Pagination was not a problem because almost all reissues into the early 1980s were based upon first edition plates (the 1976 Copyright Act extended protection to existing works for seventy-five years following date of publication). *O Pioneers!* entered the public domain in 1988, however (*Alexander's Bridge* preceded it by two years, but no one seemed to notice); *The Song of the Lark* and *My Ántonia* followed in short order, and cheap editions proliferated. Because the textual landscape of Cather studies has shifted radically in recent years, a first step for teachers and scholars working with Cather will be to assess the reliability and authority of editions.

Important stimuli for Cather studies include materials now being made available by the Willa Cather Scholarly Edition. Each volume of this new edition traces a Cather text as it emerged from the complicated historical processes of creation and transmission. Each volume provides textual plus historical apparatuses: a critical text of Cather's work; a textual essay describing and interpreting changes she made through various versions of it; a historical essay presenting a biography of the work, the circumstances of its conception, composition, and reception; and explanatory notes providing information relevant to the meaning of the text, including identifications of locations, literary references, persons, historical events, and specialized terminology. *O Pioneers!* (1992) and *My Ántonia* (1994) are in print; and *A Lost Lady* (1997) is in production, each having been awarded the MLA's Committee on Scholarly Editions emblem for having met the highest standards in scholarly editing; *Obscure Destinies, Death Comes for the Archbishop, The Professor's House*, and *Shadows on the Rock* are in the pipeline. Perhaps tellingly and certainly sadly, the Cather Edition is the first long-term editorial project for a woman author to be associated with the MLA's Committee on Scholarly Editions (the only other work written by a woman to be awarded CSE's emblem was the single volume of Virginia Woolf's *Melymbrosia*).

An important complement to the Scholarly Edition's notes is *A Reader's Companion to the Fiction of Willa Cather*, written by John March and edited by Marilyn Arnold with Debra Lynn Thornton; it presents allusions, persons, and quotations in Cather's writing published in books and magazines following her graduation from the University of Nebraska in 1895. With fuller information available about Cather's sources comes the opportunity for comprehensive studies of a range of subjects, including one that Cather always denigrated—working up material from published sources, a subject that has been handled only piecemeal so far.

We need fuller knowledge about and access to Cather's journalistic writing, until now represented by Bernice Slote's *The Kingdom of Art: Willa Cather's First Principles and Critical Statements 1893–1896* and William M. Curtin's two-volume *The World and the Parish: Willa Cather's Articles and Reviews, 1893–1902*. Both were pioneering publications in demonstrating the extent of Cather's early writing; because they were edited to present "Willa Cather's ideas of art" (Cather, *The Kingdom of Art* vii) and to "trace Willa Cather's development as a writer" (Cather, *The World and the Parish* xix); however, both tended to omit Cather's comments on ephemeral subjects and local circumstances—precisely the kinds of materials of special interest to cultural studies. We need ready access to Cather's journalistic writing in its entirety; the ideal would be an updated and extended edition that would expand upon, rather than attempt to replace, the superb work done by Slote and Curtin. As fuller editions are available, the need for a concordance that would facilitate the tracings of ideas and allusions through Cather's texts intensifies.

Though Cather suppressed her juvenilia, arguing that a writer should be granted the privilege of a farmer to discard his bad apples, literary

critics are likely to align themselves with Henry James, who in the opening paragraph of his first preface wrote that the author, "[a]ddicted to
'stories' and inclined to retrospect . . . fondly takes, under this backward
view, his whole unfolding, his process of production, for a thrilling tale,
almost for a wondrous adventure" (4). Until now treated primarily as
storage sites for the allusions and ideas that later appear in the mature
writing, the journalistic essays and reviews will offer insight into how
Cather developed her voice, negotiated a relationship with her subjects
and her readers, and gained skill in writing a portrait and in creating a
scene.

Joan Crane's *Willa Cather: A Bibliography* (1982) provides a starting
place for retrieval of basic materials. Crane offers a chronological listing
of all books by Cather in first and subsequent editions and the states,
issues, and printings deriving therefrom; in her discussion of each work,
Crane includes information about circumstances surrounding and details
of its production. Crane also lists works edited and poems written by
Cather (including musical settings), short fiction, articles, reviews, and
essays, plus translations of Cather's novels and stories. For Cather's
student writing, however, Crane provides only a selective listing, and
scholars interested in the juvenilia should begin with Slote's "Checklist of
Willa Cather's Critical and Personal Writing, 1891–1896" in *The Kingdom
of Art* and Curtin's "Bibliography of Articles and Reviews" in *The World
and the Parish*. Although Crane's bibliography continues to serve scholars
well for work with Cather's professional writing, we need a full and
updated checklist of her juvenilia.

The next decade of Cather studies will see readier access to Cather's
other writing. L. Brent Bohlke's untimely death forestalled the volume he
was preparing as a complement to *Willa Cather in Person: Interviews,
Speeches and Letters* (1986); plans for that volume are now proceeding. In
1993, *The Life of Mary Baker G. Eddy and the History of Christian Science* "By
Willa Cather and Georgine Milmine" was published, Cather's authorship
for the first time fully acknowledged. David Stouck, in his introduction
and afterword, provides full details concerning Cather's involvement in
the book, discusses her fidelity to facts and her concern with psychology
and philosophy, and interprets the book's relation to Cather's later
fiction. Work is progressing on a reissue of Cather's *The Autobiography of
S. S. McClure*, tentatively scheduled for 1998 from the University of
Nebraska Press.

By providing information about locations of Cather letters available in libraries, Margaret O'Connor's "A Guide to the Letters of Willa Cather" has, since 1974, provided a starting place for work with Cather's correspondence, work that required traveling to repositories throughout the United States (if scholars had the needed time and money). The alternative to traveling has been reliance upon others' paraphrases and interpretations, a notoriously problematic enterprise (see Acocella's response to O'Brien's reading of a "smoking gun" passage from a letter to Louise Pound, for example). Because restrictions against publishing the letters are unlikely to be lifted in the foreseeable future, an expanded guide to them is sorely needed, one that would include summaries of their contents as well as correspondence retrieved in the past two decades: twenty-one letters to Dorothy Canfield Fisher (Madigan); twenty pages of an adolescent Cather's holograph letters to Mrs. Helen Stowell (Bennett); five letters to Thomas G. Masaryk discovered in Prague (Halac), and more. The ongoing search for Cather-related correspondence promises to be especially fruitful in the collections and files of persons who worked with her and knew her.

As a corollary aid, a guide to sales of Cather-related materials would be of interest to scholars working on literary reputation and the marketplace (as well as to collectors). There is considerable irony in the prospect of a volume titled *Cather at Auction*, however; such a project would have been reprehensible to a writer who saw with painful clarity the potential for the Mrs. Beasleys and Molly Tuckers to "have their chance at last" by swarming like ants over someone's effects, once their owner has lost her power of resistance (*A Lost Lady* Book 2, chapter 5).

Understanding Cather means reading what she read, past and present; and it means reading her sources as she read them, George Sand and Anatole France in the original rather than in translation. Thirty years after the fact, Slote still provides the best discussion we have of Cather's reading from her childhood through her university years (Cather, *The Kingdom of Art* 37–43). Needed is a checklist of Cather's reading that would update Slote's list and track her reading through her lifetime by her references in reviews, correspondence, speeches, interviews, and (of course) fiction. Such a checklist would enable others to carry on the important influence study begun with regard to Russian, American, and French writers (see below), and it would encourage the book-length views needed to interpret the formation of Cather's aesthetics within these traditions. Finally, with its citations of contemporary writers—

Virginia Woolf and May Sarton, Sigmund Freud and William James—a checklist of Cather's reading would also support a fuller consideration of Cather within her time.

A complement to a checklist of Cather's reading would be a checklist of references *to* Cather. The influence studies have been primarily backward-looking: that is, scholars have made important contributions by discussing how Cather drew upon the classics (Ryder, Thurin), the Russians (Harris; Stouck, "Willa Cather and the Russians"), Dante (Murphy), Whitman (Anders), Daudet (Woodress, "Willa Cather and Alphonse Daudet"), and others. However, beyond generalizing about the high regard in which other writers hold Cather, critics have limited their forward-looking explorations to isolated examples: for example, Faulkner responded to *The Professor's House* in *Mosquitoes*, and Cather replied to Faulkner in "Before Breakfast" (Skaggs, "Thefts and Conversation"). The literary conversations have continued: Alice Munro wrote "Dulse" as a response to "Before Breakfast" (Thacker); E. A. Mares wrote his play *I Returned and Saw under the Sun* as a response to *Death Comes for the Archbishop*; Toni Morrison addressed Cather directly in *Playing in the Dark* and then indirectly in *Beloved*; Lynn Sharon Schwartz embedded allusions to Cather throughout *Disturbances in the Field*, as did Douglas Unger in *Leaving the Land*. A survey of addresses and allusions to Cather is a first step to understanding what has been Cather's influence upon and relationship to contemporary writers, as well as succeeding generations of writers.

A collection of contemporary reviews of Cather's fiction would serve as an additional resource for reception studies. The volume I envision would reprint a representative selection of the reviews themselves, along with supplementary materials (e.g., letters and memoranda at Houghton Mifflin and Knopf concerning marketing and publicity, representative advertising copy).

Two biographies initiated the last decade of Cather studies. With *Willa Cather: A Literary Life* (1987), James Woodress has written what will remain the standard. Reliable in its accuracy, as well as in the fullness of its information, and admirably clear in its style, Woodress's book is basic to any work in the field. Published that same year, Sharon O'Brien's *Willa Cather: The Emerging Voice* provided the catalyst for a wave of feminist readings, many of them highly derivative in drawing upon Nancy Chodorow through O'Brien and assuming Cather's lesbianism. Hermione Lee's *Willa Cather: A Life Saved Up* provides solid and insightful interpretation woven together by basic biographical information. Whereas the Woodress biography will continue to serve scholars well, Cather studies is rapidly outstripping *Willa Cather: The Emerging Voice*, and the need is increasingly apparent for biographies that deal more broadly and critically with theory and that take into account the scope of Cather's writing (O'Brien concludes with *O Pioneers!*). A biography in preparation by Cynthia Griffin Wolff may begin to address that need; additional biographies are sure to follow.

Also, I look forward to a different kind of biography—one that would more fully place Cather's writing against her professional background. Such a biography would give as much attention to Cather's interaction with her publishers and editors as has been devoted to her interactions with family and friends. Reading Cather's correspondence with Ferris Greenslet (her editor at Houghton Mifflin), and with Alfred A. and Blanche Knopf (she published with Knopf from 1920 until her death) brings one close to the circumstances of a professional writer in the early twentieth century who had to negotiate with regard to aesthetic and commercial matters. Such a biography would explore Cather's participation in literature as cultural production, and it would include, perhaps, an ethnography/sociology of the book as Cather knew it in the Southern culture of her Virginia childhood, in the frontier town of Red Cloud and at the University of Nebraska, then in Pittsburgh and in New York City's publishing circles. James L. W. West III's *American Authors and the Literary Marketplace since 1900* provides a starting place for investigating the relationship between aesthetic and commercial factors in the production of American literature.

Additional biographical research is needed to expand and deepen our understanding of Cather's friends, family, and associates. While Sarah Orne Jewett's mentoring of Cather is now standard fare in Cather studies, relatively little attention has been devoted to other relationships. Edith Lewis, her companion for nearly four decades, has received the critical equivalent of her apocryphal burial at Cather's feet; she is characteristically dismissed as an aside: "the first officer" serving Cather, her Captain (Sergeant 202), "Cather's 'stand-in'" (Woodress 201), and the "self-effacing and servile" companion to Cather (Yongue 14). Marilyn Arnold, in her introduction to a reissue of *Willa Cather Living*, lays the ground-work for further study of Lewis and the Cather-Lewis relationship, and we can now hope that others will follow up on Arnold's lead to learn more about Lewis, a woman of independence and achievement in her own right: a copyeditor at *McClure's*, an advertising writer at J. Walter Thompson, a poet and memoirist. As is the case with so much in Cather studies, scholars need to set aside preconceptions and conduct the research.

Similarly, fuller recognition of the circle of Cather's friendships and acquaintanceships lies ahead. Noting that Cather's "stay in Boston was richly productive of friendships," Woodress provides names and details to help scholars to begin exploring that circle: "Ferris Greenslet of Houghton Mifflin, who became her publisher; Margaret Deland, writer; Louise Imogen Guiney, poet; Louis Brandeis, future Supreme Court justice, his wife and her sister Pauline Goldmark, social worker; Laura Hills, painter" (*Willa Cather* 195). Other periods and places of Cather's life involved other circles, all deserving far more attention than they have until now received. Again, Woodress's *Willa Cather: A Literary Life* provides a starting place.

Cather's own participation in the literary marketplace was more extensive than has been generally acknowledged. Cather published in magazines remarkable for their variety: the women's magazine *Home Monthly* and the muckraking *McClure's*, as well as *Harper's, Century, Smart Set, Collier's, Saturday Evening Post, Woman's Home Companion*, and *Ladies Home Journal*, to name but a few. Moreover, Cather made purchasing decisions about fiction at *Home Monthly* and at *McClure's*. Neo-Marxist questions may prove fruitful: What are the processes of textualization? How do they reflect and, possibly, influence institutional patterns?

Reputation studies until now have resembled the incestuous inbreeding of critics responding to other critics. We would do well to look more fully at Cather's role in creating her own reputation by her acts of selection and revision, her participation in marketing, and her attempts to direct the terms by which her writing is read. Her essays have been read primarily for the principles of her art; a next step is to consider their role in creating the aesthetic that would safeguard her freedom to write and ensure her books a long future. Cather's essay "The Novel Démeublé" appeared in the *New Republic* shortly before *A Lost Lady* was published, for example, and reviewers echoed the essay's principles in praising Cather's novel. Lying ahead is also a study of the marketing of Cather's novels: the disappointing (to Cather's mind at least) marketing of her first novels by Houghton Mifflin and the successful marketing of her later novels by Knopf.

Inspired by feminist criticism and theory, studies on the narrative forms of women's writings have proliferated this past decade: Ann Romines's *The Home Plot: Women, Writing, and Domestic Ritual* and Helen Fiddyment Levy's *Fiction of the Home Place: Jewett, Cather, Glasgow, Porter, Welty, and Naylor* include Cather among the writers whom they interpret within maternal communities (Levy) and according to domestic rituals of housekeeping (Romines). The next decade will contain, I hope, significant studies of Cather's use of popular culture and art forms; after all, Ouida as well as Shakespeare, melodrama as well as drama, formed Cather's imagination.

To read Cather's fiction within the context of its magazine publication is to take initial steps in the cultural dialogics for which her writing is calling. Stories from Cather's early Pittsburgh period are characteristically dismissed as hackwork written to fill pages of the *Home Monthly*; however, when read within the pages of a magazine devoted to domesticity, the marriage plot in "Nanette: An Aside" takes on a satiric edge. Cather's involvement with *McClure's* meant immersion in social, political, and cultural issues of the day, and "Paul's Case: A Study in Temperament" is one story when read in a short story anthology, quite another when read alongside *McClure's* discourses on sociology and urban psychology.

Writing of the prospects for literary studies these days, one confronts issues of manner as well as substance, "the heightened contentiousness," as Gerald Graff politely calls it, "of present-day academic culture" (359). In Cather studies this contentiousness is more evident—strangely enough—in critics' attitudes toward Cather than in their attitudes toward one another. Like Niel Herbert trying to call up the shade of Mrs. Forrester to demand the secret of her ardor, so biographers, scholars, and critics have attempted to get at the real Cather, to "prove" her lesbianism, racism, sexism, and the like, and then to contest her definitions, appropriations, and silences. I expect that in the next decade we will see scholars returning to the writing itself, responding more fully to its possibilities in terms of the notion of "text" as Barthes uses it, not as a "finished, closed product, but as a production in progress, 'plugged in' to other texts, other codes (this is the intertextual), and thereby articulated with society and history in ways which are not determinist but citational" (135).

Prospects for Cather studies include expanding the context, also, from the last decade's intense gaze upon Cather herself to reading her within literary and intellectual currents. I interpret Cather within literary traditions of British romanticism and her romanticism as an early stage of modernism (*The Voyage Perilous: Willa Cather's Romanticism*); Phyllis Rose, in a superb essay, reads Cather's fiction as embodying "certain aesthetic ideals of modernism—monumentality, functionalism, anonymity" ("Modernism: The Case of Willa Cather"), and Jo Ann Middleton interprets modernism in terms of the narrative spaces ("vacuoles") of Cather's texts (*Willa Cather's Modernism: A Study of Style and Technique*). We need fuller consideration of Cather within currents of French and (especially) American romanticism, as well as within the cultural, social, and political contexts that formed these movements.

Looking more fully at the intersection of social commentary and literary genre in Cather's time means recognizing a dialogics of culture by which one explores the conversations of literary texts with contemporary social, cultural, and political texts. (Significantly, cultural scientists such as Malinowski and Veblen mapped anthropological discourse during her time.) Guy Reynolds's *Willa Cather in Context: Progress, Race, Empire* points the way by reading Cather's commentary on American society and culture, engaging such issues as immigration and assimilation, theories of progress, the role of science, and evolutionary theory.

It is here, I believe, that the most significant shift in Cather studies is occurring. Whereas in earlier decades Cather studies consisted largely of writing *about* Cather, work today is increasingly writing *through* Cather to address larger concerns. Rose's "Modernism: The Case of Willa Cather" illustrates the shift: Rose interprets Cather's modernism, of course, but, more importantly, she draws upon Cather to offer an expanded understanding of modernism itself. More recent longer studies reveal a similar shift: in *Bergson and American Culture: The Worlds of Willa Cather and Wallace Stevens*, Tom Quirk uses Cather to interpret American sensibility in the early years of the twentieth century; in *Willa Cather and the Myth of American Migration*, Joseph R. Urgo uses Cather to explicate migration as the "keystone" American experience and the prototypically American mode of thought; and in *Willa Cather in Context: Progress, Race, Empire*, Reynolds demonstrates that Cather invites consideration of volatile issues basic to American culture.

"To note an artist's limitations is but to define his genius," Cather wrote of Sarah Orne Jewett ("The Best Stories of Sarah Orne Jewett" 54); the same point might be made for Cather herself. Coming years will bring, I anticipate, fuller acknowledgment that for the intricacies of marriage negotiations, including divorce, a reader should turn to Wharton, not Cather. Cather's genius lay in writing of those matters about which she had firsthand experience, and her significance lies in resonances between her experience with that of the nation in terms of class, ethnicity, race, and politics, to name but a few. Unlike James, Wharton, and Woolf, Cather wrote of class from a vantage point derived from professional achievement rather than inherited status; her writing (like her life) demonstrates exceptional flexibility in its movements among class as regionally and culturally inscribed. Yet basic questions remain to be addressed. What was Cather's experience of and idea about class? And how does it relate to the "gift of sympathy" by which her writing is so regularly described? Moreover, Cather invites inquiry concerning the self-representation and performance basic to mobility in a capitalist society. The subject is illuminated by insight from feminist and gender critics of the past: Bartley Alexander, Thea Kronborg, Alexandra Bergson, Marian Forrester, Godfrey St. Peter, Lucy Gayheart—all present issues of the commodification of gender in a consumer culture.

Questions concerning Cather's treatment of ethnicity and race deserve far fuller and more substantial attention than they have received until now. With notable exceptions (Wasserman, "Cather's Semitism," for example), critics have too often isolated passages from their textual and historical bearings, then served them up as evidence to "prove" a predetermined critical or political stance. What we need are serious and sustained studies that read passages in context, consider Cather's writing as a whole, interpret issues within the cultures of their time, and incorporate a critical awareness of our own time. The engagement I'm calling for on race, for example, would include Cather's review of the collection of paintings called "racial studies" by Hubert Vos in Washington, DC, in 1901. (So far as I know, no one writing on Cather and race has included this essay, retrievable only by going beyond others' editing to its original publication.) The interested scholar would read Cather's review alongside other contemporary reviews of the Vos exhibition, other cultural documents about race (including fiction), and, of course, Cather's other writing then and later.

An exploration of politics will surely develop in Cather studies. A political Cather is an oxymoron, scholarly consensus would have it: John H. Randall III wrote that "Willa Cather had no use for politics" (12), and James Woodress that "political and economic issues . . . interested her very little" (*Willa Cather* 100). Yet Cather was most decidedly political in the Aristotelian tradition, which saw politics as a manifestation of art and the state as formed out of an intuitive sense of justice. And I suspect that Cather was far more engaged in the modern sense of "political" than we have acknowledged: her writing concerns power that is often at odds with democracy's grounding in a social condition of equality and respect for the individual within the community, and it regularly addresses specific institutional instances of the conflict.

The point is, of course, that we need to examine Cather's references to political events, beginning with her letters, essays, and reviews, and then to interpret such references in her fiction. Robert W. Cherny's work reading Cather against the populist movement provides one foray into this arena; there is a long way to go, beginning with setting aside preconceptions and seeing what is there. After all, Cather's explicit political writing ranges from an essay on the sinking of the battleship *Maine* in 1898 to letters on Mussolini and the rising threat of fascism, and reading her texts against a background of contemporary political events promises to be revealing.

Ethical criticism is—or should be—related to questions of political discourse as well as those of gender, race, and ethnicity. Ahead in Cather studies will be inquiries not only into the issues of appropriation, colonization, and multicultural diversity so central to our national discourse today, but also into questions fundamental to the humanities. What is literature's role in the cultural politics of its—and our—time? *Poetic Justice: The Literary Imagination and Public Life*, Martha Nussbaum's exploration of the role of aesthetic structures (including those of narrative) in ethical reasoning, provides one prolegomenon to such inquiry (see also her "Narrative Emotions"), while Michael Bérubé's *Public Access: Literary Theory and American Cultural Politics* positions academic literary debates directly within current political discourse.

Read within their historical moments, Cather's texts represent the interstices of tensions, conflicts, and possibilities forming and reforming in a society. Responding directly to issues of the time and setting the stage (as well as preparing her readers) for her books, Cather's letters on writing exist in counterpoint to her fiction as a cultural dialogic. Read independently, her 1936 essay "Escapism" has been interpreted as a manifesto of disengagement. Why don't the reformers engage directly in political debate by way of the pamphleteers, Cather asks, rather than presenting their facts "in a coating of [the] stock cinema situations" of the social protest novel (23). Yet when read within Cather's oeuvre,

"Escapism" articulates Cather's sensitivity to political issues when she was on the brink of writing her most directly political novel, *Sapphira and the Slave Girl*.

In making contextual readings, scholars in the next decade will require fuller engagement with Cather's oeuvre rather than with single texts. Cather resembles Whitman in presenting readers with an evolving opus, and like Faulkner she remained loyal to the fictional world that she created. Until now we've scarcely moved beyond noting that Cather conceived of her characters as ghosts for whom she sought bodies; it's high time that we more fully explored her blurring of boundaries between fact and fiction, her mutations of places and communities, the "conversations" of characters with one another as well as with the "real" world upon which Cather drew.

Beginning with the early 1970s, much of the vitality and some of the absurdity in Cather studies have resulted from feminism and gender studies. The next decade will see, I believe, a return to questions of aesthetics, now informed by heightened sensitivity to gender and (one would hope) to class, race, and ethnicity as well. In "'Only the Feeling Matters': Willa Cather's Sexual Aesthetics," Anders has provided one example of an aesthetic study by placing Cather's fiction in a homosexual tradition of male friendship and gay texts ranging from classical literature to nineteenth-century French novels and the poetry of Whitman, then by interpreting ways in which the unnamed subject of homosexuality contributed to Cather's characteristically subtle and elusive style.

Whitman criticism "has yet to contextualize *Leaves* itself in Whitman's even larger and more complex endeavor to unite prose and poetry in the service of an emerging democratic aesthetics," writes Ed Folsom; the same might be said of Cather, with the addendum that work moving toward an understanding of genre in Cather is promising. Richard H. Millington makes the case for Cather as a cultural critic and historian by reading *My Ántonia* as "a contest between two kinds of narrative" (Jim Burden's novelistic appeal to a solitary reader's forward movement versus storytelling's appeal to a communal response); drawing upon Benjamin's "The Storyteller," Millington suggests that in writing an epic in prose fiction, Cather resists "monologic ideologies" by releasing storytelling into "amplitude" (688, 694, et passim).

Important work is needed involving voice, that most elusive yet fundamental of qualities that has only begun to be addressed in Cather studies. Preliminary work suggests possibilities: Cather's démeublé style anticipates that of Hemingway (Love); structural linguistics helps us to recognize patterns of that style (Giltrow and Stouck); and performance theory drawn from the folklorists is useful in interpreting storytelling (Funda). The more substantial work possible with book-length studies is heralded by Elsa Nettels's interpretation of voice and discourse against a background of Victorian cultural ideas of gendered speech.

Some truisms of Cather studies remain. Cather's later writing remains slighted (Cather's comment that "the world broke in two in 1922 or thereabouts" remains the touchstone in placing her work chronologically), despite arguments for its complexities by Skaggs in *After the World Broke in Two: The Later Novels of Willa Cather* and Carlin in *Cather, Canon, and the Politics of Reading*. With the rise of Cultural Studies, I expect that the imbalance will be addressed. It was, after all, in her later works that Cather shifted her focus from the aspirations of the individual to the cultures of communities. Similarly, Cather's stories remain slighted, treated as a separate genre in books (Arnold; Wasserman, *Willa Cather*; Meyering), but seldom as part of an evolving opus. Cultural geography invites a revisioning of the idea of place in Cather, particularly of those places beyond Nebraska. David Harrell's research on allusions to the Southwest in *The Professor's House* and Gary Brienzo's reading of Cather's treatment of the Northeast through *Shadows on the Rock* provide useful guidance. Cather's travel writings, until now generally overlooked, will offer their own commentaries on place.

Other subjects remain unexplored. Cather, so long identified with aspiring youth, wrote equally powerfully of aging, as Romines has pointed out in "Willa Cather and the Coming of Old Age." Demographers remind us that our population is aging, and as it does I expect that we'll see literary studies respond and that Cather will again be providing a productive forum. The link between Cather and music is another given in Cather studies, long sustained by Richard Giannone's fine book on the subject. John H. Flannigan's essays on the musicality of Cather's writing—work informed by gender theory—invite a revisiting of this subject more broadly. Cather and the visual arts remains a wide-open subject, its treatment thus far consisting largely of analogies of Cather's writing to the work of particular artists, and commentary on these analogies. Those scholars who have written of the subject more broadly have demonstrated its promise (John J. Murphy, Al-Ghalith). Fortunately, we have a first-rate guide to the field: Polly Duryea's "Paintings and Drawings in Willa Cather's Prose: A Catalogue Raisonné" (1993) lists references in

Cather's texts to artists, paintings, drawings, illustrations, and tapestry; unfortunately, it is available only as a dissertation. Finally, we have the happy prospect of major work on Cather and religion in a forthcoming book by John J. Murphy.

Collaborative work is essential to first-rate interdisciplinary scholarship and criticism, yet interdisciplinary work in Cather studies (as elsewhere) has too often meant that someone grounded in literature learns something about another field—psychology, music, or the visual arts, for example—and writes of and from the interaction of the disciplines. "To bring two or more disciplines into significant interaction with one another requires considerable mastery of the subtleties and particularities of each," Giles Gunn has cautioned; such expertise is seldom acquired "without extensive research and reflection" (239). We need to encourage extended collaborative work in Cather studies (I am thinking here of the Giltrow-Stouck study of Cather's style as a model) and to work to change institutional structures that in the past have too often encouraged narrow disciplinary specialization.

One collaborative project might involve a revisioning of that staple of Cather studies—her writing about the land—but now informed by principles of ecocriticism. "Must literature always lead us away from the physical world, never back to it?" asks Lawrence Buell in *The Environmental Imagination: Thoreau, Nature Writing, and the Formation of American Culture* (10–11). It is a question that we might ask as we read Cather, arguably America's fiction writer most deeply committed to representing nature as such. An alternative to poststructuralist theory, ecocriticism would read Cather in terms of her representation of the environment and in terms of the relationship between text and referent. Again, research would do well to inform criticism here, to follow up on preliminary work on Cather's training at the University of Nebraska during the years that Charles Bessey was founding American botany, and his students Roscoe Pound and Frederick Clements were doing pioneering work in ecology (Rosowski, "Willa Cather's Ecology of Place").

As Cather's texts are increasingly included among reading lists of high school and college curricula, pedagogical questions will result in important work in Cather studies. Saying that she wanted to protect her books from the assigned reading of a classroom, Cather resisted paperback sales, the precondition to broad classroom adoption. Books designed for teachers provide one model (Murphy, *"My Ántonia": The Road Home*; Rosowski, *Approaches to Teaching Cather's "My Ántonia"*). What we need now are studies of the activity of reading as it exists within the class-room. What "happens" to a Cather text in the schools, colleges, and universities where it is taught? What questions are posed of it by students and by their teachers? What readings do—and do not—result?

Thus far I've written of prospects for Cather studies within the academy. More important, to my mind, are prospects for extending conversations outward. During her 1994 MLA Presidential Address, Patricia Meyer Spacks challenged those within the academy to pose the question, "So what?" in explaining ourselves as teachers of language and literature, for "we urgently need to make ourselves comprehended." I wholeheartedly agree, adding only that Cather provides an ideal forum for responding to the culture war that has divided the profession and the nation.

So prospects for Cather studies include consideration of the place of language and literature in the public realm. As Spacks has noted, "We need to remind ourselves, our students, and the public of what everyone perhaps remembered more consistently in the past: that the skills we teach and the texts we analyze—even, or especially, new texts, and old ones explored in new ways—bear directly on perplexities of common experience" (356–57). We might do well to remember with humility that the upsurge in academic writing on Cather is recent; Cather's readers—the ones she identified as hers—have known all along that her writing gives great pleasure sustainable over lifetimes and generations.

What do I mean by this? We make much of turning to noncanonical writers, reading the private papers and diaries of "ordinary people" alongside those of published authors. We would do well to turn to non-canonical readers also, to ask what it is that draws them to Cather's writing; and then we would do well to listen, setting aside our theories of the moment ("interpretive communities," for example), so that we might be "sensitive to the reader who completed the novel's reality," remembering "that readers [are] autonomous beings, selecting novels by choice and for pleasure" (Baym 46). Who were (are) Cather's "real readers," what were (are) the circumstances of their reading, and what did (do) the reviews of her books tell about their expectations? Such questions call for empirical research, for which I suggest going beyond notices in academic journals to the newsletters of reading circles, beyond the *New York Times* reviews to include those of hometown papers. Nina Baym's *Novels, Readers, and Reviewers: Responses to Fiction in Antebellum America* provides one model of such inquiry; Cathy N. Davidson's *Revolution and the Word: The Rise of the Novel in America* provides another.

Cather studies have long been supported by a broad sense of the "Cather community." The Willa Cather Pioneer Memorial and Educational Foundation (WCPM) in Red Cloud provides a means of bringing together academics with laypersons by sponsoring annual spring conferences and the *Willa Cather Pioneer Memorial Newsletter/The Willa Cather Society* (edited by John J. Murphy) and by helping the University of Nebraska–Lincoln and other universities and/or colleges to sponsor international seminars on Cather that attract, from throughout the world, students and faculty, academics and laypersons of all ages, for week-long residencies on Cather-related programs.

Any "prospects" essay stops rather than concludes, its ending not defined by a natural sense of closure so much as dictated by the limits of its author's imagination and the number of pages available for it. Nowhere is that fact more evident than in Cather studies, where we are working with literature that is proving itself so richly responsive to the multiple readings and various questions we are bringing to it. "Would reference to the difficulty of articulating 'the incommunicable future' of Cather scholarship be too easy a way out?" Richard Kopley asked of this ending. I gratefully saw the aptness of the allusion, not because its use is easy, but because his question testifies to the point with which I began. Cather's importance lies in the ways in which her ideas are inscribed into our culture, her language inscribed into our language, and, when one is working with such a writer, the future of Cather studies is bright indeed.

WORKS CITED

Acocella, Joan. "Cather and the Academy." *New Yorker* (27 Nov. 1995): 56–71.

Al-Ghalith, Asad. "Cather's Use of Light: An Impressionistic Tone." *Cather Studies 3*. Lincoln: U of Nebraska P. 267–82, forthcoming.

Anders, John. "'Only the Feeling Matters': Willa Cather's Sexual Aesthetics." Diss. U of Nebraska-Lincoln, 1993.

Arnold, Marilyn. "Introduction." *Willa Cather Living: A Personal Record* by Edith Lewis. xxxv–xliv.

Barthes, Roland. "Textual Analysis of Poe's 'Valdemar.'" Trans. Geoff Bennington. *Untying the Text: A Post-Structuralist Reader*. Ed. Robert Young. Boston: Routledge & Kegan Paul, 1981. 135–61.

Baym, Nina. *Novels, Readers, and Reviewers: Responses to Fiction in Antebellum America*. Ithaca, NY: Cornell UP, 1984.

Bennett, Mildred R. "New Letters from Willa Cather." *Western American Literature* 23 (1988): 223–26.

Bérubé, Michael. *Public Access: Literary Theory and American Cultural Politics.* London: Verso, 1994.

Bohlke, L. Brent. *Willa Cather in Person: Interviews, Speeches, and Letters.* Lincoln: U of Nebraska P, 1986.

Brienzo, Gary. *Willa Cather's Transforming Vision: New France and the American Northeast.* Selinsgrove, PA: Susquehanna UP, 1990.

Buell, Lawrence. *The Environmental Imagination: Thoreau, Nature Writing, and the Formation of American Culture.* Cambridge, MA: Belknap Press of Harvard UP, 1995.

Carlin, Deborah. *Cather, Canon, and the Politics of Reading.* Amherst: U of Massachusetts P, 1992.

Cather, Willa. *The Autobiography of S. S. McClure.* Introd. and afterword by Robert Thacker. Lincoln: U of Nebraska P, forthcoming.

———. "The Best Stories of Sarah Orne Jewett." *Willa Cather on Writing* 47–59.

———. "Escapism." *Willa Cather on Writing* 18–29.

———. *The Kingdom of Art: Willa Cather's First Principles and Critical Statements 1893–1896.* Ed. Bernice Slote. Lincoln: U of Nebraska P, 1966.

———. *A Lost Lady.* Ed. Charles Mignon and Frederick Link, with Kari Ronning. Historical essay by Susan J. Rosowski, with Kari Ronning; explanatory notes by Kari Ronning. Lincoln: U of Nebraska P, forthcoming.

———. *My Ántonia.* Ed. Charles Mignon, with Kari Ronning. Historical essay and explanatory notes by James Woodress. Lincoln: U of Nebraska P, 1994.

———. "Nanette: An Aside." *Willa Cather's Collected Short Fiction* 405–10.

———. "The Novel Démeublé." *Willa Cather on Writing* 35–43.

———. *O Pioneers!.* Ed. Susan J. Rosowski and Charles W. Mignon, with Kathleeen Danker. Historical essay and explanatory notes by David Stouck. Lincoln: U of Nebraska P, 1992.

———. "Paul's Case." *Willa Cather's Collected Short Fiction* 243–61.

———. *Sapphira and the Slave Girl.* New York: Knopf, 1940.

———. *The World and the Parish: Willa Cather's Articles and Reviews, 1893–1902.* 2 vols. Ed. William M. Curtin. Lincoln: U of Nebraska P, 1970.

———. *Willa Cather on Writing: Critical Studies on Writing as an Art.* New York: Knopf, 1949.

———. *Willa Cather's Collected Short Fiction: 1892–1912.* Ed. Virginia Faulkner. Lincoln: U of Nebraska P, 1970.

Cather, Willa, with Georgine Milmine. *The Life of Mary Baker G. Eddy and the History of Christian Science.* Introd. And afterword by David Stouck. Lincoln: U of Nebraska P, 1993.

Cherny, Robert W. "Willa Cather and the Populists." *Great Plains Quarterly* 3 (1983): 206–18.

Crane, Joan. *Willa Cather: A Bibliography.* Lincoln: U of Nebraska P, 1982.

Davidson, Cathy N. *Revolution and the Word: The Rise of the Novel in America.* New York: Oxford UP, 1986.

Duryea, Polly. "Paintings and Drawings in Willa Cather's Prose: A Catalogue Raisonné." Diss. U of Nebraska–Lincoln, 1993.

Flannigan, John H. "Thea Kronborg's Vocal Transvestism: Willa Cather and the 'Voz Contralto.'" *Modern Fiction Studies* 40 (1994): 737–63.

———. "Words and Music Made Flesh in Cather's 'Eric Hermannson's Soul.'" *Studies in Short Fiction* 32 (1995): 209–17.

Folsom, Ed. "Prospects for the Study of Walt Whitman." *Resources for American Literary Study* 20 (1994): 1–15. Reprinted in the present volume (133–54).

Funda, Evelyn. "'The Breath Vibrating Behind It': Intimacy in the Storytelling of Ántonia Shimerda." *Western American Literature* 29 (1994): 195–216.

Giannone, Richard. *Music in Willa Cather's Fiction.* Lincoln: U of Nebraska P, 1968.

Gibaldi, Joseph, ed. *Introduction to Scholarship in Modern Languages and Literatures.* New York: Modern Language Association, 1992.

Giltrow, Janet, and David Stouck. "Willa Cather and a Grammar for Things 'Not Named.'" *Style* 26 (1992): 91–113.

Graff, Gerald. "The Scholar in Society." Gibaldi 343–62.

Gunn, Giles. "Interdisciplinary Studies." Gibaldi 239–61.

Halac, Dennis. "Ever So True: Willa Cather & T. G. Masaryk." *New Criterion* 12.3 (1993): 36–40.

Harrell, David. *From Mesa Verde to "The Professor's House."* Albuquerque: U of New Mexico P, 1992.

Harris, Richard C. "First Loves: Willa Cather's Niel Herbert and Ivan Turgenev's Vladimir Petrovich." *Studies in American Fiction* 17 (1989): 81–91.

James, Henry. "Preface to 'Roderick Hudson' (Volume 1 in The New York Edition)." *The Art of the Novel.* New York: Scribners, 1962. 3–19.

Lee, Hermione. *Willa Cather: A Life Saved Up.* Issued in the United States as *Willa Cather: Double Lives.* New York: Pantheon, 1989.

Levy, Helen Fiddyment. *Fiction of the Home Place: Jewett, Cather, Glasgow, Porter, Welty, and Naylor.* Jackson: UP of Mississippi, 1992.

Lewis, Edith. *Willa Cather Living: A Personal Record.* Athens: Ohio UP, 1989.

Love, Glen A. *"The Professor's House*: Cather, Hemingway and the Chastening of American Prose Style." *Western American Literature* 24 (1990): 295–311.

Madigan, Mark. "Willa Cather and Dorothy Canfield Fisher: Rift, Reconciliation, and *One of Ours*." *Cather Studies 1*. Lincoln: U of Nebraska P, 1990. 115–29.

March, John. *A Reader's Companion to the Fiction of Willa Cather*. Ed. Marilyn Arnold with Debra Lynn Thornton. Westport, CT: Greenwood P, 1993.

Mares, E. A. *I Returned and Saw under the Sun*. Albuquerque: U of New Mexico P, 1989.

Meyering, Sheryl L. *A Reader's Guide to the Short Stories of Willa Cather*. New York: G. K. Hall, 1994.

Middleton, Jo Ann. *Willa Cather's Modernism: A Study of Style and Technique*. Rutherford, NJ: Fairleigh Dickinson UP, 1990.

Millington, Richard H. "Willa Cather and 'The Storyteller': Hostility to the Novel in *My Ántonia*." *American Literature* 66 (1994): 689–717.

Morrison, Toni. *Beloved: A Novel*. New York: Knopf, 1987.

———. *Playing in the Dark: Whiteness and the Literary Imagination*. Cambridge, MA: Harvard UP, 1992.

Murphy, John J. "Cather's New World Divine Comedy: The Dante Connection." *Cather Studies 1*. Lincoln: U of Nebraska P, 1990. 21–35.

———. *"My Ántonia": The Road Home*. Boston: Twayne, 1989.

———, ed. *Willa Cather Pioneer Memorial Newsletter/ The Willa Cather Society*. Red Cloud: Willa Cather Pioneer Memorial and Educational Foundation, 1957–.

Nettels, Elsa. *Language and Gender in American Realist Fiction: Howells, James, Wharton, and Cather*. London: Macmillan, 1996; Charlottesville: UP Virginia, forthcoming.

Nussbaum, Martha C. "Narrative Emotions: Beckett's Genealogy of Love." *Ethics* 98 (1988): 225–54.

———. *Poetic Justice: The Literary Imagination and Public Life*. Boston: Beacon P, 1995.

O'Brien, Sharon. *Willa Cather: The Emerging Voice*. New York: Oxford UP, 1987.

O'Connor, Margaret. "A Guide to the Letters of Willa Cather." *Resources for American Literary Study* 4 (1974): 145–72.

Quirk, Tom. *Bergson and American Culture: The Worlds of Willa Cather and Wallace Stevens*. Chapel Hill: U of North Carolina P, 1990.

Randall, John H., III. *The Landscape and the Looking Glass: Willa Cather's Search for Value*. Boston: Houghton Mifflin, 1960.

Reynolds, Guy. *Willa Cather in Context: Progress, Race, Empire*. London: Macmillan, 1996.

Romines, Ann. *The Home Plot: Women, Writing, and Domestic Ritual*. Amherst: U of Massachusetts P, 1992.

———. "Willa Cather and the Coming of Old Age." *Texas Studies in Literature and Language* 37 (1995): 394–413.

Rose, Phyllis. "Modernism: The Case of Willa Cather." *Modernism Reconsidered*. Ed. Robert Kiely, with John Hildebidle. Cambridge, MA: Harvard UP, 1983. 123–45.

Rosowski, Susan J. *The Voyage Perilous: Willa Cather's Romanticism*. Lincoln: U of Nebraska P, 1986.

———. "Willa Cather's Ecology of Place." *Western American Literature* 30 (1995): 37–51.

———, ed. *Approaches to Teaching Cather's "My Ántonia."* New York: Modern Language Association, 1989.

———, ed. *Cather Studies*. Lincoln: U of Nebraska P, 1990–.

Ryder, Mary Ruth. *Willa Cather and Classical Myth: The Search for a New Parnassus*. Lewiston, NY: Edwin Mellen P, 1990.

Schwartz, Lynne Sharon. *Disturbances in the Field*. New York: Harper & Row, 1983.

Sergeant, Elizabeth Shepley. *Willa Cather: A Memoir*. 1953. Lincoln: U of Nebraska P, 1963.

Skaggs, Merrill Maguire. *After the World Broke in Two: The Later Novels of Willa Cather*. Charlottesville: UP of Virginia, 1990.

———. "Thefts and Conversation: Willa Cather and William Faulkner." *Cather Studies 3*. Lincoln: U of Nebraska P, 1996.

Smith, Barbara Herrnstein. *Contingencies of Value: Alternative Perspectives for Critical Theory*. Cambridge, MA: Harvard UP, 1988.

Spacks, Patricia Meyer. "Reality—Our Subject and Discipline." MLA Presidential Address 1994. *PMLA* 110 (1995): 350–57.

Stouck, David. Introduction. Cather, *The Life of Mary Baker G. Eddy and the History of Christian Science*. By Willa Cather and Georgine Milmine. *Life* xv–xxviii.

———. "Willa Cather and the Russians." *Cather Studies 1*. Lincoln: U of Nebraska P, 1990. 1–20.

Thacker, Robert. "Alice Munro's Willa Cather." *Canadian Literature* 134 (1992): 42–57.

Thurin, Erik Ingvar. *The Humanization of Willa Cather: Classicism in an American Classic*. Lund, Sweden: Lund UP, 1990.

Unger, Douglas. *Leaving the Land*. 1984. Lincoln: U of Nebraska P, 1995.

Urgo, Joseph R. *Willa Cather and the Myth of American Migration*. Urbana: U of Illinois P, 1995.

Wasserman, Loretta. "Cather's Semitism." *Cather Studies 2*. Lincoln: U of Nebraska P, 1993. 1–22.

————. *Willa Cather: A Study of the Short Fiction.* Boston: Twayne, 1991.

West, James L. W., III. *American Authors and the Literary Marketplace since 1900.* Philadelphia: U of Pennsylvania P, 1988.

Woodress, James. *Willa Cather: A Literary Life.* Lincoln: U of Nebraska P, 1987.

————. "Willa Cather and Alphonse Daudet." *Cather Studies 2.* Lincoln: U of Nebraska P, 1993. 156–66.

Woolf, Virginia. *Melymbrosia: An Early Version of "The Voyage Out."* Ed. Louis A. DeSalvo. New York: New York Public Library, 1982.

Yongue, Patricia L. "Edith Lewis Living." *Willa Cather Pioneer Memorial Newsletter* 33 (1989): 12–15.

12

T. S. Eliot

Sanford Schwartz

As we approach the end of the modern century it is difficult to assess the prospects of the century's most celebrated poet. In the last few decades several factors have combined to create an unfavorable climate for the study of T. S. Eliot. In the first place, the Eliot Estate has earned a reputation for keeping zealous watch over unpublished manuscripts and other archival sources. With some justification, scholars calculate that they have little hope of gaining access to documents that would provide the basis for significant new work, and therefore they turn to more inviting areas of study. Second, Eliot has already received an enormous amount of attention, and it is easy to assume that, barring the release of new materials, the available terrain has been virtually exhausted. But if overprotection and overexposure aren't sufficient to ward off the prospective student, there is also the problem of Eliot's sagging reputation in the academy and the attendant suspicion that he may eventually lose his once-secure niche in the literary pantheon. The thirty years since his death have not been kind to Eliot, and in recent years the perpetual allegations of misogyny, anti-semitism, and crypto-fascism have made his name virtually synonymous with political incorrectness. Eliot may well survive the current slump in his fortunes, but under present conditions it requires a certain degree of professional resolve to commit oneself to prolonged research without the security of tenure or an independent income.[1]

With all of these difficulties it may still be premature to foreclose on Eliot either as a major author or as a rewarding focus of study. In fact, the prospects for new research have recently taken a favorable turn. After many years, the Eliot Estate has begun to acknowledge the need for editions of his unpublished manuscripts, and the long-awaited appearance of his 1926 Clark Lectures (*The Varieties of Metaphysical Poetry*, ed. Ronald Schuchard) and his unpublished early poems in the Berg Collection of the New York Public Library (*Inventions of the March Hare*, ed. Christopher Ricks) may bode well for the future. The publication of new materials should also help to dispel the impression that the work of previous generations has left contemporary scholars with little or nothing to do. The vast accumulation of commentary during Eliot's lifetime was based almost entirely on the final, published versions of the poems and on a limited selection of his essays. It was also informed by a swarm of critical assumptions that have long since come into question. Just as belated publication of Eliot's doctoral thesis (1964) and the manuscripts of *The Waste Land* (1971) and *Four Quartets* (Gardner [1978]) influenced the first round of posthumous revaluation, a sustained wave of new editions, coupled with the rethinking of literary modernism currently under way, has the potential to launch another and perhaps more momentous reassessment of his work.[2]

The excellent editions of the Clark Lectures and the Berg Collection poems offer a promising start, but much more needs to be done to facilitate future work. The outlook for a new cycle of research is at least partially dependent upon the availability of reliable, well-annotated editions of Eliot's published collections of poetry and prose, and upon ready access to his many unpublished and uncollected writings. At present there are no scholarly editions of Eliot's published poetry or plays, and in most cases we know little about his transactions with his publishers and the sometimes complex process of publication. We also lack a complete edition of Eliot's published prose. A casual glance at Donald Gallup's bibliography will reveal that the available volumes of literary criticism— *The Sacred Wood* (1920), *Selected Essays* (1932), *The Use of Poetry and the Use of Criticism* (1933), *On Poetry and Poets* (1957), *To Criticize the Critic* (1965)—contain only a small sampling of Eliot's prose, and many of these are in versions revised for book publication and complicated by discrepancies between British and American editions (Schuchard). Hundreds of additional essays, reviews, book introductions, and other miscellaneous pieces (including many discovered after Gallup's 1969 volume) must be retrieved individually from a wide array of periodicals, newspapers, and books.[3] The situation is even more dire with respect to the unpublished prose. Thus far Valerie Eliot has issued only one volume of correspondence (1898–1922), and although the thousand or so letters Eliot sent to Emily Hale are sequestered in Princeton's Firestone Library until 2020, the release of the other unpublished correspondence would be a welcome event. In addition, Eliot's many student essays and notebooks have never been published, and an allegedly extensive collection of miscellaneous papers remains entirely off-limits to scholars. At the moment, it is impossible to know whether needed editorial projects will be realized or the restrictions lifted in the immediate future. On the basis of recent developments, however, scholars now have reason to hope that Eliot's executors will see the wisdom of continuing to unlock the archives and commissioning the type of comprehensive edition that a writer of his magnitude deserves.[4]

The same uncertainty clouds the prospects for biographical research. For three decades Mrs. Eliot has attempted to honor the statement in her husband's will that his executors should not "facilitate or countenance the writing of any biography of me." This impediment has not prevented scholars from setting out on their own, and as a result of their efforts, along with a host of memoirs and reminiscences, we know a good deal about the elusive man behind the public masks. The most satisfying overview, Peter Ackroyd's *T. S. Eliot: A Life*, shows how much can be done without full access to the documentary evidence.[5] Of the more specialized studies, Lyndall Gordon's detective work in *Eliot's Early Years* and *Eliot's New Life* offers many leads that should occupy scholars for years to come. One of the most promising areas of biographical research has been Eliot's familial and cultural heritage—his distinguished New England pedigree, his childhood in turn-of-the-century St. Louis, and the influence of his talented mother, Charlotte Stearns Eliot. Scholars pursuing this line of inquiry should consult the books by Gordon, Sigg, Soldo, and the recent work of several younger scholars—Abboud, Chinitz, Daümer, and Oser among others—who are in the process of fleshing out Eliot's distinctive identity as an American writer. On another front, the relationship between Eliot and his first wife, Vivien Haigh-Wood, requires more attention than it receives. The entanglements of this union are so complex and disheartening that judicious scholars are often inclined to leave the matter alone. But in light of the recurrent assaults on Eliot's character, especially the loathsome figure portrayed in Michael Hastings's play, *Tom and Viv*, the public deserves a sensitive, thorough, and dispassionate examination of this sorrowful relationship.[6] We also have much to learn about Eliot's subsequent life, which remains partially concealed behind the prosaic routines and the cultivated public persona of his later years. Recent studies of writers such as Djuna Barnes (Plumb) reveal how little we actually know about his professional relationships and his labors as an editor during his long tenure at Faber & Faber. Beyond these or any other individual episodes of his life lies the enduring enigma of Eliot the man. After so much has been written it may sound ungenerous to assert that Eliot remains something of a mystery, but the innumerable readers who have pondered the complex temperament behind the voices of "Prufrock," *The Waste Land,* and "Ash-Wednesday" can well appreciate the scale of the problem.

Whatever the prospects for new editions and biographical studies, students of twentieth-century literature are now faced with the task of reinterpreting Eliot's oeuvre and reassessing his place in modern literary and cultural history. From the pioneering essays of F. O. Matthiessen and Cleanth Brooks to the magisterial studies by Helen Gardner, Grover Smith, and Hugh Kenner, Eliot was well served (some say too well served) by a legion of scholars and critics who oriented an entire generation of readers to his difficult art. The New Critics—above all Cleanth Brooks, with his emphasis upon paradox and irony—provided a mode of analysis that seemed perfectly tailored to Eliot's verse and underwritten by his own critical authority. Despite the subsequent appearance of much excellent scholarship, the work of this generation has never been superseded, and it remains the point of departure for any serious undertaking that hopes to do more than reinvent the wheel. Nevertheless, these classic studies were conducted without the benefit of the manuscripts of *The Waste Land* and *Four Quartets,* the unpublished early poems, and other crucial sources that have enriched and partially transformed our knowledge of Eliot's career. Furthermore, the limitations (as well as the enduring merits) of their interpretive practices have become increasingly apparent in the wake of the massive sea-change in literary criticism that has taken place since the sixties.

Contemporary Eliot scholars realize that they stand on the shoulders of giants, but they are also aware that their predecessors consolidated a certain image of Eliot that neglects or miscasts certain features of his work. Combining the trickle of new materials with the recent flood of new ideas, they are gradually freeing Eliot from his putative association with the poetics of Brooks, Ransom, and Tate. These developments are largely ignored outside the company of Eliot scholars, but they are slowly leading to a reconsideration of Eliot's poetry, his plays, and his wide-ranging efforts in philosophy, literary criticism, culture, politics, and religion. To some extent the current impetus derives from an exploration of the traditions that inform Eliot's prose, but, as we shall see, it is also driven by several additional factors: a sharper awareness of Eliot's distinctive if submerged roots in American culture; the reconfiguration of the concept of modernism in light of its encounter with feminist criticism, cultural studies, and the notion of postmodernism; and a new historical and sociological inquiry into processes through which Eliot was publicized, canonized, and subsequently disavowed in the country of his birth.

The reading of Eliot's poetry has been at once static and dynamic since the demise of the New Critical hegemony. The critical orientation has remained unchanged insofar as the very success of mid-century criticism instituted an approach to his verse, along with a definition of modernism, that a later and often less receptive generation of readers continues to employ. This conception of Eliot provides a conveniently still target, but it conceals the somewhat more fluid reality of the last few decades, during which there have been various sporadic attempts to translate new forms of criticism into new readings of the poems. In the initial revolt against New Criticism, scholars of the sixties and early seventies accented the continuities between Romanticism and Modernism and discovered the personal Eliot within the supposedly impersonal poetry.[7] By contrast, the poststructuralist turn of the ensuing years, which had a significant impact on the study of Pound, Stevens, Williams, and other modern poets, rarely touched Eliot's verse. A few critics—among them William Spanos, Gregory Jay, Harriet Davidson, Michael Beehler, and in a different way John Paul Riquelme—suggested some of the paths that might be pursued, but for the most part Eliot's ties to the old dispensation seemed to preclude any association with the new. The current outlook is still unclear, but the efforts of the eighties might still bear fruit with the appearance of the poems in the Berg Collection and the return to a more historical and contextually oriented criticism. Ricks's edition of the early unpublished poems is once again calling attention to Eliot's appropriation of the Victorians, the French Symbolists, and late nineteenth- and early twentieth-century poets and poetic conventions in Britain, France, and the United States.[8] This new phase of research into Eliot's influences and allusive practices will undoubtedly alter our view of his early verse, and may also have implications for the later poetry, especially *Four Quartets*, which has recently become the focus of renewed attention (Cooper; Ellis; Kearns, "Doctrine"; Lobb; Murray). To many, it may still seem as if Eliot's poetry has been analyzed so extensively that there is little prospect for constructive new work. But as his most distinguished readers have readily confessed, Eliot remains a notoriously difficult and elusive poet, and as we continue to unlearn the formidable paradigms of earlier criticism and situate his work in new historical and cultural contexts, the students of the next generation may be viewing his poetry in a very different light.

The same may be true of the plays, which are often ignored or consigned to the status of handmaiden to the poetry. On the whole, little has changed since the appearance of the major studies of the sixties: Denis Donoghue's *The Third Voice: Modern British and American Verse Drama*, David E. Jones's *The Plays of T. S. Eliot*, Carol Smith's *T. S. Eliot's Dramatic Theory and Practice*, and E. Martin Browne's *The Making of T. S. Eliot's Plays*. Smith's book, which situates the plays in the context of their classical prototypes and Eliot's own reflections on myth, ritual, and drama, opened an especially productive line of investigation that Phelan and other contemporary scholars have successfully explored. The time may have come, however, for some new forms of inquiry into Eliot's lifelong interest in the theater. Randy Malamud's compendium, *T. S. Eliot's Drama: A Research and Production Sourcebook*, is the natural starting point for future research, while his critical study, *Where the Words Are Valid: T. S. Eliot's Communities of Drama*, attempts to pave the way toward a new appreciation of Eliot's theatrical achievement. The latter should be read in conjunction with John Xiros Cooper's recent discussion of the sociopolitical contexts that inform the plays of the thirties and forties. Another site of potentially useful research is Eliot's relationship to British and American theatrical traditions, highbrow as well as popular, and in particular his use of the conventions of the London stage in the decades before and after World War II. This work would build upon some recent studies of Eliot's first effort, the fragmentary *Sweeney Agonistes* (drafted in 1924), which exhibits his intimacy as well as his complex involvement with the popular arts (Chinitz, Roby). Such research may not incite a stampede back to Eliot, but it may demonstrate that Eliot's plays are not merely an appendage to the poetry, and that beyond *Murder in the Cathedral*, his one acknowledged dramatic masterpiece, his theatrical works merit some consideration in the history of twentieth-century drama.

The future study of Eliot's poems and plays will be influenced significantly by the ongoing reassessment of his essays and other expository writings. Eliot's prose has always played a major role in the interpretation of his verse, and his talent for literary discussion has been admired even by those who challenged his authority and contested his judgments. These days, however, the publication of new materials and the shifting perspectives of recent literary criticism are lending new significance to Eliot's literary, philosophical, and cultural essays. During Eliot's lifetime, scholars relied primarily on *The Sacred Wood, Selected Essays,* and other collections of literary criticism, supplemented by *The Idea of a Christian Society* and *Notes Towards the Definition of Culture.* These volumes now stand alongside other sources that have commanded increasing attention over the last few decades, most notably the doctoral thesis, the Clark Lectures, and the multitude of uncollected pieces in periodicals, newspapers, and other publications. Some of these sources have already reoriented our approach to Eliot's work, and if the scholarship of the last decade is any indication, the revisionary process should continue to yield substantial returns for the foreseeable future.

Although Eliot spent many years preparing for a professional career as a philosopher, it was only with the 1964 publication of his dissertation (completed in 1916) that scholars began to pay serious attention to this element of his intellectual life. Much has been done since then to uncover Eliot's wide-ranging education (Lentricchia, McDonald), and to explicate his philosophical essays and explore their implications for his other writings.[9] But given the sometimes daunting complexity of Eliot's philosophical prose, the range of traditions on which he drew, and the absence of an edition of his student papers, the task of appropriation is far from complete. There are at least two current overviews of Eliot's early intellectual development (Gray, Skaff), and several detailed monographs devoted to specific aspects of his studies, most notably the influence of Indic traditions (Kearns, *Indic;* Sri) and early twentieth-century American philosophy (Jain). Even so, not enough has been written on his encounter with Aristotle and the ancient Greeks; Kant and the German idealists; the Austrian school of Brentano, Meinong, and Husserl; or on his intensive study of the social sciences.[10] Moreover, as a result of the contemporary tendency to identify Nietzsche, James, and other turn-of-the century thinkers with the "postmodern" watershed in philosophy, scholars have recently begun to probe the "postmodern" character of Eliot's philosophical orientation and its consequences for his poetry and other writings (Riquelme; Schwartz, "Post-Modernizing"; Sharratt; Shusterman). Richard Shusterman, for instance, has shown that Eliot's later reflections on language, interpretation, and tradition bear a striking resemblance to those of Adorno, Derrida, Gadamer, Rorty, and other luminaries of the contemporary scene. Drawing primarily on essays from the thirties and forties, Shusterman transforms Eliot the New Critic into Eliot the post-modern theorist, endowed with a prescient awareness of the radically historicist and nonfoundational philosophy that would not come to the fore until well after his death.

Shusterman's provocative research underscores the need for further reassessment of Eliot's literary criticism. So much has been written, but most of it is based on a handful of essays and mired in the critical controversies of a bygone era. Contemporary Eliot scholars are rightly exasperated by the slim range of reference employed in current literary debate, which often relies on little more than a few snippets from "Tradition and Individual Talent" or the notorious *After Strange Gods*. Yet even Eliot scholars are prone to rely on a small fund of materials and an interpretive framework that has been in place for many years. Still in its infancy is the examination of Eliot's different rhetorical strategies in the numerous outlets and institutional contexts in which his work appeared (Badenhausen, Jeffreys). So is the analysis of the often subtle shifts in voice, argument, and allusion as he proceeded from one piece to the next, or from the original to the revised version of the same essay. In addition, surprisingly few scholars have engaged in detailed study of the moment-by-moment relations between the prose and the poetry over the course of time. Ronald Bush, a notable exception to the rule, has used this form of inquiry to illuminate some of the dark corners and otherwise imperceptible shifts in Eliot's poetic practice. In this respect, his *T. S. Eliot: A Study in Character and Style* provides a prototype for future research.

The need for further investigation is even greater when it comes to the cultural, political, and religious essays. For many decades Eliot has been chained to his infamous 1927 statement that his predilections were "classicist in literature, royalist in politics, and anglo-catholic in religion." This remark is not so much erroneous as it is reductive, especially in a cultural climate where classicism, royalism, and Anglo-Catholicism have mutated into elitism, fascism, and anti-semitism (Paul Morrison). One does not have to endorse or excuse Eliot's views to recognize that he is a far more complex figure than the caricature that appears in many recent accounts, which replace a lifetime of sustained and often nuanced reflection into a handful of impolitic tags (usually from the late twenties or early thirties) revealing Eliot at his worst. Even in this inhospitable atmosphere, Eliot scholars could be doing more to prepare the way for a more honest reckoning with this aspect of his career. Anyone who doubts the sophistication or significance of Eliot's ventures into cultural theory should consult the recent studies by Jeffrey Perl and Richard Shusterman. From a historical perspective, we should also reconsider Eliot's immersion in early twentieth-century social thought and the extensive reading related to his seventeen-year editorship of the *Criterion* (Ali, Margolis). In addition, it would be worthwhile to revisit Roger Kojecky's highly informative book, *T. S. Eliot's Social Criticism*, which tells the story of the poet's participation in various discussion groups that considered the much debated issue of social reconstruction before and after the Second World War. Using society minutes and other documents, Kojecky describes the settings in which *The Idea of a Christian Society* and *Notes Towards the Definition of Culture* were originally conceived, and reveals among other things the significance of Eliot's friendship with social philosopher Karl Mannheim. Wolfgang Wicht has begun to examine the Mannheim connection, but otherwise little has been done to follow up on Kojecky's study, which provides the documentary basis for a more sensitive understanding of Eliot as a cultural philosopher and lays the groundwork for the study of an intriguing if largely forgotten episode in modern intellectual history.

There is already a substantial literature on Eliot's political identity—including lengthy studies by John R. Harrison; William Chace; Craig Cairns; Michael North, *Political Aesthetic*; Kenneth Asher; and Michael Tratner—many of them calling attention to the profound influence of Charles Maurras and the French reactionary tradition. David Thompson's recent dissertation, "Criticism and the Vichy Syndrome," reveals just how complicated these debts can be and points the way to a new and timely approach to the cultural politics of a deeply divided era. On the later politics, John Xiros Cooper's *T. S. Eliot and the Ideology of Four Quartets* breaks new ground and provides a paradigm for future criticism by situating Eliot's poems and plays within the changing sociopolitical situation of the thirties and forties. New directions are also apparent in Robert Fleissner's *T. S. Eliot and the Heritage of Africa*, and in Michael North's pioneering essay, "Old Possum and Brer Rabbit: Pound and Eliot's Racial Masquerade," which opens up a new horizon on the problems of race, nation, ethnicity, and gender that play a prominent though not easily definable role in Eliot's poetry and prose. A number of critics have written on the representation of women and the difficult issue of gender in Eliot's works, though by their own admission a great deal more needs to be done (see Pinkney; Gordon, *New Life*; Gibert-Maceda). While most of these studies refuse to let Eliot off the hook, taken together they attest not only to the troubled individual plagued by personal insecurity and inherited prejudice but also to a political intelligence far more balanced and flexible than that of the intractable ideologue portrayed in the culture wars of our own time.

Eliot's essays on culture and politics are closely tied to the religious concerns that were always central to his intellectual life. At Harvard, Eliot studied Sanskrit and Indian philosophy, and many scholars have examined the influence of Indic traditions on his later poetry and prose. Of the many studies devoted to this topic, Cleo Kearns's book has the distinctive virtue of showing how Eliot's encounter with Vedanta and Buddhism was mediated by a long line of Western Orientalists, including his own Harvard professors, who translated and interpreted many of the principal texts. Kearns also suggests that we should look more carefully at Eliot's later religious essays—especially his emphasis upon the "frontiers" between different traditions—which speak to present-day concerns with the meeting of major world cultures and the problems of multicultural identity in an era of accelerated global change. Strangely enough, however, it is not Eliot's attraction to other spiritual traditions but the character of his Christianity that has been insufficiently examined. Scholars regularly note Eliot's extensive debt to Dante (Manganiello), his study of sixteenth- and seventeenth-century Anglican divines, and his interest in St. John of the Cross, Julian of Norwich, and other figures to whom he alludes in his poetry. Nevertheless, we have no comprehensive study of Eliot's appropriation of Christian tradition and have only begun to probe his assimilation of modern theology, including the early influence of Jacques Maritain and neo-Thomism (Takayanagi) as well as the later influence of Paul Tillich and other neo-Orthodox theologians (Gordon, *New Life*).[11] Moreover, after his conversion, Eliot wrote extensively on religion and literature, and while critics now dwell on the harsh strictures of *After Strange Gods*, it is often forgotten that in his better moments Eliot composed some remarkably discerning and influential essays on the relations between poetry and belief. These are overlooked in part because most of the attention, it seems, is now directed to the vexing and incendiary issue of anti-semitism. The debate thus far has been framed by Christopher Ricks, Cynthia Ozick, and Anthony Julius, and its background conveniently summarized in a review essay by Louis Menand (review of Julius). Many Eliot scholars wish that the matter would quietly disappear, but precisely because Eliot has been a figure of such immense moral authority, the scandal of anti-semitism cannot and should not be brushed away so easily. At the same time, the unreflective adoption of anti-semitism as a spiritual litmus test (especially in an ambiguous case like Eliot's, which is light-years away from Pound's) not only flattens out a complex set of social and historical issues but also threatens to become an expression of the very thing it is meant to combat.

As this and other recent controversies indicate, the future study of Eliot's prose and poetry will depend to a great degree upon the new contexts in which his works are situated. One of the most vigorous developments in the last decade has come from the recognition of Eliot as an American writer and the exploration of ties to American culture. Much of this research focuses on biographical matters: Eliot's New England patrimony and the Unitarian heritage of his family; the landscape, culture, and the mélange of dialects in his native St. Louis; and the seven years he spent as a student in Boston. Such work has enabled scholars to illuminate Eliot's numerous though often indirect references to American writers, and more importantly, to uncover the thinly veiled presence of characteristically American propensities of mind and manner. During the eighties, this line of inquiry was pursued by Ronald Bush ("Nathaniel Hawthorne"), Lyndall Gordon, Gregory Jay, Eric Sigg, and John Soldo. Thus far in this decade there have been articles by Richard Badenhausen, Donald Childs, Mark Jarman, and A. D. Moody ("American Strain"), among others, as well as several promising dissertations: Robert Abboud's "Eliot's Crossing: America and T. S. Eliot," David Chinitz's "Jazz and Jazz Discourse in Modernist Poetry: T. S. Eliot and Langston Hughes," Elizabeth Daümer's "A Literary Mother and a Literary Son: Charlotte Eliot and T. S. Eliot," and Lee Oser's "The Letter and the Spirit: T. S. Eliot and American Poetry." This new research, which has only begun to find its way into books and journals, suggests that we will continue to hear a good deal about the American Eliot in the coming years. It will undoubtedly change the way we read Eliot's poetry, and, with its focus upon his background and early years in St. Louis, this work may broaden our understanding of certain facets of American cultural history at the turn of the last century.

Ultimately, the most momentous shift in the context of study is likely to come from the current rethinking of modernism as a historical phenomenon and as a pivotal notion in our cultural lexicon. It has been many years since the term "modernism" elicted the sense of all that was new and adventurous in twentieth-century culture; its once notable capacity to sum up the vital current of the contemporary has long since passed to its younger "postmodern" sibling. Nevertheless, as modernism recedes into cultural history, it is also undergoing a significant transformation, in part as a consequence of the posthumous encounter with its heir. Now that its glamour has faded, we are witnessing a considerable expansion of the modernist canon, the construction of a more internally variegated conception of the modernist enterprise, and a significant reassessment of its affiliations to intellectual, cultural, and social developments in the late-nineteenth and early-twentieth centuries. We also seem to be more alert to the social processes through which the concept of modernism was instituted, the various struggles for control over the definition of the term and the tendencies it represented, as well as the variety of alternative voices marginalized by the selective criteria it imposed. There is reason to believe that these developments portend a major change in the understanding of modernism. It now seems as if the rapidly developing work in areas such as feminist theory; Cultural Studies; the relations between the verbal and visual arts; as well as the intersection of science, technology, and the media will eventually overhaul our existing conceptions of early twentieth-century literature.[12] In light of this impending change, it is unfortunate that Eliot is still identified so closely with the New Critical account of modernism—the abiding reference point for nearly every revisionist claim—and that any new challenge to the traditional formulation is also regarded as another dagger through Eliot's heart. In fact, Eliot himself protested against the ostensibly Eliot-centered modernism that flourished under the aegis of New Criticism, and in recent years Eliot scholars have become increasingly aware that his writing often confounds the conception of modernism customarily used to contain it. In the long run, it is unlikely that the current project of reconceiving modernism will simply leave Eliot in the cold, as many critics assume; it should lead instead to a productive reexamination of his career and a rereading of his works.

As we move further away from mid-century modernism, scholars are no longer taking for granted the traditional story of its emergence or assuming the inevitability of Eliot's ascent to a position of unrivaled cultural authority. Instead, they are beginning to track the more complex story (or rather the various interconnected stories) that preceded the postwar consolidation of a particular conception of modernism. They are looking, for instance, at the specific events and institutional processes through which Eliot was appropriated and eventually canonized over the course of several decades.[13] On one side, there is the emerging study of Eliot's talents as a cultural tactician and the means by which he managed to situate himself at the crossroads of cultural debate in the second quarter of this century (Menand, *Discovering Modernism*). On the other side, there is the examination of the extraordinary influence of the New Critics (and to a considerable degree other critics such as F. R. Leavis and Edmund Wilson) in establishing Eliot's reputation within the postwar academy. But these are individual pieces of a much larger puzzle. At the moment, we have only a fragmentary and mostly anecdotal knowledge of the mechanisms of appropriation, and consequently a limited under-standing of Eliot's distinctive place in twentieth-century culture. We need a more multifaceted understanding of Eliot's appeal to intellectuals in various institutional settings and, as Harvey Teres has shown us, at both ends of the ideological spectrum. According to Jeffrey Perl, we would also benefit from a more thorough study of the perennial opposition to Eliot's authority, for as the history of twentieth-century cultural politics clearly demonstrates, Eliot has long served as a focal point for an impassioned debate over the character and course of modern culture.

The issue of reception and appropriation is closely tied to the problem of influence. It is easier to claim than to document Eliot's enormous impact on the subsequent course of Anglo-American poetry and criti-cism. For decades he was widely regarded as the exemplary poet/critic who infused new life into a tired tradition by linking prosodic experi-mentation to the complexities of the modern condition. Beneath this gen-eralization, however, lies a multitude of different responses, and the full story of the encounter between Eliot and several generations of Anglo-American poets has yet to be told (Altieri, "Eliot's Impact"; Murphy). One possibility might be a collection of essays—let's call it *Eliot among the Modern Poets*—with each chapter focusing on a particular writer's relationship to Eliot and his works. From a global perspective, Eliot may well be the most celebrated poet of the twentieth century, and, of the major American poets, his international influence is perhaps second only to Whitman's. Each year a handful of articles describe his impact upon individual poets outside the English-speaking world, but little has been done to integrate these specific accounts into any larger patterns. At the moment, there is one collection devoted to Eliot's presence in Latin America (Young), and similar collections might be assembled for Conti-nental Europe, Africa, the Middle East, and various regions of Asia. We also have a long way to go in the study of the editions, translations, and other mechanisms of transmission through which Eliot's influence has spread around the world (Hooker, Junkes-Kirchen). Finally, it would be interesting to learn more about Eliot's influence upon other aspects of twentieth-century culture—not only in literary circles (*Eliot among the Modern Critics?*) but in various arenas as far afield as religious meditation and popular stage and cinema.[14] Few poets have enjoyed such widespread diffusion of their works, and in the case of a writer as difficult as Eliot, this extraordinary phenomenon should not go unconsidered.

Finally, the community of Eliot scholars requires far more active and consistent bibliographical research. Regarding primary sources, the problems issuing from the lack of adequate editions are compounded by the absence of a complete list of the archival materials and the various poems, reviews, essays, and other writings that surfaced after the publication of Gallup's bibliography. With respect to secondary sources, we need an up-to-date account of Eliot research: Robert Canary's well-organized assessment of the scholarship is now over a decade old, and the bibliographies by Mildred Martin (supplemented by Mechthild Frank, Armin Paul Frank, and K. P. S. Jochum), Beatrice Ricks, and Sebastian Knowles and Scott Leonard stop in the later 1980s. The gap is not quite filled by Stuart Y. McDougal's chapter in *Sixteen Modern American Authors* and the annual review in *American Literary Scholarship*, which is always informative though brisk and selective in its contents. To complicate the situation further, an increasing proportion of Eliot scholarship is published by presses outside the English-speaking world and often in languages other than English. With the exception of a few European and Indian publications, the bulk of this work is virtually unknown to scholars in English-speaking countries. What will be required in the future is some coordinated effort to inform scholars of developments around the world (Armin Paul Frank, Ramaiah). There should be regularly periodic reviews of current publications in India, China, Korea, Japan, and other places where Eliot scholarship has become a thriving enterprise. The Internet seems the most promising venue for this type of communication, and the North American T. S. Eliot Society is currently developing a web-site designed to announce new publications and facilitate the international flow of information. Nevertheless, as we enter the age of instant global communication, we will continue to need the arduous and essential bibliographical work exemplified for this generation by the Canary and the Knowles and Leonard volumes.[15]

It is one thing to read and appreciate an author, and another to engage in research that goes beyond the drafting of an occasional essay. The latter can often be entangled in circumstances that have little or nothing to do with our initial interest in the author. In the case of T. S. Eliot, the prospects for future study are tied to legal, professional, and cultural considerations that are impossible to ignore. The situation would brighten instantly with the lifting of restrictions on the archives and the commissioning of a scholarly edition of the complete works. Such steps would facilitate the already formidable task of reconsidering a writer who has been at once the beneficiary and the victim of intense critical scrutiny. Legal issues notwithstanding, the coming decade should offer considerable opportunity and an interesting challenge as a new generation continues to rethink the history of early twentieth-century literature, the concept of modernism in which it has been subsumed, and the institutions within which it is examined and discussed. It is difficult to predict the outcome of this revaluation, but the course of current scholarship suggests that it will ultimately have profound effects on our understanding of Eliot. In this scholarship we no longer find the towering eminence of mid-century letters, but we can begin to discern the outlines of a new Eliot who is still a major artist and, somewhat akin to Coleridge in the previous century, a prescient twentieth-century intellectual who is far more our contemporary than we generally assume. At this point it may be premature to declare that this revaluation will free us either from the traditional view of Eliot or from the adversarial view that ultimately depends upon it. In any case, it is now becoming clear that the traditional image of Eliot, which appears to be grounded so securely in his own essays, obscures many significant features of his work, and it has taken a revolution in literary study—ironically, a revolution that has overthrown his hegemony and cast doubt on his canonical status—to launch the process of rediscovery that will loom large in the years to come.

NOTES

1. For a round table discussion of these difficulties, see Thormählen, pp. 215–32.

2. See Bolgan and Miller among other works that capitalized on the publication of Eliot's thesis, and Litz's fiftieth anniversary volume for studies inspired by the publication of *The Waste Land* manuscripts.

3. On the discovery of new writings, see for example David Bradshaw's recent attribution of eleven new reviews in the *Times Literary Supplement*.

4. One happy note: a concordance to the poetry and plays has finally appeared (Dawson, Holland, and McKitterick).

5. Ackroyd and Gordon (*New Life*) provide acknowledgments of the various archives and a valuable list of other biographical sources. See also Stuart Y. McDougal's chapter in *Sixteen Modern American Authors*, and the *Location Register of Twentieth-Century English Literary Manuscripts and Letters* for Eliot manuscripts in British libraries. The main archival sites are the Houghton Library (Harvard) and King's College Library (Cambridge). Both require the permission of Mrs. Eliot for examination and paraphrase of any unpublished material. In addition, important collections of unpublished letters are scattered throughout libraries in the United States and the United Kingdom. See also Herbert Howarth's early attempt at a biography, *Notes on Some Figures behind T. S. Eliot*, and Caroline Behr's useful compilation, *T. S. Eliot: A Chronology of His Life and Works*.

6. For a recent analysis by a medical doctor, see Anthony Fathman, "Viv and Tom: The Eliots as Ether Addict and Co-Dependent."

7. On this wave of scholarship see Bergonzi, Bornstein, Bloom, Frye, Langbaum, Kermode, and somewhat later, Spurr (*Conflicts*).

8. For specialized studies of these relationships to predecessors and contemporaries, see Christ and Tobin on the Victorians; D'Ambrosio on Edward FitzGerald; Pondrom on Symbolists and post-Symbolists; Stead on British poetry in the first decade of the century; Hargrove on Eliot's year in Paris (1910–11); and Materer, Mark Morrison, and Svarny on the situation around the beginning of World War I.

9. Earlier scholars tended to reduce Eliot to a philosophical idealist in the mold of F. H. Bradley. Among more recent studies, see Brooker, Childs, Gray, Jain, Longenbach, Michaels, Perl, Schwartz (*Matrix*), and Skaff. There is also some valuable information on Eliot's philosophical training in Harry T. Costello, *Josiah Royce's Seminar, 1913–14: As Recorded in the Notebooks of Harry T. Costello*.

10. On Eliot and Greek philosophy, see Charron and Lockerd. Gray and Skaff are quite thorough on Eliot's encounter with the social sciences of his day. See also Manganaro and Spurr ("Myths"), who examine Eliot and his contemporaries in light of recent revisionist thinking in social theory.

11. See also Surette on Eliot and the modernist interest in the occult, and Murray on Eliot and mysticism.

12. Perloff and Levenson anticipated some of these changes in the early eighties. Among more recent works on the reconfiguration of literary modernism, see Altieri (*Abstraction*), Baker, Dettmar, Felski, Kalaidjian, Nelson, Nichols, Rabaté, Rado, Scott, Stan Smith. Also consult the expanding list of journals—e.g., *English Literature in Transition, The Journal of Modern Literature,* and *Modernism/Modernity*—which are currently addressing the issue. The list is highly selective and does not include the vast literature on the concept of modernity, modernism in the other arts, and the relations between modernism and postmodernism.

13. Michael Grant's *Critical Heritage* and Graham Clarke's four-volume *Critical Assessments* offer a substantial though necessarily selective supply of documents to assist this important project.

14. Examples abound. For instance, in his *Love and Death* (1975), Woody Allen plays a nineteenth-century Russian aristocrat who composes the lines, "I should have been a pair of ragged claws/Scuttling across the floors of silent seas," and immediately tears them up with the lament, "too sentimental." Or consider the van covered with the text of *The Waste Land* in the decaying London of Stephen Freers's *Sammy and Rosie Get Laid* (1987). Some student of popular culture should also take a look at the extraordinary success of *Cats*.

15. Other resources: the North American T. S. Eliot Society, which runs a conference in St. Louis every September, sponsors sessions at the annual May conference of the American Literature Association, and issues a newsletter three times per year; the *Yeats Eliot Review* (1979–), which provides an outlet for specialized study, though it has appeared somewhat irregularly over the years.

WORKS CITED

Abboud, Robert. "Eliot's Crossing: America and T. S. Eliot." Diss. Rutgers U, 1994.

Ackroyd, Peter. *T. S. Eliot: A Life.* New York: Simon & Schuster; London: Hamish Hamilton, 1984.

Ali, Agha Shahid. *T. S. Eliot as Editor.* Ann Arbor, MI: UMI Research P, 1986.

Altieri, Charles. *Painterly Abstraction in Modernist American Poetry: The Contemporaneity of Modernism.* Cambridge, England, and New York: Cambridge UP, 1989.

———. "Eliot's Impact on Twentieth-Century Anglo-American Poetry." Moody, *Cambridge Companion* 189–209.

Asher, Kenneth. *T. S. Eliot and Ideology.* Cambridge, England, and New York: Cambridge UP, 1995.

Badenhausen, Richard. "In Search of 'Native Moments': T. S. Eliot (Re)Reads Walt Whitman." *South Atlantic Review* 57 (1992): 77–91.

———. "T. S. Eliot's Parenthical Method in the Clark Lectures." *South Atlantic Review* 61 (1996): forthcoming.

Baker, Houston A., Jr. *Modernism and the Harlem Renaissance.* Chicago: U of Chicago P, 1987.

Beehler, Michael. *T. S. Eliot, Wallace Stevens, and the Discourses of Difference.* Baton Rouge: Louisiana State UP, 1987.

Behr, Caroline. *T. S. Eliot: A Chronology of His Life and Works.* London: Macmillan, 1983.

Bergonzi, Bernard. *T. S. Eliot.* New York: Macmillan, 1972.

Bloom, Harold. *The Ringers in the Tower: Studies in Romantic Tradition.* Chicago: U of Chicago P, 1971.

Bolgan, Anne. *What the Thunder Really Said: A Retrospective Essay on the Making of the "The Waste Land."* Montreal: McGill-Queen's UP, 1973.

Bornstein, George. *Transformations of Romanticism in Yeats, Eliot, and Stevens.* Chicago: U of Chicago P, 1976.

Bradshaw, David. "Eleven Reviews by T. S. Eliot, Hitherto Unnoted, from the *Times Literary Supplement.*" *Notes and Queries* 42 (1995): 212–15.

Brooker, Jewel Spears. *Mastery and Escape: T. S. Eliot and the Dialectic of Modernism.* Amherst: U of Massachusetts P, 1994.

Brooks, Cleanth. "The Waste Land: Critique of the Myth." *Modern Poetry and the Tradition.* Chapel Hill: U of North Carolina P, 1939. 136–72.

Browne, E. Martin. *The Making of T. S. Eliot's Plays.* Cambridge, England, and New York: Cambridge UP, 1969.

Bush, Ronald. *T. S. Eliot: A Study in Character and Style.* Oxford, England, and New York: Oxford UP, 1983.

———. "Nathaniel Hawthorne and T. S. Eliot's American Connection." *Southern Review* 21 (1985): 924–33; rpt. *T. S. Eliot: An Anthology of Recent Criticism.* Ed. Tapan Kumar Basu. Delhi: Pencraft, 1993.

Cairns, Craig. *Yeats, Eliot, Pound, and the Politics of Poetry.* Pittsburgh: U of Pittsburgh P; London: Croom Helm, 1982.

Canary, Robert. *T. S. Eliot: The Poet and His Critics.* Chicago: American Library Association, 1982.

Chace, William. *The Political Identities of Ezra Pound and T. S. Eliot.* Stanford: Stanford UP, 1973.

Charron, William C. "T. S. Eliot: Aristotelian Arbiter of Bradleyan Antinomies." *Modern Schoolman* 73 (1995): 91–114.

Childs, Donald. "Etherized upon a Table: T. S. Eliot's Dissertation and Its Metaphorical Operations." *Journal of Modern Literature* 18 (1993): 381–94.

———. "T. S. Eliot's American Dissent/Descent." *Cohesion and Dissent in America.* Ed. Carol Colatrella. Albany: SUNY P, 1994. 77–94.

Chinitz, David. "Jazz and Jazz Discourse in Modernist Poetry: T. S. Eliot and Langston Hughes." Diss. Columbia U, 1993.

———. "T. S. Eliot and the Cultural Divide." *PMLA* 110 (1995): 236–47.

Christ, Carol. *Victorian and Modernist Poetics.* Chicago: U of Chicago P, 1984.

Clarke, Graham, ed. *T. S. Eliot: Critical Assessments.* 4 vols. London: C. Helm, 1990.

Cooper, John Xiros. *T. S. Eliot and the Ideology of "Four Quartets."* Cambridge, England, and New York: Cambridge UP, 1995.

Costello, Harry T. *Josiah Royce's Seminar, 1913–14: As Recorded in the Notebooks of Harry T. Costello.* Ed. Grover Smith. New Brunswick, NJ: Rutgers UP, 1963.

Cowan, Laura, ed. *T. S. Eliot: Man and Poet.* Vol. 1. Orono, ME: National Poetry Foundation, 1990.

Crawford, Robert. *The Savage and the City in the Work of T. S. Eliot.* Oxford, England: Oxford UP, 1987.

D'Ambrosio, Vinnie-Marie. *Eliot Possessed: T. S. Eliot and FitzGerald's "Rubaiyat."* New York: New York UP, 1989.

Daümer, Elizabeth. "A Literary Mother and a Literary Son: Charlotte Eliot and T. S. Eliot." Diss. Indiana U, 1990.

Davidson, Harriet. *T. S. Eliot and Hermeneutics: Absence and Interpretation in "The Waste Land."* Baton Rouge: Louisiana State UP, 1985.

Dawson, J. L., P. D. Holland, and D. J. McKitterick. *A Concordance to the Complete Poems and Plays of T. S. Eliot.* Ithaca, NY: Cornell UP, 1995.

Dettmar, Kevin J. H., ed. *Rereading the New: A Backward Glance at Modernism.* Ann Arbor, MI: U of Michigan P, 1992.

Donoghue Denis. *The Third Voice: Modern British and American Verse Drama.* Princeton, NJ: Princeton UP, 1959.

Eliot, T. S. *After Strange Gods: A Primer of Modern Heresy.* London: Faber; New York: Harcourt, 1934.

———. *The Complete Poems and Plays of T. S. Eliot.* New York: Harcourt, 1952; London: Faber, 1969.

———. *For Lancelot Andrewes: Essays on Style and Order.* London: Faber & Gwyer, 1928; Garden City, NY: Doubleday, 1929.

———. *The Idea of a Christian Society.* London: Faber, 1939; New York: Harcourt, 1940.

———. *Inventions of the March Hare: Poems 1909–1917.* Ed. Christopher Ricks. London: Faber, 1996; New York: Harcourt, 1997. Poems in the Berg Collection notebooks.

———. *Knowledge and Experience in the Philosophy of F. H. Bradley.* London: Faber; New York: Farrar, 1964. Eliot's doctoral dissertation.

———. *The Letters of T. S. Eliot.* Vol. 1, 1898–1922. Ed. Valerie Eliot. London: Faber; San Diego: Harcourt, 1988.

————. *Notes Towards the Definition of Culture*. London: Faber, 1948; New York: Harcourt, 1949.

————. *On Poetry and Poets*. London: Faber; New York: Farrar, 1957.

————. *The Sacred Wood*. 1920. London: Methuen; New York: Barnes & Noble, 1960.

————. *Selected Essays*. 1932. New York: Harcourt, 1950; London: Faber, 1951.

————. *To Criticize the Critic and Other Writings*. London: Faber; New York: Farrar, 1965.

————. *The Use of Poetry and the Use of Criticism: Studies in the Relation of Criticism to Poetry in England*. London: Faber, 1933; Cambridge, MA: Harvard UP, 1933.

————. *The Varieties of Metaphysical Poetry:*. Ed. Ronald Schuchard. London: Faber, 1993; New York: Harcourt, 1994. The Clark Lectures at Trinity College, Cambridge, 1926, and The Turnbull Lectures at The Johns Hopkins University, 1933.

————. *The Waste Land: A Facsimile and Transcript of the Original Drafts Including the Annotations of Ezra Pound*. Ed. Valerie Eliot. London: Faber; New York: Harcourt, 1971.

Ellis, Steve. *The English Eliot: Design, Language, and Landscape in "Four Quartets."* London and New York: Routledge, 1991.

Fathman, Anthony. "Viv and Tom: The Eliots as Ether Addict and Co-Dependent." *Yeats Eliot Review* 11 (1991): 33–36.

Felski, Rita. *The Gender of Modernism*. Cambridge, MA: Harvard UP, 1995.

Fleissner, Robert F. *T. S. Eliot and the Heritage of Africa: The Magus and the Moor as Metaphor*. New York: Peter Lang, 1992.

Frank, Armin Paul. *T. S. Eliot Criticism and Scholarship in German: A Descriptive Survey, 1923–1980*. Göttingen: Vandenhoeck, 1986.

Frank, Mechthild, Armin Paul Frank, and K. P. S. Jochum, eds. *A Half-Century of Eliot Criticism, 1916–1965: A Supplementary Bibliography*. Yeats Eliot Review Monograph series #1, 1978.

Frye, Northrop. *T. S. Eliot*. Chicago: U of Chicago P, 1963.

Gallup, Donald. *T. S. Eliot: A Bibliography*. A Revised and Extended Edition. New York: Harcourt, 1969.

Gardner, Helen. *The Art of T. S. Eliot*. London: Cresset P, 1949; New York: E. P. Dutton, 1950.

————. *The Composition of "Four Quartets."* Oxford, England, and New York: Oxford UP, 1978.

Gibert-Maceda, M. Teresa. "T. S. Eliot on Women: Women on T. S. Eliot." Thormählen. 105–19.

Gordon, Lyndall. *Eliot's Early Years*. Oxford, England, and New York: Oxford UP, 1977.

————. *Eliot's New Life*. Oxford, England: Oxford UP; New York: Farrar, 1988.

Grant, Michael. *T. S. Eliot: The Critical Heritage*. London and Boston: Routledge, 1982.

Gray, Piers. *T. S. Eliot's Intellectual and Poetic Development 1909–1922*. Atlantic Highlands, NJ: Humanities P; Brighton, Sussex: Harvester P, 1982.

Hargrove, Nancy D. "'Un Present Parfait': Eliot and La Vie Parisienne, 1910–11." Thormählen 33–58.

Harrison, John R. *The Reactionaries: A Study of the Anti-Democratic Intelligentsia*. New York: Schocken, 1967.

Hastings, Michael. *Tom and Viv*. Middlesex: Penguin, 1984; New York: Viking, 1985.

Hooker, Joan Fillmore. *T. S. Eliot's Poems in French Translation: Pierre Leyris and Others*. Ann Arbor, MI: UMI Research P, 1983.

Howarth, Herbert. *Notes on Some Figures behind T. S. Eliot*. Boston: Houghton Mifflin, 1964.

Jain, Manju. *T. S. Eliot and American Philosophy: The Harvard Years*. Cambridge, England, and New York: Cambridge UP, 1992.

Jarman, Mark. "Brer Rabbit and Brer Possum: The Americanness of Ezra Pound and T. S. Eliot." *Forked Tongues? Comparing Twentieth-Century British and American Literature*. Ed. Ann Massa and Alistair Stead. London: Longman, 1994. 21–37.

Jay, Gregory. *T. S. Eliot and the Poetics of Literary History*. Baton Rouge: Louisiana State UP, 1983.

Jeffreys, Mark. "The Rhetoric of Authority in T. S. Eliot's Athenaeum Reviews," *South Atlantic Review* 57 (1992): 93–108.

Jones, David E. *The Plays of T. S. Eliot*. Toronto: U of Toronto P, 1960.

Julius, Anthony. *T. S. Eliot: Anti-Semitism and Literary Form*. Cambridge, England, and New York: Cambridge UP, 1995.

Junkes-Kirchen, Klaus. *T. S. Eliot's "The Waste Land" Deutsch: Theorie und Praxis einer Gedichtübersetzung nach literatur und übersetzungswissenschaftlichen Gesichtspunketen*. Frankfurt am Main; New York: Peter Lang, 1988.

Kalaidjian, Walter. *Amercan Culture between the Wars: Revisionary Modernism and Postmodern Critique*. New York: Columbia UP, 1993.

Kearns, Cleo M. *T. S. Eliot and Indic Traditions: A Study in Poetry and Belief*. Cambridge, England, and New York: Cambridge UP, 1987.

————. "Doctrine and Wisdom in *Four Quartets*." Cowan 205–17.

Kenner, Hugh. *The Invisible Poet: T. S. Eliot*. 1959. New York: Harcourt, 1967; London: University Paperbacks, 1966.

————. *The Pound Era*. Berkeley and Los Angeles: U of California P, 1971.

Kermode, Frank. *Romantic Image*. New York: Vintage, 1957.

Kirk, Russell. *Eliot and His Age: T. S. Eliot's Moral Imagination in the Twentieth Century.* New York: Random House, 1971.

Knowles, Sebastian D. G., and Scott A. Leonard. *T. S. Eliot: Man and Poet. Volume II: An Annotated Bibliography of a Decade of T. S. Eliot Criticism, 1977–1986.* Orono, ME: National Poetry Foundation, 1992.

Kojecky, Roger. *T. S. Eliot's Social Criticism.* London: Faber; New York: Farrar, 1971.

Langbaum, Robert. *The Poetry of Experience: The Dramatic Monologue in Modern Literary Tradition.* New York: Random House, 1957.

Lentricchia, Frank. *Modernist Quartet.* Cambridge, England, and New York: Cambridge UP, 1994.

Levenson, Michael. *A Genealogy of Modernism: A Study of English Literary Doctrine 1908–1922.* Cambridge, England, and New York: Cambridge UP, 1984.

Litz, A. Walton, ed. *Eliot in His Time: Essays on the Occasion of the Fiftieth Anniversary of "The Waste Land."* Princeton, NJ: Princeton UP, 1973.

Lobb, Edward, ed. *Words in Time: New Essays on "Four Quartets."* Ann Arbor: U of Michigan P, 1993.

Lockerd, Benjamin G., Jr. "The Heraclitean Exchange of Elements in *Four Quartets.*" *Modern Schoolman* 73 (1995) 47–58. See also Lockerd's *Aethereal Rumours: Eliot's Physics and Poetics.* Lewisburg, PA: Bucknell UP, forthcoming.

Longenbach, James. *Modernist Poetics of History: Pound, Eliot, and the Sense of the Past.* Princeton, NJ: Princeton UP, 1987.

Malamud, Randy. *T. S. Eliot's Drama: A Research and Production Sourcebook.* Westport, CT: Greenwood P, 1992.

———. *Where the Words Are Valid: T. S. Eliot's Communities of Drama.* Westport, CT: Greenwood P, 1994.

Manganaro, Marc. *Myth, Rhetoric, and the Voice of Authority: A Critique of Frazer, Eliot, Frye and Campbell.* New Haven, CT: Yale UP, 1992.

Manganiello, Dominic. *T. S. Eliot and Dante.* London: Macmillan, 1989.

Margolis, John D. *T. S. Eliot's Intellectual Development, 1922–1939.* Chicago: U of Chicago P, 1972.

Martin, Mildred, ed. *A Half-Century of Eliot Criticism: An Annotated Bibliography of Books and Articles in English, 1916–1965.* Lewisburg, PA: Bucknell UP, 1972.

Materer, Timothy. *Vortex: Pound, Eliot, and Lewis.* Ithaca, NY: Cornell UP, 1979.

Matthiessen, F. O. *The Achievement of T. S. Eliot: An Essay on the Nature of Poetry.* 1935. 3rd ed. New York and London: Oxford UP, 1958.

Mayer, John T. *T. S. Eliot's Silent Voices.* Oxford, England, and New York: Oxford UP, 1989.

McDonald, Gail. *Learning to Be Modern: Pound, Eliot, and the American University.* Oxford, England, and New York: Oxford UP, 1993.

McDougal, Stuart Y. "T. S. Eliot." *Sixteen Modern American Authors: A Survey of Research and Criticism since 1972.* Vol. 2. Ed. Jackson R. Bryer. Durham, NC: Duke UP, 1990. 154–209.

Menand, Louis. *Discovering Modernism: T. S. Eliot and His Context.* Oxford, England, and New York: Oxford UP, 1987.

———. "*T. S. Eliot, Anti-Semitism, and Literary Form* by Anthony Julius." *New York Review of Books* 53 (1996): 34–41.

Michaels, Walter Benn. "Philosophy in Kinkanja: Eliot's Pragmatism." *Glyph: Textual Studies* 8 (1981): 170–202.

Miller, J. Hillis. *Poets of Reality: Six Twentieth-Century Writers.* Cambridge, MA: Harvard UP, 1965.

Moody, A. D. *Thomas Stearns Eliot: Poet.* 1979. 2nd ed. Cambridge, England, and New York: Cambridge UP, 1994.

———. "T. S. Eliot: The American Strain." *The Placing of T. S. Eliot.* Ed. Jewel Spears Brooker. Columbia: U of Missouri P, 1991. 77–89.

———, ed. *The Cambridge Companion to T. S. Eliot.* Cambridge, England, and New York: Cambridge UP, 1994.

Morrison, Mark. "Performing the Pure Voice: Elocution, Verse Recitation, and Modernist Poetry in Prewar London." *Modernism/Modernity* 3 (1996): 25–50.

Morrison, Paul. *The Poetics of Fascism: Ezra Pound, T. S. Eliot, Paul de Man.* Oxford, England, and New York: Oxford UP, 1996.

Murphy, Russell Elliott. "Eliot's Grandchildren: The Poet of *The Waste Land* and the Generation of the Sixties." Cowan 83–89.

Murray, Paul. *T. S. Eliot and Mysticism: The Secret History of "Four Quartets."* London: Macmillan, 1991.

Nelson, Cary. *Repression and Recovery: Modern American Poetry and the Politics of Cultural Memory, 1910–1945.* Madison: U of Wisconsin P, 1989.

Nichols, Peter. *Modernisms.* Berkeley and Los Angeles: U of California P, 1995.

North, Michael. *The Political Aesthetic of Yeats, Eliot, and Pound.* Cambridge, England, and New York: Cambridge UP, 1991.

———. "Old Possum and Brer Rabbit: Pound and Eliot's Racial Masquerade." *The Dialect of Modernism: Race, Language, and Twentieth-Century Literature.* New York: Oxford UP, 1994. 77–99.

Oser, Lee. "The Letter and the Spirit: T. S. Eliot and American Poetry." Diss. Yale U, 1995.

Ozick, Cynthia. "A Critic at Large: T. S. Eliot at 101." *New Yorker* (20 Nov. 1989): 119–54; rpt. *What Henry James Knew and Other Essays on Writers.* London: Jonathan Cape, 1993. 10–68.

Perl, Jeffrey. *Skepticism and Modern Enmity: Before and After Eliot.* Baltimore: Johns Hopkins UP, 1989.

Perloff, Marjorie. *The Poetics of Indeterminacy: From Rimbaud to Cage.* Princeton, NJ: Princeton UP, 1981.

Phelan, Virginia. *Two Ways of Life and Death: "Alcestis" and "The Cocktail Party."* New York: Garland P, 1990.

Pinkney, Tony. *Women in the Poetry of T. S. Eliot: A Psychoanalytic Approach.* London: Macmillan, 1984.

Plumb, Cheryl J., ed. *Nightwood: The Original Versions and Related Drafts.* Normal, IL: Dalkey Archive P, 1995.

Pondrom, Cyrena. *The Road from Paris: The French Influence on English Poetry, 1900–1920.* Cambridge, England, and New York: Cambridge UP, 1974.

Rabaté, Jean-Michel. *The Ghosts of Modernity.* Gainesville: UP of Florida, 1996.

Rado, Lisa, ed. *Rereading Modernism: New Directions in Feminist Criticism.* New York: Garland, 1994.

Ramaiah, L. S. *Indian Responses to T. S. Eliot: A Bibliographical Guide to Writings in English.* Calcutta: Writers Workshop, 1988.

Ricks, Beatrice, ed. *T. S. Eliot: A Bibliography of Secondary Works.* Metuchen, NJ: Scarecrow P, 1980.

Ricks, Christopher. *T. S. Eliot and Prejudice.* London and Boston: Faber, 1988.

Riquelme, John Paul. *Harmony of Dissonances: T. S. Eliot, Romanticism, and Imagination.* Baltimore: Johns Hopkins UP, 1991.

Roby, Kinley E., ed. *Critical Essays on T. S. Eliot: The Sweeney Motif.* Boston: Hall, 1985.

Schuchard, Ronald. "American Publishers and the Transmission of Eliot's Prose." *Modernist Writers and the Marketplace.* Ed. Warren Chernaik, Warwick Gould, and Ian Williston. London: Macmillan; New York: St. Martin's P, 1996. 171–201

Schwartz, Sanford. *The Matrix of Modernism: Pound, Eliot, and Early Twentieth-Century Thought.* Princeton, NJ: Princeton UP, 1985.

———. "Post-Modernizing Eliot: The Approach from Philosophy." *Modern Schoolman* 73 (1995): 115–27.

Scott, Bonnie Kime, ed. *The Gender of Modernism: A Critical Anthology.* Bloomington: Indiana UP, 1990.

———. *Reconfiguring Modernism.* Bloomington: U of Indiana P, 1995.

Sharratt, Bernard. "Eliot: Modernism, Postmodernism, and After." Moody, *Cambridge Companion* 223–35.

Shusterman, Richard. *T. S. Eliot and the Philosophy of Criticism.* New York: Columbia UP; London: Duckworth, 1988.

Sigg, Eric. *The American T. S. Eliot: A Study of the Early Writings.* Cambridge, England, and New York: Cambridge UP, 1989.

Skaff, William. *The Philosophy of T. S. Eliot: From Skepticism to a Surrealist Poetic, 1909–1927.* Philadelphia: U of Pennsylvania P, 1986.

Smith, Carol H. *T. S. Eliot's Dramatic Theory and Practice: From "Sweeney Agonistes" to "The Elder Statesman."* Princeton, NJ: Princeton UP, 1963.

Smith, Grover. *T. S. Eliot's Poetry & Plays: A Study in Sources & Meaning.* 1956. 2nd ed. Chicago: U of Chicago P, 1974.

Smith, Stan. *The Origins of Modernism: Eliot, Pound, Yeats and the Renewal of Rhetorics.* London and New York: Harvester Wheatsheaf, 1994.

Soldo, John J. *The Tempering of T. S. Eliot.* Ann Arbor, MI: UMI Research P, 1983.

Spanos, William. "Repetition in *The Waste Land*: A Phenomenological Destruction." *Boundary 2* (1979): 225–85.

Spurr, David. *Conflicts in Consciousness: T. S. Eliot's Poetry and Criticism.* Urbana: U of Illinois P, 1984.

———. "Myths of Anthropology: Eliot, Joyce, Lévy-Bruhl." *PMLA* 109 (1994): 266–80.

Sri, P. S. *T. S. Eliot, Vedanta and Buddhism.* Vancouver: U of British Columbia P, 1985.

Stead, C. K. *The New Poetic: Yeats to Eliot.* London: Hutchinson, 1964.

Surette, Leon. *The Birth of Modernism: Ezra Pound, T. S. Eliot, W. B. Yeats, and the Occult.* Montreal: McGill-Queen's UP, 1993.

Svarny, Erik. *"The Men of 1914": T. S. Eliot and Early Modernism.* Philadelphia: Open UP, 1988.

Takayanagi, Shun'ichi, S. J. "T. S. Eliot, Jacques Maritain, and Neo-Thomism." *Modern Schoolman* 73 (1995): 71–90.

Teres, Harvey. "Remaking Marxist Criticism: *Partisan Review*'s Eliotic Leftism, 1934–1936." *American Literature* 64 (1992): 127–53.

Thompson, David. "Criticism and the Vichy Syndrome: Charles Maurras, T. S. Eliot and the Forms of Historical Memory." Diss. U of Chicago, 1996.

Thormählen, Marianne, ed., *T. S. Eliot at the Turn of the Century.* Lund, Sweden: Lund UP, 1993.

Tobin, David. *The Presence of the Past. T. S. Eliot's Victorian Inheritance.* Ann Arbor, MI: UMI Research P, 1983.

Tratner, Michael. *Modernism and Mass Politics: Joyce, Woolf, Eliot, Yeats.* Stanford: Stanford UP, 1995.

Wicht, Wolfgang. "T. S. Eliot and Karl Mannheim: Cultural Reconstruction vs. the Destruction of Culture." *Zeitschrift für Anglistik und Amerikanistik* 36 (1988): 197–204.

Young, Howard, ed. *T. S. Eliot and Hispanic Modernity (1924–1993).* Denver: Society of Spanish and Spanish-American Studies, 1994.

13

Ernest Hemingway

Michael S. Reynolds

Seventeen years ago I said in Yeatsian tones that it was time for us to relearn our trade, to do well what best becomes scholars. With the territory marked off and a few good guides, I urged all to become explorers, charting empty spaces on the Hemingway map (Oldsey 22–23). It seems appropriate, therefore, to review the work for which I had such high hopes and to speculate about the work that remains. By any measure, recent years have been more productive than anyone could have imagined. In his lively posthumous career, Ernest Hemingway has published more books from the grave than he did during the last twenty years of his life: *A Moveable Feast, Islands in the Stream, The Dangerous Summer, The Garden of Eden,* and *Selected Letters.* Since 1980, more than thirty scholarly books, twelve collections of essays, and hundreds of articles have been published, filling in the map of Hemingway studies.

Some areas are now much richer in detailed topography. Seventeen years ago we did not have easy access to the important journalism from Hemingway's formative years in Europe. Today we have *Dateline: Toronto* and the missing Toronto *Star* stories as well. Seventeen years ago we knew little about Hemingway's reading. Today we have a catalog of his Cuban library (Brasch and Sigman) and a list of his pre-1940 reading (Reynolds, *Hemingway's Reading*). Seventeen years ago we had only Carlos Baker's "life story" of Hemingway, but not his literary biography. Today we have competing versions: Meyers, Griffin, Lynn, Mellow, my own work, and more to follow. We now know more about Ernest Hemingway than about our own fathers. Seventeen years ago we did not have the work of Paul Smith, Bernice Kert, Frederic Svoboda, John Raeburn, Linda Wagner-Martin, Mark Spilka, Joe Flora, Susan Beegel, Jim Phelan, Debra Moddelmog, Jerry Kennedy, Robert Fleming, Jacqueline

Tavernier-Courbin, Kenneth Johnston, or Gerry Brenner, to name the more obvious players.

Much of this activity is due to a single cause: the Hemingway collection of letters and manuscripts housed in the John F. Kennedy Library. An obvious effect of this collection can be seen in Paul Smith's *Reader's Guide to the Short Stories of Ernest Hemingway*, which, among its many gifts, gives us the first chronology for the writing of the stories and describes the manuscripts involved. Smith's book, heavily dependent on the Kennedy Library, is the tool that will take criticism of the short stories up to the next level of complexity.

Without access to these manuscripts and letters, many of us would be leading far different, far poorer scholarly lives. In 1976 at the Alabama Hemingway conference, I gave the only paper based on manuscript study. In my opening remarks, I said: "The text itself is no longer enough. . . . no serious critic can afford to avoid the manuscripts, for if he does, he will sleep uneasy, wondering what he has missed" (Noble 115). Today such a warning is unnecessary; everyone knows about the manuscripts, which have been both blessing and bane. Without them, much of our work would not have been possible, but because these manuscripts are so rich with implications, they have made articles almost too easy to publish. As Jackson Benson predicted fourteen years ago, on the basis of the manuscripts, "we could fill *American Literature* with articles for two hundred years and never even get to the really good material" (Noble 35). That is what we've been doing, skimming the cream, leaving much of the tedious work for the next generation.

So let me suggest what we have not been doing and what most obviously remains to be done. First, the tools of the trade need resharpening, and new ones need to be forged. If we are going to take Hemingway studies into the next century, we must find electronic means of assisting the process, or we will find our work terribly time-consuming, flawed by ignorance, and inaccurate. Already the lapsed time between the conception of a fresh idea, its publication, and its effect in the marketplace is measured in years; if technology and science moved at our pace, we would still be driving the Model-A. What we need is better and more informative bibliographies in hypertext and on CD-ROM; bibliographies that can be searched by key words in linked sequences; bibliographies that have abstracts of the articles, that have indexes of the books; on-line bibliographies that are continually updated by users and authors. Since most scholars are already using their PCs for composition of essays and storage of research, it would be a simple matter to put our Hemingway work on-line via the Mosaic system. If we were to do so, I could, for example, open my note files from the *Paris Tribune*, the *Key West Citizen*, and the *Havana News* to anyone who wanted to use them.

I have recently proposed a hypertext CD-ROM that would combine the two volumes of the Hanneman bibliography, the Larson bibliography, and *Hemingway's Reading*. The user would get hypertext abstracts of the articles in Hanneman. With the *Reading*, he or she would get indexes of books Hemingway read, author information, the table of contents of magazines read, and more annotation. The user would also be able to sort reading material by year, by subject, by genre, by author, by publisher, or any combination: e.g., a listing of all the books Hemingway read before 1940 on elephant hunting in the order in which he read them.

We also need to put all published Hemingway texts on-line or on CD-ROM. I, for one, am tired beyond measure of searching through *Death in the Afternoon*, *Green Hills of Africa*, and *A Moveable Feast* for accurate quotations, references to bullfighters and place names, and those quotations that one vaguely remembers but can never find when they're needed. Peter Hays at the University of California at Davis will share his disk facsimile of *In Our Time*, which he developed for his concordance. Using scanners, we should be able to make all the texts available either on-line or on disk for scholarly use. Particularly as copyrights on Hemingway material begin to run out, we must get accurate texts in place electronically if we are ever to produce the standard Hemingway editions.

An equally useful and necessary task is the arduous business of dating the manuscripts, particularly the fragments. Seventeen years have passed since the opening of the Hemingway collection in the Kennedy Library and twenty-three since the manuscripts first became accessible, yet we still cannot say with any certainty when Hemingway wrote about Philip Haines, when he wrote *A Moveable Feast*, or when he began *The Garden of Eden*. There are literally hundreds of undated manuscript fragments in the Kennedy Collection; many of these may be crucial to the literary biographer and textual critic, but until someone establishes the apparatus for accurate dating, they remain largely anecdotal.

To accomplish the editing task before us, we shall have to develop some essential tools. We need, for example, a method for dating the numerous Hemingway fragments, notes, and unpublished texts, most of which are in the Hemingway collection at the Kennedy Library. Using typed and dated Hemingway letters as the known quantity, we could establish the characteristics of Hemingway's numerous typewriters, owned and borrowed. Applying that information to the Kennedy Library's typescripts, we could group them at least into recognizable periods. Then a study of the paper, watermarks, and ribbons might narrow the time frame. A second and complementary tool would allow careful analysis of changes in Hemingway's handwriting over time, isolating those identifying characteristics that would aid in dating the holograph fragments and undated letters, of which there are hundreds. Unpublished fragments could be quickly compared with published texts if they were on CD-ROM.

Finally we need a comprehensive and electronic means of searching the Hemingway manuscripts and letters held in public libraries. An on-line bibliography of this material would give us the usual archivist's description of the manuscript or letter, and would add dating, when known, and a brief abstract, while it would call attention to related items. To create any of these tools, we must first educate a handful of young scholars with the requisite forensic and bibliographic skills, not to mention the dedication and enthusiasm, required for such tasks.

Our apparent lack of interest in accurate textual studies is both curious and appalling. We still have not developed the expertise required for this work. The standard edition of Hemingway's canon may remain on the other side of the horizon, but there is nothing preventing us from doing the textual descriptions. When 25 percent of a major author's work is published posthumously under the direction of several editorial hands, responsible scholars should describe the editorial changes. There's nothing flashy about writing the descriptions, no theoretical axes to grind, no politics involved, but it is satisfying, substantial, and lasting. Most important, such descriptions will keep us from making foolish mistakes and saying silly things about the available texts.

In the next twenty-five years, we should edit all of Hemingway and produce the standard and variorum editions that we so sorely lack. The reediting task will require intense and collaborative work under guidelines yet to be established. Electronic networking will make this task easier, as will electronic tools for comparing texts, but this monumental task will require enormous goodwill and cooperation on the part of all involved. As a first stage, someone, like James L. W. West III at Penn State's Center for the History of the Book, needs to group the first generation of editors to work out the parameters of the problem, locate the materials, and begin the task. For all but Hemingway's posthumous publications, we frequently have holograph drafts, typescripts, and corrected galleys. In every present text, there are unrealized omissions, unnecessary deletions, and outright errors at all three stages. It is not too soon to begin the corrective work on *In Our Time* and *The Sun Also Rises*. Needless to say, such work must be carried out with the probity of a priest and the precision of a cartographer.

Every Hemingway text we have is flawed, but his posthumous work is a disaster area. Jacqueline Tavernier-Courbin's *Ernest Hemingway's "A Moveable Feast"* describes in specific detail the revisions Hemingway made and the specific changes and deletions made by his editors. *Islands in the Stream*, pieced together anonymously by Carlos Baker from a complex manuscript, is, according to Robert Fleming, the best edited of the posthumous work. No one has yet compared typescripts and text of *The Dangerous Summer*, edited by Michael Pietsch. About the editing of *The Garden of Eden*, there is general scholarly agreement that no major American author has been worse served by his publisher. The novel in print, which lost half its plot and much of its focus in editing, bears so little resemblance to the book Hemingway wrote that scholars can speak only to the manuscript versions.

If Rose Marie Burwell is on the right track, and I believe she is, then scholars, critics, and publishers have badly misread what Hemingway referred to as his trilogy and what may become his tetralogy with the addition of the unpublished African manuscript. *A Moveable Feast*, *Islands*, *Garden*, and the African story have as a common theme the public and private life of the artist in our time. (See Robert Fleming's *The Face in the Mirror*.) Written between 1946 and 1960, these stories have overlapping characters, settings, and conflicts; parts of one story were sometimes moved to another as Hemingway worked on two and sometimes three of these books at the same time. Because the scholars who came of age after World War II generally wanted Hemingway to continue writing as he had in his early period, they were ill prepared to embrace a postmodernist Hemingway, whose experiments did not fit their expectations. Before these texts can be well edited and republished authoritatively, we must not only reconstruct the writing of each, but also reach some agreement about Hemingway's post–World War II agenda.

Bibliography, textual dating, textual studies: these are the basic kinds of scholarship that we need but that few of us are practicing—and even fewer are passing the requisite skills on to their graduate students. While studying Hemingway's marginalized characters, we need to rehabilitate marginalized skills.

We now have almost a half-century of Hemingway biography and criticism that anyone new to this field must first absorb, even as he or she remembers that the explications and agendas of the World War II generation tell as much about the flaws and values of the Eisenhower years as they do about Hemingway's texts. The unified field theories of the 1950s and 1960s, which imposed order on a disorderly life and its works, are no longer as convincing as they once were. One must think of Hemingway's texts and the critics' commentaries as bench-marks on an out-of-date map, forcing the user to resurvey each point to verify its accuracy.

Since Carlos Baker's first and still most factually comprehensive *Hemingway: A Life Story*, there have been more biographies of Hemingway written than of any other single American author. These include Peter Griffin's *Along with Youth: Hemingway, the Early Years*, and *Less Than a Treason: Hemingway in Paris*; Kenneth S. Lynn's *Hemingway*; Jeffrey Meyers's *Hemingway: A Biography*; Scott Donaldson's *By Force of Will: The Life and Art of Ernest Hemingway*; James Mellow's *Hemingway: A Life without Consequences*; my own trilogy, *The Young Hemingway*, *Hemingway: The Paris Years*, and *Hemingway: The American Homecoming*; Gregory Hemingway's *Papa: A Personal Memoir*; James McLendon's *Papa: Hemingway in Key West*; Norberto Fuentes's *Hemingway in Cuba*; John Raeburn's *Fame Became of Him: Hemingway as a Public Writer*; Mary Hemingway's *How It Was*; Bernice Kert's *The Hemingway Women*; as well as Jack Hemingway's autobiography, *Misadventures of a Fly Fisherman*, Gioia Diliberto's *Hadley*, Carl Rollyson's *Nothing Ever Happens to the Brave: The Story of Martha Gellhorn*; and Peter Viertel's *Dangerous Friends: At Large with Hemingway and Huston in the Fifties*. Enough, many say, enough. Who can bear to hear once more of who did what to whom in Max Perkins's office that dusty afternoon so long ago? What can we possibly be told that we have not heard five times before?

The answer depends upon the scale of the map you require. If what you want is the broader view, choose the 1:500,000 scale map, which is ideal for general navigation. If your need is for a more detailed map, one that would allow you to spend a week in Dordogne without getting lost, choose a 1:50,000 scale. If you are going to do any cross-country hiking, you need a 1:10,000 scale map. The map is never the territory itself, and a biography is never the life itself—one must allow amply for the many faces of Ernest Hemingway now amongst us. But a literary biography of

Hemingway should be more interested in the writer than in the public man, more interested in his text and its immediate context than in glorifying or denigrating Hemingway the husband, the friend, or the father. We should recall W. H. Auden's eulogy of Yeats: "You were silly like us: your gift survived it all." It is Hemingway's "gift" that should be at the heart of our studies, not his "silliness."

Like maps, biographies are written at different scales. Consider, for example, studies of those Hemingway years 1926 through 1929, when he broke his contract with Liveright, finished *The Sun Also Rises*, divorced Hadley, married Pauline, wrote *Men without Women* and *A Farewell to Arms*, moved to Key West, and buried his father. Baker, Meyers, and Mellow, each with his own virtues, cover this period at a scale of one year to every ten pages; my coverage of this period is written at one year to fifty-five pages. Having written her incomparable book, *Letters from the Lost Generation*, Linda Miller is now writing about the hysterical summer of 1926 at Antibes on a scale of three months to two hundred pages. Like maps, each book has its limitations and its particular uses; each has its flaws and omissions due to information that has not yet surfaced.

So many scholars prefer to work with selected Hemingway texts; we have not been interested in seeing him whole. To complete Hemingway's literary biography, we must stop ignoring his so-called nonfiction, including the *Esquire* "Letters," and begin reconstructing the complex Hemingway: man of letters; stylist; natural historian; outdoorsman; sometime alcoholic; sometime Catholic; journalist; navigator; avid reader; and authority on bullfighting, military tactics, political revolutions, and marlin fishing. We must also stop trying to create a single person who never changed, who was always Ernest Hemingway of the grey-bearded photographs; we must stop reading his life retrospectively, interpreting his early texts on the basis of his later ones. We must allow the man to change over time, to change his mind, his style, and his objectives. Despite all generalizations to the contrary, Ernest Hemingway was experimenting with structure, genre, and style to the very end of his life.

If one is interested only in Hemingway's early period (1915–29), then one needs no further biographies, for most of the crucial information is available. If one's field is the middle period (1930–45), then one is on far less certain ground. During the so-called Key West years, Hemingway produced more writing than during any other decade of his life: one volume of short stories, one play, two volumes of nonfiction, the *Esquire* letters, his African short stories, and two novels. Seventeen years ago I called it the truly unexplored territory that would be the most rewarding field during the next decade. I was wrong. There was plenty of territory to explore, but few scholars made the safari. I do not understand why we haven't done better by Hemingway's thirties. Why don't we know as much about Hemingway in Key West as we do about him in Paris? Why don't we know more than the barest surface detail about those months in Havana when he was writing *For Whom the Bell Tolls*?

For the period just after 1940, we know even less about Hemingway's literary biography than we do for the thirties. I cannot date a single significant manuscript as having been written between 1940 and 1945. For a literary biographer, the absence of a record of composition is the equivalent of a blank space on a map. Why would the most popular American author stop writing for five years? His biographers say it was the war that stopped him. But during the Spanish Civil War he managed to write two novels, a handful of short stories, one play, and portions of a movie script.

For the middle period, we still lack the kind of detailed literary history/biography that we have for the early period. We know very little about the background and composition of *Death in the Afternoon, Green Hills of Africa, To Have and Have Not, The Fifth Column,* and *For Whom the Bell Tolls*. No one has yet given the attention to the writing of these texts that it deserves. We still do not appreciate Hemingway's experimentation during the middle period; we do not understand how it builds toward *For Whom the Bell Tolls*. We know little about the effects of his relationship with Martha Gellhorn on his writing; we need a careful and detailed reading of the fiction she wrote from 1936 through 1945. (When I asked her for an interview, which she declined, she told me to read what she had published and I would not need the interview.) We still do not have the complete story of Hemingway's active and ideological involvement in the Spanish Civil War—though, fortunately, William Watson, who has been researching the period for some time, is on the verge of publishing what should be the whole story. For all the belittling of Hemingway's counter-espionage activities in Cuba (1940–43), no one has yet tracked down his reports, which are probably buried in the State Department papers in the National Archives. At the Kennedy Library, we have his notes from the period and Colonel Charles Lanham's sanitized narrative; we have the transcript of the military hearing on the charges that Hemingway the journalist was actually participating in the fighting; and we have his own fictional version, "A Room on the Garden Side." What we lack are the field reports and battle narratives that are probably stored somewhere. No one has brought all of this information to bear on those few days in the Hurtgenwald—5 November 1944–4 December 1944—when Hemingway came close enough to death and destruction to smell its breath: an experience as traumatic as any other in his life, an experience that contributed heavily to his postwar writing.

Hemingway's late period (1945–61) remains almost as murky as it was twenty years ago. Slowly the letter caches are surfacing, and survivors are telling their stories: Peter Viertel, Norberto Fuentes, Slim Keith. The more we learn, however, the more muddled the period becomes. Only now is the chronology of the period coming clear. We have only the vaguest outlines of what and when Hemingway wrote during these sixteen years, and most of our knowledge of that period is flawed. We know a lot about Hemingway's relationship with Maxwell Perkins (Berg), but very little about his total relationship with the Scribners, junior and senior, and their publishing house. The Scribner author archives have only recently been opened at Princeton. We know a good deal about the development of the public persona (Raeburn), but we don't understand why Hemingway was never a target of the 1950s communist witch-hunts. His unequivocal support of the Loyalist cause in the Spanish Civil War should have left him vulnerable to the House UnAmerican Activities Committee, which ruined the lives of many writers far less complicit than Hemingway. Nor do we understand Hemingway's complex medical history—including treatment for hypertension, depression, high cholesterol, hemochromotosis, and paranoia—not to speak of the impact of the medications on his ability to write. Medical records recently opened at the Kennedy Library give partial evidence, perhaps enough to reconstruct the treatments and medications that could not prevent his suicide and may have contributed to it. Crucial to all of the unanswered questions are the Hemingway letters, some of which have not yet come to light. A recent full-scale biography spends 270 pages covering Hemingway in the 1920s, 90 pages on the 1930s, and 25 pages on the 1940–45 period. Just when you thought you did not need to read another Hemingway biography, I'm saying that we still have much to learn.

When Mary Hemingway went to Cuba in 1961 to retrieve her dead husband's literary estate, she discovered his statement forbidding publication of his letters. The typed note was dated 20 May 1958 (How It Was 504). At that moment in Washington, DC, Ezra Pound was about to be released from St. Elizabeths Hospital for the insane, while in New York, the *Paris Review* was publishing its now-famous interview with Hemingway. On his writing table at the Finca, Hemingway was then struggling for closure with his Paris memoirs, with *The Garden of Eden*, and with his life itself. He signed the note with his literary past weighing heavily upon him, and by writing the note called attention to the autobiography in letters that he had been somewhat consciously writing since his early Paris days.

Whether Hemingway was serious or not in his injunction was soon a moot point. In 1980, Mary Hemingway and Charles Scribner, Jr., prevailed upon Carlos Baker to edit and annotate *Ernest Hemingway: Selected Letters*. For scholars, who had for twenty years been forced to paraphrase, *Selected Letters* was a great relief, but only a few realized that the complete letters would run to three or four volumes. The task of collecting and annotating still lies years before us, for we will be well into the next century before all the letters surface. Meanwhile there is much we can do to prepare for that time.

Some of us need to be scouting in the more sparsely detailed areas of the map, looking for Hemingway correspondence that has not yet come to light. We have only a few of Hemingway's letters to Augustus Pfeiffer, the driving force behind Richard Hudnut Cosmetics' far-flung empire and Pauline's wealthy uncle and benefactor. Between 1927 and 1940, Uncle Gus was Ernest's financial advisor, political sounding board, surrogate father, and literary angel. When Hemingway needed historical materials for *Death in the Afternoon*, Uncle Gus directed his minions in Spain to collect them. Extrapolating from his letters in reply to Hemingway, one senses that Hemingway's letters to Gus Pfeiffer should provide a wealth of evidence for Ernest's political development through the thirties. Somewhere those letters probably exist.

Somewhere else may be the Hemingway letters to Charles Sweeney, that mysterious soldier of fortune whom Hemingway first met in Constantinople during the Greco-Turkish War and with whom he remained in contact as late as 1946, when he hunted with Sweeney in Utah. Given Hemingway's now-obvious fascination with military aspects of political revolutions and the lives of revolutionaries, literary historians would be grateful for any correspondence with Sweeney, who, for thirty years, went to every major or minor war available. Equally interesting, for different reasons, would be Hemingway letters to Philip Percival, Alfred Rice, and Marlene Dietrich.

Although Hemingway's complete collected letters cannot be published until the post-1940 letters have surfaced and Martha Gellhorn's lock on her Hemingway correspondence is removed, there are a number of valuable collections that could be published while we are waiting for the magnum opus. Having only one side of a correspondence is never as interesting as having both sides set in historical context. There are some now-complete Hemingway correspondences that would be major additions to literary history. Someone should edit and place in context the Hemingway–Ezra Pound–Archibald MacLeish correspondence, which, running from 1923 to 1958, is one of the most interesting and argumentative literary correspondences of American modernism. Most, if not all, of this correspondence resides in a handful of libraries: the Kennedy, the Lilly, the Beinecke, the Firestone, and the Library of Congress. Another interesting collection would be both sides of Hemingway's correspondence with painters: Joan Miro, Mike Strater, Waldo Peirce, Luis Quintanilla, and others. Studies of the sort I am suggesting are more than a collection of letters. One must provide the narrative bridges, explain the silences, and establish the historical contexts that enrich the letters.

Even though Hemingway scholars have been, as a group, almost exclusively interested in the much-romanticized public lives of the literary twenties to the neglect of Hemingway's middle and late periods, there remain several difficult studies related to the early period still to be done. J. Gerald Kennedy's recent book, *Imagining Paris*, has taken us to the next level of Hemingway work: the effect of intersections on the development of the artist. For several years we have known what Hemingway read from Sylvia Beach's lending library, but no one has yet analyzed the immediate and long-range impact of Hemingway's Paris reading on his career. The most valuable literary history we have is the correspondence between Hemingway and Scribners publishing house. A well-annotated edition with the necessary narrative bridges, chronology, and index would be a nice four-year task for a pair of scholars. More difficult and necessary is a summing up and judicious analysis of Hemingway's lifelong literary relationships with Gertrude Stein, Ford Madox Ford, Ezra Pound, and James Joyce—not who said what to whom, but how the work of each mentor contributed to Hemingway's artistic career, not only in Paris, but right up to his death.

Literary biography is, of course, only a small part of the work to be done. The number of women writing about Hemingway is growing annually, and part of their interest is in gender studies. Rather than allow uninformed critics who have read only "The Short Happy Life of Francis Macomber" to continue dismissing Hemingway as a misogynist, we need to write the serious gender studies for our time. Gender theory, which has changed how we teach many male writers, is opening Hemingway's texts in new ways. But the writing of the serious gender studies will take balanced readers, ones who do not confuse Hemingway's public image with his fiction; ones dedicated enough to read all the texts, reserving judgments and eschewing political ends; ones more interested in Hemingway than in the agenda of others. For models, one might look to Mark Spilka's *Hemingway's Quarrel with Androgyny* and Robert Scholes and Nancy Comley's *Hemingway's Genders*.

Hemingway's nonfiction continues to be the most neglected part of his canon. If we can stop reading *Green Hills* as autobiography, perhaps we can deal responsibly with Hemingway's use of the hunter as metaphor for the writer. That step will lead us toward an improved reading of *Death in the Afternoon*, which remains a garbage dump we pick through for pithy quotes while ignoring the heart of its matter. Like more than one modernist and postmodernist, Hemingway frequently wrote about the problems of being a writer. One of the things we're told that Nick leaves behind him on Big Two-Hearted River is the need to write. The story itself becomes as much an extended metaphor about writing as a story about fishing. Hemingway's bullfighters, fishermen, hunters, and boxers are all, at some level, metaphors for his trade. To continue to neglect his nonfiction, which totals about 30 percent of his total work, is to leave about 30 percent of our map uncharted.

Much remains to be learned also about Hemingway's narrators and the structure of the stories they tell, a field of study not so much neglected as slighted. Good work is being done, but not nearly enough. The point of view in Hemingway's short fiction is seldom simple and almost never consistent. In his several experiments, he breaks every rule for writing short stories. We've been so enthralled with guessing what he left out of stories that we've missed a good deal of what he put into them. I have learned more about Hemingway's craft from working with an undergraduate on the manuscript draft of "Fathers and Sons" than I have from most of the criticism of the past seventeen years. We need new tools, new leadership, and new direction; we need better training. James Phelan's work, *Reading People, Reading Plots*, is a necessary part of our future if we are ever to describe accurately this amalgam that we call Hemingway studies.

We also need genre studies that incorporate the best of what has been said with a comprehensive overview. We still cannot say much about Hemingway and the structure of the novel. No, he is not using the same structure time and again. Yes, he does know what he's doing. He's read his Joyce, his Conrad, and his Ford Madox Ford, and he uses them as well as anyone else from his generation. Anyone who continues to treat him as a simple-minded novelist lacking in structural finesse needs to change writers or actually read all Hemingway's texts. Even more necessary is the genre study that remains to be done on Hemingway's short stories. We have plenty of ways to read the stories as stories. The manuscript studies are accumulating. But we need to appropriate the best of Paul Smith, Joseph Flora, and others who have written so well about the stories and to bring their work to bear on the generic changes Hemingway wrought with his frequently experimental short fiction.

Incredible as it may seem, we still do not have a decent study of Hemingway's several styles. Back in the old days, his style was always reduced to impressionistic metaphors—staccato, hard-bitten, hard athletic prose. Between then and now the whole theory and practice of stylistics has undergone a revolution—but when it got around to Hemingway, the results were so theoretical and statistical that no one but specialists could read them. Much to be desired is a study of his styles using contemporary theory, but theory presented in a way that is readable, persuasive, and interesting to the general academic reader. And where are the linguists and the semioticians who should be working on Hemingway? Why hasn't someone applied the techniques of discourse analysis to Hemingway's text? If the new rhetoric is useful in analyzing how students learn to write, why can't its methodology be applied to Hemingway manuscripts and their revisions? And when will those with interests in the environment, the terrain, and landscape painting bring their knowledge to bear on Hemingway's rich texts? The projects of which I speak are not traditional literary studies, and most of us are poorly trained to undertake them. However, that fact does not excuse us from urging graduate students into these areas.

Wherever one looks in the sciences, the action is at the interfaces between established disciplines: biochemistry, biophysics, artificial intelligence, astrophysics. Wherever disciplines join, possibilities multiply. Realizing the need for multiple skills and training, scientists and engineers usually work in teams. One seldom sees a single-author paper in a scientific journal. Only in the humanities do we still insist that everyone work alone, resulting in each knowing too little about too much. It is time to work together. We must encourage jointly written essays, studies that bring together linguists, rhetoricians, narratologists, and literary theorists; we must turn the divisive pluralism of our departments into a strength. A sympathetic medievalist and a sensible rhetorician could join a Hemingway scholar grounded in American culture to survey Hemingway's lifelong interest in and use of his medieval reading. I suggest that we begin to work in teams on such projects and that we set new standards for our trade.

Now that theory is losing some of its religious fervor, perhaps we will see applications that are more interested in understanding the complexity of Hemingway's texts than in converting the unbelievers. A theoretically based scholar—one so confident in his or her approach that there is no need to argue theory with us—will find Hemingway's middle and late texts fertile fields. The best example I can offer of a useful theoretical work on Hemingway is the Scholes and Comley book, *Hemingway's Genders*, which uses gender theory without reciting its catechism. Another area ripe for remapping is the intersection of Hemingway's texts with the performing and fine arts. Someday we will get past his 1924 statement about wanting to write in the manner that Cezanne painted to examine the influence of motion pictures on his narrative; musical counterpoint in his structuring his fiction; and classical music and opera in his work.

Many of the tasks I suggest are not for the very young; who would risk tenure on long-term projects such as these? What remains to be done in Hemingway studies will cost one dearly in time lost in unlighted alleys and the dead-end roads of frequently tedious research. Patience, humility, and dedication are the tolls for passage. But there are sufficient established scholars amongst us who could do the work, if only they would take the lead. Carlos Baker and Philip Young are both dead. We, their aging children, are finally on our own. Like Eliot's old men, we must become explorers, the longer the trip the better, for there is nothing so satisfying as a long-term task.

There is a larger issue at stake here than merely filling in blanks on the Hemingway map. Because we have been far too interested in the public man, Hemingway is in danger of becoming merely a cultural icon we use on T-shirts and in advertising campaigns. Because we have focused our attention almost exclusively on Hemingway's fiction of the 1920s, he is in danger of becoming a period author rather than a major writer whose entire canon matters. I suspect that we don't write about Hemingway's 1930s because we don't teach his works of that decade. Who among us teaches *Across the River* or *To Have and Have Not* with any regularity? If Hemingway scholars are not interested in his work after 1929, no one else is going to be. Like Sartre's existential man, we must behave as if with our every act we were setting a professional standard.

WORKS CITED

Baker, Carlos. *Ernest Hemingway: A Life Story.* New York: Scribners, 1969.

Beegel, Susan F. *Hemingway's Craft of Omission.* Ann Arbor, MI: UMI Research P, 1980.

———, ed. *Hemingway's Neglected Short Fiction: New Perspectives.* Ann Arbor, MI: UMI Research P, 1989.

Berg, A. Scott. *Max Perkins: Editor of Genius.* New York: Dutton, 1978.

Brasch, James D., and Joseph Sigman. *Hemingway's Library: A Composite Record.* New York: Garland, 1981.

Brenner, Gerry. *Concealments in Hemingway's Works.* Columbus: Ohio State UP, 1983.

Burwell, Rose Marie. *Hemingway: The Postwar Years and the Posthumous Novels.* New York: Cambridge UP, 1996.

Diliberto, Gioia. *Hadley.* New York: Ticknor & Fields, 1992.

Donaldson, Scott. *By Force of Will: The Life and Art of Ernest Hemingway.* New York: Viking, 1977.

Fleming, Robert E. *The Face in the Mirror: Hemingway's Writers.* Tuscaloosa: U of Alabama P, 1994.

Flora, Joseph. *Ernest Hemingway: A Study of the Short Fiction.* Boston: Twayne, 1989.

———. *Hemingway's Nick Adams.* Baton Rouge: Louisiana State UP, 1982.

Fuentes, Norberto. *Hemingway in Cuba.* Trans. Consuelo E. Corwin. Secaucus, NJ: Lyle Stuart, 1984.

Griffin, Peter. *Along with Youth: Hemingway, The Early Years.* New York: Oxford UP, 1985.

———. *Less Than a Treason: Hemingway in Paris.* New York: Oxford UP, 1990.

Hanneman, Audre. *Ernest Hemingway, A Comprehensive Bibliography.* Princeton, NJ: Princeton UP, 1967.

———. *Supplement to "Ernest Hemingway: A Comprehensive Bibliography."* Princeton, NJ: Princeton UP, 1975.

Hays, Peter. *A Concordance to Hemingway's "In Our Time."* Boston: G. K. Hall, 1990.

Hemingway, Ernest. *The Dangerous Summer*. New York: Scribners, 1985.

——. *Dateline: Toronto*. Ed. William White. New York: Scribners, 1985.

——. *Death in the Afternoon*. New York: Scribners, 1932.

——. *Ernest Hemingway Selected Letters, 1917–1960*. Ed. Carlos Baker. New York: Scribners 1981.

——. Esquire "Letters" in *By-Line: Ernest Hemingway*. Ed. William White. New York: Scribners, 1967.

——. *The Fifth Column and the First Forty-Nine Stories*. New York: Scribners, 1938.

——. *For Whom the Bell Tolls*. New York: Scribners, 1940.

——. *The Garden of Eden*, New York: Scribners, 1986.

——. *Green Hills of Africa*. New York: Scribners, 1935.

——. *In Our Time*. New York: Boni & Liveright, 1925; New York: Scribners, 1930.

——. *Islands in the Stream*. New York: Scribners, 1970.

——. *A Moveable Feast*. New York: Scribners, 1964

——. *The Sun Also Rises*. New York: Scribners, 1926.

——. *To Have and Have Not*. New York: Scribners, 1937.

Hemingway, Gregory H. *Papa: A Personal Memoir*. Boston: Houghton Mifflin, 1976.

Hemingway, Jack. *Misadventures of a Fly Fisherman*. Dallas, TX: Taylor, 1986.

Hemingway, Mary Welsh. *How It Was*. New York: Alfred A. Knopf, 1976.

Johnston, Kenneth G. *The Tip of the Iceberg: Hemingway and the Short Story*. Greenwood, FL: Penkevill, 1987.

Keith, Slim. *Slim: Memories of a Rich and Imperfect Life*. New York: Warner, 1990.

Kennedy, J. Gerald. *Imagining Paris: Exile, Writing and American Identity*. New Haven, CT: Yale UP, 1993.

Kert, Bernice. *The Hemingway Women*. New York: Norton, 1983.

Larson, Kelli A. *Ernest Hemingway: A Reference Guide 1974–89*. Boston: G. K. Hall, 1990.

Lynn, Kenneth S. *Hemingway*. New York: Simon & Schuster, 1987.

McLendon, James. *Papa: Hemingway in Key West*. Rev. ed. Key West, FL: Langley P, 1990.

Mellow, James R. *Hemingway, A Life without Consequences*. Boston: Houghton Mifflin, 1992.

Meyers, Jeffrey. *Hemingway: A Biography*. New York: Harper and Row, 1985.

Miller, Linda Patterson. ed. *Letters from the Lost Generation: Gerald and Sara Murphy and Friends*. New Brunswick, NJ: Rutgers UP, 1991.

Moddelmog, Debra. *Readers and Mythic Signs: The Oedipus Myth in Twentieth-Century Fiction*. Carbondale: Southern Illinois UP, 1993.

————. "The Unifying Consciousness of a Divided Conscience: Nick Adams as Author of *In Our Time*." *American Literature* 60 (1988): 591–610.

Noble, Donald R., ed. *Hemingway: A Revaluation*. Troy, NY: Whitson, 1983.

Oldsey, Bernard, ed. *Ernest Hemingway: The Papers of a Writer*. New York: Garland, 1981.

Phelan, James. *Reading People, Reading Plots: Characters, Progression, and the Interpretation of Narrative*. Chicago: U of Chicago P, 1989.

Plimpton, George. "The Art of Fiction, XXI: Ernest Hemingway." *Paris Review* 5 (1958): 60–89.

Raeburn, John. *Fame Became of Him: Hemingway as a Public Writer*. Bloomington: Indiana UP, 1984.

Reynolds, Michael. *Hemingway: The American Homecoming*. Oxford: Blackwell, 1992.

————. *Hemingway: An Annotated Chronology*. Detriot: Omnigraphics, 1991.

————. *Hemingway: The Paris Years*. Oxford: Blackwell, 1989.

————. *Hemingway's Reading, 1907–1940: An Inventory*. Princeton, NJ: Princeton UP, 1981.

————. *The Young Hemingway*. Oxford: Blackwell, 1986.

Rollyson, Carl. *Nothing Ever Happens to the Brave: The Story of Martha Gellhorn*. New York: St. Martin's, 1990.

Scholes, Robert, and Nancy Comley. *Hemingway's Genders*. New Haven, CT: Yale UP, 1994.

Smith, Paul. *A Reader's Guide to the Short Stories of Ernest Hemingway*. Boston: G. K. Hall, 1989.

Spilka, Mark. *Hemingway's Quarrel with Androgyny*. Lincoln: U of Nebraska P, 1989.

Svoboda, Frederic Joseph. *Hemingway & "The Sun Also Rises": The Crafting of a Style*. Lawrence: UP of Kansas, 1983.

Tavernier-Courbin, Jacqueline. *Ernest Hemingway's "A Moveable Feast": The Making of a Myth*. Boston: Northeastern UP, 1991.

Viertel, Peter. *Dangerous Friends: At Large with Hemingway and Houston in the Fifties*. New York: Doubleday, 1992.

Wagner-Martin, Linda W., ed. *Ernest Hemingway: Six Decades of Criticism*. East Lansing: Michigan State UP, 1987.

14

Zora Neale Hurston

Michael Awkward and Michelle Johnson

Side-splittingly funny and moving moments in *In Search of Our Mothers' Gardens* offer a record of Alice Walker's search for Zora Neale Hurston's final resting place during the early 1970s, a search that took her, ultimately, to a Fort Pierce, Florida, burial ground filled with unchecked vegetation and inhospitable spirits. In large part because of Walker's efforts to recover her authorial forebear's discarded literal and literary body and Robert Hemenway's seminal contribution, *Zora Neale Hurston: A Literary Biography*, scholars over the last two decades have had access, if not to Hurston's literal body, to the lively, complex spirit manifested in her literary corpus.

Unsure about the precise location of Hurston's body, Walker nonetheless sumptuously marks her closest approximation of Hurston's resting place with a tombstone made of Ebony Mist that inscribes the younger writer's sense of her forebear's place in the American literary firmament:

ZORA NEALE HURSTON
"A GENIUS OF THE SOUTH"
NOVELIST   FOLKLORIST
ANTHROPOLOGIST
1901   1960

As remarkable as Walker's gesture still appears to us more than two decades after Hurston's rediscovery—particularly in light of Harold Bloom's popular speculations on the anxiety of literary influence—we are struck nonetheless as much by what Walker's inscription fails to record as by its rich recognitions. We now know, for example, that Hurston was born at least a decade before 1901, and that she contributed significantly to other discursive forms, particularly the essay (some of whose best examples Walker made widely available through a Feminist Press collection of Hurston's writings, *I Love Myself When I Am Laughing*) and autobiography (which Walker does not mention apparently because, as she acknowledges in her writings, she dislikes the liberties that Hurston takes with the narrative of her self-making).

If we see Walker's list as not only partial, but also motivated by the contingencies of value that, according to Barbara Herrnstein Smith, condition all evaluative acts, then we can respond to the strategic partiality of scholarly renderings of Hurston's thematics, racial and gendered politics, aesthetics, and formal and disciplinary negotiations. Like Whitman's famous persona, Hurston was a vast figure containing multitudes, including sometimes perplexing contradictions. Explorations of her work must attend to its formulation on race and gender. To do Hurston justice, however, scholarship must operate with as expansive a concept of African Americanist and feminist—or, as we will argue below, gender—studies as possible.

Scholars taking up the subject of Zora Neale Hurston's work and life must be concerned with investigating more fully all of her texts and the expansive contexts in which she and her texts were produced. These scholars should aim for richer assessments of the individual texts themselves, of their relations to one another and to the work of black diasporic and other American writers, and of the fullness of Hurston's achievement.

Assessments of the nature of Hurston's current status vary widely. For example, as late as 1990, Robert Hemenway, using academic rank as a measure of canonicity, argued that Hurston "has a precarious hold at the untenured assistant professor level—the jury being still out on the nature of her achievement," while Ernest Hemingway is "good, but not of the first rank (an associate professor, who seems to repeat himself)" (30). Using the same two figures' "contrasting fortunes," however, Wendy Steiner asserted just five years later that Hurston's work has become central to literary and cultural studies in the academy, whose abiding methodologies privilege the return of the repressed, the suppressed, and marginalized, while an already well-known Hemingway's "virile chest-thumping and despair have become clichéd" (148). We believe that Hurston's place is much more secure than her distinguished biographer suggests (perhaps in an attempt to make no more than modest claims for the impact of his own contributions to American literary history). But while she is now widely recognized as an important, canonical writer, the celebration of Hurston may be short-lived if, as in Steiner's rendering, our attention is confined primarily to one text—*Their Eyes Were Watching God*—and to revisiting already much-traveled interpretive ground pertaining to that novel's narrative strategies, its representation of black gender relations, and the issue of a black woman's search for voice.

Nevertheless, we recognize that the canonicity of that text and the cult of personality that has developed around Hurston—as represented in the Broadway plays, festivals, T-shirts, postcards, and other paraphernalia that celebrate her colorful personality—have had significant benefits for Hurston scholarship, not the least of which is the fact that others of her texts are now widely available for the first time. Indeed, the shift in Hurston's fortunes has been accompanied by a shift in her publishers from the University of Illinois Press to HarperCollins (which has, under Henry Louis Gates, Jr.'s editorship, reprinted virtually all of her writings) and, in 1995, the Library of America, for whom Cheryl Wall has contributed a beautiful two-volume set of Hurston's writings, *Novels and Stories* and *Folklore, Memoirs, and Other Writings* (in which all of Hurston's work referred to in this essay is collected). If it is true that, as Hurston's best-known protagonist, Janie of *Their Eyes Were Watching God*, says of her dead husband, Tea Cake, "he could never be dead until she herself had finished feeling and thinking" (183), then clearly Hurston has achieved a level of literary immortality virtually unprecedented for American writers of African descent.

But we encounter competing versions of Hurston circulating in the popular and critical imaginations—the black feminist par excellence, the race woman, the diasporic visionary whose anthropological work anticipated and helped clear the way for current fascination with notions of a Black Atlantic inspired in part by Paul Gilroy, the controversial iconoclast, the cultural nationalist, the politically naive conservative, the literary foremother. These competing versions make it seem at times that her readers and scholars have been even less reliable in their location of the body of Hurston's work than Walker was in discovering her literal body's remains, and that the perhaps unresolvable identities hamper our ability to discover the meaning of her work.

If, as Steiner claims, Hemingway's value to Americanist scholarship has diminished because his meanings are overdetermined, part of Hurston's importance may well lie in the fact that, with each new significant scholarly discovery, her corpus resists such stock—and, of course, even in Hemingway's case, patently simplistic—representations. Hence, we make no effort here to resolve the contradictions between the available versions of Hurston. We are, nevertheless, convinced that the future research likely to be influential in the resolution of these contradictory narratives must engage the entirety of her discursive project. We recognize, however, that in its concentration on selected works, Hurston scholarship is not significantly different from that of the other writers included in this volume. (Critical work on Hurston texts other than *Their Eyes Were Watching God* is clustered primarily around the folklore collection *Mules and Men*, which is viewed by many as a model of participatory ethnographic narrative, and the autobiography *Dust Tracks on a Road*, whose most insightful critics see it as a provocative rendering of subjective indeterminacy.)

Whereas it may not be possible effectively to enliven the clichéd understandings of the works of a figure such as Hemingway—as Michael Reynolds argues in this volume, scholars seem generally unprepared to engage Hemingway either from a postmodernist or a "serious gender studies" perspective—perceptions of Hurston are still being actively formed and re-formed, established, debated, and defended. We believe that because of these still-active debates, future scholarship has the capacity to impact the shape and direction not only of Hurston's career and the analyses of black and women's texts, but, among other things, of American modernism, gender and cultural studies, and autobiographical and narrative theory.

Consider, for example, the potential fruits of exploring Hurston's work in the context of the widely accepted view that one of the great modernist subjects is "the exploration and questioning of the relations between the sexes" (Steiner 147). Scholarship on *Their Eyes Were Watching God* has for some time now been focused on what Carla Kaplan terms "the erotics of talk," a phrase that pertains in this context to Janie's desires to achieve verbal self-actualization—voice—and felicitous heterosexual coupling. Tracing what we might call a metaphorics of violence in Hurston's texts—and it appears in nearly all of the fictive texts and in the anthropological and autobiographical works as well—encourages not merely a recognition of a pattern evident throughout her corpus, nor simply more persuasive readings of Janie's murder of her third husband, Tea Cake, but a first step toward a comprehension of violence's transracial and transgendered significance to a modernist project framed by two brutal world wars, the bloody dismantling of Jim Crow, and the volcanic discord that accompanied the boisterous struggles for women's, gay and lesbian, and other minority civil rights.

Further, given the centrality of the image of pollination to the novel, both in the much-discussed backyard scene, in which Janie experiences nature orgasmically, and in her "love thoughts" about Tea Cake, whom she believed could be the bee to her blossom, Janie's childlessness is a subject that scholars might profitably explore. Indeed, one issue that has barely been discussed in examinations of Hurston's fictive rendering of Eatonville is its strange absence of children. Given the concern of modernist texts such as Hemingway's *A Farewell to Arms* and black texts such as Nella Larsen's *Quicksand* and James Weldon Johnson's *The Autobiography of an Ex-Colored Man* with the procreative consequences of sexual expression, scholars must begin to explain what it means for our understanding of Hurston that what Ann duCille and others demonstrate to be this novel's powerful critique of the institution of marriage fails, in its rendering of Janie's travails, to consider the pleasures and dangers of reproduction.

Hurston scholarship would profit not only by exploring underexposed topics in much-discussed texts, but also by an active decentering of facets of her personality and work that scholars have already located and examined. At the same time, we need to expand our vision so as better to contextualize her corpus vis-à-vis the historical and cultural patterns that both inform it and against which it struggles. While we have become entranced by her striking personality, the compelling themes she engages, and the maverick quality of her methodology and behavior, we must remind ourselves that much of Hurston's genius is firmly rooted in the clarity of vision that compelled her to document and refigure multiple components of American cultures. Because Hurston explored important aspects of black culture in the 1920s, 1930s, and 1940s, we run the risk of obscuring much of the nature of the dynamic shifts within black culture if we limit the body of Hurston scholarship to analyses of gender and culture.

We are calling, in other words, for a more energetically historicized, contextualized, and comparativist Hurston scholarship. And while the type of project we envision will undoubtedly present challenges to some literary scholars because of her work in other forms, the shift in focus of many literary critics to Cultural Studies suggests that investigators are quickly becoming more intellectually adroit at exploring new contexts. Exploration needs to include examining her work in relation both to

African American and/or women's literature and culture and to white and/or male American authors and anthropologists. Such examination will undoubtedly yield marked refigurations of our understanding of a number of discourses.

Because Hurston engaged and recorded the dynamic nature of African American cultures as both an author of fiction and an anthropologist, literary scholars must more fully engage her nonfiction. The lack of fuller attention to Hurston's anthropological work and the ways in which it informs her fiction results in part from the fact that her work's most influential scholarly investigator, Robert Hemenway, concludes in "Eatonville Anthology" that Hurston was primarily a "creative artist." That assertion suggests that her ultimate movement away from anthropology can be seen as a function of both her fundamental ambivalence about the tenets of anthropology and her commitment to the creative venture. The discourse on the partial truths possible in anthropological investigation and on the blurred lines between creative and scientific ethnography has grown since the publication of Hemenway's essay, allowing us to recognize the fluidity of Hurston's negotiations of these narrative forms more acutely than her biographer was able to in 1972.

By examining Hurston's role as anthropologist, we can more clearly discern the similarities to and deviations from the practices of other anthropologists such as Franz Boas, Ruth Benedict, Hortense Powdermaker, Katherine Dunham, and Jane Belo. We can begin to understand more fully the ways in which Hurston uses her ethnographies and fiction to engage issues posited by her contemporaries who were also concerned with a systematic investigation of culture. But at the same time that we compare these methodological and theoretical approaches, it is imperative that we discern Hurston's relationships with key anthropologists, such as Boas, and lesser-known anthropologists, such as Jane Belo. Assumptions that Boas greatly influenced Hurston because she studied under him need to be tested systematically by means of close comparisons of the two figures' anthropological output and theorizing. If, in fact, Boas was such a great influence on her anthropological work, we need to understand why in her letters to Langston Hughes she credits Hughes, rather than Boas, with ideas for the structure and content of her Southern folklore collecting.

And while we must explore Boas's influence on Hurston's work, we must also discern the extent to which Hurston's findings may have influenced Boas's and his colleagues' approaches to cultural analysis. We know, for instance, that Boas introduced Otto Klineberg to Hurston, whom she put in touch with informants in the South. In order to gain a clearer understanding of the contours of her contributions to the development of American cultural analysis, we need to examine Klineberg's research to determine Hurston's influence on its direction and outcome.

Even as we seek to understand Hurston's texts in the context of her anthropological setting, we must also situate her work within African American cultural experiences and the ideological perspectives that seek to explain them. At least since the pioneering work of Melville Herskovits, a foundational ideological concern in the study of African American cultures has been the extent to which cultural beliefs, forms, and norms originating in Africa are manifest throughout the African diaspora in general and in the United States in particular. Advocates of the "tabula rasa" perspective, such as E. Franklin Frazier, and scholars who argue for the retention of West African beliefs and practices, such as Herskovits, debated energetically such issues as African American acculturation and the manifestations of African cultural and spiritual tenacity during the first half of the twentieth century.

In the coming years, we must establish more convincingly Hurston's early and influential membership in the African retention school. Hurston not only argued for the influence of West African ritual throughout the diaspora, but also carefully documented African-inflected rituals that appear in the Americas. Because of the careful work of Gwendolyn Midlo-Hall, we now are aware, for instance, that the specific practices that Hurston attributes to Dr. Grant and Dr. Duke in "Hoodoo in America" and *Mules and Men*, respectively, are linked to a Senegambian tradition of acknowledging the living spirit of roots and plants prior to harvesting them for human use. Hurston's work may hold further examples of the ways in which West African traditions are retained in African American cultures, and while her corpus provides the anthropologist or historian with documentation of Africanist presence in African American cultures, it also illuminates aspects of the world view that Hurston brings to her fiction.

Hoodoo appears as a theme in Hurston's work from her first published short story, "John Redding Goes to Sea" in 1921, and continues to be featured in her series "Hoodoo and Black Magic" until the year before her death. We must therefore explore the ways in which she understood and crafted the results of her lengthy and extensive field work, and engage in a sustained discussion of Hurston and her work on Hoodoo and Voodoo. Her representations of Hoodoo shift from rendering it as a limiting superstition in "John Redding Goes to Sea," to figuring it as a destructive social and spiritual force in *Jonah's Gourd Vine*, to positing it as a liberatory practice in *Moses Man of the Mountain*. Our consideration of her shifting perspectives raises critical questions of ideology, methodology, and epistemology.

When considering Hurston's cultural and intellectual context concerning Hoodoo and Voodoo, we must also carefully clarify how her relationships with Langston Hughes and Carter G. Woodson may have informed her research on such foundational issues as methodology and access to practitioners. Likewise, we will benefit from a clearer understanding of how Hurston compares with other contemporaries, such as Rudolph Fisher, Richard Wright, and Claude McKay, who, in varying degrees, discuss Hoodoo, "superstition," and Obeah. It will also be crucial to explore how negritude writers treat African spirituality particularly, since thinkers such as Senghor insist that McKay and Hughes are influential figures in their intellectual development. Moreover, we will benefit from extending the conversation that Hurston started in her critical review of Robert Tallant to determine how her conclusions about Hoodoo and Voodoo compare with those of other Hoodoo, Root Medicine, and Voodoo scholars like Lyle Saxon and Katherine Dunham.

We must not only establish a diasporic cultural connection and assert the influence of West African traditions in these cultures, but also consider how Hurston engages another primary theme in African diasporic studies: slavery. Hurston commented on the results of slavery in her short stories, novels, essays, and ethnographies, yet her perspectives range from recognizing the horror and the resultant rage in "Magnolia Flower" to claiming that slavery was a necessary price to pay in exchange for some benefits of western culture in "How It Feels to Be Colored Me." We must carefully examine the original material that Hurston collected and published in the admittedly heavily plagiarized "Cudjo's Own Story of the Last African Slaver." Through this project we can discern how her research connects with other folklore collections that reconstruct the lives of African Americans who were formerly enslaved.

Earlier we argued that it is crucial for scholars to focus their critical attention beyond *Their Eyes Were Watching God* to a wider range of fictive texts. We want to suggest below how an expansive vision might further enliven Hurston scholarship by situating her work in the context of a number of central literary, critical, and cultural concerns. Take, for instance, the example of *Moses Man of the Mountain*, which, despite Hemenway's insistence that it is one of Hurston's masterpieces, has received scant critical attention, in part because this eclectic novel is difficult to place comfortably in the same context as the most widely discussed Hurston works, which can be more easily situated in terms of extant discussions of African American culture, feminist discourse, or other popular contemporary theoretical concerns.

While a closer reading of even the more widely discussed Hurston texts might cause us to question the insistence of scholars during the previous three decades that Hurston is a feminist thinker in a late twentieth-century sense, certainly a sophisticated gender analysis—one that benefits from, among other things, an emerging, increasingly complex men's studies—could be brought usefully to bear in explications of *Moses Man of the Mountain*. Perhaps because Hurston draws so heavily from an established patriarchal biblical tradition, she offers an undoubtedly masculinist treatment of Moses, whom she renders as a paternalistic nationalist, but critiques only minimally for such perspectives. Yet, given the context of her larger body of work, a detailed analysis of gender in Hurston requires more sustained treatments of *Moses* and its female characters Miriam, Zipporah, and Jochebed.

The method and outcome of cross-cultural analysis in the diaspora are subjects to which we can usefully return to expand upon (among other recent revisitings) Ann duCille's provocative investigation of Hurston's last novel, *Seraph on the Suwanee*. Before duCille, before—for that matter—Hemenway, Hurston's engagement of white characters was read as an appeal to a white audience and an abandonment of African American cultural tradition. Given contemporary interest in the politics of race and gender, a compelling point of entry might be to discuss why and how she felt qualified to write a novel about capitalism, class, sexuality, violence, gender, and culture among Florida whites. Indeed, a careful examination of this text in the context of her later essays that criticize racism in the United States may reveal a more complicated notion of how she viewed relationships between southern African Americans and whites and provide an illuminating reading of *Seraph on the Suwanee*.

Revisiting Hurston's neglected work suggests another area for fruitful research: Hurston's relationship to other insightful investigators of twentieth-century American Southern culture, including William Faulkner, Carson McCullers, and Flannery O'Connor. Analysis of this relationship should also extend the transracial gaze to white efforts to "write" black culture and other African American efforts to "write" white culture, such as those found in works by Richard Wright, Eugene O'Neill, Julia Peterkin, Sherwood Anderson, Ann Petry, and Lorraine Hansberry.

Close attention to the figuration of violence in *Seraph* is crucial to our understanding of that novel, though quite a number of critics go to great lengths to minimize its significance or ignore it altogether. For example, Lillie Howard ignores the most blatant act of what she calls "chauvinism," and, as recently as 1994, John Lowe suggests that Hurston did not, in fact, intend to suggest that Jim rapes Arvay. The question of sexual and emotional violence emerges when we consider Jim and Arvay's relationship, and might be seen profitably in the context of other depictions in Hurston's corpus. Hurston examines the ways in which fear, insecurity, habit, love, illusion, and sexual fulfillment both inform and disrupt notions and/or experiences of "true love." While we may find the romantic/sexual relationships in Hurston's texts upsetting, even unsettling, we must examine their tensions and question Hurston's recurring rendering of these tensions.

Reading *Seraph on the Suwanee* against other texts by African American authors who explore white culture is just one possibility as we consider the many writers with whom Hurston bears comparison. Highlighting the artistic and ideological differences between Hurston and Richard Wright, scholars have put forward important comparisons of their work as well as of their various criticisms of one another. As well, critics have provided numerous comparisons between Walker's *Color Purple* and Hurston's *Their Eyes Were Watching God*. While these are important comparisons, and each of these authors' works, particularly Wright's, encourage even deeper critical investigation, Hurston's corpus calls for a broader cast of authors against which to examine a wide range of themes and approaches.

For example, though scholars have emphasized Hurston's and Langston Hughes's friendship and the ensuing schism over the authorship of their co-authored *Mule Bone*, virtually no comparative analysis of their creative output exists. Likewise, Hurston's oeuvre should be related to that of other writers of the twenties and thirties, including Claude McKay, Rudolph Fisher, Nella Larsen, and Jean Toomer, in order to investigate more fully, among other topics, the ways in which these authors represent their central characters' relationships to African American folk culture.

Additionally, because of the significance of Hurston's environmental awareness and use of nature imagery, her work also carries with it important correlations with and divergences from that of nineteenth-century authors such as Charles Chesnutt, Ralph Waldo Emerson, Henry David Thoreau, and Sarah Orne Jewett. By exploring connections between her work and that of her contemporaries of the first half of the twentieth century such as Toomer, Willa Cather, Meridel Le Sueur, William Faulkner, Ann Petry, and John Steinbeck, we can begin to examine how these writers' notions of nature, industry, modernity, and culture intersect with or differ from Hurston's. Finally, just as critics have explored connections between Walker and Hurston, we must investigate the extent to which her work compares with that of contemporary writers such as Toni Cade Bambara, Gloria Naylor, Paule Marshall, Ishmael Reed, and Randall Kenan, in part to understand precisely how important themes that Hurston addressed such as spirituality, enslavement, gender, and relations to the natural world are taken up by subsequent African American authors.

Hurston is a writer whose stock rose in the academy to some extent as a consequence of the spaces created for previously marginalized texts by poststructuralist theorists and by feminist and Afro-Americanist scholars. Scholarship on her work should strive to render the meanings of her career as faithfully as possible. But it should also recognize that we are doomed to offer biased, incomplete, and limited readings that, like Hurston's own perspectives on crucial matters such as slavery, are neither definitive nor immutable. While it is our duty as Hurston scholars and "witnesses for the future" to collect and make Hurston's work available to subsequent generations, our activities do not ensure— Walker's memorable formulation notwithstanding—that by "collect[ing them] again . . . , bone by bone" (92) we will achieve a unified vision of their significance and power.

Walker's osseous image foreshadowed developments at the 1991 Eatonville Festival of the Arts, where some of its organizers discussed moving what Walker marked as Hurston's remains from their Fort Pierce location to Eatonville in an effort to prevent developers from destroying the center of her imaginative and anthropological universe. This plan seems the ultimate in—and certainly, from a variety of vantage points, the most self-serving of—Hurston recovery projects. While it appears that this effort has been abandoned, it speaks to the intensity of the urges of Hurston's biological and spiritual successors to make use of and reclaim her, bone by bone, in a quite literal sense. And if this use of Hurston's remains appears unseemly, we should keep in mind that Hurston herself never recoiled from the subject of death. From her first short story, "John Redding Goes to Sea," to *Seraph on the Suwanee*, Hurston examined the ways in which the lifeless body is read and interpreted by those whom its spirit leaves behind.

As we embark upon future projects in Hurston scholarship, we must be careful about the uses to which we are willing to put her bodily remains to serve our own interests. Yet we must also remember the crucial components of Hurston's work that symbolically embrace an Africanist notion of the simultaneous existence of life and death. Hurston leaves us what is no longer a living body, yet through our efforts to invigorate the body of Hurston scholarship, we can uncover new life and new meanings for the living.

WORKS CITED

Anderson, Sherwood. *Dark Laughter*. New York: Boni & Liveright, 1925.

Bambara, Toni Cade. *The Salt Eaters*. New York: Vintage, 1980.

Benedict, Ruth. *Race and Racism*. 1945. London: Routledge & Kegan Paul, 1983.

Bloom, Harold. *The Anxiety of Influence*. New York: Oxford UP, 1973.

Boas, Franz. *Anthropology and Modern Life*. New York: Norton, 1962.

Cather, Willa. *Sapphira and the Slave Girl*. 1940. New York: Vintage, 1975.

Chestnutt, Charles. *The Conjure Woman*. 1899. Ann Arbor: U of Michigan P, 1969.

duCille, Ann. *The Coupling Convention*. New York: Oxford UP, 1994.

Dunham, Katherine. *Island Possessed*. Garden City, NJ: Doubleday, 1969.

Frazier, E. Franklin. *Black Bourgeoisie*. New York: Free Press, 1957.

Gates, Henry Louis, Jr. *The Signifying Monkey: A Theory of Afro-American Literary Criticism*. New York: Oxford UP, 1989.

Gilroy, Paul. *The Black Atlantic*. Cambridge: Harvard UP, 1994.

Hansberry, Lorraine. *Les Blancs*. New York: Random House, 1972.

Hemenway, Robert. "The Personal Dimension in *Their Eyes Were Watching God*." *New Essays on "Their Eyes Were Watching God."* Ed. Michael Awkward. Cambridge, MA, and New York: Cambridge UP, 1990. 29–50.

———. *Zora Neale Hurston: A Literary Biography*. Urbana: U of Illinois P, 1977.

————. "Zora Neale Hurston and the Eatonville Anthology." *The Harlem Renaissance Remembered*. Ed. Arna Bontemps. New York: Dodd, Mead, 1972. 190–214.

Hemingway, Ernest. *A Farewell to Arms*. New York: Scribners, 1929.

Herskovits, Melville. *The Anthropology of the American Negro*. New York: Columbia UP, 1930.

Holloway, Joseph. ed. *Africanisms in American Culture*. Indianapolis: Indiana UP, 1990.

Howard, Lillie. *Zora Neale Hurston*. Boston: Twayne, 1980.

Hurston, Zora Neale. *Dust Tracks on a Road*. 1942. Urbana: U of Illinois P, 1984.

————. *Folklore, Memoirs, and Other Writings*. Ed. Cheryl A. Wall. New York: Library of America, 1995.

————. "Hoodoo in America." *Journal of American Folk-lore* 44 (1931): 317–417.

————. *I Love Myself When I Am Laughing—and Then Again When I Am Looking Mean and Impressive*. Ed. Alice Walker. Old Westbury, NY: Feminist P, 1979.

————. *Jonah's Gourd Vine*. 1934. New York: HarperCollins, 1990.

————. "Magnolia Flower." *The Complete Short Stories*. Ed. Henry Louis Gates, Jr., and Sieglinde Lemke. New York: HarperCollins, 1995. 33–40.

————. *Moses Man of the Mountain*. 1939. New York: HarperCollins, 1990.

————. *Mules and Men*. New York: HarperCollins, 1990.

————. *Novels and Stories*. Ed. Cheryl A. Wall. New York: Library of America, 1995.

————. Review of *Voodoo in America*, by Robert Tallant. *Journal of American Folk-lore* 60 (1947): 436–38.

————. *Seraph on the Suwanee*. 1948. New York: HarperCollins, 1990.

————. *Their Eyes Were Watching God*. 1937. New York: Perennial, 1990.

Hurston, Zora Neale, and Langston Hughes. *Mule Bone*. New York: Harper-Collins, 1993.

Jewett, Sarah Orne. *The Country of Pointed Firs and Other Stories*. 1896. Garden City, NY: Doubleday Anchor Books, 1954.

Johnson, James Weldon. *The Autobiography of an Ex-Colored Man*. 1912. New York: Hill & Wang, 1960.

Kaplan, Carla. *The Erotics of Talk*. New York: Oxford UP, 1995.

Kenan, Randall. *Visitation of Spirits*. New York: Anchor, 1989.

Klineberg, Otto. *Race and Psychology*. Paris: Modern Sciences, 1951.

Larsen, Nella. *Quicksand and Passing*. 1929. New Brunswick, NJ: Rutgers UP, 1986.

Le Sueur, Meridel. *I Hear Men Talking and Other Stories*. Minneapolis: West End P, 1984.

Lowe, John. *Jump at the Sun: Zora Neale Hurston's Cosmic Comedy*. Urbana: U of Illinois P, 1994.

Marshall, Paule. *Praisesong for the Widow*. New York: Dutton, 1983.

McKay, Claude. *Banana Bottom*. New York: Harper, 1933.

Midlo-Hall, Gwendolyn. *Africanisms in Colonial Louisiana: The Development of Afro-Creole Culture in the 18th Century*. Baton Rouge: Louisiana State UP, 1992.

Naylor, Gloria. *Mama Day*. New York: Vintage, 1988.

O'Neill, Eugene. *The Emperor Jones*. Cincinnati, OH: Stewart & Kidd, 1921.

Peterkin, Julia. *Scarlet Sister Mary*. Indianapolis: Bobbs-Merrill, 1928.

Petry, Ann. *The Street*. Boston: Houghton Mifflin, 1946.

Powdermaker, Hortense. *After Freedom: A Cultural Study in the Deep South*. 1939. New York: Russell & Russell, 1986.

Saxon, Lyle, Edward Dreyer, and Robert Tallant, eds. *Gumbo Ya-Ya: Folk Tales of Louisiana*. 1945. New York: Pelican, 1991.

Senghor, Leopold. *Afrique Africaine*. Lausanne: Clairefontaine, 1963.

Smith, Barbara Herrnstein. *Contingencies of Value*. Cambridge, MA: Harvard UP, 1988.

Steinbeck, James. *The Grapes of Wrath*. New York: Viking P, 1939.

Steiner, Wendy. *The Scandal of Pleasure: Art in the Age of Fundamentalism*. Chicago: U of Chicago P, 1995.

Thompson, Robert Farris. *Flash of the Spirit*. New York: Vintage, 1983.

Toomer, Jean. *Cane*. New York: Boni & Liveright, 1923.

Walker, Alice. *The Color Purple*. New York: Washington Square P, 1982.

———. *In Search of Our Mothers' Gardens: Womanist Prose*. San Francisco: Harcourt Brace Jovanovich, 1983.

Wright, Richard. *Lawd Today*. New York: Walker, 1963.

15

William Faulkner

Thomas L. McHaney

An anonymous essayist in a 1954 *Times Literary Supplement* issue devoted to the American South put the case for Faulkner succinctly: Faulkner is, the author wrote, "poetically, the most accurate man alive." The writer and critic Randall Stewart used the phrase for the title of an essay in 1962, which is where many first encountered it, but we can now say, thanks to some detective work by Suzanne Marrs (24), that the phrase (and the essay) was Eudora Welty's. If Welty's judgment is even a little bit true, then the study of Faulkner's texts remains an enterprise worthy of the time and effort. Despite thousands of essays and hundreds of books, Faulkner's biography, his times, and his texts remain open to many possibilities for good new research.

Joseph Blotner's *Faulkner: A Biography* has held up strongly, especially his revised one-volume abridgement. Michael Millgate's *The Achievement of William Faulkner* is still in print and remains the best general critical introduction to Faulkner, with a reliable short biographical chapter as well. However, recent trends in representing Faulkner's life do not make me hopeful. Such biographies as those by Stephen Oates and Frederick Karl have not served the Faulkner field (or their major source, Blotner) well. Psychologically reductive, they sniff along in Blotner's tracks looking for odorous detail to highlight, portraying Faulkner's life as wretched and his art as psychologically determined or accidental. As a result, perhaps, a feminist reviewer of a recent account of Faulkner's career began her piece by asserting unequivocally that Faulkner was a "mean little man, a drunk, a womanizer, a snob" and a "Southern Partisan" racist (Roberts). As I read the life, however, there is little evidence for such an assessment of the person who wrote the great psychological novels of the late twenties and early thirties. Faulkner's Hollywood affair, later, was a mono-amour set against an ill-begun marriage that nonetheless endured. As to racism, the most damaging reports are of doubtful authority. At the time of Faulkner's death, friends and admirers far more liberal than he, of both sexes, defended him against that charge. We can document that he showed far more courage on sensitive issues of race and social justice than most ministers and politicians and academics of his time. Regarding his bouts of depression or drinking, the counterpoint is that Faulkner repeatedly took responsibility for cares—local and global—that he could have avoided. Despite some cruel losses and disappointments, he loved, and received love from, many other people, male and female, young and old. Like those Old Testament figures whose lives he adapted into modern fiction, Faulkner often transcended, without perfecting, the kind of flawed life that characterizes most of humanity. If he expressed in his work some of the moral earnestness of the patriarchs, he also exhibited in the fiction, and occasionally in his daily life, a rich humor, frequently self-deprecating, a humor lacking in both the prophets and their God. He was also a man of many masks, as even the photographic record—much of which Faulkner arranged—shows (Cofield). A new biography that concentrates solely on the intellectual and professional aspects of Faulkner's career would be welcome. By constructing small, dense volumes on Hemingway (e.g., *The Young Hemingway*), Michael Reynolds has shown what microbiography can accomplish.

Details for important periods of Faulkner's life remain to be found and used to tell circumstantially how William Faulkner of Oxford, Mississippi, bootstrapped himself into a world-class artist. Faulkner's most formative years are not fully recorded. Above all, his reading requires a much more detailed accounting. To cite a single example, a study of Faulkner's opportunities to discover classical American writing would be very valuable. It should take into account his and his acquaintances' reading of the literary journalism, academic scholarship, and cultural history of his time (Van Wyck Brooks, Bernard DeVoto, Henry Adams, Raymond Weaver, Thomas Beers, and so on), as well as his reading of Emerson or Melville, to name an important pair.

Not all that Faulkner could have learned about Southern history from reading books was reliable, as his own observations and meditations ultimately proved to him. But now Faulkner's South is newly documented, and this fact should prove a great advantage to future scholarship. The history and roles of all the South's peoples; the nature of its agriculture and commercial life; the diversity of its geography and language; and the South and such topics as hunting, sharecropping, populism, religion, small-town life, transportation, the Great Migration and the role of the WPA, and a great deal more, are now reconsidered in excellent monographs. Even the pictorial record is richer than at any time before. New Faulkner biography must take account of this rich lode. Not only did Faulkner imagine the past more accurately than many of his contemporaries, including historians, but also he observed the changing contemporary scene more acutely, and he appears to have intuited much of what he wrote very accurately simply because he meditated hard on both his regional culture and the way humans behave. To write about him well, however, we need to know all that he might have learned from his reading, as well as from family and regional lore. Joel Williamson's *William Faulkner and Southern History* is an interesting attempt to provide such knowledge.

Although many published materials were worked into Blotner's initial and revised versions of the life, the broad sweep of both works required omitting much detail, and a great many documents have appeared since the 1984 revised version. Tom Dardis has recently shown how the record can be improved, writing about Faulkner's relationship to Harrison Smith, the editor who accepted *The Sound and the Fury*, and about the publisher Horace Liveright (*Firebrand*). James Watson's edition of a long-suppressed cache of important Faulkner letters (*Thinking of Home*) is a reminder that the Faulkner archives may continue to grow.

Susan Snell's study of Faulkner's friend and mentor, the lawyer Phil Stone of Oxford, shows what can be done by concentrated research on the Oxford of Faulkner's youth. Snell presents an account that is the fullest yet because she did not go looking for a place that predicted or centered upon Faulkner or his fiction. A thorough version of Faulkner's early life must take into account not only, as Snell does, the ways in which Stone's education folded into Faulkner's, but also the ways in which other people of town and university touched Faulkner. As a bright boy underfoot locally, he knew the legal and commercial life of the courthouse square well, and it is likely that he knew more about intellectual life on the Ole Miss campus than is yet recorded. James Lloyd's *Lives of Mississippi Authors* provides some information about Ole Miss faculty and students who might have served as conduits of information to Faulkner, but much more research in this area is required. We also must not overlook the influence upon Faulkner of information filtered through African

American memory and opinion. Faulkner once remarked that he learned a great deal in his father's livery stable from hostlers and drivers, and his funeral sermon for Caroline Barr attests to her influence. It would be a mistake to assume, however, that all Faulkner learned from African Americans is confined to spheres of town labor and agriculture directly visible to the white middle class. A deep investigation, like Susan Snell's work on Stone, directed into the African American communities of Oxford, might throw new light on one of Faulkner's most important subjects.

Since Faulkner's death in 1962, the canon of his writing is much enlarged, and though much bibliographical information regarding Faulkner's works is available in Meriwether (*Literary Career*), Skei, Brodsky and Hamblin, and guides to collections, a standard primary bibliography of Faulkner, with full information about each of the books, stories, and other pieces, remains a major desideratum. Many of Faulkner's primary works still receive little scholarly attention, or only passing interest. Posthumous editions of previously unpublished writing are still too little used for Faulkner studies. The aborted comic novel *Elmer*; the early attempt at writing a Snopes novel, *Father Abraham*; and *Uncollected Stories* are only the most obvious examples. These texts, along with the facsimiles and transcriptions of handmade books that Faulkner gave to special friends during his apprenticeship (*Mayday, Marionettes*), deserve more individual attention than they have received. Two different examples of how one might proceed with such works are Martin Kreiswirth's study of the early writing's influence in *The Sound and the Fury* and Judith Sensibar's discussion of the poetry in the development of Faulkner's career (*Origins of Faulkner's Art*). The Hollywood screenplays, available in various editions since Faulkner's death—all listed in the *Bibliography of American Fiction* section on Faulkner (McHaney, "William Faulkner")—likewise merit use in discussions of Faulkner's principal trade, the writing of fiction.

As with the posthumous publications, Faulkner's manuscripts and typescripts are not used as much as they should be in current scholarship. Photographic facsimiles of many Faulkner manuscripts and typescripts are now widely available in libraries, and a wealth of material remains in specific public manuscript collections. There are published guides to special collections at Tulane (Bonner), Southeastern Missouri (Brodsky and Hamblin), and the University of Mississippi (Kinney and Fowler). Complementing an early account of the University of Texas collection (Langford, "Insights") is James Watson's introduction to recently opened material gathered initially by the late Carvel Collins (Watson, "Carvel Collins"). Early catalogues of the Linton Massey Faulkner Collection at the University of Virginia (Crane and Freudenberg, Massey) are useful, but should be supplemented by lists available in the manuscripts division at the University of Virginia library. Catalogues of Carl Petersen's private collection (*Each in Its Ordered Place* and *On the Track of the Dixie Limited*) provide a glimpse of materials now dispersed into public and private hands, most of which can be tracked down. Special guides exist for poetry manuscripts (Sensibar, *Faulkner's Poetry*), film scripts (Kawin), and short story materials (Skei). The 25-volume Garland facsimile edition of the Virginia and New York Public Library manuscripts and typescripts (Blotner, McHaney, Millgate, Polk) includes lists of relevant manuscript holdings in all known collections, and the editors have written brief essays about each work's composition and publication, preludes to more detailed treatments. In a special publication, *Mississippi Quarterly* made available a list of Faulkner-related material in his hometown newspaper (Lloyd, *The Oxford "Eagle"*). Published catalogues of established Faulkner collections and of temporary library exhibitions often have unique value of their own, reproducing documents, manuscripts, transcriptions, letters by and to Faulkner, inscriptions by and to him, fugitive pieces of poetry or prose, and legal documents. (A list of catalogues through 1988 is in the Faulkner entry in volume 1 of the *Bibliography of American Fiction* [McHaney, "William Faulkner"].) Many years ago, the collector Louis D. Brodsky sought members of Faulkner's Ole Miss circle who were not the writer's main friends and found many previously unknown manuscripts, books with inscriptions, and other Faulkner life records. Similarly conducted searches among Faulkner's less remarked acquaintances elsewhere (or, by now, their heirs) from New Orleans and Paris, from such Mississippi towns as Pascagoula, Clarksdale, Greenville, and Charleston, or from Hollywood and New York might prove equally fruitful. Even so simple a resource as Brodsky's collection of books inscribed by Faulkner to others reminds us that inscriptions record and date the writer's whereabouts and encounters, helping us to log his travels and, in some cases, his relationships. Thomas Verich's census of copies of the limited signed edition of *Go Down, Moses* and the list of inscribed books in the Brodsky collection (Brodsky and Hamblin, volume 1) are excellent examples of tracking and recording signed and dated Faulkner items. Close reading of the Brodsky catalogues (Brodsky and Hamblin) and of those devoted to the collections of Linton Massey in Virginia (Crane and Freudenberg, Massey) and Carl Petersen in Illinois ought to be part of every Faulkner scholar's preparation.

Although the record for finding and publishing Faulkner's early work is good, the project of making all his writing widely available remains incomplete. We need collected editions of the poetry, the nonfiction prose, the short stories and sketches, and an enlarged edition of the letters. Now there are the *Selected Letters* (Blotner) and the early fugitive letters to his parents (Watson, *Thinking of Home*), but not all of Faulkner's correspondents have yet made their holdings available. No census exists of such materials as Faulkner's own graphic art, photographs of him, audio recordings of his readings and interviews, films in which he appeared, or legal documents. An annual update of the appearance of such life records in collections or catalogues would be a good feature for *The Faulkner Journal* or someone's web-site.

As the Faulkner canon is enlarged, the critical record for Faulkner grows more vast, but it can be searched with increasing ease in a variety of bibliographies (Bassett; Inge; McHaney, *Reference Guide*). Such works always require updating, and a new generation of scholars will have to reevaluate what has been done, but surely access to the past should slow the flow of pieces devoted to overly familiar stories, novel scenes, or characters. The Faulkner essays in *American Literary Scholarship: An Annual* (treating 1963 to the present) and annual essays about Faulkner scholarship published from 1978 through 1987 in the *Mississippi Quarterly* annual Faulkner issue (summers) provide additional help by evaluating each year's scholarship. Summary essays on Faulkner in *Sixteen Modern American Authors: A Review of Research and Criticism*, Volumes 1 and 2 (Meriwether, "William Faulkner"; Cohen, Krause, and Zender), winnow years of scholarship even more stringently, and these essays require a supplement already. Such tools guide students to new tasks and away from shopworn subjects or approaches. They should be used regularly by editors considering manuscripts, as well as by those seeking to publish.

In the last decade, most of the major Faulkner novels became available in "corrected" editions sold as trade hardbacks, paperbacks, and Library of America volumes, of which there are three so far. That one scholar, Noel Polk of Southern Mississippi, did all the textual work—comparing typographical errors, undoing editorial meddling, and seeking the restoration of the author's intentions—is a miracle of discipline and energy.

But the subject is by no means closed. The Faulkner "corrected" editions, which come from trade publishers, lack much of the apparatus of modern textual editions. Polk has published, in a small edition, *An Editorial Handbook for William Faulkner's "The Sound and the Fury,"* but so far neither the evidence and argument in that account nor the less documented work on Faulkner's other texts has attracted serious review in literary journals. Although Polk has good cooperation from Random House and the Library of America for his project, and his training and track record as a textual scholar legitimize his undertaking, the lack of scholarly debate is a disservice to Polk's gift to the field and should be corrected. Despite so much recent work, the final word on the development and form of Faulkner's texts may not be in yet; in 1987, the University of Virginia acquired a handwritten draft of Faulkner's second novel, *Mosquitoes*. This discovery challenged assumptions about the composition not only of *Mosquitoes* but also of other early work. Subsequent discoveries may provide documentation that challenges other assumptions.

As textual and bibliographical scholarship is completed, much can be done to apply the results to the critical enterprise. Editors, teachers, and critics need to adopt standards for the texts they use and cite. *The Faulkner Journal* and the annual Faulkner issues of *Mississippi Quarterly* insist upon "corrected" texts as sources in their essays, but many journals and presses still allow citation from whatever sources their authors provide. The newer criticism, skeptical of all projects except its own, has done nothing to improve the situation. Yet textual study is valuable not only because it corrects, but also because it builds a foundation for study of a writer's habits of composition, for the correct sequencing of works— especially short stories—and for stylistic analysis. Ultimately, nothing but a concerted outcry will suffice to strike very corrupt texts from the "Works Cited" pages of journals and critical books. A definitive "collected" edition of Faulkner is much overdue, and it is certainly time for us to consider variorum and hypermedia versions of such great books as *The Sound and the Fury, Light in August,* and *Absalom, Absalom!*

Noel Polk's textual labor also informs another too little used version of Faulkner's texts, one of particularly strong potential value to the critic: the computer-generated concordances to the published fiction, long and short (see McHaney's "William Faulkner" for the complete list). The earliest published concordances use the findings of textual scholarship to cite variant readings between different versions of Faulkner's work. Concordances finished more recently cite "corrected" texts. The concordances were published in hard covers through UMI Press (before it ceased publishing) and are still available through the parent company, University Microfilms International, which offers also a less expensive microfiche version. Faulkner critics ignore these valuable tools at their peril, or at least to their own disadvantage. The Faulkner concordances offer extremely useful access to facets of Faulkner's diction and syntax, to his creation of idiolects and image patterns, and to his invention of language. The concordances contain vocabulary lists arranged alphabetically and in terms of frequency of occurrence, and statistical analyses of Faulkner's diction. A few of the concordances include essays that point out how critics might use them—for example, Cleanth Brooks on *As I Lay Dying* and André Bleikasten on *The Sound and the Fury*. In an era influenced by literary theory based on discourse analysis and grounded in linguistics, psychology, and analytical philosophy, we should find much value in the word lists in concordances and in the greater ease of access to specific word forms and phrases. An example of what close attention to the "idiolects" of Faulkner characters and narrators can achieve is Irena Kaluza's *The Functioning of Sentence Structure in the Stream-of-Consciousness Technique of William Faulkner's "The Sound and the Fury": A Study in Linguistic Stylistics*, a work published long before the appearance of the concordances. The value and availability of the concordances could be increased enormously if they were gathered onto a single database source—the emergent CD-ROM technology, for example—so that all texts could be searched at once, if one desired.

The most useful journal-based literature on Faulkner doubtless is by now absorbed into book-length studies or selective anthologies of criticism, but despite hundreds of essays on the major works, only a few of Faulkner's novels have received individual book-length studies, and none of these monographs by any means closes discussion of the text in question. Good books that successfully discuss the composition of Faulkner's novels are rare—Fadiman on *Light in August* and Schoenberg on *Absalom, Absalom!* are useful; Langford on *Absalom, Absalom!* is not—a fact that indicates both the difficulty of such projects and the need for more of them. Annotations to Faulkner's novels are currently offered in two series, one of these from Garland and edited by James B. Meriwether, and another from the University Press of Mississippi, conceived by the late James Hinkle and now under the overseership of Noel Polk. Books in these series provide documentation for sometimes obscure facts used by Faulkner, and they can lead scholars to previously undocumented

Faulkner reading or allusions, but much of their space is devoted to a record of how often Faulkner paraphrases himself (see McDaniel or Ruppersburg). The tracking down of allusions and sources in Faulkner's major works remains in its infancy. Useful annotations to the stories, sketches, poetry, and essays will be as valuable as salient annotations to the novels. Because Faulkner omitted, obscured, or significantly altered important allusions between early drafts and final forms of his texts, the annotations to published works should be checked against manuscripts. The author sometimes left evidence in early forms of texts that he constructed his "obscurities" deliberately.

As Lothar Hönnighausen shows in *William Faulkner: The Art of Stylization*, the fin-de-siècle aesthetic that evolved into modernism touched Faulkner early through a variety of means. There were the obvious sources in literary and graphic art, and even Oxford newspaper advertisements were replete with the period's characteristic imagery. National and regional media also brought a great deal into Faulkner's life. Faulkner's travels took him to such hotspots of modernism as Paris, New York, and New Orleans. In his own backyard, as well as on the new phonograph recordings of the era, jazz duplicated the richly allusive montages and improvisations of Eliot, Picasso, and Joyce, a phenomenon taken up recently by Craig Werner in *Playing the Changes*. It is not for nothing that Louis Armstrong was described on a poster for one of his early performances as "Master of Modernism." Faulkner spent more time close to the early scenes of this new music than most of his Jazz Age contemporaries. His awareness of it is a centerpiece in *Soldiers' Pay* and a more subtle effect in *Mosquitoes*. An examination of Faulkner's understanding of this influence is yet to be written.

Robert Penn Warren once pointed out that "non-Southern, even non-American, critics . . . not knowing Southern life firsthand . . . have sometimes been freer to regard the fiction as a refraction in art of a special way of life and not as a mere documentation of that way of life" ("Introduction: Faulkner: Past and Present"). These non-American critics, of whom we now recognize the second and third generation in such countries as France or Japan, have wielded tools fashioned by Russian formalists, structuralists, phenomenologists, deconstructionists, New Historicists, Marxists of various hues, and devotees of Cultural Studies. But the best of them—Bleikasten, Gresset, Hönnighausen, and Pitavy, for example—are also careful readers of the complete body of Faulkner's work, students of the texts and their backgrounds. Their close textual work, combined with a preference for an eclectic practical criticism, has made their projects sound, stimulating, and readable. As theory matured into applied criticism in American academia, the works of these non-American scholars became models for good work by such American critics as John Irwin, Donald Kartiganer, John Matthews, and Stephen Ross, among others, whose studies seem even more useful than when first encountered because we are more familiar with the theoretical context.

Likewise, gender studies, when not simply condemning the reading of Faulkner, has much to tell us. When we can explain how and why Faulkner's culture was both misogynist and gynolatrist, both patriarchal and gynocentric, perhaps we can better explore similar seeming contradictions in the writer's rendering of that culture. Like race studies, gender studies has to distinguish Faulkner's unmeditated bondedness with his own time from what occurred when he loosed his imagination on a human problem within the tradition of prose fiction. As we compare his work to that of the historians, we perceive more clearly how Faulkner captured the secret climate of race and the tragedy of the public climate of racism. Some feminists find a basis for seeing a similar dual rendering of gender and sexism. Faulkner's dialectics take many forms yet unremarked in criticism, reflecting contradictions both in the specific local cultures he observed and in the contradictory and perverse behavior of humankind. A Marxist historian like Eugene Genovese apparently has no trouble appreciating Faulkner's skill in capturing, through imaginative reconstruction, the complex dialectics of the world that the slaves and the slaveholders made together (115–16). Much of what is in print about Faulkner and race, Faulkner and women, or Faulkner and history is due for major transformation. A criticism that tried to make Faulkner an epitome of the Agrarian South gave us a traditionalist and conservative, an interpretation that does not quite fit even Faulkner's everyday life. But as a writer, Faulkner achieved levels of modernist abstraction rarely approached by a criticism caught up in easy suppositions about Southern mimesis and mythical cultural unity.

Similarly, if we put aside conventional genre consciousness in our reading of Faulkner, we come closer to understanding his formal achievements. Mikhail Bakhtin's practical observations in *The Dialogic Imagination* about the open-endedness and ungeneric nature of long prose fiction offer, as we are beginning to see, a stimulating approach to Faulkner's novels. Bakhtin formulated his ideas almost exactly at the same time as Faulkner made his fiction. One might, without too much forcing of the issue, say that two writers, living in similarly restrictive cultures and working out of similar reading lists (from the classics through the nineteenth century), reached the same conclusions for the same reasons. Applying Bakhtin's ideas in *Rabelais and His World* and *Problems of Dostoevsky's Poetics* to Faulkner's most Rabelaisian or Dostoevskian fiction is a natural enterprise for Faulknerians and is already under way (see, for example, Dalziel). For further research into Faulkner's various mythologies, including his mythology of time, Bakhtin's concept of the "chronotope" should also be useful. In general, challenges to the New Criticism's aloof certainty and its penchant for finding thematic unity are salutary, even as they problematize for us what reading means and how we apply it. Similarly, challenges by Cultural Studies to "givens" of national or regional or gender identity, if not made as doctrinaire as the icons they smash, are apt to find sympathy with Faulkner's interest in radical individualism and his penetration or deliberate confounding of stereotypes.

As we have had enough of the weak concept of unity, we have also had enough misplaced self-congratulation about the special virtues of Southern "place" and sufficient chauvinist rhetoric about Faulkner and the Southern penchant for storytelling. Room exists for consideration of whatever metaphors of place signify in Faulkner's work, and a major need exists for study of the different kinds of representation that he achieved by manipulating the illusion of a human voice on a printed page. Is there anyone left who regards Faulkner's writing as a merely natural outgrowth of legendary Southern qualities? Great writers make place do the important work it accomplishes in great fiction. No number of Sundays on the porch swing or nights in the hunting camp could produce *The Sound and the Fury* or *Go Down, Moses* from a mind without a sophisticated aesthetic and a dogged discipline for putting words on paper again and again. Sentimentalizing, or condescending to, the ambition and talent of Faulkner (or any Southern writer) falsifies the practice of the craft of fiction, the search for techniques commensurate to a vision of a region studied deeply.

If we give up seeking an illusory unifying figure in the carpet, scores of thematic topics still remain open in Faulkner's work. In many instances, thematic topics applied thinly to a broad range of Faulkner's works beg for full treatment as manifestations in single works. The regular international Faulkner conferences held in Europe every two years since 1979 and the Faulkner and Yoknapatawpha Conferences held at the University of Mississippi annually since 1974 have produced volumes on a variety of topics. Instead of exhausting their topics, however, these conferences have, in a sense, mainly opened them. The typical discourse of conference-going rarely lends itself to comprehensive discussion. Linking the following topics to Faulkner's work under the lens of newer criticisms might prompt many projects still waiting for thorough treatment: Art, Film, History, Humor, Idealism, Ideology, Imagination, Modernism, Mythology, Nature, Philosophy, Psychology, Race, Religion, the Southern Renaissance, Women. Victor Strandberg pointed the way to serious investigation of the possibilities years ago in a little book titled simply *A Faulkner Overview: Six Perspectives*, a work whose chapters should be regarded as six prolegomena to big singular works on the role in Faulkner's creative life of the subjects touched: religion, music, philosophy, psychology, and eros. More specifically, scholars should explore the when, where, and what of Faulkner's familiarity with the doctrines of American Protestant religion and his use of the life of Jesus of Nazareth; they should look more deeply into his absorption of history and historiography; they should take up seriously his literary relationship to what he called the three great men of his time: Marcel Proust, James Joyce, and Thomas Mann; they should investigate his relationships to such American contemporaries as Willa Cather, F. Scott Fitzgerald, and Edith Wharton; they should investigate what he might have absorbed within the climate of ideas in California during his labor there for the motion picture studios. What can be accomplished by taking Faulkner's play within the realm of ideas seriously was demonstrated early on by such different works as the late Richard Adams's *Faulkner: Myth and Motion* and Michael Millgate's "Faulkner's Masters," and more recently by Paul Douglass's Faulkner chapters in *Bergson, Eliot, and American Literature*.

Consideration of the prospects for Faulkner studies would be remiss without directing special attention to the short story career, which has been not so much scanted in the scholarly record as oversimplified. First, we re-count the short story canon. Obviously, as the publication of *Uncollected Stories* shows, the *Collected Stories* of 1951 gave us much less than half the short story canon. Add the New Orleans pieces and other prose juvenilia, more of it fiction than we once thought, and the total number of Faulkner stories is more than one hundred. To do Faulkner's story canon justice, we will need, as Hans Skei argued at a 1995 symposium in Norway on the stories, a more sophisticated aesthetic for the criticism of Faulkner's non-novelistic fiction, including genre theories for the short story as rich as those now available for the study of the novel. We must resist, for the purposes of serious study, both the "grading" of stories as somehow lesser than novels and the pursuit of the discredited concept of unity. As Skei pointed out in Oslo, we need no more apologies for Faulkner's stories, no quarrels about borderlines between genres when stories move into novels. Skei's summary work on Faulkner's short story career laid a foundation on which we have yet to build as broadly as we should. The increased availability of reliable published texts, of draft and final manuscripts and typescripts of the stories, and the publication of the concordances to the stories should make excellent new work possible.

George Garrett, who has since made his own mark in the short story, the novel, and poetry, noted in a 1959 essay on Faulkner's early literary criticism that although Faulkner joined no schools of thought, developed no critical position, and rarely made formal statements about literature, he nonetheless cultivated throughout his career several important principles in his writing: "an emphasis in all literary forms on artifice to distinguish art from life, a concept of complete fidelity to character, a devotion to the American scene, a sense of the vitality of language, and, finally, a position that art, however truthful and tragic, must be a positive statement against anarchy and chaos." Faulkner's search for fictional truth was never easy, neat, or without interference from his culture or himself. But we should learn something from the way Faulkner's work has continued to jolt new generations in unexpected parts of the world, especially where old rigidities and orthodoxies begin to break under the enduring push of human individualism. Whatever critical fashion does with Faulkner's work, his prospects among those struggling in his craft remain excellent. As to his prospects with scholars, critics, and teachers, why should we not expect great things from ourselves also?

WORKS CITED

Adams, Richard P. *Faulkner: Myth and Motion.* Princeton, NJ: Princeton UP, 1968.

American Literary Scholarship: An Annual. Ed. James Woodress, et al. Durham, NC: Duke UP, 1965–present.

Bakhtin, Mikhail. *The Dialogic Imagination.* Ed Michael Holquist. Trans. Caryl Emerson and Michael Holquist. Austin: U of Texas P, 1981.

———. *Problems of Dosteovsky's Poetics.* Trans. R. W. Rotsel. Ann Arbor, MI: Ardis, 1973.

———. *Rabelais and His World.* Trans. Hélène Iswolsky. Bloomington: Indiana UP, 1984.

Bassett, John, comp. *Faulkner: An Annotated Checklist of Recent Criticism.* Kent, OH: Kent State UP, 1983.

———, comp. *Faulkner in the Eighties: An Annotated Critical Bibliography.* Metuchen, NJ: Scarecrow, 1991.

———, comp. *William Faulkner: An Annotated Checklist of Criticism.* New York: Lewis, 1972.

———, ed. *William Faulkner: The Critical Heritage.* London and Boston: Routledge & Kegan Paul, 1975.

Bleikasten, André. *Faulkner's "As I Lay Dying."* Trans. Roger Little. Bloomington: Indiana UP, 1973.

———. Introduction. *"The Sound and the Fury": A Concordance to the Novel.* Ed. Noel Polk and Kenneth Privratsky. Ann Arbor, MI: UMI P, 1980.

———. *The Most Splendid Failure: Faulkner's "The Sound and the Fury."* Bloomington: Indiana UP, 1976.

Blotner, Joseph. *Faulkner: A Biography.* 2 vols. New York: Random House, 1974.

———. *Faulkner: A Biography.* Rev. ed. (1 vol.) New York: Random House, 1984.

———, ed. *Selected Letters of William Faulkner.* New York: Random House, 1978.

Blotner, Joseph, Thomas McHaney, Michael Millgate, and Noel Polk, eds. *William Faulkner Manuscripts.* 25 vols. New York: Garland, 1986–87.

Bonner, Thomas, Jr., comp. *William Faulkner: The William B. Wisdom Collection: A Descriptive Catalogue.* New Orleans: Tulane U Libraries, 1980.

Brodsky, Louis Daniel, and Robert W. Hamblin, comps. *Faulkner: A Comprehensive Guide to the Brodsky Collection.* 5 vols. Jackson: UP of Mississippi, 1982–88.

Brooks, Cleanth. Introduction. *"As I Lay Dying": A Concordance to the Novel.* Ed. Jack L. Capps. Ann Arbor, MI: University Microfilms, 1977.

Cofield, J. R., comp. *William Faulkner: The Cofield Collection.* Oxford, MS: Yoknapatawpha P, 1978.

Cohen, Philip G., David Krause, and Karl F. Zender. "William Faulkner." *Sixteen Modern American Authors. Volume 2. A Survey of Research and Criticism since 1972.* Ed. Jackson R. Bryer. Durham, NC: Duke UP, 1989. 210–300.

Crane, Joan St. C., and Anne E. H. Freudenberg, comps. *Honoring Linton Reynolds Massey, 1900–1974: Man Collecting: Manuscripts and Printed Works of William Faulkner in the University of Virginia Library. Exhibition Catalogue.* Charlottesville: U of Virginia Library, 1975.

Dalziel, Pamela. *"Absalom, Absalom!*: The Extension of Dialogic Form." *Mississippi Quarterly* 45 (1992): 277–94.

Dardis, Tom. *Firebrand: The Life of Horace Liveright.* New York: Random House, 1995.

———. "Harrison Smith: The Man Who Took a Chance on *The Sound and the Fury.*" *Faulkner and Popular Culture.* Ed. Ann Abadie and Doreen Fowler. Jackson: UP of Mississippi, 1990. 163–78.

Douglass, Paul. *Bergson, Eliot, and American Literature.* Lexington: U Kentucky P, 1986. 118–41, 142–65.

Fadiman, Regina. *Faulkner's "Light in August": A Description and Interpretation of the Revisions.* Charlottesville: UP of Virginia, 1975.

Faulkner, William. *Collected Stories.* New York: Random House, 1951.

———. *Elmer.* Ed. Dianne Cox. Northport, AL: Seajay P, 1984.

———. *Father Abraham.* Ed. James B. Meriwether. New York: Random, 1984.

———. *Faulkner: Novels 1930–1935: "As I Lay Dying," "Sanctuary," "Light in August," "Pylon."* Ed., with notes to the text, by Noel Polk and Joseph Blotner. New York: Library of America, 1985.

———. *Faulkner: Novels 1936–1940: "Absalom, Absalom!" "The Unvanquished," "If I Forget Thee, Jerusalem" ["The Wild Palms"], "The Hamlet."* Ed., with notes to the text, by Noel Polk and Joseph Blotner. New York: Library of America, 1990.

———. *Faulkner: Novels 1942-1954: "Go Down, Moses," "Intruder in the Dust," "Requiem for a Nun," "A Fable."* Ed., with notes to the text, by Noel Polk and Joseph Blotner. New York: Library of America, 1990.

———. "Funeral Sermon for Mammy Caroline Barr." *Essays, Speeches and Public Letters.* Ed. James B. Meriwether. New York: Random House, 1965. 117–18.

———. *Marionettes.* Limited edition facsimile. Charlottesville: UP of Virginia, 1975. Trade edition. Ed. Noel Polk. Charlottesville: Bibliographical Society of the U of Virginia, 1977.

———. *Mayday.* Limited edition. Ed. Carvel Collins. South Bend, IN: U of Notre Dame P, 1977. Typeset edition, with representative illustrations. Ed. Carvel Collins. South Bend, IN: U of Notre Dame P, 1980.

———. *Mosquitoes.* New York: Boni & Liveright, 1927.

———. *Soldiers' Pay.* New York: Boni & Liveright, 1926.

———. *The Sound and the Fury.* New York: Cape & Smith, 1929. Corrected edition. New York: Random House, 1984.

————. *Uncollected Stories*. Ed. Joseph Blotner. New York: Random House, 1988.

Garrett, George. "Faulkner's Early Literary Criticism." *Texas Studies in Language and Literature* 1 (1959): 3–10.

Genovese, Eugene D. *Roll, Jordan, Roll: The World the Slaves Made*. New York: Pantheon Books, 1974.

Gresset, Michel. *Faulkner, ou la fascination: poètique du regard*. Paris: Klincksieck, 1982. Reprinted as *Fascination: Faulkner's Fiction 1919–1936*, adapted from the French by Thomas West. Durham, NC: Duke UP, 1989.

Hönnighausen, Lothar. *William Faulkner: The Art of Stylization in his Early Graphic and Literary Work*. Cambridge, England: Cambridge UP, 1987.

Inge, M. Thomas, ed. *William Faulkner: The Contemporary Reviews*. New York: Cambridge UP, 1995.

Irwin, John T. *Doubling and Incest, Repetition and Revenge*. Baltimore: Johns Hopkins UP, 1975.

Kaluza, Irena. *The Functioning of Sentence Structure in the Stream-of-Consciousness Technique of William Faulkner's "The Sound and the Fury": A Study in Linguistic Stylistics*. Krakow, Poland: Jegellonian UP, 1967.

Karl, Frederick. *William Faulkner: American Writer*. New York: Weidenfeld & Nicolson, 1989.

Kartiganer, Donald M. *The Fragile Thread: The Meaning of Form in Faulkner's Novels*. Amherst: U of Massachusetts P, 1979.

Kawin, Bruce. *Faulkner and Film*. New York: Frederick Ungar, 1977.

Kinney, Arthur F., and Doreen Fowler. "Faulkner's Rowan Oak Papers: A Census." *Journal of Modern Literature* 10 (1983): 327–34.

Kreiswirth, Martin. *William Faulkner: The Making of a Novelist*. Athens: U of Georgia P, 1983.

Langford, Gerald. *Faulkner's Revision of "Absalom, Absalom!": A Collation of the Manuscript and the Published Book*. Austin: U of Texas P, 1971.

————. "Insights into the Creative Process: The Faulkner Collection at the University of Texas." *William Faulkner: Prevailing Verities and World Literature*. Ed. Wolodymyr T. Zyla and Wendell M. Aycock. Lubbock, TX: Interdepartmental Committee on Comparative Literature, Texas Tech, 1973.

Lloyd, James B. *Lives of Mississippi Authors, 1817–1967*. Jackson: UP of Mississippi, 1981.

————, comp. *The Oxford "Eagle," 1900–1962: An Annotated Checklist of Material on William Faulkner and the History of Lafayette County*. Mississippi State, MS: *Mississippi Quarterly*, 1976.

McDaniel, Linda. *"Flags in the Dust": Annotations to the Novel*. New York: Garland, 1991.

McHaney, Thomas L. "William Faulkner." *Bibliography of American Fiction 1919–1988.* Ed. Matthew J. Bruccoli and Richard Layman. Vol. 1. New York: Facts on File, 1991. 173–85. Reprinted, updated but slightly condensed, in *Essential Bibliography of American Fiction: Modern Classic Writers.* Ed. Matthew J. Bruccoli and Judith S. Baughman, with a Foreword by George Garrett. New York: Facts on File, 1994. 1–20.

———, comp. *William Faulkner: A Reference Guide.* Boston: G. K. Hall, 1976.

Marrs, Suzanne. *The Welty Collection: A Guide to the Eudora Welty Manuscripts and Documents at the Mississippi Department of Archives and History.* Jackson: UP of Mississippi, 1988.

Massey, Linton R., comp. *"Man Working," 1919–1962: William Faulkner, A Catalogue of the William Faulkner Collections at the University of Virginia.* Charlottesville: Bibliographical Society of the U of Virginia, 1968.

Matthews, John. *The Play of Faulkner's Language.* Ithaca, NY: Cornell UP, 1982.

Meriwether, James B. *The Literary Career of William Faulkner: A Bibliographical Study.* Princeton, NJ: Princeton U Library, 1961. Rpt., Columbia, SC: U of South Carolina P, 1971.

———. "William Faulkner." *Sixteen Modern American Authors: A Review of Research and Criticism.* Ed. Jackson R. Bryer. Durham, NC: Duke UP, 1973. 223–75.

Millgate, Michael. *The Achievement of William Faulkner.* New York: Random House, 1966. Rpt., Athens: U of Georgia P, 1989.

———. "Faulkner's Masters." *Tulane Studies in English* 23 (1978): 143–55.

Oates, Stephen B. *Faulkner: The Man and the Artist.* New York: Harper & Row, 1987.

Petersen, Carl. *Each in Its Ordered Place: A Faulkner Collector's Notebook.* Ann Arbor, MI: Ardis, 1975.

———. *On the Track of the Dixie Limited: Further Notes of a Faulkner Collector.* La Grange, IL: Colophon Book Shop, 1979.

Pitavy, François L. *Faulkner's "Light in August."* Trans. Gillian Cook. Bloomington: Indiana UP, 1973.

Polk, Noel. *An Editorial Handbook for William Faulkner's "The Sound and the Fury."* New York: Garland, 1985.

Reynolds, Michael. *The Young Hemingway.* Oxford, England: Basil Blackwell, 1986.

Roberts, Diane. "South's 'Sacred Monster.'" *Atlanta Journal-Constitution* (16 April 1995): K10.

Ross, Stephen. *Fiction's Inexhaustible Voice: Speech and Writing in Faulkner.* Athens: U of Georgia P, 1989.

Ruppersburg, Hugh M. *Reading Faulkner: "Light in August": Glossary and Commentary.* Jackson: UP of Mississippi, 1994.

Schoenberg, Estella. *Old Tales and Talking: Quentin Compson in William Faulkner's "Absalom, Absalom!" and Related Works*. Jackson: UP of Mississippi, 1977.

Sensibar, Judith. *The Origins of Faulkner's Art*. Austin: U of Texas P, 1984.

Sensibar, Judith, with the assistance of Nancy L. Stegall. *Faulkner's Poetry: A Bibliographic Guide to Texts and Criticism*. Ann Arbor, MI: UMI P, 1988.

Skei, Hans. *William Faulkner: The Short Story Career: An Outline of Faulkner's Short Story Writing from 1919 to 1962*. Oslo: Universitetsforlaget, 1981.

Snell, Susan. *Phil Stone of Oxford: A Vicarious Life*. Athens: U of Georgia P, 1991.

Stewart, Randall. "Poetically the Most Accurate Man Alive." *Modern Age* 6 (1962): 81–90.

Strandberg, Victor. *A Faulkner Overview: Six Perspectives*. Port Washington, NY: Kennikat P, 1981.

Verich, Thomas M. "*Go Down, Moses and Other Stories*: A Preliminary Census of the Limited, Signed Edition of 100 Numbered Copies." *Mississippi Quarterly* 44 (1991): 337–45.

Warren, Robert Penn. "Introduction: Faulkner: Past and Present." *Faulkner: A Collection of Critical Essays*. Ed. Robert Penn Warren. Englewood Cliffs, NJ: Prentice-Hall, 1966. 1–22.

Watson, James G. "Carvel Collins' Faulkner: A Newly Opened Archive." *Library Chronicle of the University of Texas* 20 (1991): 17–35. Rpt., *Mississippi Quarterly* 44 (1991): 257–72.

——, ed. *Thinking of Home: William Faulkner's Letters to His Mother and Father, 1918–1925*. New York: Norton, 1992.

[Welty, Eudora.] "Place and Time: The Southern Writer's Inheritance." *Times Literary Supplement*. 17 September 1954: xlviii.

Werner, Craig. *Playing the Changes: From Afro-Modernism to the Jazz Impulse*. Urbana: U of Illinois P, 1994.

Williamson, Joel. *William Faulkner and Southern History*. New York: Oxford UP, 1993.

16

Richard Wright

Keneth Kinnamon

Compared to the other author studies treated in this volume, Wright studies are still in their infancy. Nevertheless, even before biographies by Constance Webb and Michel Fabre and the critical studies by Edward Margolies, Dan McCall, Russell C. Brignano, Keneth Kinnamon, and David Bakish—all published in the six years from 1968 to 1973—there was a substantial body of essays and reviews, some of them helpful. A glance at some of this early work and a look at the achievements of the last three decades will establish our bearings before we scout the terrain of that large territory of Wright scholarship still to be explored.

From 1933 through 1960, the year of his death, close to eight thousand printed items on Wright appeared. Most are insignificant as criticism, though they do document the worldwide interest in his work, fill in biographical details, provide information on his publishing history, and the like. The more important reviews, many by prominent critics and writers of the middle third of the century, can be found in John Reilly's useful *Richard Wright: The Critical Reception*.

In addition to reviews, serious critical attention to Wright began during his lifetime. Among his friends and protégés, Ralph Ellison wrote thoughtful essays in the forties on *Uncle Tom's Children*, *Native Son*, and *Black Boy*, and James Baldwin's 1949 attack on *Native Son* in "Everybody's Protest Novel" began one of the more celebrated literary quarrels of the twentieth century. Their early and later writings on Wright are essential reading for any student of the author. The same could be said for Edwin Berry Burgum's "The Promise of Democracy and the Fiction of Richard Wright" (223–40) and "The Art of Richard Wright's Short Stories" (241–59), perhaps the best early treatments of *Native Son* and *Uncle Tom's Children*. Criticism of Wright before his death was necessarily tentative, but it had the compensatory freshness of a first response, and it joined many issues that were to be addressed more fully in subsequent criticism and scholarship: art vs. propaganda, black nationalism vs. racial integration, the geography of racial experience, the use of violence in fiction, Marxist ideology, determinism and volition, naturalism and existentialism, the Third World and anticolonialism, the problems and opportunities of expatriation, and others.

The first book on Wright, Constance Webb's *Richard Wright: A Biography*, is almost as much a memoir as a biography, for its chronology is sometimes confused, its focus is on the man rather than his work, and its interpretation of Wright's personality is perhaps too generous. Much better is Michel Fabre's thoroughly researched and judicious full-scale life, *The Unfinished Quest of Richard Wright*. An intellectual and literary biography, Fabre's work presents Wright as a powerful witness against racism, but also as a writer-thinker in quest of a universally applicable definition of the essentially human. Of the other three biographies, John A. Williams's *The Most Native of Sons* is a short life for young readers, and Margaret Walker's *Richard Wright: Daemonic Genius* may be safely ignored. Addison Gayle's *Richard Wright: Ordeal of a Native Son* adds to Webb and Fabre important new information on governmental surveillance and harassment of Wright.

In addition to Fabre and Gayle, memoirs and autobiographies by such friends as Baldwin, Horace Cayton, Frank Marshall Davis, Ellison, Ollie Harrington, Chester Himes, and William Gardner Smith will interest the student of Wright's life. Grace McSpadden White and Jack B. Moore are both informative, the former on Wright's Memphis years and the latter on his trip to the Gold Coast. *Conversations with Richard Wright*, edited by Keneth Kinnamon and Michel Fabre, collects interviews with the author conducted at various stages of his career. By the time this essay is published, one hopes that Julia Wright's eagerly anticipated memoir of her father will have appeared. It will give a much needed view of Wright as parent and husband.

At the same time that biographical facts were being established by Webb and Fabre, critical interest was booming. As if to compensate for the unjust neglect that Wright suffered in the 1950s and early 1960s, in the five years from 1969 through 1973 five critical books were published, two additional books collected critical responses to *Native Son*, two pamphlets on Wright came out in established series, and three journals published special issues on Wright (one of these issues appearing two years later as a book)—not to mention a Wright issue of *Negro Digest* appearing in 1968. Such a bountiful first harvest inevitably contained some redundancy, but the five books and two pamphlets generally complement each other. Edward Margolies's *The Art of Richard Wright* treats both the fiction and the nonfiction, emphasizing Wright's existentialism and universalism more than racial protest. Russell C. Brignano's *Richard Wright: An Introduction to the Man and His Works* organizes its treatment around four areas: emerging racial issues, Marxism, the Third World, and rationalism versus the absurd. Focusing on Wright's career through *Native Son*, Keneth Kinnamon's *The Emergence of Richard Wright: A Study in Literature and Society* attempts to examine Wright's early works in biographical and social contexts while also analyzing their literary properties. David Bakish's *Richard Wright* is a brief monograph surveying chronologically Wright's life and work. Dan McCall's *The Example of Richard Wright* stresses the theme of racism and gives a favorable assessment of Wright's importance. Unfortunately, on numerous occasions McCall makes unauthorized and unacknowledged use of another scholar's work (Kinnamon, Review of *The Example of Richard Wright*). One should also note that Robert Bone's Minnesota pamphlet usefully sketches the picaresque pattern in Wright's work and discusses the writer's theory of history, while Milton and Patricia Rickels, writing their pamphlet for the Southern Writers Series, appropriately stress Wright's Southernness.

Space is not available to comment on the collections of essays or the special issues of journals, but a few more important pioneers of Wright scholarship require mention. John M. Reilly has published not only his collection of reviews, but also numerous thoughtful articles. Donald B. Gibson's classic 1969 essay "Wright's Invisible Native Son" changed the way we think about Wright's most important novel by focusing on Bigger Thomas as an individual human being. Like Reilly, Gibson did good bibliographical work and continued to contribute solid articles over the years. Fritz Gysin's long Wright chapter in *The Grotesque in American Negro Fiction* is the best treatment of its subject. Meanwhile, a younger generation of scholars in the seventies was busily at work on dissertations treating Wright. For that decade, *Dissertation Abstracts International* lists eighteen dissertations devoted wholly to Wright and forty-five treating him as part of a larger topic.

The 1980s and early 1990s marked new advances in Wright scholarship. Instrumental in acquiring Wright's papers for Yale, Charles T. Davis and Michel Fabre collaborated on the indispensable *Richard Wright:*

A *Primary Bibliography*, including unpublished works as well as drafts and variants of published works. Six years later came Keneth Kinnamon's massive *A Richard Wright Bibliography: Fifty Years of Criticism and Commentary, 1933–1982*, including 13,117 annotated items in many languages. This work is being slowly brought up to date with installments in the *Richard Wright Newsletter*.

In the 1960s Blyden Jackson projected a Twayne volume on Wright, of which his essay "Richard Wright: Black Boy from America's Black Belt and Urban Ghettos" was to have been the opening chapter. Although the book never materialized, Robert Felgar's *Richard Wright* appeared in the Twayne series in 1980. More original in their approaches were Joyce A. Joyce in *Richard Wright's Art of Tragedy*, a close study of literary technique, especially in *Native Son*; Eugene Miller in *Voice of a Native Son: The Poetics of Richard Wright*, a provocative if sometimes fanciful interpretation of the Wrightian aesthetic; and Robert J. Butler in his excellent *Native Son: The Emergence of a New Black Hero*, one of the very best readings of Wright's greatest work. Michel Fabre's preeminence in Wright studies was further solidified with *The World of Richard Wright*, collecting previously published articles and adding new ones; *Richard Wright: Books and Writers*, cataloging his reading; and the chapter on Wright in *From Harlem to Paris*.

No fewer than nine collections of essays have appeared since 1980. Among these, Yoshinobu Hakutani's *Critical Essays on Richard Wright* is a well-balanced compilation with an informed introduction tracing Wright's reception; some important contributions from earlier decades; and five new essays, all of them strong. A similar collection is Richard Macksey and Frank E. Moorer's *Richard Wright: A Collection of Critical Essays*. C. James Trotman's uneven *Richard Wright: Myths and Realities* collects papers from a conference, mostly by new voices in Wright studies. Keneth Kinnamon's *New Essays on "Native Son"* contains his study of the novel's composition and reception, followed by Reilly on narrative technique, Trudier Harris on the presentation of female characters, Houston A. Baker on the concept of place and black gender roles, and Craig Werner on the work in relation to literary modernism. Arnold Rampersad's *Richard Wright: A Collection of Critical Essays* contains a judicious overview of Wright's career by the editor, followed by fifteen essays published from 1981 to 1991, a chronology, and a bibliography. Robert J. Butler's *The Critical Response to Richard Wright* includes reviews as well as later critical essays concerning *Native Son, Black Boy, The*

Outsider, and *Eight Men.* A final section presents six essays, three reprinted and three not previously published, on issues arising from the Library of America edition of Wright and the recently published novella, *Rite of Passage.*

In such a condensed survey as this, only a few highlights can be mentioned from the book chapters and journal articles on Wright published during the last decade and a half. Certainly a student should consult the treatment of Wright in Gibson's *The Politics of Literary Expression,* Charles T. Davis's *Black Is the Color of the Cosmos,* Michael G. Cooke's *Afro-American Literature in the Twentieth Century,* Trudier Harris's *Exorcising Blackness,* Houston A. Baker's *Blues, Ideology and Afro-American Literature,* Valerie Smith's *Self-Discovery and Authority in Afro-American Narrative,* Melvin Dixon's *Ride Out the Wilderness,* and Charles Scruggs's *Sweet Home.* On the controversial subject of Wright's portrayal of women, in addition to the essays by Baker and Harris mentioned above, Maria K. Mootry's "Bitches, Whores, and Women Haters," Shirley Anne Williams's "Papa Dick and Sister-Woman," and Miriam DeCosta-Willis's "Avenging Angels and White Mothers" are all provocative. Robert Bone's important "Richard Wright and the Chicago Renaissance" expands our understanding of Wright's early literary milieu and his influence on it, and Carla Cappetti does the same for his interest in social science in "Sociology of an Existence: Richard Wright and the Chicago School." Yoshinobu Hakutani goes well beyond the usual perfunctory remarks on the subject of "Richard Wright and American Naturalism." Keneth Kinnamon in "How *Native Son* Was Born" and Janice Thaddeus in "The Metamorphosis of Richard Wright's *Black Boy*" provide new research on Wright manuscripts and the politics of their publication. Other especially noteworthy essays on single works are Abdul JanMohamed's "Rehistoricizing Wright: The Psychopolitical Function of Death in *Uncle Tom's Children,*" Tracy Webb's "The Role of Water Imagery in *Uncle Tom's Children,*" and John Lowe's "Wright Writing Reading: Narrative Strategies in *Uncle Tom's Children*"; James A. Miller's "Bigger Thomas's Quest for Voice and Audience in Richard Wright's *Native Son*" and Ross Pudaloff's "Celebrity as Identity: Richard Wright, *Native Son,* and Mass Culture"; Patricia D. Watkins's "The Paradoxical Structure of Richard Wright's 'The Man Who Lived Underground'"; and Herbert Leibowitz's chapter on *Black Boy* and *American Hunger* in his *Fabricating Lives: Explorations in American Autobiography.*

After the acquisition of the Wright papers by the Beinecke Library in 1976, the most important stimulants to Wright scholarship have been the conference on "Mississippi's Native Son" held at the University of Mississippi in 1985; the publication in two volumes of the Library of America edition of *Lawd Today, Uncle Tom's Children, Native Son, Black Boy/American Hunger, The Outsider,* and *The Long Dream*; and the formation of the Richard Wright Circle. Organized by Maryemma Graham, the Mississippi conference brought to Wright's native state conferees from Europe and Asia as well as North America and featured a number of friends from the author's younger years as well as scholars and writers. Some of the best conference papers appeared in a special issue of *Callaloo* in 1986. The appearance of two volumes of Wright in the Library of America in 1991 not only solidified the growing consensus on his status as a canonical American author, but also occasioned a spate of reviews and essays surveying his career or addressing the complicated textual and editorial issues raised. Special praise goes to Arnold Rampersad for his detailed chronology and notes and to Mark Richardson for his careful textual scholarship. Jerry Ward and Maryemma Graham are the guiding spirits of the Richard Wright Circle, founded in 1991 with the blessing of Ellen and Julia Wright The organization issues the *Richard Wright Newsletter* twice a year and sponsors sessions on Wright at meetings of the American Literature Association.

Thus conditions are propitious for major advances in Wright scholarship, many of which can be completed by the centennial of Wright's birth in 2008. What is needed?

We should know more about Wright's life. Rampersad's useful chronology in the Library of America edition suggests how valuable a truly exhaustive chronology would be, one that records all datable events, drawing on diaries, letters, engagement calendars, biographies, memoirs, newspaper items, financial records, and the like. Albert J. Von Frank's recent *An Emerson Chronology* could serve as a model for such a work, one that only an indefatigable researcher should undertake. An even more formidable task awaits the next biographer of Wright, who should approach the subject from a fresh perspective and utilize fully information that has not yet been disclosed or discovered. This biographer should begin by studying carefully Fabre's invaluable preface to the second edition of his biography, written almost a quarter century after the first. With characteristic intellectual honesty, he acknowledges certain shortcomings in his treatment of Wright's literary relations and his personal life. Whether or not a psychoanalytical approach is taken, the next major biographer of Wright should pay full attention to such matters. We need to know more about Wright the husband and father, about his personality, about his love life, about his medical history, about the circumstances of his death. In short, we need a fuller sense of Wright the man as well as of Wright the writer. Two able scholars are now seriously considering a new biography. Essential to the new biographer, whoever she or he may be, will be the cooperation of Wright's surviving family and friends and the relaxation of restrictions on the use of materials in the Wright Archive at Yale. Wright has been dead longer than Hemingway, Faulkner, and Hughes. It is time for information about him to be as readily available to serious scholarly investigators as that about his great contemporaries.

In this regard, publication of Wright's correspondence must have a high priority. Some twenty-five years ago Fabre and Margolies prepared a selection for publication, but were unable finally to secure permission from the Wright estate to bring out the volume. In 1973 Margolies published an important essay on "The Letters of Richard Wright," whetting our appetite for the documents themselves. One hopes that the volume will appear quickly. What is needed in the long run is a multivolume scholarly edition of all of Wright's letters—many of which are still in private hands—with full editorial apparatus and perhaps a selection of letters written to Wright. Clearly such a project would require substantial institutional and foundation funding and a dedicated team of scholars prepared to make a long-term commitment. The pioneering Wright scholars, now in their sixties, would probably be quite happy for such a task to devolve on their younger colleagues. Preliminary work should get under way as soon as possible. Especially urgent is the task of locating Wright letters in the hands of recipients and their heirs before these letters are lost or destroyed.

The appearance of the Library of America edition in 1991 not only recognized Wright's canonical status but also underscored the need for more textual scholarship. Of the five works included by the Library of America, only *Uncle Tom's Children* is printed as first published; the others were all subjected to various kinds of editorial intervention beyond Wright's control. But what of *12 Million Black Voices, Savage Holiday, Black Power, The Color Curtain, Pagan Spain, White Man, Listen!, The Long Dream, Eight Men,* and *Rite of Passage*? These await textual scholars prepared to trace the process of composition, revision, proofreading, and publication to establish a suitable copy-text. The Library of America could sponsor or supervise such work, leading to two more Wright volumes to join the first two, one of these containing *12 Million Black Voices, Black Power, The Color Curtain, Pagan Spain, White Man, Listen!,* and such essays as "Blueprint for Negro Writing," "The Ethics of Living Jim Crow," *How "Bigger" Was Born,* and "I Tried to Be a Communist," and the other including *Savage Holiday, The Long Dream, Eight Men,* and *Rite of Passage.* As the first two volumes of the edition showed, textual scholarship stimulates criticism and can have important interpretive consequences.

Another important editorial task involves publication of additional posthumous works. *Eight Men, Lawd Today!, American Hunger,* and *Rite of Passage* all appeared after Wright's death, but much manuscript material worth assembling, editing, and publishing remains in the Beinecke Library. Quite properly, the Wright estate will determine what appears and when, but one hopes that *Rite of Passage* is the harbinger of several works to come. The early novel "Tarbaby's Dawn," the subject of a dissertation by Virginia Whatley Smith, should certainly reach print. Wright's "Almos' a Man," one of his best short stories, is an episode from this manuscript of over three hundred pages. At the other end of Wright's career came "Island of Hallucinations," a sequel to *The Long Dream,* treating Fishbelly's life in Paris. A projected third volume in this trilogy would have taken Fishbelly from Europe to Africa and finally back to the United States. Much longer than "Tarbaby's Dawn," "Island of Hallucinations" would add a new dimension to the Wright canon. Much longer still is the manuscript of "Little Sister," a novel about black women, begun immediately after the completion of *Native Son.* In addition to these three novels, a new collection of short stories and novellas could be assembled from the Beinecke, including such intriguing titles as "The Colored Angel," "Doodley-Funn," "Graven Image," "Pimp Situation," "Song of the Bleeding Throat," "A Strange Girl," and "When the World Was Red."

A collection of Wright's unpublished essays, statements, and speeches would be helpful for a fuller understanding of his literary sensibility and his wide-ranging interests in politics, culture, social and racial issues, and autobiography. Wright wrote, in addition to his published book reviews, many reports on manuscripts under consideration for publication or for selection by the Book-of-the-Month Club. Many of these reports are ephemeral, but others are worth retrieving. Other literary pieces have obvious importance: "The Future of Literary Expression," "On Litera-ture," "Personalism," "Writers and Their Art," "Writing from the Left." Similar lists could be made for unpublished essays on racial and political issues. Of special interest are some of Wright's unpublished autobio-graphical writings, notably the long "Memories of My Grandmother," which Eugene Miller has put to good use in *Voice of a Native Son.* The compiler of a volume of Wright's uncollected prose will have scores of manuscripts from which to choose.

Very little has been written on Wright's interest in drama, ranging from the successful dramatization of *Native Son* with Paul Green to musi-cals. When Bruce Dick completes his study of the drama in Wright's career, we will know whether a collection is feasible. There can be no question, however, of the need to publish Wright's poetry. It falls into three main categories: agitprop verse, blues, and haiku. The first appeared in left magazines of the thirties, but only a few of the dozens of blues and thousands of haiku have appeared in print. Written at the end of his life, the haiku are of high quality if the few that have been pub-lished are representative. It might be difficult to find a publisher willing to print all four thousand haiku, but surely the eighty-page manuscript that Wright prepared and submitted in the last year of his life could come out. A companion volume of blues poems would be welcome.

As any reader of *Black Boy* knows, Wright was an autodidact whose reading altered his perception of reality ("new ways of looking and see-ing"), as well as stimulated his creative imagination. In his *Richard Wright: Books and Writers,* Fabre laid the groundwork for studies of influ-ence and intertextuality, but much remains to be done in addition to Charles Scruggs on Mencken, Robert Butler on Zola and Farrell, Yoshinobu Hakutani on Dreiser, Eugene Miller on Stein, Fabre on the French existentialists, Tony Magistrale on Dostoevsky, Alvin Starr on Stephen Crane and Farrell, Fred L. Standley on Baldwin, Claudia Tate on Kierkegaard, Kinnamon on Angelou, and William Goede on Ellison, et al. Wright states that *Main Street* was his "first serious novel" (*Black Boy* 218) in the program of intensive reading stimulated by Mencken in Memphis, but where is a substantial essay on Wright and Sinclair Lewis? What is the relation of *Uncle Tom's Children* to *Dubliners* or *Winesburg, Ohio* or *In Our Time*? Comments are frequent on Wright's relation to American naturalism, but what about his relation to George Moore and Thomas Hardy? A good study of Wright's influence on militant black writers of the 1960s and 1970s is much needed, and his impact on African writers and Frantz Fanon would repay closer study. Research opportunities in this area abound.

Certain topics call for book-length studies. Amritjit Singh is working on a book about Wright and the Third World, but a broader book on Wright and politics would also be useful. Such a work would explore the Communist and post-Communist stages of Wright's ideological journey, giving full attention to the political dimension of his imaginative writing as well as of his nonfiction. With a more intensive focus, scholars might retrace Wright's steps in Spain and Indonesia, doing for *Pagan Spain* and *The Color Curtain* what Jack B. Moore has done for *Black Power*. Political as well as literary considerations certainly shaped the reception of Wright's books at home and abroad. A full-scale reception study would necessarily be based on Kinnamon's bibliographical labors, but he leaves this important task to some other scholar. A book on Wright and religion would be welcome. In the area of sexual politics, a good book on Wright and women would be an important contribution. Such a book would do well to avoid polemics, to treat Wright's relation to the women in his life as well as his depiction of women in fiction, and to consider unpublished as well as published writings. Whatever the theoretical or psychoanalytical perspective, if any, the author of such a work should accommodate all the relevant facts.

Such a caveat, however obvious it may seem, is equally applicable to future Wright criticism. Not many critics have looked at Wright from poststructuralist perspectives, but Abdul JanMohamed has shown that such new work can be helpful. More is sure to come. Lacanian or Foucauldian approaches might well be applied to *The Outsider, Savage Holiday*, and other works. After all, Wright himself was deeply interested in psychological as well as social and political theory. Contrary to some early opinion, Wright's work and life are diverse and rich enough to reward various scholarly and critical approaches. We no longer have to argue Wright's importance. Let us dedicate our efforts to further and fuller explorations of its dimensions.

WORKS CITED

Anderson, Sherwood. *Winesburg, Ohio.* New York: B. W. Huebsch, 1922.

Baker, Houston A., Jr. *Blues, Ideology and Afro-American Literature: A Vernacular Theory.* Chicago: U of Chicago P, 1984.

Bakish, David. *Richard Wright*. New York: Ungar, 1973.

Baldwin, James. *Nobody Knows My Name: More Notes of a Native Son*. New York: Dial, 1961.

———. "Everybody's Protest Novel." *Notes of a Native Son*. Boston: Beacon, 1955.

Bone, Robert A. *Richard Wright*. Minneapolis: U of Minnesota P, 1969.

———. "Richard Wright and the Chicago Renaissance." *Callaloo* 9 (1986): 446–68.

Brignano, Russell Carl. *Richard Wright: An Introduction to the Man and His Works*. Pittsburgh: U of Pittsburgh P, 1970.

Burgum, Edwin Berry. *The Novel and the World's Dilemma*. New York: Oxford UP, 1947.

Butler, Robert J. "Farrell's Ethnic Neighborhood and Wright's Urban Ghetto: Two Visions of Chicago's South Side." *MELUS* 18.1 (1993): 103–11.

———. *"Native Son": The Emergence of a New Black Hero*. Boston: Twayne, 1991.

———. "Wright's *Native Son* and Two Novels by Zola: A Comparative Study." *Black American Literature Forum* 18 (1984): 100–105.

———, ed. *The Critical Response to Richard Wright*. Westport, CT: Greenwood, 1995.

Cappetti, Carla. "Sociology of an Existence: Richard Wright and the Chicago School" *MELUS* 12.2 (1985): 25–43.

Cayton, Horace R. *Long Old Road*. New York: Trident P, 1965.

Cooke, Michael G. *Afro-American Literature in the Twentieth Century: The Achievement of Intimacy*. New Haven, CT: Yale UP, 1984.

Davis, Charles T. *Black Is the Color of the Cosmos: Essays on Afro-American Literature and Culture, 1942–1981*. Ed. Henry Louis Gates, Jr. New York: Garland, 1982.

Davis, Charles T., and Michel Fabre. *Richard Wright: A Primary Bibliography*. Boston: G. K. Hall, 1982.

Davis, Frank Marshall. *Livin' the Blues: Memoirs of a Black Journalist and Poet*. Ed. John Edgar Tidwell. Madison: U of Wisconsin P, 1992.

DeCosta-Willis, Miriam. "Avenging Angels and White Mothers: Black Southern Women in Wright's Fictional World." *Callaloo* 9 (1986): 540–49.

Dixon, Melvin. *Ride Out the Wilderness: Geography and Identity in Afro-American Literature*. Urbana: U of Illinois P, 1987.

Ellison, Ralph. *Going to the Territory*. New York: Random House, 1986.

———. *Shadow and Act*. New York: Random House, 1964.

Fabre, Michel. *From Harlem to Paris: Black American Writers in France, 1840–1980*. Urbana: U of Illinois P, 1991.

———. *Richard Wright: Books and Writers*. Jackson: UP of Mississippi, 1990.

———. "Richard Wright, French Existentialism, and *The Outsider.*" Hakutani, *Critical Essays* 182–98.

———. *The Unfinished Quest of Richard Wright.* New York: Morrow, 1973. 2nd ed. Urbana: U of Illinois P, 1993.

———. *The World of Richard Wright.* Jackson: UP of Mississippi, 1985.

Felgar, Robert. *Richard Wright.* Boston: Twayne, 1980.

Gayle, Addison, Jr. *Richard Wright: Ordeal of a Native Son.* Garden City, NY: Anchor/Doubleday, 1980.

Gibson, Donald B. *The Politics of Literary Expression: A Study of Major Black Writers.* Westport, CT: Greenwood, 1981.

———. "Wright's Invisible Native Son." *American Quarterly* 21 (1969): 728–38.

Goede, William. "On Lower Frequencies: The Buried Men in Wright and Ellison." *Modern Fiction Studies* 15 (1969): 483–501.

Green, Paul, and Richard Wright. *Native Son (The Biography of a Young American), a Play in Ten Scenes.* New York: Harper, 1941.

Gysin, Fritz. *The Grotesque in American Negro Fiction: Jean Toomer, Richard Wright, and Ralph Ellison.* Bern: Francke Verlag, 1975.

Hakutani, Yoshinobu, ed. *Critical Essays on Richard Wright.* Boston: G. K. Hall, 1982.

———. "*Native Son* and *An American Tragedy*: Two Different Interpretations of Crime and Guilt." *Centennial Review* 23 (1979): 208–26.

———. "Richard Wright and American Naturalism." *Zeitschrift für Anglistik und Amerikanistik* 36 (1988): 217–26.

Harrington, Ollie. "The Last Days of Richard Wright." *Ebony* (Feb. 1961): 83–86, 88, 90, 92–94.

Harris, Trudier. *Exorcising Blackness: Historical and Literary Lynching and Burning Rituals.* Bloomington: Indiana UP, 1984.

Hemingway, Ernest. *In Our Time.* New York: Boni & Liveright, 1925.

Himes, Chester. *My Life of Absurdity.* Garden City, NY: Doubleday, 1976.

———. *The Quality of Hurt: The Autobiography of Chester Himes.* Garden City, NY: Doubleday, 1972.

Jackson, Blyden. "Richard Wright: Black Boy from America's Black Belt and Urban Ghettos." *CLA Journal* 12 (1969): 287–309.

JanMohamed, Abdul R. "Rehistoricizing Wright: The Psychopolitical Function of Death in *Uncle Tom's Children.*" *Richard Wright.* Ed. Harold Bloom. New York: Chelsea House, 1987. 191–228.

Joyce, James. *Dubliners.* London: Grant Richards, 1914.

Joyce, Joyce A. *Richard Wright's Art of Tragedy.* Iowa City: U of Iowa P, 1986.

Kinnamon, Keneth. "Call and Response: Intertexuality in Two Autobiographical Works by Richard Wright and Maya Angelou." *Studies in Black American Literature* 2 (1986): 121–34.

————. *The Emergence of Richard Wright: A Study in Literature and Society.* Urbana: U of Illinois P, 1972.

————. "How *Native Son* Was Born." *Writing the American Classics.* Ed. James Barbour and Tom Quirk. Chapel Hill: U of North Carolina P, 1990.

————. Review of *The Example of Richard Wright*, by Dan McCall. *Journal of English and Germanic Philology* 70 (1971): 180–86, 753–54.

————, ed. *New Essays on "Native Son."* Cambridge, England: Cambridge UP, 1991.

Kinnamon, Keneth, and Michel Fabre, eds. *Conversations with Richard Wright.* Jackson: UP of Mississippi, 1993.

Kinnamon, Keneth, with the help of Joseph Benson, Michel Fabre, and Craig Werner. *A Richard Wright Bibliography: Fifty Years of Criticism and Commentary, 1933–1982.* Westport, CT: Greenwood, 1988.

Leibowitz, Herbert. *Fabricating Lives: Explorations in American Autobiography.* New York: Knopf, 1989.

Lowe, John. "Wright Writing Reading: Narrative Strategies in *Uncle Tom's Children.*" *Modern American Short Story Sequences: Composite Fictions and Fictive Communities.* Ed. J. Gerald Kennedy. Cambridge, England: Cambridge UP, 1995. 52–75.

McCall, Dan. *The Example of Richard Wright.* New York: Harcourt, Brace, 1969.

Macksey, Richard, and Frank E. Moorer, eds. *Richard Wright: A Collection of Critical Essays.* Englewood Cliffs, NJ: Prentice-Hall, 1984.

Magistrale, Tony. "From St. Petersburg to Chicago: Wright's *Crime and Punishment.*" *Comparative Literature Studies* 23 (1986): 59–70.

Margolies, Edward. *The Art of Richard Wright.* Carbondale: Southern Illinois UP, 1969.

————. "The Letters of Richard Wright." *The Black Writer in Africa and the Americas.* Ed. Lloyd W. Brown. Los Angeles: Hennessey & Ingalls, 1973. 101–16.

Miller, Eugene E. "Richard Wright and Gertrude Stein." *Black American Literature Forum* 16 (1982): 107–12.

————. *Voice of a Native Son: The Poetics of Richard Wright.* Jackson: UP of Mississippi, 1990.

Miller, James A. "Bigger Thomas's Quest for Voice and Audience in Richard Wright's *Native Son.*" *Callaloo* 9 (1986): 501–6.

Moore, Jack B. "Black Power Revisited: In Search of Richard Wright." *Mississippi Quarterly* 41 (1988): 161–86.

Mootry, Maria K. "Bitches, Whores, and Women Haters: Archetypes and Typologies in the Art of Richard Wright." Macksey and Moorer 117–27.

Pudaloff, Ross. "Celebrity as Identity: Richard Wright, *Native Son*, and Mass Culture." *Studies in American Fiction* 11 (1983): 3–18.

Rampersad, Arnold, ed. *Richard Wright: A Collection of Critical Essays.* Englewood Cliffs, NJ: Prentice-Hall, 1995.

Reilly, John M., ed. *Richard Wright: The Critical Reception.* New York: Burt Franklin, 1978.

Rickels, Milton, and Patricia Rickels. *Richard Wright.* Austin, TX: Steck-Vaughn, 1970.

Scruggs, Charles. "Finding Out about This Mencken: The Impact of *A Book of Prefaces* on Richard Wright." *Menckeniana* 95 (1985): 1–11.

———. *Sweet Home: Invisible Cities in the Afro-American Novel.* Baltimore: Johns Hopkins UP, 1993.

Smith, Valerie. *Self-Discovery and Authority in Afro-American Narrative.* Cambridge, MA: Harvard UP, 1987.

Smith, Virginia Whatley. "Richard Wright's *Tarbaby Series.*" Diss. Boston U, 1988.

Smith, William Gardner. "Black Boy in France." *Ebony* (July 1953): 32–36, 39–42.

Standley, Fred L. "'. . . Farther and Farther Apart': Richard Wright and James Baldwin." Hakutani, *Critical Essays on Richard Wright* 91–103.

Starr, Alvin J. "The Concept of Fear in the Works of Stephen Crane and Richard Wright." *Studies in Black Literature* 6.2 (1975): 6–9.

———. "Richard Wright and the Communist Party—The James T. Farrell Factor." *CLA Journal* 21 (1977): 41–50.

Tate, Claudia. "Christian Existentialism in Richard Wright's *The Outsider.*" *CLA Journal* 25 (1982): 371–95.

Thaddeus, Janice. "The Metamorphosis of Richard Wright's *Black Boy.*" *American Literature* 57 (1985): 201–14.

Trotman, C. James, ed. *Richard Wright: Myths and Realities.* New York: Garland, 1988.

von Frank, Albert J. *An Emerson Chronology.* New York: G. K. Hall, 1994.

Walker, Margaret. *Richard Wright: Daemonic Genius.* New York: Warner, 1988.

Watkins, Patricia D. "The Paradoxical Structure of Richard Wright's 'The Man Who Lived Underground.'" *Black American Literature Forum* 23 (1989): 767–83.

Webb, Constance. *Richard Wright: A Biography.* New York: Putnam's, 1968.

Webb, Tracy. "The Role of Water Imagery in *Uncle Tom's Children.*" *Modern Fiction Studies* 34 (1985): 5–16.

White, Grace McSpadden. "Wright's Memphis." *New Letters* 38 (1971): 105–16.

Williams, John A. *The Most Native of Sons: A Biography of Richard Wright.* Garden City, NY: Doubleday, 1970.

Williams, Shirley Anne. "Papa Dick and Sister-Woman: Reflections on Women in the Fiction of Richard Wright." *American Novelists Revisited: Essays in Feminist Criticism.* Ed. Fritz Fleischmann. Boston: G. K. Hall, 1982.

Wright, Richard. "Almos' a Man." *O. Henry Memorial Award Prize Stories of 1940.* Ed. Harry Hansen. New York: Doubleday, Doran, 1940. 289–305.

——. *Black Boy: A Record of Childhood and Youth.* New York: Harper, 1945.

——. *Black Power: A Record of Reactions in a Land of Pathos.* New York: Harper, 1954.

——. "Blueprint for Negro Writing." *New Challenge* 2 (1937): 53–65.

——. *The Color Curtain: A Report on the Bandung Conference.* Cleveland: World, 1956.

——. "The Colored Angel." Unpublished short story, ts. James Weldon Johnson. Wright Collection Miscellaneous 350. Yale U.

——. "Doodley-Funn." Unpublished short story, ts. James Weldon Johnson. Wright Collection Miscellaneous 368. Yale U.

——. *Early Works: Lawd Today!, Uncle Tom's Children, Native Son.* Ed. Arnold Rampersad and Mark Richardson. New York: The Library of America, 1991.

——. *Eight Men.* Cleveland: World, 1961.

——. "The Ethics of Living Jim Crow." *American Stuff: WPA Writers' Anthology.* New York: Viking, 1937. 39–52.

——. "The Future of Literary Expression." Unpublished essay, ts. James Weldon Johnson. Wright Collection Miscellaneous 395. Yale U.

——. "Graven Image." Unpublished short story, ts. James Weldon Johnson. Wright Collection Miscellaneous 398. Yale U.

——. *How "Bigger" Was Born.* New York: Harper, 1940.

——. "Island of Hallucinations." Unpublished novel, ts. James Weldon Johnson. Wright Collection, 173 [1–2]. Yale U.

——. "I Tried to Be a Communist." *Atlantic Monthly* (Aug. 1944): 48–56.

——. *Later Works: Black Boy (American Hunger), The Outsider.* Ed. Arnold Rampersad and Mark Richardson. New York: The Library of America, 1991.

——. *Lawd Today.* New York: Walker, 1963.

——. "Little Sister." Unpublished novel, ts. James Weldon Johnson. Wright Collection 29 [1–4]. Yale U.

——. *The Long Dream.* Garden City, NY: Doubleday, 1958.

——. "Memories of My Grandmother." Unpublished essay, ts. James Weldon Johnson. Wright Collection Miscellaneous 474. Yale U.

——. *Native Son.* New York: Harper, 1940.

——. "On Literature." Unpublished essay, ts. James Weldon Johnson. Wright Collection Miscellaneous 133. Yale U.

———. *The Outsider.* New York: Harper, 1953.

———. *Pagan Spain.* New York: Harper, 1956.

———. "Personalism." Unpublished essay, ts. Schomburg Collection C13. New York Public Library.

———. "Pimp Situation." Unpublished short story, ts. James Weldon Johnson. Wright Collection Miscellaneous 516. Yale U.

———. *Rite of Passage.* New York: HarperCollins, 1994.

———. *Savage Holiday.* New York: Avon, 1954.

———. "Song of the Bleeding Throat." Unpublished novella, ts. James Weldon Johnson. Wright Collection Miscellaneous 763. Yale U.

———. "A Strange Girl." Unpublished novella, ts. James Weldon Johnson. Wright Collection Miscellaneous 767. Yale U.

———. "Tarbaby's Dawn." Unpublished novel, ts. James Weldon Johnson. Wright Collection 39. Yale U

———. *12 Million Black Voices: A Folk History of the Negro in the United States.* New York: Viking, 1941.

———. *Uncle Tom's Children: Four Novellas.* New York: Harper, 1938.

———. "When the World Was Red." Unpublished short story, ts. James Weldon Johnson. Wright Collection Miscellaneous 805. Yale U.

———. *White Man, Listen!* Garden City, NY: Doubleday, 1957.

———. "Writers and Their Art." Unpublished essay, ts. James Weldon Johnson. Wright Collection Miscellaneous 811. Yale U.

———. "Writing from the Left." Unpublished essay, ts. James Weldon Johnson. Wright Collection Miscellaneous 812. Yale U.

Author Index

Higdon, David Leon, 178
Higgins, Brian, 64–65, 67, 69
Hildreth, Margaret Holbrook, 114
Hill, David W., 8
Hill, Hamlin, 162, 169
Hill, Patricia, 118, 122
Himes, Chester, 316
Hirst, Robert H., 155
Hobbs, Catherine, 121
Hocks, Richard A., 188, 189–90
Hodder, Alan D., 12, 30
Hodgson, John, 47
Hoffman, Andrew, 162
Hoffman, Daniel G., 63
Holbrook, David, 208
Holland, Laurence Bedwell, 188
Holland, P. D., 256
Hollis, C. Carroll, 133
Holloway, Emory, 146
Holly, Carol, 180–82, 188
Hönnighausen, Lothar, 305
Hooker, Joan Fillmore, 254
Horne, Philip, 181
Horwitz, Howard, 13
Hovet, Theodore R., 116
Howard, June, 120
Howard, Leon, 67
Howard, Lillie, 292
Howarth, Herbert, 256
Howarth, William L., 25, 27
Howe, Irving, 11, 186, 202, 204
Hubbell, George Shelton, 9
Huggins, Nathan, 106
Hughes, Gertrude Reif, 12
Hull, William Doyle, II, 45
Hulpke, Erika, 178
Hutch, Richard A., 9
Hutcheon, Linda, 206
Hutchinson, George, 133, 135, 148
Hyneman, Esther F., 41

Inge, M. Thomas, 302
Inness, Sherrie A., 207
Irey, Eugene F., 65
Irwin, John T., 43, 306

Jackson, Blyden, 318
Jackson, David K., 41
Jacobs, Robert D., 47
Jacobson, Marcia, 189

Jain, Manju, 247, 256
James, C. L. R., 74
Jameson, Fredric, 76, 148
JanMohamed, Abdul R., 319, 324
Jarman, Mark, 251
Jay, Gregory, 245, 251
Jeffreys, Mark, 248
Jobe, Stephen H., 180
Jochum, K. P. S., 254
Johnson, Barbara, 71
Johnson, Glen M., 7, 13
Johnson, Linck C., 14, 27, 29
Johnson, Michelle, 5, 283–94
Johnston, Kenneth G., 267
Jolly, Roslyn, 183
Jones, David E., 246
Jordan, Cynthia, 45
Joseph, Mary J., 189
Joslin, Katherine, 203, 212
Joyce, Joyce A., 318
Julius, Anthony, 250
Junkes-Kirchen, Klaus, 254
Justin, Henri, 51

Kalaidjian, Walter, 257
Kaluza, Irena, 304
Kanadey, V. R., 148
Kaplan, Amy, 210
Kaplan, Carla, 286
Kaplan, Fred, 120, 162, 180, 183, 185
Kaplan, Justin, 143, 162
Kaplan, Sidney, 78
Kappes, Carolyn, 23
Karcher, Carolyn L., 78–79
Karl, Frederick, 297
Karsner, David, 145
Kartiganer, Donald M., 306
Kaston, Carren Osna, 184
Katz, Jonathan, 22
Kawin, Bruce, 301
Kearns, Cleo M., 245, 247, 250
Keith, Slim, 274
Kelley, Alita, 165
Kelley, Mary, 121, 124
Kelley, Wyn, 73
Kennedy, J. Gerald, 43, 266, 276
Kenner, Hugh, 244
Kermode, Frank, 256
Kert, Bernice, 266, 271
Ketterer, David, 166

Subject Index